# ENGLAND IN THE AGE OF
# SHAKESPEARE

# ENGLAND IN
# THE AGE OF
# SHAKESPEARE

—⚹—

*Jeremy Black*

INDIANA UNIVERSITY PRESS

This book is a publication of

Indiana University Press
Office of Scholarly Publishing
Herman B Wells Library 350
1320 East 10th Street
Bloomington, Indiana 47405 USA

iupress.indiana.edu

Manufactured in the United States of America

Cataloging information is available from the Library of Congress.

ISBN 978-0-253-04230-9 (hardback)
ISBN 978-0-253-04231-6 (paperback)
ISBN 978-0-253-04234-7 (ebook)

1 2 3 4 5   23 22 21 20 19

*For Eluned Dorkins*

# CONTENTS

# PREFACE

The west yet glimmers with some streaks of day;
Now spurs the lated traveller apace,
To gain the timely inn.

—*Macbeth*, III, iii

OR ENTER THE THEATER AND see the First Murderer speak
these lines as he prepares to kill Banquo and his son, Fleance,
at Macbeth's behest. The audiences of Shakespeare's day knew
that they were seeing a play, but playwrights sought to capture
the understanding of the audience and to craft works that would
resonate with their collective and individual experiences. That
situation is very different for modern audiences of Shakespeare's
plays. They go to a production, but their experiences are not the
same as their predecessors'. As a result, many who now attend
the theater spectate on the plays and register the experience as
an occasion or as a school or family obligation, as much as entering into the spirit or meaning that the play would have had for
Shakespeare's contemporaries.

In this book, I shall try to do the latter—that is, enter into
that spirit—while accepting that such an endeavor is difficult
and problematic. The responses of contemporaries (for example,

to reports of witchcraft) are unclear. There is written evidence that not all of them believed in witches. The argument cannot be readily settled by recourse to historical evidence, as there is not enough of it and it is open to varied interpretations. Clues are offered by the status of the character that makes comments in a play. Is the character a credible witness? Is he or she joking? Are we supposed to believe him or her? The plays moreover are structured so as to suggest differing views, but that is not the same as encouraging the audience to feel some equality of skeptical response toward the characters and their views. This is a point demonstrated by the likely response to *Macbeth*, where the protagonist, his wife, and the witches are all clearly and repeatedly presented in a strongly hostile light.

If "all the world is a stage," then that stage and its historical setting repay continued examination. Such is the approach taken in this book, which focuses on Elizabethan and Jacobean England but also ranges further, both historically and geographically. The stress will be on presenting the current historical understanding of Shakespeare's world with an emphasis that will extend our interpretation of the plays. This book, then, is a historical account of the interacting political, social, economic, and cultural contexts in which Shakespeare's plays were written, performed, and received and which helped to shape and influence his contemporaries. His age is understood primarily as his lifetime (1564–1616), but we must also consider the previous generation, the memories of which could readily be recovered by and for Shakespeare. Some of the audience would also have been older than the playwright. The impact of these contexts can be seen in the themes, plots, language, and presentation of the plays.

This book is lightly footnoted, but both footnotes and the "Selected Further Reading" section at the end are intended to direct readers toward relevant scholarship. That scholarship is crucial, but even more so is seeing, listening to, or at least reading the plays. Engaging directly with the works is valuable whatever the medium selected; and the expansion of available media over the last century has greatly increased the number of ways in which Shakespeare can be presented and approached. So also with translations of Shakespeare into the cultures and occasions, as well as languages, of many other peoples.

For myself, this book brings back memories of over half a century, from childhood onward, of going to Shakespeare's plays in many places, but most notably Arundel, Cambridge, Exeter, London, Newcastle, Oxford, Plymouth, and Stratford; in open-air variety (from pouring rain to soft evenings) and in closed-in intensity; and with many different people. Recollections can be bittersweet, but these plays have been a cause and occasion of many memories. The echoes of these memories and in particular of those with whom I went to the theater are with me now. I would like in particular to thank my beloved father for taking me, then an impressionable young adult, for the first time to see the Royal Shakespeare Company (RSC): a commanding and dynamic production of *Henry V* in Stratford in 1975, with Alan Howard in the royal role, one played without the antiwar critique, more especially anger, that is at the fore in so many recent productions. Living in North East England from 1980 to 1996, I benefited greatly from the RSC bringing its productions to the provinces, especially in the shape of Newcastle's excellent Theatre Royal and the Playhouse. More recently, the open-air productions in the Rougemont Gardens in Exeter have occasioned family outings, as well as providing another linkage back to Shakespeare himself, for Rougemont Castle features in *Richard III* with a brief mention. The Bristol-based company Tobacco Factory has offered some especially memorable productions in the South West.

I first saw Shakespeare onstage at my school, Haberdashers' Aske's, notably a lively production of *Much Ado About Nothing*, and another of *Julius Caesar* with the battle scenes made disorientating by stroboscopic lighting, and I first acted onstage there as a very young "Wall" in *A Midsummer Night's Dream*, an appropriately limited part. Yet again, I am reminded of how lucky I was to go to such an imaginative school. The decision of Michael Fitch, our teacher, to squeeze the entire A-level English course into one year and spend the other year on a Grand Tour through English literature, which he felt was a necessary part of education, provided another term of Shakespeare to add to *Macbeth* and *Antony and Cleopatra*, which were the set texts we had to cover. We also dealt with his contemporaries, including Thomas Kyd, while Thomas Middleton's *The Revenger's Tragedy*[1] was another set text. I irritated Michael by telling him that I preferred the plays of John Webster, notably his tragedies, *The Duchess of Malfi* and *The White Devil*, but benefited from the opportunity to discuss *Hamlet* and *King Lear* with such a fine teacher and also from comparing Shakespeare's *Antony and Cleopatra* with John Dryden's *All for Love; or, The World Well Lost*, his version of the story. Michael had scant time for theory, once sardonically remarking that "a phallic object is anything longer than it is broad."

This teaching also provided me with the encouragement, when young, to go to the theater myself, benefiting from transport by the London tube and from inexpensive matinee tickets, moving forward as soon as the lights went down, from the back row to more expensive but empty seats nearer the stage. Sir Laurence Olivier as Shylock and Paul Scofield as Prospero proved especially memorable, but I also liked the vigorous productions at the Young Vic.

"He was not of an age but for all time!" Ben Jonson's assessment in his poem "To the Memory of My Beloved the Author, Mr William Shakespeare" (1623) is still so apt. The insistent nature of Shakespeare's imagery can be found across the range of world culture. Moreover, the presentation of Shakespeare has offered accounts for England at the time, as well as of many other periods and cultures. The coverage and style in individual productions, as well as in works based on or referring to Shakespeare, varied greatly. For example, Olivier's *Henry V* (1944) opened with a panorama of London in about 1600, but it was a model shot, and, thereafter, the first act took place within the theater. In contrast, far more authentic images of street life appeared in the film *Shakespeare in Love* and in "The Shakespeare Code," a 2007 episode of the hugely popular British television series *Doctor Who*. In the latter, Doctor Who visits Shakespeare's London, informing his black companion that Africans then lived in London (as indeed they did), thus helping to ground an idea of identity that was of current relevance.

Variety is still very much to the fore at present. For example, the 2017 program of the Theatre Royal, Plymouth, included Yukio Ninagawa's production of *Macbeth*, part of a tour reviving the highly successful 1985 production, which is performed in Japanese with English subtitles. There was also Brett Dean's *Hamlet*, a new opera based on the play, with the central issue being how vengeance was thwarted by introspection.

For this book, I have benefited from lecturing on Shakespeare's England for the University of Virginia Summer School in Oxford and at Radley College and from the advice of Jonathan Barry, Karen Edwards, Bill Gibson, Johanna Luthman, Andrew McRae, Steven Parissien, Nigel Ramsay, Laura Sangha, Nigel Saul, Mark Stoyle, Richard Wendorf, Neil York, and two anonymous readers, on all or sections of an earlier draft. Eileen Cox has helped on particular points. It is a great pleasure to dedicate the book to Eluned Dorkins, a good friend to both Sarah and to me.

The exact composition of Shakespeare's theatrical canon is a matter of great controversy, while the dating of many individual plays is unclear.[2] Many commentators have doubted authorship of all or some of the plays by Shakespeare. The following should be seen as suggestions, and there is much room for debate, about dates, order, and authorship. For respected, recent attempts to discuss the entire play canon in order—their order inevitably differing from each other and from what follows—see Harold

Bloom, *Shakespeare and the Invention of the Human* (1998); Marjorie Garber, *Shakespeare after All* (2004); and Gary Taylor, John Jowett, Terri Bourus, and Gabriel Egan (editors), *The New Oxford Shakespeare: The Complete Works* (2017).

| | |
|---|---|
| 1588–93 | *The Comedy of Errors* |
| 1588–94 | *Love's Labor's Lost* |
| 1590–91 | *Henry VI, Part II* |
| 1590–91 | *Henry VI, Part III* |
| 1591–92 | *Henry VI, Part I* |
| 1592 | *Arden of Faversham* (part authorship) |
| 1592–93 | *Richard III* |
| 1592–94 | *Titus Andronicus* |
| 1593–94 | *The Taming of the Shrew* |
| 1593–98 | *The Two Gentlemen of Verona* |
| 1594 | *Edward III* (anon. and Shakespeare) |
| 1594–96 | *Romeo and Juliet* |
| 1595 | *Richard II* |
| 1594–96 | *A Midsummer Night's Dream* |
| 1595–96 | *King John* |
| 1596–97 | *The Merchant of Venice* |
| 1597 | *Henry IV, Part I* |
| 1597–98 | *Henry IV, Part II* |
| 1598–1600 | *Much Ado About Nothing* |
| 1599 | *Henry V* |
| 1599 | *Julius Caesar* |
| 1599–1600 | *As You Like It* |
| 1599–1600 | *Twelfth Night* |
| 1600–01 | *Hamlet* |
| 1597–1601 | *The Merry Wives of Windsor* |
| 1601–02 | *Troilus and Cressida* |
| 1604 | *All's Well That Ends Well* |
| 1603–04 | *Othello* |
| 1604 | *Measure for Measure* |

| 1605 | *King Lear* |
| 1605 | *Macbeth* |
| 1606–07 | *Antony and Cleopatra* |
| 1605–08 | *Timon of Athens* |
| 1607–09 | *Coriolanus* |
| 1608–09 | *Pericles* |
| 1609–10 | *Cymbeline* |
| 1610–11 | *The Winter's Tale* |
| 1611 | *The Tempest* |
| 1612–13 | *Henry VIII*, coauthored |
| 1613 | *The History of Cardenio*, lost, coauthored |
| 1613–14 | *Two Noble Kinsmen*, coauthored |

## NOTES

1. The anonymous play published in 1607 has also been attributed to Cyril Tourneur, but Middleton's authorship is now generally accepted.

2. See, for example, J. Peachman, "Why a Dog? A Late Date for *The Two Gentlemen of Verona*," *Notes and Queries*, 252 (2007): 265–72.

# ENGLAND IN THE AGE OF
# SHAKESPEARE

# ONE

# THE IMAGINATION OF THE AGE

UNCERTAINTY HELD AT BAY: THAT was the experience of life and the molder of personality in early-modern England, the England of the sixteenth and seventeenth centuries. Man in the state of nature was described by Thomas Hobbes in *Leviathan* (1651), his masterpiece (of political thought and much else), as "solitary, poor, nasty, brutish and short," and this phrase describes much of Shakespeare's world. The sudden pitfalls of life, notably the fatal accidents and the tragic illnesses that snuffed out life with brutal rapidity, could be explained not only by the harsh injustices of chance but also by the impact of evil and malevolence.

These elements were repeatedly seen in Shakespeare's plays; indeed, they gave the plays much of their plot, their dynamic energy, and their atmosphere. Characters could be defined in terms of how they responded to chance, evil, and malevolence. In turn, evil and malevolence worked in part, notably in the tragedies, by exploiting character, as with Iago's cloyingly seductive manipulation of Othello and the witches' provocation of Macbeth and his wife, a provocation that is a seduction of another type.

All around them, contemporaries saw a battle between good and evil, a battle that was the cause of dread and fear—with jokes about it, as with the Porter's speech in *Macbeth*, very much being "gallows humor." Evil and malevolence, whatever their source and purpose, operated in and through the varied settings of life. The dark, both literally and metaphorically, was particularly important, as with the villainy in *Much Ado About Nothing.* This is a villainy dependent upon the misidentification that the dark makes far easier. The modern world can overcome darkness, with electric lighting and with global navigation systems. By contrast, in Shakespeare's world, the dark was a pervading, spreading sphere; although, in the open-air theater in this period, when darkness falls in a play, the staging brings on more lights.

Darkness might not always be a token of menace, danger, and uncertainty. It could be a setting for romance and witty confusion. Moreover, in *A Midsummer Night's Dream,* which is set in and outside Athens, Oberon orders Puck to prevent Demetrius and Lysander from fighting:

> overcast the night;
> The starry welkin cover thou anon
> With drooping fog as black as Acheron;[1]
> And lead these testy rivals so astray,
> As one come not within another's way. (III, ii)

The play demonstrates the vulnerability of humans to supernatural agencies, albeit to comic effect, as with Bottom being given the head of an ass (donkey). The humorous confusion of nighttime comic mischance is also seen in other plays, as in the highway robbery in *Henry IV, Part I* in which the Chamberlain tells Gadshill: "you are more beholding to the night than to fern-seed for your walking invisible" (II, i). The "seed" of the fern was believed to convey invisibility. However, alongside the romance of the evening in *A Midsummer Night's Dream* and humorous confusion elsewhere in Shakespeare's work there is nighttime horror, terror, and evil. In contrast, pastoral plays very much employ daytime settings.

Nighttime fear especially befell travelers, both literal and figurative, whether simply unable to see their route or to grasp the menaces that might face them. In *King Lear,* the Fool sees the dark as part of the moral blindness that has overcome Lear and his kingdom and become the dominant tone of the latter: "out went the candle," and he observes, "we were left darkling" (I, iv). Lear, in turn, is reborn through his experience into a degree of clarity, but he cannot regain what he has lost.

More generally, the dark was a world outside human understanding, not to mention outside human control. Like All Hallows' Eve (Halloween, October 31), when the dead walked on the earth, the dead king walks at night in *Hamlet*, but he fades away at daybreak, aware that his realm is that of nighttime: not just nighttime imaginings but also nighttime reality. The ghost of this king is a part of a wider struggle, between Christian good and spirits, that is outlined in the first scene of the play. Aware of this struggle, Hamlet is concerned about the danger of being misled. Marcellus sets the ghost's response at daybreak in terms of a wider struggle between good and evil, observing:

> It faded on the crowing of the cock.
> Some say that ever 'gainst that season comes
> Wherein our Saviour's birth is celebrated,
> The bird of dawning singeth all night long:
> and then, they say, no spirit can walk abroad;
> The nights are wholesome; then no planets strike,
> No fairy takes, nor witch hath power to charm,
> So hallow'd and so gracious is the time. (I, i)

Lady Macbeth calls on the assistance of darkness, crying:

> Come, thick Night,
> And pall thee in the dunnest smoke of Hell,
> That my keen knife sees not the wound it makes,
> Nor Heaven peep through the blanket of the dark,
> To cry, "Hold, hold!" (I, v)

Macbeth's evil and increased lack of self-control, each a product of diabolical forces working on his narcissism, is measured by his willingness to call on the dark to cover the murder of his erstwhile friend, now imagined rival, Banquo, when he declares:

> Come, seeling Night,
> Scarf up the tender eye of pitiful Day,
> And, with thy bloody and invisible hand,
> Cancel, and tear to pieces, that great bond
> Which keeps me pale!—Light thickens; and the crow
> Makes wing to th' rooky wood;
> Good things of Day begin to droop and drowse,
> While Night's black agents to their prey do rouse. (III, ii)

This was a world of nightmare; and the role of the dark in the life of the imagination was both aspect and product of a more generalized sense of fear, one that was in no way restricted to the dark, although focused there.[2] The witches brought onstage in *Macbeth* operate in the dark or in misty vapors. Caliban, the "born devil" of *The Tempest*, is a "thing of darkness" (IV, i; V, i). In this play, the (dead) witch Sycorax is a malign as well as mysterious counterpoint to Prospero's white magic, a witch passing on her poison through her son, Caliban. His plans may be thwarted, but they are vicious and dangerous and provide much of the drama of the play.

The approach of playing Caliban as the victim of Western colonialism and of treating Prospero and Miranda as having selfish reasons to stigmatize him unfairly, and thus as unreasonable in their criticism, represents a different power relationship. This relationship also captures the idea of a monstrous "other," although, in this case, one in which sympathy is directed to the supposed "monster." Moreover, Caliban's otherness has frequently been represented by his color.[3] This contrast with the account of Caliban's diabolical origins involves a very different reading of the play; however, it is one that makes more sense to some modern audiences.

In their malevolence and deceit,[4] the devil and the witches were real for contemporaries, including playgoers, representing a directing and leading part of the potent and varied legions of evil.

In *All's Well That Ends Well*, the Clown refers to serving a great prince: "The black prince, sir, alias the prince of darkness, alias the devil . . . he is the prince of the world" (IV, v). Satan, limbo, and furies return as subjects of "talk" in that play (V, iii). In *The Comedy of Errors*, the courtesan is decried, inaccurately, as "the devil's dam . . . she comes in the habit of a light wench" (IV, iii). In *Othello*, Iago rejoices in the birth of his plot, exulting that

> Hell and night
> Must bring this monstrous birth to the world's light. (I, iii)

In practice, however, it is a plot based on the envy of one human for another. In *The Tempest*, the storm at sea that sinks the ship leads the desperate Ferdinand to exclaim as he leaps into the sea:

> Hell is empty,
> And all the devils are here. (I, ii)

Magic is certainly at play, although one that, it turns out, is not malign, because it is called forth by Prospero, who is presented as a generally positive figure, notably in the magical safety of both ship and crew.

References to hell are commonplace in Shakespeare's plays, although not always menacing. Sir John Falstaff, in *The Merry Wives of Windsor*, refers to being thrown into the river Thames, "like a barrow of butcher's offal," offering an explanation, incidentally, of why the Thames downstream at London was so filthy—only for him to be saved because it was not "as deep as hell." Indeed, "the shore was shelvy and shallow" (III, v). Mrs. Page, speaking of him, says: "The spirit of wantonness is, sure, scared out of him: if the devil have him not in fee-simple, with fine and recovery, he will never, I think, in the way of waste, attempt us again" (IV, ii).

There are many references in Shakespeare to the devil as a figure of malevolent deceit, but also to rather different devils. In *Othello*, Cassio reflects: "It hath pleased the devil drunkenness to give place to the devil wrath. . . . Every inordinate cup is unblest, and the ingredient is a devil" (II, iii). These references reflect not the emptiness of the language of hell and the devil but its universality so that, alongside Satan, there are often lesser devils. Villains, moreover, can mistake the good as diabolical, as when Sebastian in *The Tempest*, responding to Prospero's knowledge of his treacherous plan, remarks, "The devil speaks in him" (V, i).[5]

The Last Judgment, the divine judgment at the end of the human world, was still a present fear even if, following the Protestant Reformation earlier in the sixteenth century, images of it were banished from churches, the interiors of most of which were eventually whitewashed. The Christian world picture provided plentiful ground for fear, with millenarian, apocalyptic, and eschatological anxieties drawing heavily on the biblical Book of Revelation. In *Henry VI, Part I*, Henry Beaufort, Cardinal-Bishop of Winchester, comments on Henry V, the son of his legitimate half brother:

> He was a king bless'd of the King of Kings [i.e., God].
> Unto the French the dreadful judgment-day
> So dreadful will not be as was his sight.
> The battles of the Lord of Hosts he fought. (I, i)

There were more immediate issues and episodes. James VI of Scotland (r. 1567–1625) and I of England (r. 1603–25), for whose court *Macbeth* may well have been produced, wrote against witches and was believed to be the target of their diabolical schemes, notably of the North Berwick (Scotland) coven of witches. Banquo was regarded as James's ancestor and was presented thus by Shakespeare in *Macbeth*.

James later recanted his opinions and, if anything, became a force for moderation in the treatment of witches.[6] But belief in witchcraft was abundantly present in recent history, Scottish, English, and Continental. An earlier king of Scotland, James III, in 1479, had accused one of his brothers, John, Earl of Mar, of witchcraft. Mar died soon after in mysterious circumstances.

Several witches were condemned for melting a wax image of James and were burned to death.

Thirty-eight years earlier, Eleanor Cobham had been accused of using a witch to entrap her husband, Humphrey, Duke of Gloucester, a younger brother of Henry V, and of hiring an astrologer to melt a wax image of his nephew, Henry VI, in order to kill him and to obtain the throne for Humphrey. In *Henry VI, Part II*, Shakespeare shows Eleanor as consulting a fortune-teller, the witch Margery Jordan, and having the fiend Asmath conjured forth. Margery is burned alive as a consequence.[7] The contentious and topical nature of witchcraft accusations was linked to these accusations being brought against Queen Elizabeth's mother, Anne Boleyn, in 1536, although she was not finally charged with witchcraft.

Witchcraft was an indictable crime. It encapsulated the threat to orthodoxy and what was believed to be the relationship between the real nature of evil and both inner and public conflicts. Contemporary concerns about witchcraft also provide a way in which later historians could see both types of conflict.[8]

In Shakespeare's lifetime, news of witches was spread in the relatively new culture of print—in learned treatises, chapbooks, printed ballads, and engravings. Examples included Reginald Scot's *The Discoverie of Witchcraft* (1584), although Scot was a vehement skeptic, George Gifford's *A Dialogue Concerning Witches and Witchcraftes* (1593), and John Cotta's *The Trial of Witchcraft* (1616). The news spread by print accounts of trials was also important, such as the *Most Strange and admirable discovery of the three Witches of Warboys* (1593) and *The Witches of Northamptonshire* (1612). The last reported an episode that allegedly happened to William Avery and his sister, Elizabeth Belcher, who had been bewitched because, it was claimed, she had hit a witch:

> Riding homewards in one coach, there appeared to their view a man and a woman riding both upon a black horse. Master Avery having spied them afar, and noting many strange gestures from them, suddenly...cried out...That either they or their horses should presently

miscarry. And immediately the horses fell down dead. Whereupon Master Avery rose up praising the grace and mercies of God that had so powerfully delivered them, and had not suffered the foul spirits to work the uttermost of their mischief upon men made after his image, but had turned their fury against beasts.[9]

Shakespeare was far from alone in mentioning witches and in putting them onstage. In *The Witch of Edmonton* (c. 1621), a play by William Rowley, Thomas Dekker, and John Ford, an old woman named Elizabeth Sawyer becomes a witch, after having made a pact with the devil—a common theme in witch accounts. At the same time, the play, which also features a devil dog, is a rather sophisticated one that presents Elizabeth Sawyer as a woman forced by a hostile society into behaving like a witch. Indeed, the play treats several of the "establishment" figures as distinctly more evil in motivation than her, which is a parallel to John Webster's *The Duchess of Malfi* (1613).

Parliamentary statutes against witchcraft were passed in 1563 and 1604, the first arising from a connection drawn between Catholicism and magical conspiracy that reflected alleged Catholic attempts to conjure spirits over Elizabeth's chances of dying from smallpox in 1562, a death that would have pushed the Catholic Mary, Queen of Scots to the fore for the succession. The 1604 act made even the benevolent conjuring of spirits a capital offense. However, the toll of executions under Elizabeth I, although higher than at any other time in English history except the 1640s, remained relatively low, in part probably because the justices of the peace (JPs) wished to avoid the dangerous communal fractures that energetic witch-hunting could provoke and reveal.[10]

Concern about witches bridged elite and populace, church and state. However, at the same time, there was a contrast between the category of witchcraft imposed by the law and the less defined but still potent traditional religious and folklore beliefs. The frequency of curses in discussion and disputes and the concern to which they gave rise focused attention on the practice of directing harm and on the linked power of bewitchment.

This was a theme that Shakespeare could use with captivating or malign intention, language, and energy, as in *A Midsummer Night's Dream* and *Macbeth* respectively. The apparitions that the witches show Macbeth are even more unsettling and mysterious than are the witches themselves. Conversely, in *The Tempest*, Prospero uses "the rabble," over whom he has given power to Ariel, to produce an attractive masque for Ferdinand and Miranda (IV, i). In *Twelfth Night*, as part of a blackly comic (even bleakly comic) plot, the imprisoned Malvolio is treated as if he is inhabited by a "fiend," in fact by "Satan" (IV, ii).

In contrast, Laertes's angry outburst to Hamlet—"The devil take thy soul" (V, i)—captures a real harm to accompany Laertes's very physical attempt to throttle Hamlet, a harm that is more lasting and terrifying than that intended to Hamlet's body. This is a play in which the question of guilt for the death of Hamlet's father sits within the more general one of the abiding struggle for salvation. For Hamlet to kill his uncle Claudius, the king, he has to feel justified, and Hamlet is strongly challenged by his unease and uncertainty, before being energized by his conviction of his uncle's guilt. At first, Hamlet doubts the ghost of his father, in a fashion similar to but more incapacitating than Macbeth's doubts about being led astray by the witches. He muses:

> The spirit that I have seen
> May be the Devil, and the Devil hath power
> T'assume a pleasing shape, yea and perhaps
> Out of my weakness, and my melancholy,
> As he is very potent with such spirits,
> Abuses me to damn me. (II, ii)

There was also a degree of ambivalence about the supernatural, an ambivalence captured by the presence and attitudes of spirits working at the behest of good forces, notably Puck in *A*

*Midsummer Night's Dream* and, more problematically, Ariel in *The Tempest*. Their power is shown greatly to surpass those of humans. With Puck and Ariel, this is not only a matter of their speed. In addition, Puck is protean, which is a key element of his magical character, and he is, at once, able to work for good or bad. As he boasts:

> Sometimes a horse I'll be, sometimes a hound,
> A hog, a headless bear, sometimes a fire,
> And neigh, and bark, and grunt, and roar, and burn,
> Like horse, hound, hog, bear, fire, at every turn. (III, i)

In the last scene of *The Tempest*, Ariel is shown as feeling human sympathy and a degree of pity that Prospero comes to more reluctantly (V, i). Belief in fairies was widespread, and while the church had traditionally presented them as demons, fairies were treated far more favorably in popular culture.[11]

Accusations of witchcraft in England arose from a wide range of causes, including refusals of charity and personal quarrels, but the fear of real evil was at the core of witchcraft allegations. It was believed possible to cause harm to person and property by using magical means and to do so as part of a rejection of society and Christianity. Demonic possession could be seen at work[12] and was believed to be more generally present.

To keep away such fates and curses as a whole, it was appropriate and even necessary to turn to white magic. Such magic ranged widely, including both the teachings and practices of Christianity (practices that in turn were very varied) and the semi- (or un-) Christianized magical beliefs that brought meaning, comfort, and a precarious safety to many. Many people, especially before the Reformation, relied on lucky charms and traveled to sacred sites, such as springs: holy wells were especially numerous in Cornwall and Wales. The wearing of crucifixes, the making of the sign of the cross (which was very important to both social practice and the iconography of the period), the reverence shown to religious images, and the saying of prayers were all aspects of a world in which the doings of the day were suffused with Christian thought, expression, and action. The sign of the cross was designed to ward off evil. Moreover, illiterate people drew a sign of the cross as a substitute for writing their signature.

The vocabulary of most of Shakespeare's characters reflects this focus. The inability to talk of salvation is a clear indicator of Macbeth's guilt and is one that he nervously repeats and repents after the murder of Duncan:

> Listening their fear, I could not say "Amen,"
> when they did say, "God bless us."
> . . . . . . . . . . . . . . . . . . . . . . . . . .
> wherefore could not I pronounce "Amen"?
> I had most need of blessing, and "Amen"
> Stuck in my throat (II, ii)

In the pressure of the moment, his wife fails to appreciate his point, but she is eventually driven to the false repentance of suicide. In contrast, a would-be king slayer, Caliban, at the close of *The Tempest*, is brought to realize his folly and to "seek for grace"—in other words, redemption (V, i). In the same scene, however, Antonio, another would-be king slayer and, unlike Caliban, a human, indeed a baptized Christian, fails to confront his sin. It is in part as a result but also more generally that the resolution of that play is uncertain, varied, and can be played differently, for example, in the relationship between Ariel and Prospero but also regarding the future of Antonio, who remains a malcontent and thus a threat, as well as a means for evil.

The new religious practices of the Protestant Reformation did not lessen the conviction of direct providential intervention in the affairs of man and of a daily interaction of the human world and the wider spheres of good and evil. Instead, there was room to accentuate and focus these beliefs. To the established Protestant Church—the Church of England—Catholicism was superstitious, even a system of superstition. In addition, to many (but not all) Protestants, the Catholic Church served the goals of the devil, and, therefore, individual Catholics could be seen in this light. However, that was not invariably the case. Indeed, links of family, friendship, kinship, and community cut across this division, although sometimes also focusing on it (for example, in inheritance disputes).

Evil, malevolence, and the inscrutable workings of the divine will all seemed the only way to explain the sudden pitfalls of the human condition. There was a widespread certainty that forces of good and evil battled for control of the world and throughout the world. This was a society that, in terms of the Augustinian belief in the struggle between the City of God and that of the devil but also drawing on wider and older anxieties and traditions, was shadowed by spirits, good and bad. These spirits were seen and believed to intervene frequently in the life of humans, on a pattern also present in other contemporary cultures, for example those of Buddhist Japan and Hindu India.

This belief brought together Christian notions—in particular, providentialism (a conviction of God's direct intervention in the life of individuals); the intercessionary role of clerics, sacraments, prayer, and belief; and the real existence of heaven, hell, and the devil—with a related and overlapping group of ideas, beliefs, and customs that were only partially Christianized. The latter also testified to a mental world that was not entirely explicable in terms of Christian theology nor under the spiritual sway and ecclesiastical authority of the Church of England.[13] This was a world, for both the elite and the masses, of good and evil, of knowledge in magic and magic in knowledge, of fatalism, of the occult, and of astrology and alchemy.

There were many overlaps, tensions, and fault lines between these practices, tendencies, and categories and the individuals and communities, experiences, and perceptions involved. In part these overlaps, tensions, and rift lines reflected the ambiguities and confusions of contemporary thought, as can be seen in the plays of the period. In addition, consistency or clarity were not the tasks, or, at least, not the prime tasks, of playwrights; and this was readily apparent both in the case of individual characters and regarding plays as a whole.

Astrology, almanacs, and witchcraft were all part of the context of stories and the process of their plots, and could variously be benign and malign. Life, fertility, health, livelihood, and fortune in war or love all were at stake in a form of control and pursuit of knowledge that replicated that associated with the oracles of antiquity. The tales of antiquity, notably as told in Ovid's *Metamorphoses*, which was extensively drawn on by Shakespeare, describe unpredictable change but also change that reflected the transformative ability of phenomena, including change of shape and the coming, loss, and recovery of life. These were stories about becoming. Ovid was Shakespeare's favorite classical writer, and most of his references to classical mythology relate to stories in that work, which he knew both in Latin and in the 1567 English translation. Although Shakespeare refashioned what he read,[14] the influence of the *Metamorphoses* is especially strong in *A Midsummer Night's Dream*, *Titus Andronicus*, and *The Winter's Tale*, but it can also be seen elsewhere, for example, in *The Tempest*. Shakespeare's classical education at Stratford left an important legacy in his writings, including in subjects, plots, characterization, symbolism, and language. So also with his references to the Bible.[15]

With reference to astrology and almanacs, the impact of the zodiac was seen in the understanding of both character and change, while constraining or explaining the role and impact of what might otherwise be seen as random chance. This crucial issue fired up the debate between determinism and free will, a debate found throughout Shakespeare's works as in those of all other playwrights of the period. This issue could be horrific, as when the spell-casting witches lure Macbeth to regicide and the loss of his soul, or comic, as when lovers seek to persuade their intended. Shakespeare's characters frequently refer to the zodiacal sign under which they were born. Thus, in *All's Well That Ends Well*, Parolles is told he must have been born under Mars when it was moving backward because he is inclined to flee when fighting (I, i).

Familiarity with the heavens united the new learning of the Elizabethan Renaissance with the old learning from the Middle Ages, two worlds that Shakespeare straddled and drew on. His characters regularly make astrological references. In *Much Ado About Nothing*, Don John says to Conrade, a fellow villain: "I wonder that thou—being, as thou sayest thou art, born under Saturn—goest about to apply a moral medicine to a mortifying mischief" (I, iii). This is a reference to the gloomy and "saturnine" character of those born under this sign but also an acceptance that free will can play a role. In the same play, Beatrice, a far more positive character, remarks, "there was a star danced, and under that was I born" (II, i). At the start of *Cymbeline*, the First Gentleman observes:

> our bloods
> No more obey the heavens. (I, i)

In *Twelfth Night*, Sir Toby Belch points out to Sir Andrew Aguecheek that they were both "born under Taurus" (I, iii) and should therefore be able to dance. In *King Lear*, as part of a more general questioning in the play of purpose, morality, and causation, there is a bitter attack on astrology and the zodiac. However, the attack is given to the morally bankrupt (and illegitimate) villain Edmund, an allocation that, arguably, compromises, if not invalidates, the argument:

> This is the excellent foppery of the world, that when we are sick in fortune, often the surfeit of our own behaviour, we make guilty of our disasters the sun, the moon, and the stars; as if we were villains by necessity, fools by heavenly compulsion, knaves, thieves, and treachers [traitors], by spherical predominance, drunkards, liars,

and adulterers by an enforced obedience of planetary influence, and all that we are evil in by a divine thrusting on. An admirable evasion of whoremaster man, to lay his goatish disposition to the charge of a star! My father compounded with my mother under the Dragon's tail, and my nativity was under Ursa Major, so that it follows I am rough and lecherous. 'Sfoot! I should have been that I am had the maidenliest star in the firmament twinkled on my bastardizing. (I, ii)

Astrology meant a geography as well as a moral sphere that needed to be navigated. This was a geography of the factors that affected fate, a geography that, in practice, brought the occult into peoples' lives and enabled its possibilities to be understood. Indeed, the measurement, presentation, and understanding of physical space on the earth's surface scarcely exhausted the geographies of Shakespeare's world. The geography of the stars appeared far more present than that of distant continents, in part due to the influence, if not control, that the zodiac was believed to wield over peoples' lives. The zodiac was part of an ordered world. In *Troilus and Cressida*, although his argument is aimed at specific ends, as well as being a reflection of his somewhat tricky character, Ulysses also offers a much-quoted general account when he declares:

Degree being vizarded,
The unworthiest shows as fairly in the mask.
The heavens themselves, the planets, and this centre
Observe degree, priority, and place,
Insisture, course, proportion, season, form,
Office, and custom, in all line of order;
And therefore is the glorious planet Sol
In noble eminence enthroned and sphered
Amidst the other; whose medicinable eye
Corrects the ill aspects of planets evil,
And posts, like the commandment of a king,
Sans check, to good and bad: but when the planets
In evil mixture to disorder wander,
What plagues, and what portents, what mutiny,

What raging of the sea, shaking of earth,
Commotion in the winds, frights, changes, horrors,
Divert and crack, rend and deracinate
The unity and married calm of states
Quite from their fixure! O, when degree is shaked,
Which is the ladder to all high designs,
The enterprise is sick. How could communities,
Degrees in schools, and brotherhoods in cities,
Peaceful commerce from dividable shores,
The primogenitive and due of birth,
Prerogative of age, crowns, sceptres, laurels,
But by degree, stand in authentic place?
Take but degree away, untune that string,
And, hark! what discord follows. (I, iii)

Thus, the world, and not just the earth but the wider world within which the earth was located, had order and therefore purpose, and humans needed guidance to understand this order and its underlying structure. This guidance had to have both a mental and a physical component. The zodiac gave a key form to this structure and explained how it operated and how best it could and should be understood.

The magician was a great guide, for the magician could range beyond Christian magic to conjure up evil or to seek to lessen it. At the same time, the magician, not least for dramatic effect, moral purpose, and Christian belief, had to leave room for individual will and action. Prospero is the most impressive instance of Shakespeare's magicians, but he is scarcely alone. As king of the fairies, Oberon, in *A Midsummer Night's Dream*, is another. He is able, for example, according to Titania, to take "the shape of Corin," a mythical lover, in order to woo Phillida (II, i). Seeking to understand as well as direct, with the latter very much dependent on the former, the magicians could scan the skies and indeed generally did so. But the magicians also looked at a full range of means to gauge the future, many of which involved reading natural runes on the earth: from human health to animal or other equivalents.

This was a guidance that was notable in Shakespeare's London, as can be seen from the great reputation enjoyed by John Dee (1527–1608), a leading mathematician and cartographer. On the Continent, the court of the (Holy Roman) Emperor Rudolf II (r. 1576–1612), located in Prague, the capital of the kingdom of Bohemia, was a major center of astrology, and Rudolf was greatly interested in the spirit world, the occult, and alchemy.[16] Those involved sought to be at the cutting edge of advances in astronomy, mathematics, and other subjects; they were not "reactionary" figures. More humble astrologers lacked such patronage, facilities, and education but benefited from the reputation of the prominent and from the knowledge and information provided by relevant publications.

Again, this was a world that was well understood and presented by Shakespeare. Fortune-telling was a matter of small talk among young men discussing marital prospects, as much as a risk to souls, as in *Macbeth*, or an engagement with affairs of state. In *Henry IV, Part I*, Owen Glendower (Owain Glyndŵr) and Harry Hotspur row about the astral signs that allegedly accompanied the birth of the former, a vainglorious figure keen to assert and demonstrate the drama of his life. Astrological speculation also played a part in conspiracies, such as the unsuccessful one of Perkin Warbeck in the 1490s by discontented Yorkists against Henry VII.[17]

Belief in the devil was related to apocalyptic ideas, and these ideas encouraged great interest in astronomy. Astronomy was regarded as enabling predictions about astral movements that could then be aligned with astrological theses. Moreover, both comets and horoscopes were linked to political reflection. Thus, experimentation, in the form of astronomy, was designed to support an established and all-encompassing interpretative pattern. Portents and signs were looked for as a means of prophecy. Given the extent to which modern scholarly opinion credits sunspot activity with responsibility for the climatic deterioration that affected agriculture, social stability, and much else during the sixteenth and seventeenth centuries,[18] the interest in those centuries in astronomy and astrology appears more reasonable, albeit totally different in character, context, cause, and consequence to the modern scholarly approach.

Astronomy was a key element in the discussion and understanding of fate and one that was developing rapidly. Thus, Thomas Addison's *Arithmetical Navigation* (1625) provided detailed knowledge about the effective use of maritime charts and about the celestial bodies. The heliocentric system of Nicolas Copernicus (1473–1543), which held that the earth moves about the sun, was rapidly disseminated by print, while the *Rudolphine Tables* (1627) of Johannes Kepler (1571–1630) provided tables of planetary positions based on his discovery that the orbits of planets were elliptic and on his ability to ascertain their speeds. Kepler, the author of *Astronomia Nova* (1609), succeeded the Danish astronomer Tycho Brahe (1546–1601) as court astronomer to Rudolf II.

Copenhagen was an important center of astronomy under both Frederick II (r. 1559–88), father of James I's wife, Anne, and patron of Brahe, and Christian IV (r. 1588–1648), her brother, and this offers a different linkage between the two courts from that suggested by *Hamlet*. Kepler's *Harmonice Mundi* (*The Harmony of the World*, 1619), reflected both his continuing research in planetary motion and the belief that astronomy was necessary to understand the inherent design and order of the universe and, therefore, its capacity for good. Kepler also saw the impact of music on human emotions as an aspect of cosmic harmony. He argued that humans vibrate in sympathy to the universe's divine order and also respond to the disruptions of this order that are related to dissonance. To Kepler, musical counterpoint was analogous to the interlocking nature of planetary orbits.

There was an interest in the idea of other inhabitants of the cosmos, which helped to explain concern with the moon, where such inhabitants were believed to exist. In *The Tempest*, Stephano tells Caliban that he had been "the man i' th'moon" and had come from the moon to the island (II, ii), while Prospero describes Caliban's mother, the witch Sycorax, as

one so strong
That could control the moon, make flows and ebbs (V, i)

The last line indicates her power to cause change. The predictive power of the imagination was seen in written accounts of fictional lunar voyages, such as Kepler's *Somnium* (*Dream*) of about 1609 and Francis Godwin's *The Man in the Moone: or A Discourse of a Voyage Thither* (1638). Playwrights, however, did not turn to the topic of journeys to the moon.

Astronomical research encouraged an interest in mathematical understandings of the cosmos and its workings. This was particularly seen in the work of Shakespeare's contemporary Galileo Galilei (1564–1642), professor of mathematics at Padua and then mathematician to Cosimo II, Grand Duke of Tuscany (r. 1609–21). His earliest publication, *Le Operazioni del compass geometrico e militare* (1606), focused on military engineering, not navigation, but there was an emphasis on using an instrument (a compass) and on the importance of applying mathematical rules. Subsequently, Galileo's empirical research focused on the newly invented telescope. First appearing at The Hague in 1608, this was an instrument greatly improved by Galileo.

Moreover, in revealing what he had discovered with his telescope—which, by the close of 1609, magnified twenty times—Galileo's *Sidereus Nuncius* (*The Sidereal Messenger*, 1610) transformed the understanding of the moon by showing it to be like the earth: uneven and with mountains and valleys. Such a similarity challenged the view of an essential contrast between the nature and substance of the earth and the heavens, an argument made by Aristotle. Drawing on the authority of the latter, the thinkers of medieval Christendom had seen the moon as being like the planets, perfect in shape and orbit and unchanging, whereas the earth was prone to change and decay. As a result, the earth was believed to be the appropriate setting for redemption. By revealing that Jupiter had four satellites, Galileo also showed that the earth's moon was not unique. In 1613, Galileo's astronomical ideas were attacked on scriptural grounds, and, subsequently, formal proceedings were launched against him.[19]

White magic and science were not polar opposites, although there were differences between them. To contemporaries, both alchemy and astrology, while studies of mysteries, were also intellectual pursuits and sciences, part of the longstanding overlap of natural and supernatural phenomena and analysis.[20] In contrast, in the value judgment of the period, "magic" was the technique either of the humble (wise women) or of the suspect (ritual magicians). In 1456–57, the English government licensed groups of prospectors to continue their efforts to transmute base metal into bullion; but alchemy, alas, was not to be a substitute for taxation. The alchemical enthusiasms of Henry Percy, Ninth Earl of Northumberland (1564–1632), led him to be known as the "wizard earl." He was a patron of key figures in geographical enquiry, including Thomas Harriot (see chap. 12).

Far from being considered miraculous, such beliefs had a rationality in contemporary terms that helped to make them central to ways of understanding the world. In *The Tempest*, Prospero is a learned figure, able to direct storms and to use his power for both good and ill. Indeed, he has mastery over death, boasting that

> graves at my command
> Have waked their sleepers, oped [opened], and let 'em forth
> By my so potent art. (V, i)

This ability indicates the unfixed nature of death, and that is repeatedly a theme in Shakespeare's plays or language.

However, as with other such potent figures and entities, Shakespeare felt that he needed to confront the question of how far such power takes free will away from the other characters in the play.

Without free will, there can be no guilt, no search for grace, no apology, and no redemption. To dramatic effect, while also capturing theological, psychological, and philosophical uncertainties, the interplay of determinism and free will repeatedly plays a major role in the plays. This interplay reflects and interacts with the ambiguities of personality and also captures some of the issues involved in audience judgment and response. Thus, the future Richard III accepts the murdering fate for which "was I ordained" (*Henry VI, Part III*, V, vi), a choice of words that underlines the sacrilegious character of killing the anointed monarch, a sacral figure.

The contemporary belief in predestination was connected to providential thought, each creating a sense of determinism. The interplay of determinism and free will can be seen both in the responses of individuals and in the difficulties faced by those trying to control particular situations. Despite being a potent magician, Prospero is not able to direct enemies until "a most auspicious star" comes into play (*The Tempest*, I, ii). Julius Caesar seeks to take advantage of superstition in order for Calphurnia, his wife, to become pregnant, which is essential if he is to found a dynasty (as Pompey had done), observing that

> The barren, touched in this holy chase,
> Shake off their sterile curse (I, ii)

But when faced by the option of a prescient warning by a soothsayer—"Beware the Ides of March" (March 15)—he dismisses him as "a dreamer" (I, ii). This is presented as an aspect of Caesar's hubristic pride, but (as well as, not instead) it is not clear how much free will he has. So also for other characters. In that play, the conspirator Cassius makes a vigorous rejection of determinism as part of the longstanding dialogue with his coconspirator, Brutus, through which a whole series of ideas is explored:

> Men at some time are masters of their fates;
> The fault, dear Brutus, is not in our stars,
> But in ourselves, that we are underlings. (I, ii)

In *King Lear*, Edgar vanquishes his half brother, the evil Edmund, and then tells him:

> The gods are just, and of our pleasant vices
> Make instruments to plague us. (V, iii)

This is a verdict on evil, for Edmund's malice has played on the faults of their father, the Earl of Gloucester. Such malice is within but, crucially, is not simply internal. Instead, this malice is part of the real presence of evil in this world, a real presence that seeks to thwart good by working on human clay. Thus, Adam's Fall, the original act of human sin, is reenacted by individuals and across human history. Indeed, if the good call on God or, depending on the setting, the gods, so also can the evil, as when the villainous Claudius, operating in the Christian world, tells Hamlet that the latter's grief "shows a will most incorrect to Heaven . . . 'tis a fault to Heaven" (I, ii). Othello claims that Desdemona has "gone to burning hell!" only for Emilia to call him "a devil" (V, ii). Othello realizes that no one can control his or her fate but, due to his crime, regards himself as destined for hell, crying out:

> O cursed, cursed slave! Whip me, ye devils,
> From the possession of this heavenly sight!
> Blow me about in winds, roast me in sulphur,
> Wash me in steep-down gulfs of liquid fire! (V, ii)

This is a vivid recollection of images of the fate of the damned. Iago is called a "demi-devil" who has "ensnared" Othello's "soul and body" (V, ii). The future Richard III "will buzz abroad [spread] such prophecies" as will doom his brother Clarence, and thus he fulfils the prophecy of Henry VI, one that draws on the ominous portents of Richard's birth (*Henry VI, Part III*, V, vi).

White magic of a type was seen with the touch of the monarch, although it was not regarded as magic. Royal "touching" to cure scrofula (the King's evil—a skin disease), a quasi-magical sign of royal majesty, was observed in *Macbeth* in the case of King Edward the Confessor of England (r. 1042–66), a holy figure to whom the ability was usually traced in England. The practice of touching for scrofula was abandoned in 1603 by James I, who was also against making the sign of the cross, only to be reinstated by him in 1605 and to become more common under Charles I (r. 1625–49), Charles II (r. 1660–85), and James II (r. 1685–88). Having been dropped by William III (r. 1689–1702) and reinstated by Anne (r. 1702–14), "touching" was not abandoned permanently until by George I (r. 1714–27).

Very differently, as an instance of love magic—to bind someone's life with magic, Shakespeare has Othello deploy references to white magic in order to explain the significance of the handkerchief he has given Desdemona:

> OTHELLO: That handkerchief
>   Did an Egyptian to my mother give;
>   She was a charmer, and could almost read
>   The thoughts of people. She told her, while she kept it
>   'Twould make her amiable and subdue my father
>   Entirely to her love; but if she lost it
>   Or made a gift of it, my father's eye
>   Should hold her loathed, and his spirits should hunt
>   After new fancies. She, dying, gave it me,
>   And bid me, when my fate would have me wive
>   To give it her. I did so; and take heed on 't;
>   Make it a darling like your precious eye.
>   To lose't or give't away were such perdition
>   As nothing else could match.
> DESDEMONA: Is't possible?
> OTHELLO: 'Tis true. There's magic in the web of it.
>   A sibyl that had numbered in the world
>   The sun to course two hundred compasses,
>   In her prophetic fury sewed the work;
>   The worms were hallowed that did breed the silk,
>   And it was dyed in mummy which the skilful
>   Conserved of maidens' hearts. (III, iv)

Mummy was a substance derived from embalmed bodies that allegedly had magical qualities. In this case, the dye was made from the hearts of virgins. Egypt was a noted source of mystery and "charmer" means enchantress. Othello is depicted in the play as a successful warrior but an unsophisticated and simple person and therefore possibly credulous.

Understood as intermediaries with the knowledge that was present in this wider world, individuals involved with the occult were frequently prominent figures. Moreover, the understanding of intellectual developments was one in which skills related to the occult could be central. Thus, the well-connected John Dee wished to be able to receive information from angels so as to establish a reliable guide to God's plans.[21] Far from the relationship with God being seen as one mediated solely by the Church and unchanging until the Second Coming of Christ brought human time to the climax of judgment, there was a belief that this relationship could be created anew by other means. Indeed, Dee was in some respects a Prospero figure, albeit without the personal majesty or even regality, let alone the sexual probity, of the latter. Dee recorded conversations with angels in his "angelic laboratory," where experimentation apparently served to advance the cause of true religion. Ultimately, the requisite information for understanding the Book of Nature and redeeming nature depended on the angels, but human effort could help draw it forth. Dee's conversations with angels looked back to medieval magical traditions and folk religion.[22] Far from being an isolated figure, Dee, who enjoyed the favor of Elizabeth I, had many rivals in magical learning and service.

Contemporary thought had both complexity and unity. Belief in prediction, astrology, alchemy, and the occult was apparently especially strong in England in the early seventeenth century. Astrology itself represented a powerful continuation from medieval thought, a continuation that was made stronger and more dynamic both by the attempt to revive the supposed purity of its ancient roots and by the incorporation of new astronomical and mathematical knowledge. Thus, astrology should not be automatically typecast as a redundant system of information and insight. Indeed, astrology benefited from a range of recent and new developments, for, not least with its almanacs, printing was as much about astrology and strange providences—for example, interventions by divine or diabolical agents or sightings of peculiar animals—as it was about a more secular account of life. This was not a new situation. In the later medieval West, secret alphabets had increased in quantity, and whole manuscripts were written occasionally using them. The same was true of the world of print.

Knowledge that was secret, in source and form, was a significant concept that drew on Neoplatonic theories of essential form and truth and the belief that truths, while not inscrutable, were encrypted, notably by suprahuman agencies, and that astrological and other wisdom was necessary to decode them.[23] "Rapt in secret studies" (I, ii), Prospero in *The Tempest* is a potent instance of such knowledge. Official concern about such activity, always a factor, was enhanced as a result of the Reformation, which pushed heresy to the fore as an issue and thus encouraged attempts to control the expression of opinion.

The true path of Christian virtue and salvation was apparently challenged not only by false prophets, indeed pseudochurches, laying claim to the word of Jesus, but also by a malevolent world presided over by the devil, a world that could be seen as including these prophets and operating through them. The future Richard III compares himself to Judas, a powerful image, when kissing Edward IV's sons at the close of *Henry VI, Part III* (V, vii).

As already mentioned, the Christian world picture provided many grounds for fear, with millenarian, apocalyptic, and eschatological anxieties drawing heavily on the Bible's Book of Revelation. Already potent prior to the Reformation, not least in response to such calamities as savage epidemics and the Ottoman (Turkish) advance into the Balkans, these anxieties became stronger as a consequence of the Reformation and of the accentuation of this Ottoman threat; Turkish armies assailed Vienna in 1529 and Malta in 1565, albeit unsuccessfully in each case. Warfare and the rise of evil power and powers were seen as signs of the approach of the millennium. The Reformation, which began in 1517, encouraged millenarian anxieties, as did repeated political and environmental crises, such as rebellions and outbreaks of epidemic diseases. Together, these factors fueled belief in a powerful, ambitious, and remorseless devil, one endlessly challenging the existing order.

The linkage of human events with the natural world was expressed not only in terms of zodiacal influence but also with reference to disturbances in the natural phenomena of the world that accompany major events, as, most conspicuously, with the assassinations of Duncan in *Macbeth* and of Julius Caesar. Lenox, a Scottish thane in Duncan's party, comments on the first:

> The night has been unruly: where we lay,
> Our chimneys were blown down; and, as they say,
> Lamentings heard i' th' air; strange screams of death,
> And, prophesying with accents terrible
> Of dire combustion, and confused events,
> New hatched to the woeful time, the obscure bird
> Clamoured the livelong night: some say, the Earth
> Was feverous, and did shake. (II, iii)

"Dire combustion" may be a reference to the Gunpowder Plot of 1605. The night before he is assassinated, Caesar notes, "Nor heaven nor earth have been at peace tonight," and Calphurnia, his wife, tells him what the watch in Rome has seen:

> A lioness hath whelped in the streets,
> And graves have yawned and yielded up their dead;
> Fierce fiery warriors fought upon the clouds
> In ranks and squadrons and right form of war,
> Which drizzled blood upon the Capitol;
> The noise of battle hurtled in the air,

Horses did neigh, and dying men did groan,
And ghosts did shriek and squeal about the streets. (II, ii)

This leads Caesar to reflect on free will:

CAESAR: What can be avoided
Whose end is purposed by the mighty gods?
Yet Caesar shall go forth; for these predictions
Are to the world in general as to Caesar.
CALPHURNIA: When beggars die, there are no comets seen;
The heavens themselves blaze forth the death of princes.
CAESAR: Of all the wonders that I yet have heard,
It seems to me most strange that men should fear,
Seeing that death, a necessary end,
Will come when it will come. (II, ii)

Othello responds to his murder of his wife by crying:

Methinks it should be now a huge eclipse
Of sun and moon, and that th'affrighted globe
Should yawn at alteration. (V, ii)

The last means that the world should split open. Othello also refers to the influence of the spheres in order to lessen his responsibility:

It is the very error of the Moon.
She comes more nearer Earth than she was wont
And makes men mad. (V, ii)

At the same time, anxieties were not always expressed in apocalyptic terms. Instead, there were more immediate responses, those in particular associated with more humble characters, especially if lowlifes. Thus, Mistress Overdone, a Vienna brothel keeper in *Measure for Measure*, complains: "what with the war, what with the sweat, what with the gallows and what with poverty, I am custom-shrunk" (I, ii). Austria was at war with the Turks from 1593 to 1606, but the reference to the war would have resonated with an English audience whose long war with Spain had just drawn to a close.

Science, or, rather, all the various sciences, could be regarded as adjuncts of theology, itself the "queen of sciences." The sciences were aspects of knowledge as a unity, with God's work and intentions reflected across the material world. Christian thinkers sought better to understand the workings of a cosmos created by a Christian God. Moreover, useful knowledge cannot be defined and understood simply in modern terms. For example, the balance of the four humors was regarded as important for the health of rulers and their realms, and the balance was a typical theme in alchemical prophecies.

There was an assumption that human nature responded naturally to opportunities and constraints, the sympathetic Claudius remarking in *Measure for Measure* that he was arrested because of

> too much liberty . . .
> As surfeit is the father of much fast,
> So every scope by the immoderate use
> Turns to restraint. Our natures do pursue,
> Like rats that ravin down their proper bane,
> A thirsty evil, and when we drink we die. (I, ii)

The Church had originally set its face against any systematic "scientific" enquiry, on the grounds that man was only intended to know the mind of God as interpreted by the Church. Yet, in practice, there was a range of responses. Natural philosophy, the predecessor of modern science, was understood as a discipline that looked to God and the Bible, as well as to Nature. Early Protestants similarly, although rejecting the intermediary role of the Church, believed that all necessary knowledge was to be found in the scriptures and therefore had to be found there. Religious themes were to the fore. Many, accordingly, were wary of the alchemists' search for the springs of hidden natural forces, as there was apparently a magical dimension to this search.

Meanwhile, the humanistic learning and tendencies of the Renaissance encouraged a critical reading of sources. Moreover, the response to the exploration of a suddenly wider world, notably the Americas, greatly tested existing intellectual categories, particularly as animals and plants unknown to classical writers, especially Aristotle and Pliny, the great classifiers, were discovered. As a consequence of new knowledge, the validity and thus authority of current explanatory systems were called into question.[24] So also with earlier notions of geography and anthropology: commentators had to confront a range of peoples that had not been within the knowledge of their predecessors.

In London, there was a largely unregulated ferment of interest in the physical and natural worlds. New equipment, in the shape of the telescope and the microscope, was to qualify existing ideas even more in the seventeenth century.[25] Meanwhile, the Reformation had challenged the authority of the Catholic Church, not only in what would today be seen as explicitly religious terms but across the field of knowledge as a whole, especially in judging truth. This questioning was not incompatible with religious issues, for such topics as the treatment of the relics of saints, an important aspect of Catholic religious practice, involved both religion and the linked discussion of truth.

The role of the Reformation in scientific developments was therefore indirect but very important. Indeed, the assault on the monopolistic position of the Catholic Church entailed an attack on its role as a source and guarantor of truth. For example, the Gregorian reform of the longstanding Julian calendar in 1582 by Pope Gregory XIII was unacceptable to Protestant Europe precisely because it had papal validation. This assault on the position of the Catholic Church was also an attack that encompassed the established nature of university scholarship because that was Church based.[26]

The question of truth was pushed to the fore in many of Shakespeare's plays, with questions as to the real nature of phenomena, such as those that are shown to Hamlet, Macbeth, and Pericles (who sees Diana as in a vision), and, separately, as in *The Winter's*

*Tale* and even, very differently, *The Comedy of Errors*, over identity. When Macbeth asks if he sees a dagger before him, he is asking what is happening; but he is doing so in a way that draws powerfully on uncertainty as to phenomena and observation. That human perception is uncertain is a key point that is not abstract philosophy but a matter of personal salvation in the war between good and evil. The staging of this is not simply an artifice to draw attention to being in the theater but also a presentation of human dilemmas in the context of the dilemma of being human.

The crisis centered on the methods to be used for the establishment, authorization, and protection of truth was given greater force by the extent of intellectual curiosity and the related willingness to challenge the traditional knowledge represented by the Church's endorsement of Aristotle. In England, Francis Bacon (1561–1626) addressed the issue. The son of the Lord Keeper and a cousin of Robert Cecil, Bacon played a significant political role and, under James I, was Lord Chancellor from 1618 to 1621. He argued for authentication not in terms of institutions—notably the Church, which now very obviously could offer only a contested authority, especially in England—but, instead, with reference to the method employed. "Experimental learning" was seen as providing a universally valid approach able to comprehend the course of nature. Indeed, experimentation, a positive not a contemplative approach, was crucial to the research that led to William Harvey's account of the circulation of the blood. Experimentation, publication, and a pursuit of utility were all significant to the vitality of science in London.[27]

Drawing on the rise of expertise in Elizabethan England (including in mathematics), the place of scholars and experts in government business, and the role of entrepreneurial projecting, Bacon suggested that God actually intended man to recover that mastery over nature that he had lost at Adam's Fall: it was (along with the Reformation), he argued, part of the preparation for the Second Coming of Christ—which was a frequent lodestone and at least ostensible goal for commentators. Thus, scientific inquiry became not only a legitimate pursuit but almost a religious duty for the devout Protestant. Empirical perception, and thereby objectivity, was a way in which God revealed the order of life; and research in this form was therefore necessary.[28] As an instance of empirical research, dissection was important in acquiring and displaying information about the body.

Knowledge was reconceptualized in terms of the creation of theory in the light of the evidence gained by observation, rather than being thought of as a demonstration of theory in the form of a syllogism. Writers and painters, knowing nature through imitating it, offered a parallel to this gathering and expression of evidence. This idea of knowing nature through imitation became immensely influential among the English intelligentsia later in the seventeenth century.

The notion of mastery over nature, however, was not one that playwrights always tended to address positively. Instead, they could prefer, as in Marlowe's powerful and dramatic *Doctor Faustus* (c. 1592), to see dangerous necromancy and pride at work, with the danger pushed to the fore as the work of diabolic forces, which are able to act because Faustus revokes his baptism and abjures scriptures. Faustus strikes a deal with Lucifer in which he gains the use of magic for twenty-four years but agrees then to go to hell. It was claimed in 1632 by William Prynne, a hostile critic, that actual devils had appeared on the stage during a performance.

Alongside empiricism, there was also a continuing emphasis on the role of classical knowledge. This was seen as being of value for modern natural philosophy (science), as well as for dealing with such practical issues as calendar reform. Thus, in addition to instruments, books played a major role in establishing and verifying knowledge. New scientific ideas were frequently heavily dependent on earlier learning. For example, Harvey (1578–1657), in his *De Motu Cordis* (*On the Motion of the Heart and Blood*,

1628), drew on Aristotelian concepts in his rejection of the ideas of Galen (129–c. 210) about the circulation of the blood. Far from being transformative, scientific ideas and their reception were responses to the world conditioned by the specificities of existing circumstances. In particular, nonempirical ideas of proof continued to be significant in a culture in which textual authority, notably the Bible, was central. The authority of Aristotelian principles remained important for many, not least for philosophical categories and the classification of knowledge and in the argument that there was no barrier between the things that are and people's understanding of them and thus that there was no real role for the free will of rational intellectual thought and for skepticism.

Most of the population was unaware of the new science. Moreover, empiricism was not regarded as necessarily incompatible with traditional forms of Christian and occult knowledge, for example, miracles and astrology—indeed, far from it.[29] In *The Comedy of Errors*, Antipholus of Syracuse remarks of Ephesus:

> They say this town is full of cozenage;
> As, nimble jugglers that deceive the eye,
> Dark-working sorcerers that change the mind,
> Soul-killing witches that deform the body,
> Disguised cheaters, prating mountebanks,
> And many such-like liberties of sin. (I, ii)

In practice, however, no jugglers are shown, which may be a comment on this belief. At any rate, Londoners might have found the energy of Ephesus both familiar and attractive.

As already mentioned, it was generally accepted that astrological anatomies and zodiacs were keys to human character, revelations of Providence, and guides to the future; that extraterrestrial forces intervened in the affairs of the world, especially human and animal health and the state of the crops and the weather; and that each constellation presided over a particular part of man.

Much of literature addressed the human relationship with the divine. This was seen not only in works explicitly on devotional, philosophical, and ethical topics but also in the world of imaginative literature. Here there were classic themes of sin and redemption and a journeying toward salvation but also the related intervention of the superhuman in human life, both past and present. This intervention took a number of forms, as divine judgment, or, at least, the impact of a purposeful divine Providence, and the superhuman manifested themselves in different ways. The range not only encompassed the historical and high- drama but also the "star-crossed lovers" of romance, as in *Romeo and Juliet* (Prologue), and the confusion of mistaken identities repeatedly seen in the comedies. The manifestation of ghosts, as in *Hamlet, Julius Caesar, Macbeth, Cymbeline,* and *Richard III,* was an important link between past and present, that of the living dead, one that reflected the immanence in the human world of beings from the spirit sphere. This immanence was pushed to the fore as a result of the Reformation's abandonment of purgatory as a means to locate and help the dead.[30]

As a vivid instance of this immanence, at once psychologically arresting and a real presence, Brutus is shown as oppressed by his central role in the murder of Caesar. This is the culmination of the most emotionally charged relationship of *Julius Caesar,* one of murderously disloyal friendship. In his military camp near Sardis, Brutus is visited by the ghost of Caesar but does not really know what he sees, asking,

> this monstrous apparition ...
> ... Art thou any thing?
> Art thou some god, some angel, or some devil,

He earns the reply that the ghost is "Thy evil spirit" (IV, iii). The ghost tells Brutus that they shall meet again at Philippi. At the climactic battle there, where his cause goes down to total defeat, Brutus exclaims:

> O Julius Caesar, thou art mighty yet!
> Thy spirit walks abroad, and turns our swords
> In our own proper entrails. (V, iii)

Shakespeare thus offers a powerful account of guilt and retribution, one given physical form with the ghost. Shakespeare adds
to the ghost the claim that it is that of Caesar. Seeing the ghost
leads Brutus, indeed, to conclude "my hour is come" (V, v) and
to resolve on suicide.

This is at once a description of what Brutus did do,[31] a more
noble fate than that of Macbeth at Dunsinane or Richard III at
Bosworth—and a product of the difference between classical
values and Christian teachings. Cassius, Antony, and Cleopatra,
each in their own way honorable as well as flawed, are all shown
killing themselves, while, in contrast, Macbeth, who lives in the
Christian era, declares:

> Why should I play the Roman fool, and die
> On mine own sword? whiles I see lives, the gashes
> Do better upon them. (V, viii)

Although this was not Macbeth's motivation, Christian teaching
decried suicide, treating it not only as dishonorable but also as a
sin because of a defiance of the divine capacity for mercy, as well
as of the teachings of the Church. A warrior, Othello commits
suicide, which is, at once, an aspect of his depiction as a Moor,
psychologically truthful, and a product of the play as a bloody
revenge tragedy, and one, moreover, as with much of the genre,
with an Italian setting, albeit among the Italians in Cyprus. In
contrast, the suicides of Pyramus and Thisbe in *A Midsummer
Night's Dream* are part of the comedy, distanced by being in the
comic play within the play and thus a contrast to the tragedy of
suicidal young love in *Romeo and Juliet*, a tragedy made more
potent by its being unnecessary.

The inherent connections between the earth and salvation
were aspects of a world in which God was present and active,
able and willing to act in the world as part of a wider process of
spiritual travel and action through spaces that were immediate.[32]
This situation linked the modern to the classical world, for, in

*Cymbeline* Jupiter descends in thunder and lightning to upbraid "you petty spirits of region low ... you ghosts" for pressing him on behalf of the condemned Posthumus; the ghosts are those of family members (V, iv).

Salvation was not an outcome that had to await death. Instead, in a universe bounded temporally by the Fall and the apocalypse, time and space took on meaning in terms of the divine will and spiritual redemption. "The wills above be done!" declares Gonzalo as the ship splits in the dramatic opening scene of *The Tempest* (I, i). Redemption could be seen in the case of individual characters, such as Lear, and the language employed was frequently religious, as with Lear's meritorious daughter, Cordelia, of whom it was observed

> she shook
> The holy water from her heavenly eyes
> That clamour moistened. (IV, iii)

Uncertain of his situation, and specifically as to whether he is in hell, Lear subsequently awakes to tell Cordelia in truly memorable lines:

> You do me wrong to take me out o'th'grave:
> Thou art a soul in bliss; but I am bound
> Upon a wheel of fire, that mine own tears
> Do scald like molten lead.
> . . . . . . . . . . . . . . . . . .
> You are a spirit, I know. (IV, vii)

*King Lear* is set in pre-Christian times, indeed is one of the English "history plays," but, as in those plays set in classical Rome, Christian themes are to the fore. Alongside classical ideas and references, notably to Oedipus, such themes are especially prominent in *King Lear*—although more for Gloucester and Lear, both of whom experience redemption, than for Cordelia, who ends up as a sacrificial figure. She is ostentatiously meritorious, in so far as such a phrase can be employed to describe a character who is a pure moral center. Forgiveness of others and a surrender of the goods of the world are presented in *King Lear* as key elements in redemption, the forgiveness depending in part on the self-knowledge that becomes an important part of that play. Self-knowledge, however, cannot itself redeem, as is shown throughout by Iago and, more hesitantly, by Macbeth.

### CONCLUSION

In addition to tensions about free will and salvation, and alongside continuities and ambiguities in religious practice and thought, the Protestant Reformation had caused a profound psychological crisis, one that helped explain the problems faced by those trying to enforce the new religious settlement and also by those seeking to keep magical elements in accord with Christianity.[33] Traditional patterns of exposition, faith, and observance were put under great strain and, in part, shattered. For example, the belief in the efficacy of prayers for the souls of the dead in purgatory, to help them toward salvation, was fundamental to monasticism as well as to chantries. Its disappearance, or at least discouragement, represented a major and disturbing discontinuity in emotional and religious links between the generations, as well as of a crucial link between the earth and the supranatural.

In this new ecclesiology, doubt was probably a condition of both life and death. This condition was captured by Hamlet: it is clearly linked to his indecisiveness and a central part of the inaction that characterizes much of the play. The same condition is seen to affect Claudius in *Measure for Measure*. Unfairly treated by Angelo's arbitrary and hypocritical interpretation of the law and denied mercy, Claudius contemplates his own imminent execution, declaring:

Death is a fearful thing.
. . . . . . . . . . . . . . . . .
to die, and go we know not where;
To lie in cold obstruction and to rot;

This sensible warm motion to become
A kneaded clod; and the delighted spirit
To bathe in fiery floods, or to reside
In thrilling region of thick-ribbed ice;
To be imprison'd in the viewless winds,
And blown with restless violence round about
The pendant world; or to be worse than worst
Of those that lawless and incertain thoughts
Imagine howling: 'tis too horrible!
The weariest and most loathed worldly life
That age, ache, penury and imprisonment
Can lay on nature is a paradise
To what we fear of death. (III, i)

Doubt can be linked to the notion that "Shakespeare's hallmark is ambiguity. If plays have any social value it must be because the conflict of opinion contained in dialogue allows audiences to think the previously unthinkable."[34] Possibly so in modern terms, but that would have been far less the case in Shakespeare's lifetime.

Alongside doubt, there is repeatedly in Shakespeare an affirmation of value and values, including in *Measure for Measure* by the thwarted villain, Angelo. Most powerfully, Macbeth, in his final battle, realizes that he has been misled by the second apparition brought forth by the witches. In a culmination of his metaphysical despair, Macbeth speaks to the audience as much as to himself:

be these juggling fiends no more believ'd,
That palter [equivocate] with us in a double sense;
That keep the word of promise to our ear,
And break it to our hope. (V, viii)

His vanquisher, Macduff, bearing Macbeth's head, proclaims "the time is free" (V, ix). Modern directors sometimes stage the closing scene to suggest that Macduff will try to overthrow the new king, Malcolm, but that is not Shakespeare's play, no more than it is to present *Henry V* as an antiwar play. Instead, it is the moral order that is affirmed in *Macbeth*, one already seen in the court of Edward the Confessor, where Malcolm had taken refuge. The king is shown using his touch to cure scrofula, a gift discussed in Holinshed, while, employing the language of Christianity, Malcolm affirms goodness and proclaims continuity and the defeat of the devil:

> Angels are bright still, though the brightest fell:
> Though all things foul would wear the brows of grace,
> Yet Grace must still look so. (IV, iii)

The human devil, Macbeth, "Hell-hound" according to Macduff, once so promising to Duncan, is defeated, and with him, the devil.

## NOTES

1. A river in Greece. In Greek mythology, souls were ferried across Acheron to enter hell.

2. C. Kolslofsky, *Evening's Empire: A History of the Night in Early-Modern Europe* (Cambridge, 2011).

3. Paul Brown, "'This Thing of Darkness I Acknowledge Mine,' *The Tempest* and the Discourse of Colonialism," in *Political Shakespeare: New Essays in Cultural Materialism*, ed. Jonathan Dollimore and Alan Sinfield (Manchester, 1985), 48–71.

4. D. G. Denery, *The Devil Wins: A History of Lying from the Garden of Eden to the Enlightenment* (Princeton, NJ, 2015).

5. S. Clark, *Thinking with Demons* (Oxford, 1997); M. Harmes and V. Bladen, eds., *Supernatural and Secular Power in Early-Modern England* (Farnham, UK, 2015); M. Gibson and J. Esra, *Shakespeare's Demonology: A Dictionary* (London, 2017).

6. G. Wills, *Witches and Jesuits* (Oxford, 1995); B. P. Levack, *Witch-Hunting in Scotland: Law, Politics and Religion* (London, 2008).

7. N. Levine, *Women's Matters: Politics, Gender and the Nation in Shakespeare's Early History Plays* (Newark, DE, 1998); L. Manley, "From Strange's Men to Pembroke's Men: 2 *Henry VI* and *The First Part of the Contention*," *Shakespeare Quarterly*, 54 (2003): 253–87.

8. P. Elmer, *Witchcraft, Witch-Hunting and Politics in Early-Modern England* (Oxford, 2016).

9. M. Gibson, "Devilish Sin and Desperate Death: Northamptonshire Witches in Print and Manuscript," *Northamptonshire Past and Present* 51 (1998): 15–21.

10. M. Stoyle, "'It Is But an Olde Wytche Gonne': Prosecution and Execution for Witchcraft in Exeter, 1558–1610," *History* 96 (2011): 151; and *Witchcraft in Exeter, 1558–1600* (Exeter, 2017).

11. R. F. Green, ed., *Elf Queens and Holy Friars: Fairy Beliefs and the Medieval Church* (Philadelphia, 2016).

12. A. French, *Children of Wrath: Possession, Prophecy and the Young in Early Modern England* (Farnham, UK, 2015).

13. F. W. Brownlow, *Shakespeare, Harsnett, and the Devils of Denham* (Newark, DE, 1993).

14. J. Kerrigan, *Shakespeare's Originality* (Oxford, 2018).

15. N. Shaheen, *Biblical References in Shakespeare's Plays* (Newark, NJ, 1999).

16. R. J. W. Evans, *Rudolf II and His World: A Study in Intellectual History, 1576–1612* (Oxford, 1973).

17. I. Arthurson, *The Perkin Warbeck Conspiracy, 1491–1499* (Stroud, UK, 1994).

18. G. Parker, *Global Crisis: War, Climate Change and Catastrophe in the Seventeenth Century* (New Haven, CT, 2013).

19. T. Mayer, ed., *The Roman Inquisition: Trying Galileo* (Philadelphia, 2015).

20. R. Bartlett, *The Natural and the Supernatural in the Middle Ages* (Cambridge, 2008).

21. G. Parry, *The Arch-Conjuror of England: John Dee* (New Haven, CT, 2012).

22. D. E. Harkness, *John Dee's Conversations with Angels: Cabala, Alchemy, and the End of Nature* (Cambridge, 1999).

23. P. Curry, *Prophecy and Power: Astrology in Early Modern England* (Cambridge, 1989); W. Eamon, *Science and the Secrets of Nature: Books of Secrets in Medieval and Early Modern Culture* (Princeton, NJ, 1994); A. Geneva, *Astrology and the Seventeenth Century Mind: William Lilly and the Language of the Stars* (Manchester, 1995).

24. A. Barrera-Osorio, *Experiencing Nature: The Spanish American Empire and the Early Scientific Revolution* (Austin, TX, 2006).

25. D. Harkness, *The Jewel House: Elizabethan London and the Scientific Revolution* (New Haven, CT, 2008).

26. A. Weeks, *Paracelsus: Speculative Theory and the Crisis of the Early Reformation* (Albany, NY, 1997).

27. Harkness, *Jewel House*.

28. J. Solomon, *Objectivity in the Making: Francis Bacon and the Politics of Inquiry* (Baltimore, 1998); E. Ash, *Knowledge and Expertise in Elizabethan England* (Baltimore, 2004).

29. J. Seitz, *Witchcraft and Inquisition in Early Modern Venice* (Cambridge, 2011).

30. S. Greenblatt, *Hamlet in Purgatory* (Princeton, NJ, 2001); P. Schwyzer, *Literature, Nationalism and Memory in Early Modern England and Wales* (Cambridge, 2004).

31. K. Tempest, *Brutus: The Noble Conspirator* (New Haven, CT, 2017).

32. T. Rist, *Shakespeare's Romances and the Politics of Counter-Reformation* (Lewiston, UK, 1999).

33. S. Clark, *Thinking with Demons: The Idea of Witchcraft in Early Modern Europe* (Oxford, 1997); L. Sangha, *Angels and Belief in England, 1480–1700* (London, 2012).

34. Comments by anonymous reviewer, provided to me by Indiana University Press on November 7, 2017. Judging by the report, this reviewer is a literary scholar and not a historian.

# THE WORLD OF THE PLAYS

THE DARK, AS NOTED IN the previous chapter, was a physical presence, one particularly apparent, then and now, in open-air theatrical performances as light faded, even when lamps were lit. In twilight and at night, space shrank to the shadowy spots lit by flickering lights, and indoor theaters had act breaks in part to allow candles to be trimmed and, if necessary, replaced. The impact of the dark is difficult to understand today when we visit houses or other buildings from the period and easiest to do so only if they lack electric lights and are kept dark to protect the tapestries and paintings on display. Even then, we do not get the effect of candlelight with the shadows that it cast, shadows interspersed by moments of clarity, whether real or misleading. This is a background that makes sense of Iago's trickeries or Hamlet's doubts. For the poor of any neighborhood, the great houses would have been the only places where there was any real measure of light after dusk. At night, sight was a privilege of the rich, for candles were expensive, and England was a dark country speckled with glimmers of light. When you stare into the fire, your eyes perceive the surrounding darkness as even blacker.

When the moon did not shine, either because it had waned or because it was covered by cloud, the night was very dark. Unsurprisingly, this was a moral, as well as a physical, image and metaphor for Shakespeare. Darkness covers villainy, whether of Macbeth or of Don John in *Much Ado About Nothing*, and villains and others make reference to this linkage. Disguise is an aspect of the dark and is made easier by it, as in *Romeo and Juliet*. Context, however, is all. Subterfuge in comedies, as in *Twelfth Night*, can provide the occasion for the humor. Lighting probably meant more than it would for a modern audience. Light was linked to warmth and was central to a world in which the dark, the damp, and the cold pressed hard on people. Light was also linked to being able to see and therefore understand.

The dark brought out anxieties about animals. Animals capable of inflicting death—bears and wolves—had been wiped out in England, although not elsewhere in Europe, a point that underlined the foreignness of the latter. The native brown bear had probably been wiped out in England in the tenth century. The bears used for bearbaiting were imports. The original wild boar were probably extinct by the thirteenth century, although, for hunting purposes, James I released them into Windsor Park in 1608. Wolves are thought to have become extinct in England during the reign of Henry VII (1485–1509), and the last known one in Scotland was killed in 1680.

References to both bears and wolves are seen in Shakespeare's plays, which reflected the continued potency of the sense of threat that they encapsulated. In *The Winter's Tale*, a bear chases Antigonus off the stage, leading to the famous stage direction "Exit, pursued by a bear." The Clown then describes the bear tearing out Antigonus's shoulder bone and dining on him: "they are never curst but when they are hungry" (III, iii). Captive bears were on ready display in London in the vicious bearbaitings held in Southwark, which also was a setting for theaterland. In *A Midsummer Night's Dream*, a "headless bear" is one of the disguises used by Puck to get the Mechanicals other than Bottom to flee (III, i). The Jailer's Daughter in *The Two Noble Kinsmen* imagines that Palamon has been eaten by wolves (III, ii), while, in *As You*

*Like It*, Orlando slays the "hungry lioness" that threatens to kill Oliver (IV, iii). There were no lions in England. The Shepherd in *The Winter's Tale* worries that "the wolf" will find his two missing sheep (III, iii), and, in *Henry VI, Part III*, the Lieutenant of the Tower leaves Richard, Duke of Gloucester, the future Richard III, alone with his victim, Henry VI, who remarks: "so flies the reckless shepherd from the wolf" (V, vi). The Bible is full of references to wolves and shepherds.

Audiences would be expected to understand references to the noise made by the animals. In *The Tempest*, Prospero describes the imprisoned Ariel:

> thy groans
> Did make wolves howl and penetrate the breasts
> Of ever-angry bears. (I, ii)

There were other wild animals that were still at liberty in England: foxes raided farmsteads to attack farm animals, notably chickens; rats were a serious issue; and fears about what could be living out there rushed to the fore. Domestic animals also posed issues: rabies was a problem among the dog population.

Another aspect of the dark, including that of troubling shadows, was provided by the extent of woodland. This was greater than in modern England, and whereas woodland remains important in upland regions today, the contrast was notably so in lowland areas. Woodland served many economic purposes, especially as a source of wood and for foraging pigs, as an illustrated map of Cambridge in 1574 by Richard Lyne makes clear.

Woodland was also valuable for hunting, both in practical and in social terms, with the latter as a display of rights and shared privileges. A particular culture, that of the hunt, and occupation, that of huntsmen, were each involved. Reference to hunting, both literally and figuratively, is frequent in Shakespeare, notably in courtship but not only there. In *The Tempest*, Ariel summons up spirits to act as hunting dogs in order to drive away the conspirators proposing to murder Prospero, and they burst upon the stage to do so. Prospero remarks: "Let them be hunted soundly" (IV, i). In *The Two Noble Kinsmen*, Theseus and his party go into the woods on a May morning hunt (III, i). In *Henry VI, Part III*, Edward IV is freed from captivity when hunting "to disport himself" (IV, v). Other forms of hunting were also mentioned. In *Much Ado About Nothing*, there are comparisons between wildfowling and tricking Beatrice and Benedick into falling in love (II, iii).

Yet woodland also represented uncertainty, danger, and loss. It is striking how frequently Shakespeare's characters get lost in woodland. Indeed, in that respect it is an equivalent to the dark. In part, this is a matter of comedy and/or romance, as in *A Midsummer Night's Dream* and *As You Like It*. In the former, the lovers get lost in the wood, which provides the opportunity for comic mistakes, including the seduction of Bottom by his own imaginings as worked on by the forces of magic and happenstance. The wood is the unstructured world of disguises and surprises.

However, danger or tragedy might also be involved. Woodland gives shelter to the brigand and, in particular, to the highwayman. In *The Two Gentlemen of Verona*, the forest harbors outlaws who have committed such crimes as murder and abduction. In this, Shakespeare draws on the long literary tradition of outlawry, one based on the very varied nature of the practice.[1]

Aside from outlawry, the forest was also the scene of conflicts over hunting, with the contrary drives mentioned above, of local people seeking income and landowners wanting to protect their power and status and thus falling into dispute.[2] In contrast, the benign setting of *As You Like It* is the Forest of the Arden in Warwickshire near Stratford, although, possibly, also the far more extensive Ardennes in the Low Countries. However, the potential for menace is seen in Orlando's entry "with his sword drawn" to demand food (II, vii). Generally an attribute of men of status, drawn swords threaten to cause disorder, and Shakespeare often views them with disfavor, which can include treating them with ridicule, as in *Twelfth Night*.

So many of Shakespeare's plays focused on or made mention of the deceitfulness of courts, preeminently so in *Hamlet*, and of courtiers, as in *Measure for Measure* and, in a way, *Julius Caesar* and *Othello*. In contrast, the countryside could offer the more honest environment of the pastoral genre, as in *As You Like It*, *All's Well That Ends Well*, and *The Winter's Tale* and, to a degree, *A Midsummer Night's Dream*. Court hierarchies are challenged or subverted in moving into these different environments. This process is also seen in *The Tempest* with shipwreck and then rediscovery and rescue on Prospero's island.

Another form of uncertainty, one repeatedly found in the plays, was that of all types of traveling, including by day. Hardship, anxiety, and topography greatly exaggerated the impact and difficulties of distance. A multitude of circumstances made journeys unpredictable and hazardous, including theft and violence, breakdowns in equipment—wheels and rudders failing, axles and masts snapping, ships springing leaks, and horses bolting—and accidents caused by poor and unreliable road surfaces or by boats capsizing crossing rivers.

Roads were greatly affected by rain, especially on heavy clay soils, for example, in south Essex, the Midlands, and the Vale of Berkeley in Gloucestershire, where wheels churned up the mud into impassable quagmires; on the greensand of the Weald in Kent, Surrey, and Sussex; and in the Exe Valley in Devon. Road construction and maintenance were of limited effectiveness in marshy regions, such as the Fens and the Somerset Levels, each an extensive region where there were no real roads. In the Somerset Levels, peddlers carried packs of goods to villages that were inaccessible to wagons or even packhorses. In addition, such valleys as the Ouse, Severn, Trent, and Thames were prone to flood, and their soil was often heavy and difficult to traverse. Instead, most land routes sought to follow ridges, where the soil was drier. Many of these were routes that went back through the Middle Ages and even to pre-Roman times.

"What need the bridge much broader than the flood?" (*Much Ado About Nothing*, I, i) is a question that listeners would have understood, "flood" in this quotation meaning the flow of the river, not the extent of a flooded river. On land, spring thaws and autumn floods could bring problems. They did so in particular by sending rivers into spate, which made them dangerous, even impossible, to ford: fording was the standard means by which many rivers were crossed. Thaws and heavy rain flooded low-lying areas, such as the Somerset Levels and the Fens, and, indeed, along most rivers. The Fens were permanently flooded, and people made a living of sorts, eel catching or reed harvesting, out of that landscape. Floods played a role in Shakespeare's plots, as in the failure of the rebellion of Henry, Second Duke of Buckingham, in 1483 in *Richard III*. This rebellion indeed failed totally, in part due to the flooding of the river Severn: "by sudden floods and fall of waters, Buckingham's army is dispersed and scattered" (IV, iv), writes Shakespeare. However, that flood was more significant by making it impossible for the rebel forces to combine. Having not yet in effect been canalized, as was repeatedly done in the nineteenth century, most rivers were shallower than their modern counterparts and had broader courses with lower banks and were thus harder to bridge (although not to ford) and far readier to flood. There were no real flood-prevention schemes.

More generally, rivers and mountains featured strongly in the sense and awareness of terrain of people before the situation was changed in the late nineteenth century with the use of high explosive. We find this difficult to understand. What can the Chilterns, a range of hills that Shakespeare had to cross en route from Warwickshire to London, mean to an age that can easily blast a hole through the escarpment, as, dramatically, with the M40 motorway at Stokenchurch? The same is true of less prominent features, such as the Failand ridge, which is now carved by the M5 east of Clevedon. Rivers now can be bridged and marshlands drained.

Standards of road maintenance then were low. Upkeep was largely the responsibility of the local parish, which was a civil as well as a religious entity, and the resources for a speedy and effective response to deficiencies were lacking, as were the organization and will. It was scarcely surprising that medieval merchants, who were among the main sufferers from dreadful roads, left money for repairs in their wills. Looked at differently, the needs and resources of government were in equipoise: in the contexts of the technological, organizational, and resource limitations of the period, the rapid and predictable dispatch of messages was not of sufficient concern to ensure that England's rulers leaned hard on local elites to improve roads.

The situation did not improve during Shakespeare's lifetime, although he was one of the Stratford citizens who subscribed to contribute to the cost of promoting an act of Parliament for road repairs. Horses were the same, ships were still wooden and wind powered (sometimes also rowed in the Mediterranean and the Baltic), most roads remained dirt tracks, and the impact of the weather had not changed. Local markets and supply were much more important than today. It is understandable that details of the movements of letters and couriers and of their all-too-frequent mishaps and related uncertainties crop up regularly in the correspondence and diaries of the period and in Shakespeare's plays. They are important to the plots in many of the latter, particularly in *Romeo and Juliet*.

A network of regular and reliable long-distance wagon services did not develop in England until the seventeenth century, notably the later decades, and the first turnpike road dated from the 1660s, with a national network of such roads only coming into play in the mid-eighteenth century. In contrast to England, there were major road schemes in Japan under the Tokugawa shogunate in the early seventeenth century, particularly with the building of the lengthy Tokaido Road (and its fifty-three way stations) from the capital Edo (Tokyo) to Kyoto in order to ensure that governmental authority was readily wielded so far west.

The slowness of land travel, the difficulty of moving such bulk goods as grain and coal overland, and Britain's island character all ensured that trade and travel by river and sea, rather than on land, were far more important than today. Aside from the poor nature of the roads and the relatively few bridges, the need to feed the draft animals required to pull laden wagons led to an emphasis, instead, on water transport. Boats were more important than bridges in crossing rivers and, even more, the numerous estuaries on England's indented coastline, such as the Humber, the Tyne, the Mersey, the Dee, the Dart, the Exe, and the Thames. Ferries across bodies of water, such as the Solent or the Bristol Channel—in the latter case from Sully near Cardiff to Uphill in Somerset, and from Beachley to Aust—were significant.

The importance of rivers focused attention on those bridges that existed. Bridging points, such as Exeter over the river Exe and Oxford over the river Thames, took a central role in the communication system, as did ferries. The seven-arched medieval stone bridge over the river Tyne at Newcastle was a crucial feature of the city's local, regional, and national position. The same was true of Gloucester and the river Severn. London Bridge remained the lowest crossing point on the Thames, and there was no road crossing of the river Tamar downriver of Gunnislake.

Frequent references to the flow of rivers assume that listeners were very familiar with the experience of being on the water, as in *Two Gentlemen of Verona* when Julia tells her servant Lucetta that she will follow Proteus to Milan. She compares true love to a stream flowing naturally:

The current that with gentle murmur glides,
Thou know'st, being stopp'd, impatiently doth rage;
But when his fair course is not hindered,
He makes sweet music with th'enamell'd stones,
Giving a gentle kiss to every sedge

He overtaketh in his pilgrimage;
And so by many winding nooks he strays
With willing sport to the wild ocean. (II, vii)

So also with the death of Ophelia in *Hamlet*. Gertrude explains that, while insane, Ophelia had fallen into a "weeping brook" and eventually been pulled down by the weight of her wet clothes:

her garments, heavy with their drink,
Pull'd the poor wretch ...
To muddy death. (IV, vii)

Although with very different contexts and purposes, the two passages resonate in poetic description, with Julia's river matched by the description of the plants that Ophelia collected.

Many settlements and country houses, for example, Antony House in Cornwall and Hampton Court, were best approached by water. More generally, water—both the sea and inland waterways—had far more of an impact on people's lives than is the case today. Many towns that today lack quays and wharves were then ports, either seaports or, as a result of transshipment onto river vessels, ports linked into maritime trade. Many ports handled foreign trade, in contrast to the nineteenth century (and subsequently) when the greater size of merchantmen led to the concentration of long-distance trade on fewer harbors that had the necessary facilities for handling large ships. Examples of such sixteenth-century coastal ports included Barnstaple, Bideford, Dartmouth, and Topsham in Devon.[3] Inland ports included Langport in Somerset, as well as Bristol, Exeter, Gloucester, Lincoln, Norwich, Stratford, and York.

References to catching the tide are frequent in the plays (*Two Gentlemen of Verona*, II, iii). Urging on Cassius the need to march on and confront their enemies at Philippi, Brutus declares:

We, at the height, are ready to decline.
There is a tide in the affairs of men,
Which, taken at the flood, leads on to fortune;
Omitted, all the voyage of their life

Is bound in shallows and in miseries.
On such a full sea are we now afloat;
And we must take the current when it serves,
Or lose our ventures. (*Julius Caesar*, IV, iii)

Like light and dark, tides were Shakespearean metaphors. Captured by Warwick "the King-Maker," in *Henry VI, Part III*, Edward IV reflects:

What fates impose, that men must needs abide;
It boots not to resist both wind and tide. (IV, iii)

So also with references to the winds. In *The Comedy of Errors*, the understandably anxious Antipholus of Syracuse tells Dromio to go to the port (of Ephesus on the Mediterranean) and

if the wind blow any way from shore,
I will not harbour in this town tonight. (III, ii)

But the situation for travelers was even worse at sea than it was on the roads. Shipwreck and the problems of storm-tossed or, in contrast, becalmed journeys, of too much or too little wind, engaged the imagination of the age, a process encouraged by biblical stories and tales of exploration. Winds blowing ships onto rocky coasts were a particular threat. Storms and shipwrecks played a major role in a number of plays, both by Shakespeare, including *The Tempest, The Merchant of Venice, Twelfth Night, A Winter's Tale, Pericles,* and *The Comedy of Errors,* and by other playwrights. Apparent shipwrecks are the cause of the action in *The Merchant of Venice,* for they destroy Antonio's prospects and, therefore, make his bond fall due. Risk destroys credit, a situation that Shylock exploits. The precariousness of trade is amply demonstrated as Antonio faces the prospect of the loss of his life.

A terrible storm is also important to the plot of *Othello,* in that the destruction of the Turkish fleet preparing to invade Cyprus leaves the Venetians sent to help defend the island free to pursue the obsessive jealousies that Iago builds up. Had Othello, the general, instead had to fight the Turks, as he had done earlier, then the plot would have been very different, and his martial character would have been to the fore. At the beginning of act 2, Montano, the Venetian governor of Cyprus, gazes at the sea where the First Gentleman can see nothing bar "a high-wrought flood" or turbulent sea. Montano provides a vivid account of the vulnerability of wooden ships:

MONTANO: Methinks the wind hath spoke aloud at land;
  A fuller blast ne'er shook our battlements.
  If it hath ruffianed so upon the sea,
  What ribs of oak, when mountains [mountainous seas] melt on
    them,
  Can hold the mortise? What shall we hear of this?
SECOND GENTLEMAN: A segregation [dispersal] of the Turkish fleet:
  For do but stand upon the foaming shore,
  The chidden billow seems to pelt the clouds.
  The wind-shaked surge, with high and monstrous main,
  Seems to cast water on the burning Bear
  And quench the guards of th'ever-fixed pole [Pole Star].
  I never did like molestation view
  On the enchafed flood.
MONTANO: If that the Turkish fleet
  Be not ensheltered and embayed, they are drowned;
  It is impossible to bear it out.
THIRD GENTLEMAN: News, lads! Our wars are done.
  The desperate tempest hath so banged the Turks
  That their designment halts. A noble ship of Venice
  Hath seen a grievous wrack and sufferance
  On most part of their fleet. (II, i)

Thus, the language of report has to make up for the drama of show. Storms and shipwrecks were both important, indeed crucial and decisive, plot devices and the occasion of dramatic scenes and of vivid and often harrowing speeches. In the second scene in *Twelfth Night*, the Captain remarks:

after our ship did split,
When you and those poor number saved with you
Hung on our driving boat. (I, ii)

Later, Antonio refers to "the rude sea's enraged and foamy mouth" (V, i). *The Tempest* begins with tempest and shipwreck, Miranda, from the shore, watching "A brave vessel . . . Dashed all to pieces" (I, ii). In *The Winter's Tale*, the Clown observes from land a shipwreck in the stormy sea:

> O, the most piteous cry of the poor souls!
> Sometimes to see 'em, and not to see 'em; now
> The ship boring the moon with her mainmast,
> And anon swallowed with yest and froth, as you'd
> Thrust a cork into a hogshead . . . to make an
> End of the ship, to see how the sea
> Flapdragoned [swallowed] it; but, first, how the
> Poor souls roared, and the sea mocked them. (III, iii)

At Dunster Castle in Somerset close to the Bristol Channel, there is an allegorical painting by Hans Eworth dated 1550 of Sir John Luttrell, the owner of Dunster, depicting him emerging half naked from a storm-tossed sea, while, in the background, sailors abandon a sinking ship. Few people knew how to swim, and ships lacked safety equipment. Dutch paintings of the period, for example by Jacob van Ruysdael (c. 1628–82), include harrowing scenes of ships being sunk in storms or threatened with sinkings.

Winter voyages were harshest and most dangerous. This was true not only of long journeys but also of the numerous shorter trips that were so important for trade and transport, such as those in the Bristol Channel. More generally, journeys, both at sea and on land, that could be undertaken in the summer might be impossible in winter and to a degree that is not true today.

Making the situation even more difficult, coastal charts were frequently imperfect or nonexistent, and lighthouses absent or inadequate. Accurate timekeeping, and thus navigation, was very difficult without the instruments that were to be developed later. As a result, knowledge was unfixed, in the sense that it could not readily be related to such maps as might exist. Experience, in the shape of the views of long-lived members of the crew, was a crucial element in knowing how to respond to circumstances.

Alongside a quest for practical solutions, there was a belief that witches could direct winds. This belief was noted in *Macbeth* when a witch promises revenge on a sailor, en route from London to Aleppo in Syria, for the rudeness of his wife. In *The Tempest*, Prospero indeed can conjure up a storm.

Shipwreck was a frequent reference, and even in plays set far from the sea, as in *Two Gentlemen of Verona*:

> Go, go, be gone, to save your ship from wrack,
> Which cannot perish having thee aboard,
> Being destined to a drier death on shore. (I, i)

The following scene has Julia refer to "the raging sea" (I, ii), as she later does to "the wild ocean" (II, vii). In *The Two Noble Kinsmen*, the jailer's daughter, gone mad, imagines a shipwreck (III, iv). In *Measure for Measure*, set in inland Vienna, Angelo's jilting of Mariana is explained in terms of a shipwreck in which her brother was drowned and her dowry lost (III, i). This explanation captures the many vulnerabilities of characters, vulnerabilities that were particularly present in the case of women. Those who were well born had furthest to fall in fortune, a point demonstrated in a number of the plays.

In Clarence's dream in *Richard III* (not a play in which the sea plays a prominent role), a dream that he describes shortly before he is killed by being drowned in a butt of wine in the Tower of London, Clarence is knocked overboard into the sea:

> Lord, Lord! methought what pain it was to drown:
> What dreadful noise of water in mine ears!
> What sights of ugly death within mine eyes!
> Methought I saw a thousand fearful wracks;
> A thousand men that fishes gnaw'd upon. (I, iv)

In *Henry VI, Part II*, again not a play in which the sea plays a particular role, Queen Margaret describes a storm that includes the "vaulting sea" and "the splitting rocks" (III, ii). In *Part III*, she is given a storm-ship simile (V, iv).

As another aspect of maritime uncertainty, there was the role of piracy, a brutal instance of the way in which the routine of life could be totally overturned and one more menacing than highway robbery. As with many other plot elements, piracy was far from Shakespeare's own experience. Nevertheless, it was salient in his reimagining of his Italian sources. Piracy played a part in many of the plots, for example, *Antony and Cleopatra* and, far more, *The Comedy of Errors* and *Pericles*, and underlined the imminence of violence and the uncertainty it represented and could provoke. In *Antony and Cleopatra*, the campaign against Sextus Pompey (the surviving son of Julius Caesar's rival Pompey the Great), Menecrates, and Menas, three leading pirates in the Mediterranean, is important to the rift between the triumvirs as Antony does not approve of the other two breaking the truce with Sextus Pompey, who is shown as being more honorable.

In *Pericles*, Marina, who as a baby had narrowly escaped shipwreck, later avoids murder only to be seized by pirates and sold to a brothel in Mitylene, which, in fact, was where the prominent Algerine (Algerian) privateer Barbarossa, the leading Ottoman (Turkish) admiral of the sixteenth century, came from. In his raids, many Christians were, indeed, seized for slavery. In *Measure for Measure*, Ragozine, "a most notorious pirate" (IV, iii), dies of fever in prison in Vienna (far from the sea), ensuring that his head can be passed off as that of Claudio. In a crucial plot development, Hamlet's voyage from Denmark to England is unexpectedly cut short by a pirate attack in the North Sea, which ensures that he can return to the action in Denmark (IV, vi). Rosencrantz and Guildenstern, who sail on to England, have very different fates.

Piracy was a very real problem at the time, with, for example, Spanish pirate ships in the English Channel during the early 1590s. Contemporary attacks by Algerine privateers, including in English coastal waters and on the south coast of England, made piracy particularly pressing as an issue, and in 1621, in response, the English unsuccessfully attacked Algiers. Sycorax, the "damned witch" of *The Tempest* (I, ii) who is Prospero's opposite, was born in Algiers. There was also local piracy in English waters, as off the Wirral in 1585, piracy in which women played a role by selling stolen goods.[4]

Turning from the problems of travel, distance implied difference as well as difficulty. In the preface to his *Eneydos* (1490), a translation of a French version of the *Aeneid*, William Caxton (c. 1422–c. 1491) recounted a tale of London merchants en route to Zeeland, who stopped in nearby Kent and could not make themselves understood because the Kentish dialect was so strong. One farmer's wife supposedly thought that they were French because their language was so different. Shakespeare frequently plays with dialect as a humorous device, one often linked to travel, distance, and the bringing together of strangers, and is able to suggest distance as a result. As the London dialect was based on East Anglian and was only established in consequence of the massive migration from East Anglia into London during the fourteenth and fifteenth centuries, it was therefore a fairly young standard in the sixteenth century. As Shakespeare would have observed, regional and local differences in spoken English were far stronger than today, both in the accent and in the words employed. Furthermore, as printing continued much of the medieval dialectalism, the standardization of the printed language emerged slowly, although it was still significant.

The world not only looked but actually was very different in winter and summer, as well as in spring and autumn. This was a matter not solely for travelers but also for those in the world of work. The seasonal round of agriculture set a rhythm, creating a world that was very different to the modern one of fairly constant tasks framed by a human timetable. In Shakespeare's day, the course and success of the harvest were crucial to rural life, and human limitations were cruelly exposed in agriculture.

Shakespeare's language frequently referred to harvest conditions; and the sequence of the seasons took on an important part of its meaning in this context. The care of animals was also a frequent reference point. Speed, Valentine's servant, is introduced in *Two Gentlemen of Verona* with a discussion about whether servants are like sheep (II, i).

Shakespeare's family was well aware of agricultural conditions. In part, this was because of the backgrounds of his grandfathers and of his father-in-law: Anne Hathaway's father, Richard, was a yeoman farmer. It was also because, like most other towns, Stratford, the small town in which he grew up, was greatly influenced by developments in its rural hinterland. These circumstances would have been true for much of the population, including people in London, as many had migrated there from rural backgrounds and/or hinterlands.

Agriculture was affected by a range of problems. Animal diseases had a devastating effect in this period, not least due to the primitive nature of veterinary science. Animal births went wrong more frequently than in the present day and with more harmful consequences for both the births and the mothers. Very differently, Sir Henry Lee, Elizabeth I's host at Ditchley, Oxfordshire, in 1592, lost three thousand sheep in the great storm of 1570.

Farmers lived close to their stock, often under the same roof, as in the surviving fifteenth-century Fleece Inn in Bretforton, near Evesham (not far from Stratford), which was originally a longhouse, an early type of farmhouse. Moreover, the killing of the animals was not "sanitized" in some distant abattoir. People would have been familiar with the sights, sounds, and smells of animals being killed and butchered and with the difficulties of managing the animals accordingly. People saw blood, both animal and human, much more frequently than today. About to be murdered by the future Richard III, Henry VI reflects:

> So first the harmless sheep doth yield his fleece,
> And next his throat unto the butcher's knife. (V, vi)

Arable farming was also difficult and unpredictable, and both ways of working the land involved far more human effort than has been necessary since effective mechanical aids were introduced. Plant stocks had not yet been scientifically improved to resist disease and adverse weather conditions and to increase yields. Such tasks as harrowing, sowing, weeding, and harvesting were greatly affected by the weather. The soil type was also a very important factor in the difficulty of working the soil. Soil drainage was limited, while irrigation was not an option. The dependence of the economy on the natural order of the seasons is vividly captured in *A Midsummer Night's Dream* when Titania observes to Oberon on the impact of their dispute:

> Therefore the winds, piping to us in vain,
> As in revenge have sucked up from the sea
> Contagious fogs; which, falling in the land,
> Hath every pelting river made so proud
> That they have overborne their continents.
> The ox hath therefore stretched his yoke in vain,
> The ploughman lost his sweat, and the green corn
> Hath rotted ere his youth attained a beard.
> The fold stands empty in the drowned field,
> And crows are fatted with the murrion [diseased] flock. (II, i)

Industry was also greatly influenced by the time of the year, making both employment and the nature of work seasonal. Frozen waterways denied watermills power, as did summer drought; water power was also required for bellows and hammers, such as those in the Wealden ironworks, which were the major source of iron. In the "Little Ice Age" that characterized the period, the climate deteriorated from the higher temperatures prevalent earlier in the millennium, reducing growing and working seasons on the land and affecting transport links and the details, sights, and sounds of life. Thus, in 1564, in a great frost, the River Dee was frozen over at Chester so that football was played on it. The Thames was also affected by winter freezing, with people skating on the river and the holding of ice fairs on it. Winter was literally colder and longer than in the experience and tales of the past.

Shakespeare's characters frequently linked the weather to agriculture, as when Conrade tells Don John in *Much Ado About Nothing* that he needed to make "fair weather" in order to stay in with his brother: "It is needful that you frame the season for your own harvest" (I, iii). The net effect was to lead to continual concern about the harvest and the availability of food. This concern took the form of speculation and preparation. The likely nature of the next harvest soon became the topic of the aftermath of the last. In *Pericles*, the prince brings relief to Tarsus by providing bread to a city where hunger had reduced mothers to be ready "to eat those little darlings whom they loved" and spouses to "draw lots who first shall die to lengthen life" for the other (I, iv).

The state of food supplies results in the confrontation shown in the first scene of *Coriolanus*, with a rioting crowd spilling into the streets of ancient Rome. Complaining about the wealthy patricians, the First Citizen draws attention to the physical impact of hunger, the bluntness of his language and images driving his threat home:

> the leanness that afflicts us, the object of our misery, is as an inventory to particularise their abundance; our sufferance is a gain to them. Let us revenge this with our pikes, ere we become rakes: for the gods know I speak this in hunger for bread, not in thirst for revenge.

Menenius Agrippa, a member of the elite, tries to redirect the anger: "For the dearth [shortage of food], the gods, not the patricians, make it, and your knees to them, not arms, must help." This does not convince the citizens (I, i). Fear of such episodes was a key element in the anxieties of the prosperous in Shakespeare's England and in social policy, especially the passage of successive Poor Laws.

Seasonal conditions, notably winter ice, spring spate, and low summer water levels, hit the river traffic that was so important to the economy, often blocking it completely, and this could affect food supplies and much else. Rivers combined to form trading systems that covered much of England. For example, in the West Midlands, Shakespeare's homeland, the Severn was navigable as far inland as Bewdley, near Kidderminster, the Stratford Avon almost up to Warwick, the Wye to Hereford, and the Lugg to Leominster. All these waterways combined to enhance the importance of the Severn system, and thus of the riverports, such as Stratford, Tewkesbury, and Gloucester, and of the nearby major seaport, Bristol. So also with the Thames, Trent, and other major rivers. Some of these rivers took big boats, but many of the navigable rivers could only be used by small boats. These were also more appropriate because the banks had not been built up, and such boats were easiest to tie up.

Markets and, even more, fairs greatly registered seasonal rhythms too. Such occasions were crucial to the flow of goods and people and thus to economic activity. Industrial production is frequently misrepresented if shown in terms of static plant and processes, for most manufacturing involved a degree of outwork and assembly or, at least, of the movement of raw materials. Thus, textiles were generally finished off in workshops different from those where they were begun. This was certainly true of dyeing.

In addition, transhumance—the movement of animals, notably sheep and cattle, to summer and winter pastures—linked upland and lowland areas, for example, the South Downs and Romney Marsh in Sussex or Dartmoor and the Exe Valley in Devon, on a local, regional, and national pattern. Droving, the movement of animals, is referred to by Shakespeare, as in *Much Ado About Nothing* (II, i). More generally, there was a close interdependence between areas of economic, physical, and social difference. This was true both of the economy as a whole and of regional and local economies. For example, in Devon, the moorlands of Dartmoor and Exmoor had important commercial relationships with nearby lowland parishes. Parishes focusing on arable cultivation had a concentrated settlement pattern, with people living in villages, while those centering on animals, especially in the uplands, had dispersed settlement patterns with isolated farmsteads.

This account may seem a long way from the theater, but it is not so, whether in terms of context, plot, characterization, or language. If plays captured the drama of life, they were also an aspect of a society that, whatever its many difficulties, was recovering after the brutal travails of the fourteenth century, most clearly the major plague epidemic of 1348–51 known as the Black Death, when about a third of the population had been killed in an apparently arbitrary, as well as painful, fashion. This experience should not be sanitized by reference to the population "falling."

In the sixteenth century, by contrast, alongside continued attacks by the plague and other deadly diseases, there was a marked degree of growth, in both population size and economic activity, growth that was noted by contemporaries. This growth very much fed through into the world of things and into cultural consequences.

Indeed, Elizabethan England was a society that had more possessions than its predecessors, and the results can be seen in the fittings of Tudor houses, both halls and kitchens. The average home had fewer objects than a modern house, in large part because of the combination of low average incomes, an absence of mass production, and the limited range of products that could be turned into objects. Nevertheless, more objects survive from the sixteenth century than from the fifteenth, some of them new in form, such as printed books. As a result, Shakespeare's audiences had a larger frame of reference in which to interpret his plays.[5] Other evidence of possessions, such as probate inventories, legal records, and literary references, also suggests a marked trend toward possessing more. In *Much Ado About Nothing*, Beatrice refers to Benedick as wearing "his faith but as the fashion of his hat; it ever changes with the next block" (I, i), a block being the mold on which hats were shaped.

Increasing material consumption also invited denunciation by moralists and was seen by some as the cause of what was regarded as a major rise in crime. Gremio, a suitor to Bianca in *The Taming of the Shrew*, makes much of his wealth:

> my house within the city
> Is richly furnished with plate and gold:
> Basins and ewers to lave her dainty hands;
> My hangings all of Tyrian tapestry;
> In ivory coffers I have stuffed my crowns [money];
> In cypress chests my arras counterpoints,
> Costly apparel, tents, and canopies,
> Fine linen, Turkey cushions boss'd with pearl,
> Valance of Venice gold in needle-work,
> Pewter and brass, and all things that belong
> To house or housekeeping. (II, i)

Gremio is rejected as, elsewhere in Shakespeare's plays, are other suitors who focus on their wealth and possessions, as opposed to their character and personal qualities. Nevertheless, the world of things had important cultural consequences. Craftsmanship flourished in the manufacture of many goods. The increase in the number of musical instruments, such as lutes, probably ensured that instrumental music came to play a more prominent role, especially in genteel society. Songs were set to music, which it must be assumed people could readily play. Domestic music making was common, and the rise of broadside ballads saw a new form for popular music.[6] As a very different type of music, the visitors' and viewers' experiences of Prospero's island in *The Tempest* are suffused with magical sounds.

Books were an important part of this new world. The first one printed in England was published by Caxton in 1475: *The Recuyell [collection] of the Histories of Troy*, which was a source for

Shakespeare's *Troilus and Cressida*. Early beginnings were less important than subsequent sustained growth in the production and consumption of books and other printed material. The availability of books helped to encourage literacy, while printing became commercially attractive because of the strong demand for books that built up in the fifteenth century, as well as its use to produce such ephemera as notices, which proved very important to government. Printing had major religious and political dimensions, especially with the publication of the Bible in English as an important aspect of the Reformation, and also energized cultural production. Printing was most important for its collective functions, especially the use of the Bible and the Book of Common Prayer in church. Printing also offered the possibility of a more private and individual culture than that provided by the conspicuous consumption and display of public ceremonial. All forms of literature could readily be made available through print, and poetry, drama, sermons, and maps could be more easily disseminated.[7]

So also with accounts of travel. In 1579, a translation of Marco Polo's travels was published. Describing itself as "most necessary for all sorts of persons and especially for travellers," it provided much information on the Orient, where the Venetian Polo had traveled in the late thirteenth century, and notably on China. More followed from Ralph Fitch (c. 1550–1611): this traveler reached Goa, the major Portuguese base in India in 1583; was jailed and released; traveled on to Pegu (Myanmar), Malacca (Malaysia), and Colombo (Sri Lanka); returned to England in 1591; and had his narrative published in 1599. Shakespeare presumably read it, as Fitch's ship from London to Aleppo in 1583 was the *Tyger* and in *Macbeth* a witch calls down trouble on a sailor: "Her husband's to Aleppo gone, master o'the Tyger" (I, iii).[8] In 1598, an English translation of Jan Huygen van Linschoten's *Itinerario* (1596), the work of a Dutchman who had lived in Goa, provided more information under the title of *His Discours of Voyages into ye Easte and West Indies*. From 1580 to 1640, Goa was indirectly under the kings of Spain, as, following a conquest-enabled inheritance, they were kings of Portugal in this period.

Shakespeare's plays made frequent reference to characters reading books. In *Much Ado About Nothing*, Benedick tells a servant "In my chamber-window lies a book; bring it hither to me in the orchard" (III, ii). In *Twelfth Night*, when the upwardly mobile Malvolio thinks that Olivia's advice to him is to advance "arguments of state," he resolves to "read politic authors" (III, v). As a reminder of the range of published material, Prospero's very different knowledge is also encapsulated in books. The destruction of Prospero's books is both practical and emblematic as an end to his secret knowledge: Caliban seeks this destruction but is thwarted, only for Prospero himself to drown the books before he returns to Naples. There are also references to books and reading in plays by other writers, such as Francis Beaumont's hilarious *The Knight of the Burning Pestle* (1607).[9]

The expansion of drama was one of the highpoints of the age. In Scotland, theater developed, with works by Sir David Lyndsay (c. 1490–c. 1555) and others, but it was essentially in a court setting. In England, by contrast, public patronage and the exigencies and opportunities of the commercial marketplace were also very important. Centered on London, theater also was seen across England thanks to traveling theater companies.[10] The first visit to Stratford-on-Avon was in 1568, a year in which Shakespeare's father was bailiff, and there were frequent visits in the 1570s and early 1580s.

Purpose-built facilities followed in London, supplementing the pattern of playing in livery company halls, inns, private houses, and other temporary settings and drawing on the tradition of staging plays, for example, in grammar schools, as part of a humanist education.[11] The Theatre, the large first purpose-built public playhouse in England since Roman times, located in Shoreditch outside the bounds of the city's authority, was opened in London in 1576 and, after problems with the lease, was reassembled as the Globe in 1599, only for the latter to be burned down in 1613. The Lord Chamberlain's Men, later renamed King's Players, produced plays at both theaters. Established in 1594, the troupe proved a remarkably cohesive theatrical company, in part because it brought together the dramatist (Shakespeare) and the actors, a group that included Shakespeare.[12] This then was a background to the playwright's achievement.

Plays were staged in theaters open to the public, but the London area was also significant as being the location of the court, and Shakespeare's plays were frequently staged for the court—unsurprisingly so, as he was the principal playwright for the Lord Chamberlain's Men, then King's Players. Several plays, including *The Tempest*, are believed to have first been staged at court. This staging probably involved the revision, notably lengthening, of his plays; and that helps explain the varied lengths of surviving versions and especially the length of the generally used texts, as opposed to the shorter versions of the original plays. The tendency to focus on Shakespeare as a writer and actor for the people has led to a downplaying of his significance as a court dramatist, one very much seen with the play within a play in *Hamlet* and *A Midsummer Night's Dream*. The former very much captured court performances as an aspect of court politics.[13] The presence of the court underlined the varied dynamisms of London and its many roles within the country.

## NOTES

1. J. C. Appleby and P. Dalton (eds.), *Outlaws in Medieval and Early Modern England: Crime, Government and Society, c. 1066–c. 1600* (Farnham, UK, 2009).

2. D. C. Beaver, *Hunting and the Politics of Violence before the English Civil War* (Cambridge, 2008).

3. T. Gray, ed., *The Lost Chronicle of Barnstaple, 1586–1611* (Exeter, 1998).

4. C. Jowitt (ed.), *Pirates? The Politics of Plunder, 1550–1650* (Basingstoke, UK, 2006); J. C. Appleby, *Women and English Piracy, 1540–1720: Partners and Victims of Crime* (Woodbridge, UK, 2013).

5. S. Clegg, *Shakespeare's Reading Audiences: Early Modern Books and Audience Interpretation* (Cambridge, 2017).

6. C. Marsh, "'The Woman to the Plow; and the Man to the Hen-Roost': Wives, Husbands and Best-Selling Ballads in Seventeenth-Century England," *Transactions of the Royal Historical Society* 28 (2018): 65–88.

7. H. B. Hackel, *Reading Material in Early Modern England: Print, Gender, and Literacy* (Cambridge, 2005).

8. M. Edwardes, *Ralph Fitch: Elizabethan in the Indies* (London, 1972).

9. C. Scott, *Shakespeare and the Idea of the Book* (Oxford, 2007).

10. A. Gurr, *The Shakespearian Playing Companies* (Oxford, 1996).

11. A. Lancashire, *London Civic Theatre: City Drama and Pageantry from Roman Times to 1558* (Cambridge, 2002).

12. A. Gurr, *The Shakespeare Company, 1594–1642* (Cambridge, 2004).

13. R. Dutton, *Shakespeare, Court Dramatist* (Oxford, 2016).

# A DYNAMIC COUNTRY

THE TUDOR AGE (1485–1603) TURNED out to be the last period before the geography of England radically changed. The settlement of the Atlantic littoral of North America and the resulting major development of the Atlantic economy were to give crucial opportunities to the West Coast ports of England. This was especially so of Bristol, from which English exploration of North America had begun, and, later, of Liverpool.[1]

As yet, however, London's position had not been challenged. Instead, it had become more significant in England in the fourteenth and fifteenth centuries, especially from 1470, so that by 1500, 70 percent of England's crucial export—woolen cloth— was passing through the city. And not surprisingly, cloth figured hugely in London's trade figures. The so-called new draperies—a light worsted cloth of high quality, the market for which quickly expanded in world markets and notably with exports to Mediterranean countries—proved particularly significant.[2] Cloth exports accounted for up to three-quarters of everything that was exported from the busy wharves of London, wharves that were not banished downriver as was the case in the late twentieth century with the development of Tilbury. Indeed, boarding a ship was a move frequently mentioned in Shakespeare's plays. Born far from the sea, he was made well aware of this maritime dimension of experience as a result of living in London.

By the Tudor century, virtually all of the trade in raw wool and most of the trade in woolen cloth were in the hands of the English merchants, although the Hanse merchants of northern Germany still accounted for around 30 percent and the Italians for perhaps 15 percent of this crucial trade. There were longstanding tensions over this foreign involvement, tensions that in part reflected and strengthened xenophobia. In 1517, there were ugly May Day riots in London, directed against foreign residents. These led to foreigners fleeing abroad. In *Sir Thomas More*, a play in the writing of which Shakespeare may have had a role and which depicted these riots, mention is made of refugee foreigners, "their babies at their backs," and the protagonist denounces cruelty by ruffians, who, he warns, may come to "shark on you." There were officially no Jews in England, although undoubtedly there were some living in Bristol and London. There were also black people. The Shrovetide masque in the *Gesta Grayorum*, an account of the Christmas entertainments performed at Gray's Inn in 1594, celebrates Elizabeth and England as offering shelter to those religiously oppressed abroad, by whom Protestants were meant.

The production and trade of cloth linked city and country in a longstanding shared project that was important to the prosperity of both. There were urban/rural tensions in Shakespeare's plays, with rural figures often treated as unpolished and crude, but these tensions were less to the fore than was the case in many other countries. In large part, this reflected a degree of shared interest and linked elites that was not generally matched elsewhere. Indeed, the Shakespeare family itself saw shared interests encompassing Stratford and the Warwickshire countryside, interests clearly seen in the leather trade of Shakespeare's father.

More generally, primogeniture (inheritance by the oldest son) in landed families, which was the English pattern, encouraged the movement of younger sons into other occupations and to the towns as they sought to gain and use opportunities. More-over, there was a long pattern of marriages between landowners and urban elites, notably so as the former tried to gain from the wealth of the latter. The marriage of the sons of land to the dowry-bearing daughters of trade was longstanding and was a process encouraged by the extent to which it did not involve a loss of so-cial status for the former: attitudes to rank were far more liberal than on the Continent.[3]

Distinctions between town and country were less than they were to become by the nineteenth century. While towns were centers of manufacturing and trade, both were also extensively pursued in the countryside, just as there was much market gar-dening within town walls.[4] There were also urban orchards and pastures, the latter particularly valuable for milk, which could not be refrigerated, treated, or preserved, and which therefore went off rapidly.

The dynamism of England in Shakespeare's lifetime reflected particularly the growth of population in this period, a growth that would have been readily apparent in London and its wider region. England's population had fallen markedly in the four-teenth century and then stagnated in the fifteenth, not helped by the Wars of the Roses. The population then grew substantially in the sixteenth century. In part, this growth reflected factors particular to England, but it was more generally true of the world as a whole. Prior to the first national census in 1801, all figures are approximate, but the population of England and Wales appears to have increased from under 2.5 million in 1500 to over 4 million by 1603, and about 5 million by 1651. The impact of this change was accentuated because it followed a period of stagnation after the bubonic plague struck savagely in the Black Death (1348–51), dra-matically cutting the population,[5] and preceded another period of stagnation that lasted until the 1740s. The increase in popula-tion in the sixteenth century was due largely to a fall in mortal-ity, but a rise in fertility stemming from a small decrease in the average age of women at marriage was probably also important. Shakespeare and Marlowe were both baby boomers.

Economic growth was both quantitative (increased production) and qualitative (new methods and transport routes). Both types were important. A more integrated economy reflected the demands of a growing population and urban markets and the absence of internal tariffs (customs barriers), which was a distinctive feature of England and one that was radically different from the situation in both France and Spain. Within England, trade increasingly linked distant areas. As national markets developed, the importance of transport links and capital availability rose. At the same time, the cost and difficulty of transport, notably overland, encouraged the production of goods near to the markets for which they were destined, a situation furthered by the absence of mass production, which also lessened economic integration. The processing of rural products—grain, meat, wool, wood, hides, hops—was central to industry throughout England. Thus, rural England was dotted with breweries (as well as the alehouses where beer was drunk)[6] and mills.

There was greater agricultural and industrial production, and greater consumption as a consequence, but also a degree of social strain and related anxiety that, in a very different context, anticipated some of the factors of life seen in England more recently. Social strains echoed strongly in Shakespeare's plays, not only those that were in theory contemporaneous but also in the depiction of social tensions in the historical plays, both English and Roman, such as *Coriolanus*. Shakespeare's England saw rural peasant uprisings, as well as aristocratic conspiracies, and was repeatedly very anxious, even on the edge.

### AGRICULTURE

Particular dynamism was apparent in the growth, across the country, of agriculture, both to feed the rising population and to provide raw materials for industry, notably wool. Shakespeare's plays assumed great familiarity with agricultural life. In *The Two Gentlemen of Verona*, the play of words in the first scene between Proteus and Speed involved cuckoldry, as in sheep having horns (the symbol of cuckoldry), but there was also reference to the propensity of sheep to stray and to their need for forage: "The sheep for fodder follow the shepherd." Later, Julia refers ironically to a fox as being "the shepherd of thy lambs" (IV, iv).

The growth in agriculture brought both prosperity and employment, indeed a marked rise in both, but, as is also discussed in chapter 8, their benefits were scarcely spread equally. More consumption encouraged price inflation, but this was not matched by the comparable wage inflation since, thanks to the population rise, there were more potential workers to compete for the available jobs. Furthermore, unemployment and underemployment helped to keep wage rates low, a process encouraged by the lack of mechanisms for collective bargaining, let alone the idea of a minimum wage. Price rises for food enabled landowners to raise rents, but landless laborers did not benefit comparably. Pastoral agriculture required less labor than its arable equivalent, and there were frequent complaints as a result about sheep farming: it was said that sheep ate men, in the sense of destroying their jobs.

Contrasts over benefits were accentuated by enclosure, which entailed the reorganization of landholdings into distinct private holdings, in effect a replacement of the collective by the individual. Although criticized by Sir Thomas More in his *Utopia* (1516) as socially destructive and responsible for such problems as theft, enclosure and its consequences were pushed forward by landlords and by groups of prosperous farmers, the second contributing to the rise of the yeomanry in wealth and social position. Enclosure generally resulted in the lessening or end of common land, the communal farmland (notably in large open fields) that had provided the landless with a place to farm for their own benefit, for example, by keeping animals. A product and

aspect of social, economic, and political differentiation, the loss
of this land hit their living standards and led to much resentment.
Enclosure was a social as well as an economic process. It reflected
a decline in paternalism and a search for profit that hit the poor,
especially if such a restructuring was designed, as it often was, to
further a switch from arable to pastoral farming (notably sheep
rearing) and, therefore, to lessen the need for labor and thus to
drive people from the land.

Surveying was one aspect of landlord control and landlord-
directed change, the "improvement" that clashed with custom
as the rural economy and, with it, rural society were reshaped.
In *The Surveyor's Dialogue* (1618) by John Norden, surveyor to
the Duchy of Cornwall and an active mapmaker, the surveyor
offered an inclusive view of economic change: "Surveys are necessary and profitable both for Lord and Tenant," only to meet
with the farmer's claim, "Oftentimes you are the cause that men
lose their land." The surveyor's retort—"the faulty are afraid to
be seen . . . the innocent need not fear to be looked into"—would
have convinced few. As opposed to surveying, the idea of "the
estimated acre," the folk equivalent of surveying, was usually the
preserve of the old men of the parish who could remember older
apportionments of land. This difference underlined the tension
between oral (plebeian) and literate (elite) traditions, a tension
that underlined the pressure of economic change.[7] Another surveyor, Edward Worsop, noted, in *Sundry Errors Committed by
Land Meters* (1582): "The common people for the most part are
in great fear when survey is made of their land." This situation reflected disquiet with economic change, notably with the conversion of arable land to pasture for sheep, which was a key instance
of the search for profit and one used to castigate it as a whole, as
with the claim that sheep ate humans.[8]

Enclosure riots were frequent, especially in the Midlands in
the 1590s and 1600s, for example, in Oxfordshire. In the Midland
Revolt of 1607, over one thousand rioters in Northamptonshire,

Leicestershire, and Warwickshire were suppressed by the local gentry, with over fifty of the rioters killed, including the execution of the ringleaders. The major one, "Captain Pouch," the tinker John Reynolds, claimed to have authority from God and the king to destroy enclosures and to have in his pouch the means to protect his followers from harm. The Midlands was a region where there was much enclosure and accompanying disruption, but there were also enclosure riots elsewhere. At Osmington in Dorset in 1624, new hedges were torn down, and an effigy of the landlord was hanged, which was hardly indicative of social subordination. Economic pressures helped to dissolve deference as well as paternalism. *King Lear* and *Coriolanus* echo some of the issues raised by enclosures.

Alongside violence, litigation became far more common in English society as interests were advanced and defended. This litigation focused on debt and contracts, which were aspects of the vast expansion of credit that was so necessary for the growing economy. The practice and language of both were repeatedly important in Shakespeare's plays, as they also were in correspondence from the period.[9] The emphasis on oaths and pledges reflects the importance of contracts.

The law did not always back the most powerful. For example, landlord attacks on the rights of customary tenants in Cumbria led in 1621 to a critical public meeting and a resolution to resist the process. In 1622, James I wrote to the bishop of Carlisle, complaining about "tumultuous and evil-disposed persons, unlawful assemblies . . . and seditious libels." A group of Cumbrian lords brought an action in Star Chamber against the tenants, but, in the event, the legal resistance of the well-organized and ably led tenants blunted the assault, and the judges found for the customary rights. If justices of the peace (JPs), most of whom were landlords, in practice often had little regard for justice, they could get into serious trouble, either with the assizes or with the Privy Council, if they disregarded the law. On the other hand, it was not easy for the poor to secure the attention of these bodies, and the easiest way to bring justice to JPs was if other members of the elite criticized them, a process encouraged by factional or religious tensions.

Although food and enclosure riots were feared by the elites, a fear reflected in Shakespeare's work, there was no social explosion under Elizabeth, as there had been in 1549 under Edward VI. Instead of any revolution by the poor, there was a steady pressure of official and social constraints on the weaker members of the community. These constraints reflected and sustained social norms and the distribution of power. The constraints included measures against bridal pregnancy and illegitimacy, the insistence (in opposition to folk practices) on a formal Church wedding as the only source of a valid marriage, and attempts in some parishes to prevent the poor from marrying and having children. Illegitimacy was regarded as morally unacceptable and also as likely to cause a burden on the poor rates that were paid by wealthy parishioners. Churchwardens presented (formally reported) people to the Church courts for a wide variety of moral offences, including adultery and selling alcohol at the time of Church services; the Tudors, however, took some "moral" offenses, notably sodomy, from the Church courts into the criminal code. Religious observance by the laity was seen as central to morality.

The enforcement of Church sanctions underlined the nature of power in society and the public nature of Christian sanctions. This enforcement reflected the sense that religion and morality were not separate from each other nor jointly separate from secular life nor spheres in which individual free will could play a role. In the small town of Wimborne Minster in Dorset in the 1590s (currently a delightful spot), presentments included "the widow Sanders" for keeping "a youth in her house" (a breach of public propriety) and two men for conspicuously ignoring the demands of religious conformity: William Lucas "for playing of a fiddle in time of God's service" and Christopher Sylar "for sitting by the fire in the sermon time, and when we asked him if he would go to church he said he would go when he listeth [liked]." In *King Lear*, the "rascal beadle" whips the prostitute (IV, vi).

Justices of the peace and constables maintained a parallel jurisdiction to the Church courts, one that was firmly enforced with physical punishments. Parishes had their stocks (to punish through public, open-air detention) and their whipping posts. In practice, most crime was petty theft, and most petty theft was the poor (the most numerous group) stealing from the poor. However, there was also theft from the wealthy, not least in the form of poaching. This was a widespread practice that reflected the limitations of social subordination and the extent of low-level violence in society, as well as gentry factionalism and rites of passage for young men. The young Shakespeare was allegedly brought up for judgment for poaching before Sir Thomas Lucy (1553–1600) in his hall at Charlecote, Warwickshire, and subsequently satirized Lucy as Justice Shallow in *Henry IV, Part II* and, more clearly, *The Merry Wives of Windsor*. There are no surviving legal records to prove or disprove the poaching story, which was first recorded in the late seventeenth century, a period in which many stories about Shakespeare were first set down. Allegedly, Shakespeare was whipped at Lucy's behest. On one of her progresses, Elizabeth I visited Charlecote in 1572 when Lucy was an MP. He was an active Protestant who in the early 1580s arrested Catholics in Warwickshire, including the Arden family to whom Shakespeare was related.

The Game Acts of 1485 and 1604 were important to the judicial proceedings by which hunting was legally defined and socially segregated.[10] The reverse of poaching was legitimate hunting by the wealthy, and, as mentioned in the previous chapter, there were frequent references in Shakespeare's plays to hunting. Over poaching, as over other matters, the practice of the law greatly favored the rich. As Shakespeare powerfully and vividly suggested in *King Lear*, the poor had less access to justice, as well as looked very different:

Through tatter'd clothes small vices do appear;
Robes and furr'd gowns hide all. Plate sin with gold,
And the strong lance of justice hurtless breaks;
Arm it in rags, a pigmy's straw doth pierce it. (IV, vi)

Similarly, in his clear-cut pamphlet *Work for Armourers* (1609), the playwright Thomas Dekker condemned enclosures and the treatment of the poor. Rags, indeed, were the clothes of the poor.

In marked contrast, the wealth of landowners left a powerful legacy in the new mansions of the period, mansions that travelers would have seen and many of which can still be seen today.[11] They were not castellated or moated as hitherto because fortifications were less necessary and also viewed with disfavor. There had been an extensive abandonment of castles, in some cases from the 1470s and far more actively under the Tudors, who came to power in 1485. Dunstanburgh Castle was already much ruined in 1538 and Dunster Castle in 1542, as a consequence of a lack of maintenance for decades. In 1597, a survey found that Melbourne Castle was being used as a pound for trespassing cattle, and it was demolished for stone in the 1610s, as many monasteries had earlier been due to the Reformation. John Speed described Northampton Castle in 1610: "Gaping chinks do daily threaten the downfall of her walls." When, in 1617, James I visited Warkworth Castle, he found sheep and goats in most of the rooms. Bramber Castle, formerly a Sussex stronghold of the Howards, was in ruins. The major fortresses built in England during the sixteenth century were for frontier defense, notably Berwick and the forts on the South Coast, and not for mounting or resisting rebellion.

The land market expanded greatly as a consequence of the Dissolution of the Monasteries in the 1530s and early 1540s, and in *Arden of Faversham* (1592), which Shakespeare possibly designed/plotted and probably partly wrote, the unlawful enclosure of the lands of the abbey of Faversham is a key feature in the plot, which was based on an actual murder committed in Kent in 1551. The Dissolution also provided major opportunities for building—not

least by providing sites, monastic buildings that could be reworked, and such building materials as stone and slate. The drive
for status was a key element, one repeatedly noted by Shakespeare, in both comedies and tragedies. This drive was tapped
by James I when, in 1611, he granted the title of baronet, the only
hereditary honor that is not a peerage, to two hundred gentlemen
of good birth as a way to raise money, at a price of £1,095 each.
One of the most splendid surviving examples of the new mansions of the period is Hardwick Hall in Derbyshire, described
by contemporaries as "more glass than wall." Built in 1590–97 for
Bess of Hardwick (c. 1527–1608), whose four marriages took her
up the social scale to become Countess of Shrewsbury in 1568,
it was almost certainly designed by Robert Smythson. An out-
standing architect, he was also largely responsible for Longleat
and probably for Chastleton House. "Prodigy houses," such as
Hardwick Hall, were built with an eye to royal progresses, for
example that of Don Pedro in *Much Ado About Nothing*, and with
the needs of a visiting court reflected in their layout. Ironically,
Elizabeth built nothing of importance herself, although that was
also the case with many English monarchs, including George III
(r. 1760–1820).[12]

One of the best preserved of Elizabethan mansions is Montacute House in Somerset, the stone of which is indeed honeyed
if your honey is rich. Its history is more generally indicative of
social changes and their relationship with government and politics. Constructed in the 1590s for Sir Edward Phelips, a successful
lawyer and MP, the house was built on land sold by the Crown
after the dissolution of the nearby monastery. As part of a more
widespread process of upward social mobility, notably by gentry,
yeoman farmers, and merchants,[13] the Phelips were "new men,"
the first identifiable ancestor of Edward Phelips being his great-
grandfather, Thomas, who, in the 1460s, rose in the service of the
Brooke family from the rank of yeoman to gentleman. Thomas's son Richard became a royal official and MP and survived

accusations of extortion and of oppression of the tenants of the Grey family's estates for which he was surveyor general. Richard, however, found it difficult to satisfy the exchequer with his accounts as lessee of the customs of Poole. Richard's son Thomas was involved in a prison escape, but thereafter he followed an establishment career as officeholder and MP.

Ability, sharp practice, and social connections were all crucial to the Phelips family. By these means they sought, like other families who made their way in government, commerce, or the law, to establish a landed position. These men did not fund the construction of their great houses off the back of sheep, as did many other rising families of the period, for example, the Spencers of Althorp, Northamptonshire, or Walter Jones, a successful wool merchant who bought the estate of Chastleton and built Chastleton House in c. 1610–12. The splendor of such houses repeatedly and insistently proclaimed status. At Montacute, armorial stained glass and elaborate screen and oak paneling adorned the Great Hall, while armorial glass and an ornate plaster frieze and ceiling decorated the Great Chamber.

In addition to new mansions, there were extensions. For example, Knole in Kent, already splendid, was greatly enlarged in the 1600s by Thomas Sackville, First Earl of Dorset (1536–1608). A poet and playwright in the 1560s, he made money both as Lord Treasurer (1599–1608)—public office being generally a source of great private gain—and by the sale of timber for charcoal to fuel the important Wealden iron industry and also to housebuilders and shipbuilders. Timber from Kent was important in satisfying London demand.

In addition, more modest but still impressive country houses survive from the period. Examples include Melford Hall in Suffolk, Benthall Hall and Wilderhope Manor in Shropshire (which, when I stayed in it, was a freezing-cold youth hostel without mains electricity or sewerage), and Eastbury House, now surrounded by a housing estate in East London. These houses reflected the expansion of the number of gentlemen in the period. The gentry benefited from their access to education, their underassessment for taxation, and their central role in the law and in the agricultural and industrial expansion of the period.

Many such Tudor houses were timber framed with close studding. Their interior layout reflected the growing division between "private" and "public" space. This was a division seen in Shakespeare's plays, with their use of an alcove at the back of the stage. This alcove could be separated off with a curtain and thus provide opportunities for staging concealment and surveillance and therefore for the "discoveries" that could be important to the plot. The alcove could also be a bedchamber. Timber construction was the norm in towns, as well as the countryside. The Globe itself was a half-timbered construction.

Alongside the houses of the landed wealthy, there were the increasingly substantial houses of yeomen, merchants, married clergy, and lawyers. Chimneys and glass in windows both made a big difference, the glass windows aiding reading. Inventories revealed lots of pewter and furnishings as part of a more general spread of wealth, even luxury.[14] In *The Tempest*, to the justified concern of Caliban, his allies Stefano and Trincolo, are distracted from their intended attack on Prospero by the clothes of his that they try on (IV, i). In *The Comedy of Errors*, the golden chain that Antipholus of Ephesus orders from Angelo, the goldsmith, for his wife, Adriana, plays a major role in the plot, with Antipholus, locked out of this house, deciding to give it to the courtesan only for Angelo, by mistake, to give it to Antipholus of Syracuse. This chain was an instance of the stage properties that were important to the plays, offering a counterpoint to the generally bare stage.

## INDUSTRY

The importance of water power, provided by fast-flowing rivers and tapped by the waterwheels in mills, helped ensure that much industry was located in the countryside. For example, the first copper smelter near Neath in South Wales, built by the Mines Royal in about 1584, depended on the power of the Aberdulais Falls. The copper came from Cornwall and was shipped to South Wales, thus forming an aspect of the integrated maritime economy of the Bristol Channel. Water-powered blast furnaces, from 1494, and slitting mills, from the 1620s, made it easier to work iron. Sixteenth-century hammer ponds—that is, man-made, spring-fed ponds that provided water power for hammering wrought iron—can still be seen in the Weald south of London, including at Ludshott and Shottermill. In *The Tempest*, Prospero refers to Ariel as venting his "groans as fast as mill-wheels strike" (I, ii)—in other words, hit the water.

The countryside was far from being a bucolic idyll, not least because of the pressures linked to enclosure and inflation. Indeed, its depiction as such was part of the romantic character of several of Shakespeare's plays, such as *A Midsummer Night's Dream*. More realistically, an emphasis in England on water and wind power was seen with mills across the country. There were also particular concentrations. The Wandle, one of the tributaries of the Thames near London, was a center of water-powered grain milling designed to serve the city.

Wood and coal were the other major power sources, and the marked growth in the mining and use of the latter has led to consideration of the period as part of a "long Industrial Revolution," one that had a long prequel in terms of qualitative and quantitative developments, before the more famous taking off in *the* Industrial Revolution of the eighteenth and nineteenth centuries.[15] Coal production rose in the sixteenth and, even more, seventeenth centuries. The major production area was North East England. The amount of coal shipped from the river Tyne, notably Newcastle, rose to 400,000 tons by 1625. When the Scots invaded England in 1644, one of their objectives was to capture the North East and thereby secure coal supplies for their parliamentary allies in London. Domestic heating was a key use for coal, notably in London, but there was also increasing use for manufacturing. Coal, for example, was the main fuel in sugar refining, brewing, salt boiling, soapmaking, and brickmaking, by 1700. As a result in part of local coal, Newcastle produced about 40 percent of all the glass made in England in the seventeenth century.

Coal production also rose in Lancashire, Wales, and Central Scotland, although none was as well placed as they could not ship coal to London and East Anglia. Landlords sought to profit. Searching for coal, William, Sixth Earl of Derby, ordered surveys on his Lancastrian property at Knowsley Park in 1602, and Sir Richard Molyneux followed suit nearby in 1610.

Although coal reduced dependence on wood, as yet wood remained far more important than coal. The significance of wood is seen in the frequent reference to fires in Shakespeare's plays. In *The Tempest*, both Caliban and Ferdinand, the prince becoming the "patient log-man" (III, i), have to bring wood for Prospero, an onerous task. The use of wood for a growing population and expanding industry helped ensure that wood prices, including that of firewood, rose above inflation. This was coupled with government anxiety about the supply of timber to build ships, notably for the navy. The Statute of Woods of 1543, which was strengthened in 1570, sought to protect timber supplies. Moreover, demand for wood for iron smelting was a problem, and in 1558 an act was passed "that timber should not be felled to make coals for the burning of iron." It was reinforced in 1581 by an "Act touching Iron Mills near until the City of London and the River Thames." Concern led to Arthur Standish's *New Directions of Experience to the Commons Complaint for the Planting of Timber and Firewood*. Published in 1613, this was followed in 1615 by a second edition, the preface of which included a royal proclamation from James I, who was a supporter of the planting and care of trees. Standish lived in Cambridgeshire, or south Lincolnshire.

That James appears in a number of respects in the present work, for example, in relation to witchcraft in chapter 1, serves as a reminder that individuals had a series of roles and a variety of views. Elizabeth, for example, can appear as a ruler personally identifying herself with the reform of the coinage through a re-coinage, visiting the royal mint to that end in 1561,[16] as well as in many other lights. This provides an appropriate way to consider Shakespeare as well as his world. So also with aspects of the environment, whether human or physical. Thus, the response to the woodland discussed here is different to its consideration in chapter 1, where it appears for example as a source of darkness and a cover for mystery, unease, and banditry.

The dynamism of the economy similarly had a range of consequences. Trends that are aggregate were experienced very differently by individuals, with further variations arising from the contrasts between stages of life, contrasts that were noted by Shakespeare. He and other playwrights captured these realities, quite as much as those of the general bustle of a growing economy.

## NOTES

1. J. Black, *Geographies of an Imperial Power: The British World, 1688–1815* (Bloomington, IN, 2018).

2. N. Harte, *The New Draperies in the Low Countries and England, 1300–1800* (Oxford, 1997).

3. L. Stone and J. C. F. Stone, *An Open Elite? England, 1540–1880* (Oxford, 1984).

4. P. Clark and P. Slack, *English Towns in Transition, 1500–1700* (London, 1976); P. Clark, ed., *Cambridge Urban History of Britain*, vol. 2, *1540–1840* (Cambridge, 2000).

5. B. M. S. Campbell, *The Great Transition: Climate, Disease and Society in the Late Medieval World* (Cambridge, 2016).

6. P. Clark, *The English Alehouse: A Social History* (London, 1983); M. Hailwood, *Alehouses and Good Fellowship in Early Modern England* (Woodbridge, UK, 2016).

7. J. Norden, *The Surveyor's Dialogue*, ed. Mark Netzloff (Abingdon, UK 2010).

8. R. Hoyle, ed., *Custom, Improvement and the Landscape in Early Modern Britain* (Farnham, UK, 2011); M. A. R. Cooper, "Edward Worsop; from *The Black Art* and *Sundrie Errours* to *True Geometricall Demonstration*," http://dx.doi.org/10.1179/sre.1993.32.248.67.

9. G. West, "A Glossary to the Language of Debt at the Climax of *1 Henry IV*," *Notes and Queries* 234 (1989): 323–24.

10. R. B. Manning, *Hunters and Poachers: A Cultural and Social History of Unlawful Hunting in England, 1485–1640* (Oxford, 1993).

11. C. Platt, *The Great Rebuilding of Tudor and Stuart England: Revolutions in Architectural Taste* (London, 1994).

12. G. W. Bernard, *Power and Politics in Tudor England* (Aldershot, UK, 2000), 175–90.

13. A. T. Brown, *Rural Society and Economic Change in County Durham: Recession and Recovery, c. 1400–1640* (Woodbridge, UK, 2015).

14. L. L. Peck, *Consuming Splendor: Society and Culture in Seventeenth-Century England* (Cambridge, 2005).

15. A. Green and B. Crosbie, *Economy and Culture in North-East England, 1500–1800* (Woodbridge, UK, 2017).

16. J. Bishop, "Currency, Conversation, and Control: Politics Discourse and the Coinage in Mid-Tudor England," *English Historical Review* 131 (2016): 791.

FOUR

—〰—

# LONDON

My sovereign, with the loving citizens,
Like to his island girt in with the ocean,
Or modest Dian [Diana] circled with her nymphs,
Shall rest in London till we come to him.

—Richard, Earl of Warwick, the "King-Maker," promising
that Henry VI will be safe, *Henry VI, Part III* (IV, viii)

WHATEVER THE POLITICAL AND RELIGIOUS crises and
changes of the fifteenth and sixteenth centuries, London retained
and developed its position as the leading English city. This leadership was governmental, political, and economic—and in many
aspects of each category. Power and trade focused on London,
and each developed in a symbiotic relationship that linked capital
and country.

The countryside began right outside London, as the anonymous
"Copperplate map" of about 1559 shows very clearly. Buildings
outside the walls are depicted, including the linear development
north along Bishopsgate Street, but the general impression is of
a rapid shift to rural activities, with fields and animals depicted.
Other activities represented outside the walls include the laying

out of cloth to dry or bleach and citizens practicing their archery, which was part of a civic duty to protect country and city. In London and elsewhere, however, many of the dwellings outside the walls were shacks, the "mean cottages" that were criticized by John Stow; and these, often temporary, residences tended not to be shown, being considered inconsequential and not worthy of inclusion. This is an aspect of the way in which maps can mislead as well as present. In the suburbs could be found industrial processes that were seen as polluting, such as brickmaking, brewing, and tanning, as well as food processing, for example, butchering.

London's impact on its hinterland was an aspect of the increasing integration of England,[1] which, while allowing for regional specialisms, encouraged mobility of labor, the flipside of which was vagrancy. Shakespeare himself was a rural migrant and, later in his career, lodged with a Huguenot (French Protestant) family, part of the immigrant population from abroad. London's impact was in part characterized by the need to provide for and support the city and its people.[2] The perishable nature of fresh food combined with transport problems to ensure that market gardening focused close to London, for example, at St. Martin's Field to its west. Pastureland was also located near to the city, to provide milk and to secure pasturage for animals that had been driven (walked) to London for slaughter along drove roads. This driving was often for a long distance, for example, of turkeys from Norfolk and of cattle from the West Country and Wales. The piazza built at Covent Garden in the seventeenth century was constructed on the "great pasture," where animals were fattened up after their long walk before being slaughtered and butchered.

The London market was particularly important in the South East. Grain was moved to London from Kent, both overland and by sea from Sandwich, as well as from East Anglia. As a result, during the poor harvests of the 1590s, serving the city led to food shortage elsewhere, which exacerbated social discontent. Such discontent, however, was far less politically significant outside

London than within it. The consequences of increasing economic integration included not only such grain movements but also steps to ease trade and travel, such as the establishment of many inns, notably in market towns and transport nodes.[3]

The society of Shakespeare's London can be discerned more readily and more clearly than that of the previous century.[4] Surviving records, both private and state, are more copious. This was thanks to printing, as well as to a marked rise in both literacy and population, to more extensive governmental activity, and to the effective nationalization of the Church as a result of the Henrician Reformation, under Henry VIII (r. 1509–47). Parish registers and churchwardens' accounts help supply population figures. There are more surviving buildings than in the fifteenth century, including churches but also more secular ones, such as schools.

Trade was to the fore in the life and outlook of the city. A hugely important part in English commercial expansion was played by the Company of Merchant Adventurers of London, which developed the trade and then monopolized the export of woolen cloth until as late as 1689 and used the proceeds to fund a wide range of imports. Such products as linen, iron, hemp, and wax were all imported in bulk and complemented by a dizzying range of light manufactured goods, especially from the Low Countries (modern Belgium and Netherlands), including iron pots, books, spectacles, and cloth-making tools. Continental workshops and workers found a ready market in London. Growth there provided much prosperity, increasing the number of affluent citizens and thus greatly influencing the nature of the local market. This wealth underwrote the dominance of expenditure and credit enjoyed by London, expenditure and credit that were also important to the operations of the theatrical world there.[5]

In its strengthening role within the national economy, London benefited from being best placed to trade with Antwerp, which was readily reached by sea across the southern North Sea. Now in Belgium, Antwerp was then the leading port of the Low

Countries, and indeed of northern Europe, and the key site of northern and western Europe's trade and finance. Antwerp's fortunes, however, were to be affected greatly by the wars of religion that broke out in the Low Countries in the 1560s—namely, the Dutch Revolt—and especially by a lengthy and ultimately successful Spanish siege in 1585.

In the short term, the problems of Antwerp economically favored Amsterdam, a city across the southern North Sea that was also well located for trade from London's point of view. London was a long-term beneficiary: its population, behind that of Antwerp in 1550, had overtaken it by 1600. Many of the foreign immigrants to London in Elizabeth's reign came from the French-speaking Walloon provinces of the Low Countries, for example, the cities of Ghent and Bruges. Their move was a consequence of the disruption of the Dutch Revolt, one that prefigured the large-scale immigration of French Huguenots (Protestants) in the late seventeenth century, although Huguenots also moved in response to the French Wars of Religion in the late sixteenth century. Immigrants from the Continent were particularly active in the luxury trades, notably the silk weaving in which French immigrants were skilled.[6]

As far as foreign trade was concerned, London was also well located for trade to Scandinavia, to Iberia (Spain and Portugal), to the Mediterranean, where the key ports were Venice, Genoa, Leghorn/Livorno, Naples, and Messina in Italy, as well as Smyrna, but not Ephesus, in Asia Minor, and to the wider world. In addition, given the extent to which commerce involved transshipment, as goods were moved from one trade to another (with profit derived from this intermediary role), London also benefited from its ability to play a major part in serving trades both to the north and to the south: to the Baltic as well as the Mediterranean. As London increased its already-strong dominance of England's international trade, it became prosperous enough to contribute 24 percent of the totality of subsidies (taxes) raised in 1541–42, a position that Amsterdam was to match in the Dutch republic in the seventeenth century.

The major and sustained rise in the population provided more producers and more consumers for the English economy. So also did the role of London as an organizational center for economic activity: the opportunities that economic growth provided for mercantile enterprise made London important to the economy across England, and increasingly so. The prominence of trade was marked by the Royal Exchange opened by Sir Thomas Gresham in 1567, in emulation of Antwerp's Bourse. This was a step applauded in Thomas Heywood's play *If You Know Not Me You Know Nobody* (1605). With its offices, colonnades, courtyards, and shops, this exchange became the center of enterprise, and its success was to lead Robert Cecil—from 1605 Earl of Salisbury, and the leading minister, as Secretary of State from 1596 to 1612, Lord Privy Seal from 1598 to 1612, and Lord Treasurer from 1608 until his death in 1612—to open the competing New Exchange on the Strand in 1609. It was designed by Inigo Jones.

The emphasis on trade in a context of commercial growth and development was linked to an all-encompassing materialism that was to the fore in the depiction of merchants and men of business, both in London and in other cities, although they also played crucial roles in civic governance and philanthropy. Moreover, trade and profit could be staged, and most powerfully so by Shakespeare in *The Merchant of Venice*.[7] That play links to the law, with "the pound of flesh" becoming a lasting phrase in the English language, one seen in many works, for example, the 2016 American film *The Accountant*, which, despite its title, is a thriller.

The significance of commercial disputes was important to the strength of London as the legal center of England. This provided an important degree of national exceptionalism in the shape of the common law, as well as part of Shakespeare's audience in the form of lawyers. Indeed, the Inns of Court, which had a long tradition of theatrical performances, including *The Comedy of*

*Errors* in Gray's Inn Hall in 1594, were an important educational center and notably so for sons of the landed elite, both elder sons mindful of their future role as landlords and JPs and younger sons seeking a legal career. Many in the audience would also have been litigants or have been threatened by litigation. From very different directions, lawyers are criticized in *Hamlet* and, even more, in *Henry VI, Part II*, although giving the criticism to the dangerous, indeed murderous, demagogue Jack Cade greatly undermines it.

The law was important in Shakespeare's plays (as in those of other playwrights), and legal language was significant both in them and in his sonnets.[8] Legal process played a role in many plays, especially *The Merchant of Venice* and *Measure for Measure*. In both cases, setting the plots abroad ensured that English legal procedures did not need to be followed even if issues of law and justice were to the fore. In other plays, such as *Othello*, the law was due to play a role as part of an outcome that was also shown, in that case in the intended treatment of Iago, although, by suicide, Othello escaped trial. Informal legal process plays a role in other plays, notably *Hamlet*, *Othello*, *The Winter's Tale*, and *Henry VIII*. Moreover, many of the dramas were in a sense trials of character, notably so with *Macbeth* and for Claudius (and, very differently, Hamlet) in *Hamlet*. These trials of character brought together religious themes and legal language, while the legal processes that were shown could involve religious language.

Shakespeare's interest in rhetoric rested on the need for his characters to present cases. Rhetoric was a technical process, drawing on classical models, that was developed at the Inns of Court, where the exercises were oral and thus a form of structured language that could have theatrical characteristics.[9] Drama was in part rhetoric with action.

Aside from commerce, Shakespeare's London was a key center of manufacturing, as it continued to be until the late twentieth century but is no longer. The sights, noises, and smells of the city reflected this manufacturing; and audiences would have been very familiar with particular trades, their activities, characteristics (for example, the alleged lechery of tailors), hierarchies, and problems. The prime market for this production was the large and growing population of the city itself, as it was the largest market in England for clothes, shoes, and other goods. However, London-made goods also circulated around England and abroad.

There was a continued process of striving for new opportunities, a tendency that looks toward the present. In 1580, Peter Morice, a Dutch engineer, so impressed city authorities with the power and efficiency of his water pump (or "forcier") that he was granted permission to install an undershot waterwheel beneath one of the northern arches of London Bridge. This was used to pump fresh water to a conduit at Leadenhall, a task that reflected the importance of water supply for the growing city. Further wheels were installed over the years, including one to grind corn, another key task. None of these facilities survived the Great Fire in 1666, and the Morice wheel was one of the first structures to burn. However, waterwheels continued in use under London Bridge until John Rennie's new bridge was built in the 1820s.

Fire was a major concern in London and other cities, one that owed much to the close-packed nature of the buildings; to their flammable materials (notably wood and thatch) and contents (including straw for bedding and firewood); to the role of open fires in heating, lighting, cooking, and manufacturing; and to the absence of what would later be regarded as basic safety procedures, especially for fire prevention *and* firefighting. Thus, in Chester in 1564, thirty-three houses were destroyed in a fire. In Wymondham in Norfolk, just over half the town was hit by a fire in 1615. Helping to increase casualties, fire escapes were primitive.

Population figures are far from exact for this precensus age, but London's population grew from about 1520, in common with that of the country as a whole and with that of Europe. Although by far the leading city in Britain, London was not one of the leading

European, let alone world, cities in population terms in 1500, when it had about 50,000 to 60,000 inhabitants. At that point, the leading city in Christian Europe was Paris, with about 225,000, followed by Naples (125,000), Milan (100,000), Venice (100,000), Granada (70,000), Prague (70,000), and Lisbon (65,000). Cities in the 50,000-to-60,000 band included Genoa, Bologna, Antwerp, and Verona.

Nevertheless, London was soon on a marked upward trend. The rapid rise in its population was probably to about 120,000 in 1558, 180,000 in 1575, 200,000 in 1600, and about 375,000 to 400,000 in 1650, which amounted to a rate of increase far greater than in the fifteenth century. In contrast, the second largest city in England in 1600 was Norwich (a city that did not feature in Shakespeare's plays), with about 15,000 inhabitants. Other major cities included Bristol, Exeter, Newcastle, and York, none of which featured significantly in the plays. London's growth was made more impressive after taking into account the high death rate of its population, especially among infants and children, as the densely packed city was particularly conducive for infection, and the infectious diseases of the period were deadly and hard to counter. The rise in the population led to more overcrowding and put further pressure on sanitation.

Viewed as a longstanding pattern, the high death rate was countered by migration to London. This migration played a different demographic role from the situation today and over the last two centuries, when immigration has essentially supplemented indigenous growth. Immigration, mostly from elsewhere in England, meant that much of London's population had been born outside the city, and immigration also helped keep the average age of the population relatively low.[10]

London's numbers put major pressure on housing and employment, at the same time as they greatly added to the vitality of the city. Migrants, from home and abroad, provided labor, unskilled and skilled, and the latter contributed to the development of new trade and products, for example, in glassmaking and in brewing hopped beer, the latter introduced by the Dutch in the fifteenth century. This development reflected the major expansion that was necessary to supply the growing population.

Each migrant, domestic or foreign, represented an individual decision that life might be better in London. For many, this hope proved illusory, as, in practice, rural penury often translated into urban poverty. Moreover, urban degradation was more pernicious because of the absence of the social and community support that was more prevalent in rural parishes, although far from invariable even there.

Nevertheless, as an important advantage for London, the social system was more fluid in towns: opportunities were more plentiful, social mobility was greater, and social control laxer, with each point exemplified by the world of the theater. This contrast with rural and small-town England helped define part of London's lasting character. There was acute social differentiation in the city but not a differentiation expressed in traditional terms of deference, as that in rural England generally was. Indeed, the countryside and its values were captured for London audiences by Shakespeare. As wealth was more fluid in London, so the basis of hierarchy and deference there was different and understood to be different.

In practice, the sense of opportunity in London surpassed the reality. However, this sense contributed greatly to a feeling of energy and flux that centered there and that Shakespeare presented, as in the depiction of the Boar's Head Tavern in Eastcheap that Falstaff frequented in *Henry IV, Part I*. At the same time, the strong pride in London that its citizens felt could be matched by an engagement with a very different world, as with Londoners' fondness for reading and seeing chivalric romances.[11] The ability to hold such contradictions on the part of audiences was seen with playwrights, such as Shakespeare, and with other writers operating in specific genres.[12] Similarly, playwrights could also write in more than one genre, with Dekker producing pamphlets on life in London.[13]

The growing population led to a physical expansion of London, especially to the west, as well as into the properties seized from the Church. Twenty-three religious houses had had estates in or abutting the city, and their seizure by Henry VIII in 1536–40, during the Dissolution of the Monasteries, provided plentiful opportunities for expansion. In this way, the Reformation brought significant alterations to the fabric of London and to its suburbs beyond the city walls, and Shakespeare's audiences lived against this background. After the Dissolution, monastic buildings were used for different purposes or were demolished to provide stone and other building materials, such as lead and timber. The Blackfriars became the site for a playhouse.[14] Some sites were leveled and not used for building. Thus, the site of the priory of St. Mary Spital was turned into a setting for military practice.[15]

While expanding, London remained compact and densely built up so that the growing throngs of people ensured that it seemed crowded, indeed more so than in the past. Thomas Platter, a Swiss visitor, observed in 1599: "This city of London is not only brimful of curiosities, but so popular also that one simply cannot walk along the streets for the crowd." Platter saw "the tragedy of the first Emperor Julius," presumably *Julius Caesar*, in a straw-thatched house, which was probably his description of the new Globe theater. He subsequently saw another play, which has not been identified, at another theater, which again has not been identified.[16]

The crowds were especially dense on London Bridge, which, like other major city bridges in Europe, was, at once, a thoroughfare and, with its numerous buildings, a place of residence and center of shopping. Despite the marked rise in the city's population and its geographical expansion, London Bridge remained the sole bridge across the Thames in the London area until the mid-eighteenth century, when Westminster Bridge was built.

London Bridge was important in historical episodes significant to London's experience, for example, Cade's rebellion in 1450, which was extensively and vividly described by Shakespeare in *Henry VI, Part II.*

The large-scale use of ferries to cross the Thames was encouraged by there only being one bridge and by the spreading nature of the city. This use accentuated the crowded nature of the river, which owed much to the combination in London of sea and river traffic, since London was foremost for both and the two depended on each other. At high tide, the river was nearly half a mile wide. Passenger traffic up and down the river added to the melee. Thames watermen—with their traditional clinker-built "wherries"—were licensed by the city to operate a river-borne taxi service. Fares were regulated by act of Parliament in 1514, and apprenticeships were introduced in 1555 to help improve safety and the standard of service. The protruding bows of the wherries allowed passengers easy access to and from the hundred or so sets of river steps that were used for the purpose. In addition, all of the riverside mansions along the Strand had their own water gates giving access to this important form of transport. So also did the Tower of London, with Traitors' Gate, through which people were brought for entry into the fortress, including for questioning and all-too-inevitable execution, as with two of Henry VIII's wives: Anne Boleyn and Katherine Howard. Taking theatergoers from the city to Southwark on the south bank of the Thames was a particularly good trade for the watermen.

London as a whole became an enormous building site, with status proving a key drive to the rebuilding. This concern with status owed much to the desire to display power and politesse and to secure respect on the part of the new (and newly promoted) nobility who had benefited greatly from Henry VIII's largesse. London, indeed, offered an ideal site for display, helping to link Crown and the elite and providing a context for the development of the theater, a development that the Common Council sought to control through licensing. At the same time, display, conspicuous consumption,[17] and social pretension, including the theaters, were all castigated, if not lacerated, by moralists, both Puritans and others.

These characteristics were also mocked by some playwrights, as in the characters of Sir Petronel Flash and his wife, Gertrude, in *Eastward Ho* (1605) by George Chapman, Ben Jonson, and John Marston. The conspicuous consumption represented by the gold chain commissioned by Antipholus of Ephesus in *The Comedy of Errors* is a target. Social pretension proved a particular butt, as with Malvolio in *Twelfth Night*.

In contrast, meritorious merchants were praised in a number of plays, including Antonio in *The Merchant of Venice*, Thomas Heywood's *Edward IV* (1592) and *If You Know Not Me You Know Nobody* (1605), and Thomas Deloney's *Jack of Newbury* (1597) and *The Gentle Craft* (1597). Deloney was a silk weaver by background.

In his *London and the Country Carbonadoed and Quartered into Several Characters* (1632), Donald Lupton referred to London as "a great world" with "so many worlds in her," a version of the current description of London as a city of villages. This variety was a feature of which Shakespeare's audiences were well aware, and it also affected their perception of other cities. Already, by the time of John Norden's map of 1593, the built-up area linked London with Westminster along Fleet Street and the Strand, an area that was comparatively affluent and focused on governmental, legal, and gentry activities rather than the commerce of the city or the industry, such as shipbuilding, to the east. The Strand proved a key area for rebuilding as there were a number of episcopal palaces there that offered such opportunities.

Increasingly, as the Strand developed or at least changed, Westminster, which was a separate city, instead became the West End of London. Its prominence reflected the rise of the court and that of Parliament. Those who served in the royal government lived in

Westminster while parliamentarians lodged there during the session.[18] In his references to courts, Shakespeare replicated the suspicion and disdain that many Londoners felt for Westminster and Whitehall but also the degree of fascination that the opulence of the court offered, a contrast also apparent to writers in the seventeenth and eighteenth centuries. Much of Shakespeare's world was a matter of capturing the small intimate spaces of courts in the small intimate space of the theater, a process replicated in *Hamlet* with the use of a play within a play to further and also comment on the process. Courtiers were presented as thinking and acting in a dangerous game of power and show, one that had an inherent drama, as well as display, that the playwright was best placed to capture.

Expansion also occurred to the south of the Thames. In 1550, the city purchased the "liberties of Southwark" from the Crown so that this already populous parish—known as the "Borough" to distinguish it from the "City"—came under the latter's jurisdiction. However, it proved difficult to achieve control, and Southwark, still then part of Surrey and, therefore, outside the city, became something of a "Wild South," with little law or regulation. The failure of the Crown to implement an integrated approach to the suburbs ensured that the governance of both London and, more specifically, the suburbs were fragmented.[19]

The availability and cheapness of land made Southwark, which contained a lot of low-grade housing, attractive to entrepreneurs. Southwark and neighboring Bermondsey became major centers of the leather industry, which used the tribal tributaries of the Thames to wash away at least some of the foulness. Already a site of brothels, with part of the district known as "the Stews," Southwark became home first to rings for bull- and bearbaiting and then also to theaters. The Hope, the first combined playhouse and baiting ring, was built in 1614.[20] As in so much else, drama brought a number of processes to the fore and benefited from their interaction. More specifically, the audience would have understood such references as Macbeth's fatalistic words

> They have tied me to a stake: I cannot fly,
> But, bear-like, I must fight the course (V, vii)

The last line is a reference to the vicious bouts between chained bears and attacking dogs.

The physical expansion and differentiation of London (and of other cities), however much operating within a context of economic interdependence,[21] were linked to change, both general and specific, notably as the Reformation worked through, especially in its impact on the townscape and charities. In particular, the expansion of the suburbs created great unease in London, understood as the city.

There was also a strong sense of urban identity. Although affected by the disruption of the Reformation, this sense was present with the institutions of the city and its livery companies and also in the positive response to historical works. Stow's *Survey of London* enjoyed great popularity, but he was not alone, with Richard Grafton being a bitter rival.[22] Shakespeare's audience was probably better aware of London's history than its modern descendants would have been.

Maps of London changed greatly in the sixteenth century, not least because there were more of them. They were also different from what had come earlier. The depiction of London by the St. Albans abbey monk Matthew Paris that dated from around 1250 was essentially a pictogram. It was drawn as part of what has become known as a "road map" for pilgrims to Jerusalem, although few would actually have carried it with them on the journey, often using it instead as a devotional tool for pious contemplation at home. The journey began at London, where pilgrims could visit the shrine of Edward the Confessor at Westminster, which was shown. In the drawing, St. Paul's, with its distinctive spire, was in the center. Similarly, a woodcut image of London, with rooftops, church spires, and city wall, appeared in the *Chronicle of England*, a work published by William Caxton in 1480.

In contrast, the so-called Copperplate map showing London in about 1559, five years before the birth of Shakespeare, is the first known printed map of London. This map was very different from the images mentioned above. It offered a dense assemblage of pictures, including a real jumble of late-medieval wooden buildings, cramped streets, and courtyards, with boats on the river. Published in 1572 but surveyed perhaps twenty years earlier, and possibly a single-sheet version of the larger original "Copperplate map," a map of London was included in the *Civitas Orbis Terrarum*, a major German atlas. In this, the figures in the foreground provided the sense of a panorama, as did the three-dimensional boats and buildings. Nevertheless, it was essentially a plan. The basic shape of the walled Roman and medieval city was unchanged, with only relatively small extraurban pockets of development to the east and to the north as far as Charterhouse. Southwark, also, was still modest in scale. Of much greater significance were the extensive tracts of London west of the river Fleet between the city and Westminster, along Holborn, and especially along the Strand between Charing Cross and Whitehall. London had burst out beyond its walls, which increased the issues involved in depicting it in maps. In contemporary European cities, walls provided the main way in which cities were both delimited and shaped, but large-scale extramural growth ended that process and forced forth new depictions of cities.

The Agas map of 1591 reflected further growth in London, including the great activity on the river. The royal palace at Whitehall is shown as linked by two arches over the public road (Kinges Streate), giving access to the hunting grounds of St. James's, as well as the tiltyard for jousting. Two years later appeared a map drawn by Pieter van den Keere and usually referred to by the name of its publisher, John Norden. The coats of arms around the map were those of the twelve great livery companies. In Southwark, both "the play house" and "the beare houses" are shown. At a more detailed level, a hand-drawn map of Southwark of about 1542 is now preserved in the National Archives. It shows the many inns and churches there, as well as the manor house, pillory, stocks, and bullring. The emergence of a specialized trade in printed maps and atlases in London was a slow process. Nevertheless, as publishing, for all genres, focused in London, it was again there that ideas were formulated and images crafted. The image of London was created and reproduced even more by pageants in the streets and on the river than by maps. It was a dynamic city, and the developing and expanding theatrical world was part of this dynamism.

## NOTES

1. J. Oldland, "The Wealth of the Trades in Early Tudor London," *London Journal* 31 (2006): 143.

2. B. M. S. Campbell, J. A. Galloway, D. Keene, and M. Murphy, *A Medieval Capital and Its Grain Supply* (London, 1993).

3. J. Hare, "Inns, Innkeepers and the Society of Later Medieval England, 1350–1600," *Journal of Medieval History* 39 (2013): 477–97.

4. L. Manley, ed., *London in the Age of Shakespeare: An Anthology* (London, 1986); D. Bergeron, *Shakespeare's London, 1613* (Manchester, 2018).

5. F. J. Fisher, *London and the English Economy, 1500–1700* (London, 1990).

6. L. B. Luu, *Immigrants and the Industries of London, 1500–1700* (Aldershot, UK, 2005).

7. D. Bruster, *Drama and the Market in the Age of Shakespeare* (Cambridge, 1992).

8. B. J. and M. Sokol, *Shakespeare's Legal Language: A Dictionary* (London, 2000).

9. P. Raffield, *Images and Cultures of Law in Early Modern England: Justice and Political Power, 1558–1660* (Cambridge, 2004); Q. Skinner, *Forensic Shakespeare* (Oxford, 2014).

10. R. Finlay, *Population and Metropolis: The Demography of London, 1580–1650* (Cambridge, 1981).

11. A. Davis, *Chivalry and Romance in the English Renaissance* (Cambridge, 2003).

12. For another example, T. Hill, *Anthony Munday and Civic Culture: Theatre, History and Power in Early Modern London, 1580–1633* (Manchester, 2004).

13. A. Bayman, *Thomas Dekker and the Culture of Pamphleteering in Early Modern London* (Farnham, UK, 2011).

14. S. Dustagheer, *Shakespeare's Two Playhouses: Repertory and Theatre Space at the Globe and the Blackfriars, 1599–1613* (Cambridge, 2017).

15. S. Brigden, *London and the Reformation* (Oxford, 1989).

16. E. Schanzer, "Thomas Platter's Observations of the Elizabethan Stage," *Notes and Queries* 201 (1956): 465–67.

17. I. Archer, "Conspicuous Consumption Revisited: City and Court in the Reign of Elizabeth I," in *London and the Kingdom*, ed. M. Davies and A. Prescott (Donnington, UK, 2008), 38–57.

18. J. F. Merritt, *The Social World of Early Modern Westminster: Abbey, Court and Community, 1525–1640* (Manchester, 2005).

19. I. Archer, "Government in Early Modern London: The Challenge of the Suburbs," *Proceedings of the British Academy* 107 (2001): 139.

20. S. Mullaney, *The Place of the Stage: License, Play and Power in Renaissance England* (Ann Arbor, MI, 1988); J. Dillon, *Theatre, Court and City, 1595–1610: Drama and Social Space in London* (Cambridge, 2000).

21. I. Archer, "City and Court Connected: The Material Dimensions of Royal Ceremonial, ca. 1480–1625," *Huntington Library Quarterly* 71 (2008): 157–79.

22. I. Archer, "The Nostalgia of John Stow," in *The Theatrical City: Culture, Theatre and Politics in London, 1576–1649*, ed. D. L. Smith, R. Strier, and D. Bevington (Cambridge, 1995), 17–34; and "John Stow, Citizen and Historian," in *John Stow (1525–1605) and the Making of the English Past: Studies in Early Modern Culture and the History of the Book*, ed. I. A. Gadd and A. Gillespie (London, 2004), 13–26.

# NARRATING THE PAST

## *History Plays*

Suppose within the girdle of these walls
Are now confined two mighty monarchies,
Whose high upreared and abutting fronts
The perilous narrow ocean [the English
    Channel] parts asunder.
Piece out our imperfections with your thoughts

—*Henry V,* Prologue

SHAKESPEARE'S SIGNIFICANCE TO CONTEMPORARIES
AND subsequently included his role as chronicler of the nation's
past. This was a role he shared with other playwrights but one
that strongly characterized much of his work. Moreover, the long-
term prominence of Shakespeare has ensured that his approach
to English history has been of lasting importance, in particular
his coverage of Henry V and Richard III. In turn, the presentation of both, especially the latter, has remained controversial to
the present.

The task of staging history itself was far from easy at the time.
In part, this was due to the politically highly controversial nature of history, but there was also the problem of reconciling and

presenting contradictory accounts of the past. In addition, as with Shakespeare's use of gunpowder weaponry and maps, there was and is the issue of anachronism. This can be a mistake and also might serve to suggest incongruities that challenge the theatrical illusion. History was inherently theatrical, but staging it was not without problems,[1] and that remains the case at present, indeed possibly even more so.

The theater was scarcely alone in depicting England's history, and the past was very much present across a range of media. Works on national history came to the fore in the Tudor age. There was an emphasis on past glory, as with John Leland's 1544 defense of Geoffrey of Monmouth's account of King Arthur in his *History of the Kings of Britain* (c. 1136). Anxious to accumulate information on English history, Leland, who was allegedly appointed "King's Antiquary" in 1533, traveled extensively and wrote much, for example, *De Viris Illustribus (On Famous Men)*, although he published little. Shakespeare's interest in history in part tied in with this newfound information that enabled him to draw for his history plays on Edward Hall's *Chronicle* and on Raphael Holinshed's *Chronicles*, the second (and longer) edition of which appeared in 1587.

These works—both the chronicles and Shakespeare's history plays—provided more than accounts of particular episodes and characters. They also offered an interpretative pattern and explanatory device, notably of the fate of the Plantagenet dynasty, culminating in the Battle of Bosworth in 1485 and the dynasty's extinction with the killing there of Richard III. This pattern ensured that the plays were more than a series of episodes, that indeed they hang together as a whole, while, as individual works, they were able to take a selective approach about what to cover because of this fundamental consistency. In part, the plays were a cautionary, indeed morality, tale on the dangers of a divided realm and the evils of a succession crisis. At the level of individuals and society, church and state, politics was not seen as separate from morality. Thus, Foxe's *Book of Martyrs* (1563) was a potent account of religious struggle and, animating this account, of providential nationhood.

Aside from chronicles, there were histories in verse and historical romances. Indeed, historical material for reading was readily available.[2] From 1586, a circle of like-minded people met together fairly regularly in London and read papers to each other on antiquarian topics. While not formally a Society of Antiquaries, this was certainly a circle of them. Nor was Shakespeare alone as a playwright of the English past. George Peele's patriotic *Edward I*, written in about 1590, appears to have been popular, at least in terms of the number of performances, which is a good indication. Marlowe provided *The Troublesome Reign and Lamentable Death of Edward the Second King of England* (r. 1307–27), a powerful play printed in 1594, the year after Michael Drayton's poem about Edward's favorite, Piers Gaveston, who was killed at the order of Edward's cousin, Thomas, Duke of Lancaster. Heywood tackled the reign of Edward IV in *Edward IV, Parts I and II* (1599), a popular account that was reprinted in 1605, 1613, 1619, and 1626 and that, drawing on Holinshed's *Chronicles*, focused on Jane Shore, Edward's mistress, and her relationship with the king. The first part included a song about Agincourt.

However, no one offered the range and volume provided by Shakespeare. English history was present in *King Lear* and *Cymbeline* but was given a sequential coverage all the way from the reign of Richard II (1377–99), although only the last stages of that reign were covered, to the accession of Henry VII in 1485. There was even an afterword in the shape of a *Henry VIII* that covered only part of his reign (in full, 1509–47), culminating with the baptism of the future Elizabeth I in 1533. In addition, *The Reign of King Edward the Third*, Richard II's grandfather but immediate predecessor, a play entered in the Stationers' Register in 1595, has been attributed in whole or part to Shakespeare. Covering a much earlier reign, Shakespeare's *King John* was probably written in 1596, although there is great critical disagreement as to its dating. Edward III ruled from 1327 to 1377 and John, his great-great-grandfather, from 1199 to 1216.

Other parts of British history were also covered by Shakespeare, but they were either mythical, in the case of *King Lear,* a potent tragedy that calls Providence into question, or located in the distant shroud of time, as with *Macbeth*, a play largely set in eleventh-century Scotland, although with part in England at the court of Edward the Confessor (r. 1042–66). It was *Richard II, Henry IV, Parts I and II, Henry V, Henry VI, Parts I, II, and III,* and *Richard III* that offered an impressive sequence of eight plays that were unmatched in their sequential intensity and narrative power.[3] The Roman plays did not form a comparable whole, as only two, *Julius Caesar* and *Antony and Cleopatra*, cohered chronologically, while *Coriolanus* and *Titus Andronicus* were separate, being respectively earlier and later chronologically. Indeed, *Coriolanus* was very much from the period of republican Rome, although, like most plays set in the Roman period, the theme was one of individual hubris.

The significance and complexity[4] of the English history plays is such that a narrative of the period of the continuous coverage is offered here, one with which the plays can be compared or, at least, that helps explain them. This narrative is necessary, not least because these years were then an important part of the recovered memory of the English public, whereas now that recovered memory is weaker and, ironically, largely dependent on Shakespeare. At the same time, it is important to appreciate the degree to which Shakespeare's views were not necessarily those expressed by his characters[5] or, indeed, all contemporaries.

## RICHARD II AND HENRY IV

Richard II (r. 1377–99) is most prominent today for being king when the Peasants' Revolt occurred in 1381, but, to Shakespeare's contemporaries, he was the monarch under whom the old political order broke down with the end of the direct line of the Plantagenet dynasty; and this is the focus of Shakespeare's attention. Indeed, the Peasants' Revolt does not concern him. It was highly dramatic but separate from the other action in the reign that he sought to cover, as well as being politically problematic due to the threat from peasant rebellions during Shakespeare's lifetime, not that that prevented him from tackling the Jack Cade revolt in 1450.

The issue of dynastic legitimacy[6] was a vital theme in Shakespeare's history plays and in Tudor England. Shakespeare's immediate sources were the Tudor histories of Daniel, Holinshed, and Hall. Beyond them lay the medieval chronicles. In the case of Richard, Shakespeare relied on chronicles that were at odds with each other in their interpretations: Thomas of Walsingham, who was critical of Richard, and Creton and the author of the *Traïson et Mort*, who discussed the deposition and were sympathetic to Richard. It was a shift from a reliance on Walsingham in the first part of the play to the other two later on that helps to explain the development of the play into a form of Passion narrative that offers echoes of the fate of Jesus in the person of Richard. Furthermore, in light of this shift, audiences were given a chance to decide on the interpretation they preferred and thus to assess right and wrong themselves.

Richard had survived the Peasants' Revolt, which, in many respects, was an attempt to pressure him into changes of policy that would accord with the peasants' concept of good kingship. More serious and lasting proved the rivalry between Richard and his aristocratic opponents. This rivalry helped lead the king, from 1397, into a violent and unstable politics that was accentuated by his authoritarian tendencies, tendencies that Shakespeare did not neglect to portray. Richard's aristocratic opponents, the Appellants, were convicted of treason in 1397 and harshly, even murderously, treated, while the king extorted forced loans and blank charters from people who were terrorized by his retinue of Cheshire guards.

Moreover, the mismatch between the appearance and substance of power under Richard was exacerbated by a serious loss of prestige due to failure in war with France. This was a longstanding theme in Shakespeare's plays. In *King John*, the French, profiting from English divisions and treachery, invade England in force, but in *Edward III* the king had successfully campaigned in France. His achievements unraveled, however, during Richard's reign.

The theme of Richard's arrogance and failure was well brought out by Shakespeare. Either was tolerable in a monarch but not both. Richard is presented as arrogant—"We were not born to sue, but to command" (I, i)—and his uncle, John of Gaunt, Duke of Lancaster (1340–99), third son of Edward III, condemns the failure to stand up against France that was later also to be a charge against Henry VI, one brought forward by Shakespeare:

England ... is now bound in with shame,
With inky blots, and rotten parchment bonds:
That England, that was wont to conquer others,
Hath made a shameful conquest of itself. (II, i)

Shakespeare's play ably captured the narcissism of Richard, a narcissism that helped make him willful, unpredictable, unable to take criticism, and detached from reality. His flawed personality matched a policy drawing on the model of the French monarchy, one focused on the need for obedience to a magisterial Crown. In some respects, this stance prefigured the views associated with Henry VIII,[7] but Richard certainly lacked his ability, drive, and good fortune, although he could also show a petulant ruthlessness.

Richard's problems culminated in 1399 when he was seized and forced to abdicate by a rebellious cousin he had disinherited and exiled, John of Gaunt's son, Henry Bolingbroke. Henry became Henry IV (r. 1399–1413), the first king of the Lancastrian dynasty, which lasted until Henry VI. While Richard was absent on an expedition to Ireland, where he was unsuccessfully seeking to suppress opposition, Henry returned from exile in France, landing at Ravenspur in Yorkshire. Richard's unpopularity and political folly had left him with an overly small power base, a situation that prefigured that of Richard III in 1485, the year of Bosworth. Too few people had an interest in preserving Richard II's regime, too many an interest in ending it. Moreover (unlike with the contrast between Richard III and the future Henry VII), Richard was seen as less manly than the future Henry IV, who had served as a crusader—a point that Archbishop Arundel made in a sermon in September 1399, at the Deposition Parliament, when he portrayed Richard as a boy (*puer*) and Bolingbroke as a man (*vir*). Richard returned from Ireland in 1399 but, playing his hand badly, was outmaneuvered, as Shakespeare shows. After negotiations via Henry Percy, First Earl of Northumberland, Richard surrendered to Bolingbroke at Flint Castle. He promised to abdicate if his life was spared. Bolingbroke had won the throne without a battle as neither Richard, Duke of York (unsuccessfully in 1460), Edward IV (successfully in 1461 and 1471), or Henry VII (successfully in 1485) were to do. Richard was formally deposed in Parliament on October 1, and on October 13 Henry was crowned as Henry IV.[8]

In the play, protesting at Henry's accession, Thomas Merke (or Merks), bishop of Carlisle, predicts a cursed country, a prediction that leads to his arrest for treason:

> in this seat of peace, tumultuous wars
> Shall kin with kin, and kind with kind, confound;
> Disorder, horror, fear and mutiny
> Shall here inhabit, and this land be called
> The field of Golgotha and dead men's skulls. (IV, i)

Thus, the bishop anticipated an overthrow of the Christian offering of peace and of the moral economy under which Christianity was a better state than other religions. The reference to Golgotha brought in the biblical story. In *Henry VI, Part III*, the accuracy of this prediction is shown with the description of the Battle of Towton in 1471, as, in a powerful scene, Henry VI sees a man bringing in the corpse of his father, whom he has unwittingly killed, while another does likewise for his son (II, v).

The coup reflected the long-lasting dynastic and political problems that were to be created from rivalries between the numerous descendants of Edward III. Too many children could be as much of a problem as too few. The Ottoman (Turkish) practice of executing siblings as was done, for example, by Selim I, "the Grim," in 1512, was not practicable. The Dukes of Lancaster and York were key cadet (junior) lines of the ruling Plantagenet house, Henry, being the son of John of Gaunt, who was the third son of Edward III. Richard II was the son of Edward III's eldest son, Edward, "the Black Prince," the victor over the French at Poitiers in 1356, who, dying in 1376, had narrowly predeceased his long-lived father.

In February 1400, Richard was murdered in Pontefract Castle, where he had been imprisoned, being killed to remove a rallying point for opposition to the new king. His supporters had already tried to murder Henry in Windsor Castle. Shakespeare's depiction of Richard's violent death is at once particularly vivid and also atmospheric and troubling and is more effective than that of the murder of the king in Marlowe's *Edward II*.[9] The exact manner of Richard's death is unclear. He may well have been starved to death.

In turn, and as seriously, Henry had to face rebellions by the powerful Percy family, a mighty magnate family who wielded great strength in the north of England and had helped Henry depose Richard and, as Shakespeare shows, overcome the conspiracy of 1400. Northumberland was the third most frequent witness to Henry's early charters.[10] However, the conspirators who overthrew Richard II fell out, just as later Richard, Earl of

Warwick, "the King-Maker," in *Henry VI*, earlier an ally of his cousin Richard, Duke of York, and of the latter's eldest son, Edward IV, fell out with Edward. Moreover, Henry, Second Duke of Buckingham, in *Richard III* fell out with his former ally.

The Percy conspiracies give political content to the *Henry IV* plays and led Henry to put off his pledge to go on pilgrimage to Jerusalem. Although far from being a dominant figure in Shakespeare's plays, Henry survived successive crises. In 1403, Henry defeated and killed the Percy heir, "Hotspur," Sir Henry Percy, at the Battle of Shrewsbury, a major episode in Shakespeare's coverage of the reign. Henry's heir, the future Henry V, is shown saving the life of his father and killing Hotspur.

In *Henry IV, Part II*, the rebellions of Hotspur's father, Henry, First Earl of Northumberland, in 1405 and 1408, are depicted. He was defeated and killed on Bramham Moor in 1408. This warfare overshadowed the reign, but, looked at differently, it represented the consolidation of the new Lancastrian house, a consolidation that proved easier than it was to be for the Yorkist dynasty in 1460–71, although far less so than for the Tudors in 1485–87 or for the Stuarts in 1603. Henry IV was also lucky and skillful in foreign policy, benefiting from French and Scottish weaknesses, including conflict in France between the leading aristocrats.[11] That of course was far less interesting theatrically than the lengthy account of the relationship between Henry and his heir. This was a relationship in which the father is a distant, largely absent figure. Indeed, in some respects, Shakespeare wrote not overlapping plays but, rather, three parts of what could have been *Henry V*. Henry IV's success[12] contributed to the domestic stability of England during the reign of his eldest son, Henry V (r. 1413–22). In 1414, Henry crushed a conspiracy organized by the Lollard Sir John Oldcastle. In *Henry IV, Part I*, Falstaff's name was originally Oldcastle, following one of Shakespeare's sources, but Shakespeare changed this due to pressure from Oldcastle's descendants.

## WAR WITH FRANCE

In 1415, Henry was to thwart a conspiracy on the eve of his invasion of France on behalf of Richard, Earl of Cambridge, the son of Edward III's fourth son, Edmund, Duke of York. Condemning the culprits to what is presented as a well-deserved death, Shakespeare has Henry blame them for being led astray by French bribery to sell the people:

> to oppression and contempt,
> And his whole kingdom into desolation. (II, ii)

This is also a warning for the spectators, as England was then at war with Spain.

In light of the important changes that happened in the sixteenth century, it is very easy to rush through the fifteenth in a history of England. It was a period of economic stagnation, international decline, acute political division, and religious stasis, or at least of less economic, religious, and constitutional change than in the Tudor age that followed. Much of the importance of the fifteenth century, indeed, was that of failure. This included, posthumously, that of Henry, which, however, was not how Shakespeare and most others presented him. Henry was a warrior prince and then king, who sought to revive the claim of his great-grandfather, Edward III, to the French throne. Henry identified with the cult of St. George and was presented essentially as an assertor of Englishness in Shakespeare's play *Henry V* (1599) and thus as a contrast with Marlowe's *Tamburlaine*.

Nevertheless, Henry had no sense that the English Channel should act as a boundary to his authority. Following all his predecessors since William I, "the Conqueror" (r. 1066–87), Henry envisaged a realm that spanned the channel. Normandy seemed closer to his center of power in southern England than the margins of his possessions in the British Isles and was also a more attractive prospect for operations and expansion.

Prestige was very important. There was the sense of a great tradition to be maintained by campaigning in France and of fame to
be gained, as a way to demonstrate warrior virtues and kingly attributes, as well as manliness. Shakespeare was misleading in presenting Henry as an attractive, approachable individual, for kings
were not accessible to their subjects in the manner depicted.[13] At
the same time, it was significant that such a presentation could
and should be made. Shakespeare captured not so much a degree
of domestication in the image of monarchy, for that did not occur, but rather the character envisaged for knightly society and a
conceptualization designed to encompass the whole army.

Henry won great glory from his victory at Agincourt on
October 25, 1415, a chaotic, muddy battle in which well-motivated
and ably commanded English and Welsh archers inflicted heavy
casualties on the much larger attacking French army. The latter mistakenly operated in a way that maximized English ad-
vantages.[14] In *Henry V*, Shakespeare, with reason, presents the
French commanders as overconfident and boastful, telling Henry
of his "most assured overthrow" (IV, iii). The battle is depicted
at length, although with few specific details. This depiction is an
aspect of a more general cultural engagement both with war and
as part of a positive discussion of a formal national narrative, one
in which the war offered a view of an emergent nationalism.[15]

Providing an account of battle that is more positive than that
in Marlowe's *Tamburlaine*, not least in explaining Henry's slaughter of French prisoners, Shakespeare has Henry repeatedly give
due thanks to God. By doing so, Henry and Shakespeare linked
Providence to national success. This was on a pattern that anticipated the response to the English victory over the Spanish
Armada in 1588:

O God, thy arm was here;
And not to us, but to thy arm alone,
Ascribe we all! When, without stratagem,

But in plain shock and even play of battle,
Was ever known so great and little loss
On one part and on the other? Take it, God,
For it is none but thine!

. . . . . . . . . . . . . . . .

And be it death proclaimed through our host
To boast of this or take that praise from God
Which is his only.

. . . . . . . . . . . . . .

God fought for us. (IV, viii)

This approach, that of not attributing success to himself, is shown as an aspect of Henry's self-mastery, which was presented as a sign of his true manliness and of appropriate kingship.[16] Agincourt was also the subject of the heroic "Ballad of Agincourt" by Michael Drayton that was first printed in his *Poems Lyric and Pastoral* (1605). Some critics have found Henry a rather unpleasant warmonger. Others have found an ambiguity important as framing a discussion as to whether there can be such a thing as just war.

Agincourt was followed two years later by the start of the English conquest of Normandy. Its capital, Rouen, fell to Henry in 1419. Weakened by aristocratic disaffection, notably by a rift between the Dukes of Burgundy and the Armagnac faction after the murder of Louis of Orléans by Burgundian agents in 1407 (the manipulative Duke John the Fearless of Burgundy, in turn, was murdered in 1419), the weak, mentally ill, and defeated Charles VI of France betrothed his daughter Katherine to Henry. Indeed, Charles in 1419–20 was like Henry VI in the 1450s.

By the Treaty of Troyes of 1420, Charles recognized Henry V (and his successors) as his heir in a union of crowns between England and France.[17] Such a union was common enough at the time, being seen in the union of the kingdoms of Denmark, Sweden, and Norway in the Union of Kalmar (1397–1523) and in those of Aragon and Castile, Poland and Lithuania, and England and Scotland. Given that English troops were sent to France by

Elizabeth I to participate in the French Wars of Religion, a heroic account of past success would have been most welcome to Shakespeare's audience. Shakespeare has Charles VI hope that the marriage will lead France and England to "cease their hatred" (V, ii).

Had the highly impressive Henry lived longer, he might have created a new Anglo-French polity, although asserting control over the whole of France was a formidable task.[18] In the event, Henry died young, probably of dysentery (a killer in this period), in 1422, leaving an heir less than one year old who became Henry VI (r. 1422–61, 1470–71). Under him, the English were eventually driven out of all their French territories bar Calais and the Channel Isles. On behalf of Charles VI's son Charles VII (the brother of Katherine), Joan of Arc, a female visionary, rallied French resistance in the late 1420s, notably at Orléans, where an English siege was broken in 1429. Subsequently, although the captured Joan, accused of sorcery, was burned as a heretic in 1431, English operations ran out of impetus. Moreover, Philip the Good, Duke of Burgundy (the son and successor of the Duke John killed in 1419), a key supporter of the English cause in France, abandoned Henry in 1435. The armies of Charles VII then drove the English out, with defeats at Formigny (1450) and Castillon (1453) sealing the fates of Normandy and Gascony respectively. French cannon played a significant role in both battles.

Shakespeare devotes due attention to failures in English policy, failures that he links to personal ambition and factional politics, although the occult also plays a role. At Henry V's funeral, described in *Henry VI, Part I*, his death is blamed by the Earl of Exeter on supernatural causes, which acts as a prelude to the presentation of Joan of Arc:

> What! shall we curse the planets of mishap
> That plotted thus our glory's overthrow?
> Or shall we think the subtle-witted French
> Conjurers and sorcerers, that, afraid of him,
> By magic verses have contriv'd his end? (I, i)

Joan of Arc is shown in the play as helped by fiends whom she is able to conjure up, but she is captured because they refuse to provide more help. There are historical and religious dimensions to her presentation.[19] Macbeth, similarly, is depicted as led astray by his trust in fiends.

*Henry VI, Part II* begins in 1444 with the triumph of the English peace party as Henry is married to Margaret of Anjou, a French princess whose father, René (1409–80), was a good friend of his brother-in-law, Charles VII of France.[20] This serves Shakespeare as a way to launch the play in terms of royal failure, for, in marked contrast with the king's marriage at the close of *Henry V*, the emphasis is on concessions to France as an aspect of the treaty. Indeed, the surrender of Maine was Henry VI's own idea and was carried through at his insistence. The leader of the war party, his uncle Humphrey, Duke of Gloucester, the youngest son of Henry IV, is given a powerful speech denouncing the agreement as a death of history, one that destroys the legacy of Henry V:

> O peers of England! Shameful is this league,
> Fatal this marriage, cancelling your fame,
> Blotting your names from books of memory,
> Razing the characters of your renown, . . .
> Undoing all, as all had never been! (I, i)

It is Shakespeare who will help restore that elision. Humphrey, a wise uncle, is similar to John of Gaunt but not like King John or Richard III. However, Humphrey is killed.

After defeat at Castillon in 1453, Calais was still retained, until lost by Mary Tudor to French attack in 1558, while the claim to the French throne was only abandoned in the reign of George III (1760–1820), and the Channel Isles, the last of the Norman legacy, are still held by the Crown. Nevertheless, France was effectively lost in 1453. There were to be further invasions of France, by Edward IV, Henry VII, and Henry VIII, each of whom entertained a wish to regain the lost glory and power of the kings of England in France, as when Henry VII decided in 1489 on new coins that included the king's arms of England and France. Henry VIII mounted very expensive invasions of France, in 1512, 1513, 1522–23, and 1544, that produced short-term territorial gains, notably the cities of Tournai in 1513 and Boulogne in 1544. The 1512 expedition to southwest France (Gascony) was an attempt to sustain the medieval claims of the monarchy to the region, and the actions of his administration there drew on the models of Henry V and his brother John, Duke of Bedford (1389–1435), regent for Henry VI in France.[21]

However, the failure of these rulers to achieve their ambitions in France was important to the development of English nationhood and government and helped underline an insular character to England/Britain's subsequent European identity. Indeed, the long-term inability to sustain a territorial presence in France provided a backdrop to later English transoceanic ambitions.

### FIFTEENTH-CENTURY DIVISIONS

Defeat by France accentuated Henry VI's weaknesses as king, as well as giving the impression of failure. This failure helped precipitate the Wars of the Roses, the struggle between the houses of Lancaster (the royal line from the accession of Henry IV in 1399) and York, each of which was descended from Edward III. Like Richard II, Henry VI was not up to the task of kingship, and the contrast—between each and the heroic image, political adroitness, and skillful determination of Richard's father, the Black Prince, and Henry's father, Henry V, respectively—was striking. Henry VI was unable to intervene intelligently in disputes between aristocrats. Most notably, the chaos that descended upon northern England in the 1440s was largely due to Henry promoting the Percys at the expense of the Nevilles in Cumberland, and quite unnecessarily so. More generally, Henry was apt to mess up sensible arrangements made for him by intelligent subordinates.

Yet the number of peers of the royal blood was a potential problem, and in Richard, Duke of York (descended from Edward III's second and fourth surviving sons), Henry (descended from the third) faced a member of the royal family who felt that his status entitled him to more recognition. Henry's position was weakened by his inability to establish unity among the nobility, but so was York's.

As Shakespeare indicates, there were bitter factional rivalries throughout Henry's lengthy minority, and, during these years, leading nobles became used to ruling the country. The mutual dislike of his uncle, Humphrey, Duke of Gloucester, and great-uncle, Henry, Cardinal Beaufort, bishop of Winchester, hindered government. Humphrey remained a major source of dissension and instability until his death in 1447. This death is presented by Shakespeare as murder, against the wishes of Henry VI (*Henry VI, Part II*, III, i–ii), by the means of Beaufort and the unpopular chief minister, William de la Pole, First Duke of Suffolk. The latter had a role akin to that of the advisers close to Richard II, and this underlined the problems posed by those who had the ear of the monarch and could manipulate him.[22]

Conflict in England under Henry began with disaffection in the early 1450s about the government, disaffection that spanned aristocratic opposition to royal favoritism and the popular hostility shown in Cade's Rebellion (1450). Earlier that year, Suffolk, who had been criticized in Parliament in 1449, was impeached there, banished, and then murdered on a boat in the English Channel. Beginning in Kent, Cade's Rebellion, which is shown at length by Shakespeare in *Henry VI, Part II*, reflected the extent to which popular action was part of the wider political world. In 1450, there were also major disturbances in southern and western England. Deference might be expressed in civic rituals, but it was frequently not shown in practice. The rebellion was a product of extortion by manorial officials, as well as widespread hostility to the government, which was seen as corrupt and full of traitors. Having defeated a royal force at Sevenoaks on June 18, the rebels seized London on July 3 and killed unpopular officials. Cade lost support in London, being defeated on July 8–9 in a struggle on London Bridge. As in 1381 with the Peasants' Revolt, a royal pardon destroyed the cohesion of the rebels. Cade fled and was mortally wounded in a skirmish on July 12. His body underwent a mock trial and was then beheaded and quartered.

In the face of the rebellion, Henry had fled, an unimpressive response that helped inspire subsequent Yorkist sympathies in London. York used the occasion of Cade's Rebellion, which, as Shakespeare shows (III, i), he was rumored to have encouraged, to return from Ireland, where he was governing the English area of control, and to demand changes in the government of England.

Subsequently, in August 1453, Henry's mental and physical collapse led to York, the heir presumptive, being made Protector— only for the birth of Edward, Prince of Wales, a son to Henry, to rule out York's chances of succeeding by hereditary right. In turn, the king's far from total recovery in the winter of 1454–55 gave the court party, under Edmund Beaufort, Second Duke of Somerset, the opportunity to turn against York. On May 22, 1455, York clashed with Somerset at the first Battle of St. Albans. In the event, the "battle" was not much more than a series of political assassinations with the Yorkists picking off their rivals. But given that these rivals were in the company of the king, this was shocking. Somerset and Henry Percy, Second Earl of Northumberland, were killed, and Henry VI, who had backed Somerset, was captured. Shakespeare leaps rapidly from Cade to St. Albans, *Henry VI, Part II* ending with York's triumph:

> Saint Albans battle, won by famous York,
> Shall be eterniz'd [immortalized] in all age to come.
> Sound drums and trumpets! and to London all:
> And more such days as these to us befall! (V, iii)

The battle of St. Albans, however, did not bring stability, instead sowing the path to instability by encouraging thoughts of revenge. York lost control of the government in 1457, and fighting resumed that year, becoming more intense in 1459.

Armed opposition to Henry's favorites therefore had led to conflict from 1455 onward, with York attacking the lords closest to the king. This fighting was linked to the loss of France in 1453, which ensured that the aristocracy no longer had a useful foreign outlet for its aggression. In structural terms, the dynamics of domestic and military power had changed with the spread of what was later termed "bastard feudalism," in which lords rewarded their followers and retained their services with an annual payment of money rather than with land. The resulting clientage was dominated by powerful nobles whose willingness to raise troops was crucial to the ability of rulers to field armies. This form of patronage and clientage was not necessarily a cause of civil conflict, but in the event of a breakdown in relations between monarch and nobles, or in the ranks of the latter, it made it easier for the nobles to mobilize and sustain their strength. The extent to which the economy was in serious difficulties accentuated these problems. A loss in silver, much of which had been sent abroad to support the war in France, contributed to a fall in the total currency in circulation in England.

For Shakespeare, the dynamic between rulers and those who sought to overthrow them was both action and theme. Henry IV and Henry V had rapidly suppressed opposition to them, Henry IV successfully overcoming the powerful interest of the Percy family, crushing their rebellions in 1403, 1405, and 1408, and Henry V thwarting a conspiracy on the eve of his invasion of France. In contrast, Henry VI was unable to suppress opposition and indeed was unmanly in contemporary views. He was mentally ill and could not cope with crises, and, unlike Prince Hal (the future Henry V) during the reign of Henry IV, Henry VI's son and heir, Edward, was an infant—as, even more, was to be Edward IV's son and heir, Edward V, the elder of the so-called Princes in the Tower. The crisis of the 1450s moved from a political confrontation to a dynastic struggle, in large part due to the highly partisan York, who sought to force his way to power when his scheming failed.[23] At the battle of Northampton on July 10, 1460, the Lancastrians were defeated, several of their leaders were killed, and Henry was captured again.

Northampton, however, was not a repetition of St. Albans. Having hitherto professed his loyalty to Henry, York now transformed the situation by claiming the throne. From a sympathetic point of view, this was very much the last resort after a decade in which he had been politically marginalized by those round Henry, but it was also a breach in the settled order. In the opening scene of *Henry VI, Part III*, York is recognized as heir to Henry, but the determined and energetic, albeit unpopular, French queen, Margaret of Anjou, is not prepared to see the disinheritance of her son, Edward. The Lancastrians attacked, defeated, and killed York at Wakefield on December 29, 1460: in mockery, his severed head was adorned with a paper crown. This was scarcely chivalry in action. Shakespeare has Margaret taunt York and be the second to stab him to death (I, iv), which was not the case in the chronicles.

Margaret then defeated Richard Neville, Earl of Warwick, a key Yorkist known as "the King-Maker," at the second battle of St. Albans, north of London, on February 17, 1461, and recovered control of Henry. However, London, a major force in politics, defied Margaret, an episode that would have been part of the collective memory there during Shakespeare's lifetime. Thwarted and short of supplies, she retreated north. York's ambitious and able eldest son, Edward, next claimed the throne, as Edward IV. He was a more charismatic and energetic figure than his father and readier to resort to war. The Yorkists marched north. At Towton in Yorkshire, during a heavy snowstorm on Palm Sunday, March 29, the Lancastrians were badly defeated in a battle that may have involved as many as 60,000 troops—which would make it the battle with the greatest number of combatants on British soil. Possibly about 20,000 were killed. Shakespeare devotes four scenes to the battle.[24] The thoroughness of Edward of

York's victory, not least the bloodletting of the Lancastrians, allowed his coronation as Edward IV and brought the submission of all but the most committed Lancastrians.

Edward was able to suppress continued Lancastrian opposition in the early 1460s, in part because the Wars of the Roses were closely linked to the context of international rivalry. Rival French and Burgundian support were the key elements. The Burgundians, opponents of the French, backed the Yorkists, and, to bring stability, Edward had to win over the French. In 1463, he was able to negotiate a truce with Louis XI of France, who promised to abandon the Lancastrians and to end the Auld Alliance with Scotland. This left Scotland exposed and led it, later that year, to agree to a truce with England. Neither was to support the other's rebels. Earlier, Edward had backed Clan Donald against the Scottish crown. Now Scotland abandoned the Lancastrians. The sequel was Lancastrian defeats at Hedgeley Moor and Hexham in 1464 in northern England, which again, as earlier with the Percys, was a center of opposition to London-based governments. Henry was captured in 1465.

However, the Yorkist interest fractured when Warwick, "the King-Maker," resenting a loss of influence, rejected his younger cousin Edward and turned to the Lancastrians. Warwick and Edward clashed over diplomacy and, more pointedly, over Edward's favor for the Woodvilles, relatives of the queen who challenged Warwick's dominance at court. Prefiguring Henry VIII's favor for Anne Boleyn, and the problems this created for Cardinal Wolsey, leading to his fall in 1529, the very fact that Edward had secretly married Elizabeth Woodville in 1464 showed that there were limits to Warwick's dominance. He had been negotiating a French marriage for Edward. Shakespeare has Warwick complain:

When you disgraced me in my embassade,
Then I degraded you from being King,
And come now to create you Duke of York.
Alas, how should you govern any kingdom
That know not how to use ambassadors. (*Henry VI, Part III*, IV, iii)

After defeating the Herberts, Edward's allies, at Edgecote on July 26, 1469, and capturing Edward soon after, Warwick seized power. However, he could not maintain his authority, and in 1470 he fled to France, with Edward regaining power. There Warwick was reconciled with the exiled Margaret of Anjou and committed himself to the restoration of Henry. This was one of the most striking realignments in the opportunistic politics of the period and one that demonstrated how far power, rather than principle, dominated some aristocratic strategies.

With the help of Louis XI, Warwick and his son-in-law, Edward's disloyal brother, George, Duke of Clarence, invaded England in September 1470. In October, Edward was deposed and forced to flee into exile, and Henry, freed from imprisonment, was restored as king. Had that remained the outcome, then Shakespeare would have had to confront a very different history, with implications for the characterization of his figures, a characterization to which eventual success and failure contributed greatly.

What Shakespeare, at the close of *Twelfth Night,* termed "the whirligig of time" (V, i), instead brought Edward back again in March 1471, benefiting from an alliance with Charles the Bold, Duke of Burgundy, Louis XI's principal opponent. Seizing the initiative, Edward invaded and regained the throne through battle. Moving fast, he defeated and killed Warwick in thick fog at Barnet, north of London, on April 14. Warwick had been betrayed by Clarence. Edward then defeated the Lancastrians at Tewkesbury on May 4, the latter a battle in which he used cannon with success in the early stages. Henry's son, Edward, Prince of Wales, was murdered after being captured at Tewkesbury: he and other leading Lancastrians were dragged from sanctuary in the abbey. Henry himself was killed in the Tower of London. Shakespeare had to show this "whirligig" but benefited from contemporaries being more familiar with the events than would be the case now—hence the need for this narrative.

Edward IV then ruled with little opposition until he died in 1483, building up his political allies.[25] Nevertheless, there were still Lancastrian risings in the country and divisions within the ruling house. Clarence had betrayed Warwick and rejoined Edward in 1471 but was sentenced to death in 1478 for treason. He was promptly secretly executed in the Tower of London, according to contemporaries drowned in a butt of malmsey wine, an episode shown by Shakespeare in *Richard III* (I, iv) and in the film *Theatre of Blood* (1973), a pastiche of Shakespearean killings presided over by Vincent Price who plays a failed Shakespearean ham actor. This is one of the most vivid homages to "the Bard of Avon." In practice, the future Richard III was not responsible for Clarence's death.

The Wars of the Roses provided Shakespeare and others with a plethora of exciting events to recount, offering a very different account to that presented by editions of leading medieval literary works, notably Robert Crowley's 1550 edition of Langland's *Piers Plowman* and Thomas Speght's 1598 and 1603 editions of Chaucer. The Wars of the Roses also ensured that there was the problem of making sense of frequent and often bewildering quick changes and of preventing them from making the plays, in whole or part, appear a confused jumble. This is a situation that is far more the case for modern audiences, not least because they are confused by references to individuals as counties and places—York, Northumberland, and so forth—which is an aspect of their titles. Indeed, that usage has attracted satirical coverage.

The problem of coherence was accentuated by the lack of a royal center. Henry VI was not only not a hero, as his father had been, but he also lacked the central significance that Richard II had offered. Moreover, there was no character comparable to Prince Hal in *Henry IV*, and certainly not the sons of Henry VI and Edward IV.

The lack of psychological drama comparable to that of Shakespeare's tragedies or of *Julius Caesar* and *Antony and Cleopatra* ensured that the tragedy in the English history plays was that of the kingdom or particular dynasties rather than of individuals. The fate of Henry VI was presented as the punishment for Henry IV's sin in deposing and murdering Richard II. The fate of the Princes in the Tower, the sons of Edward IV, was the punishment for the sin of the Yorkists seeking the throne and, in particular, for the murder of Henry VI's son, Prince Edward. The fate of Richard III was the retribution for his many cruelties, a process comparable to that which was Macbeth's destiny. Shakespeare shows Richard stabbing Henry to death, as well as joining Edward IV and Clarence in killing the defiant Prince Edward. The deposition of a monarch thus creates a lasting crisis, one for the country as a whole but also for those directly responsible. This was a lesson for Shakespeare's audiences, one that was of relevance given uncertainties over the succession to Elizabeth I.

Weak government, notably with Henry VI, is presented by Shakespeare as a terrible problem but, even so, as less serious than the evil of presumption. The latter is the active, almost (with Richard III) diabolical, force. The whole is given depth by the use of language, as well as by the plotting, with the imagery drawing on resonant understandings of power. Themes of the debilitating consequences of internal dissidence had long been a staple in the presentation of history. These themes gained new prominence in the context of the religious division and strife of the sixteenth century, division that posed a particularly serious threat in the case of conspiracies. Although not directly relevant to Shakespeare's history plays, this context was an important aspect of their background.

Edward died at forty in 1483, solvent and with England at peace but too early to leave his elder son Edward V as an adult successor. Unlike in 1422, when the far younger Henry VI had been left to grow up as king while a strong regent, his uncle, John, Duke of Bedford, directed affairs, there was a disputed succession in 1483—which might also have been the consequence had

Henry VI died as king to be succeeded by Edward, Prince of Wales. Edward IV's surviving brother, Richard, Duke of Gloucester, fearful of a Woodville takeover and what that might mean for him but also ambitious, direct, and ruthless, in a way that Henry VI's uncles had not been, moved swiftly in the last stage of the tension and rivalry between brothers that Shakespeare displays so well. Richard seized power in April 1483, declaring his nephews, the twelve-year-old Edward V and his younger brother, Richard, Duke of York, bastards, and sending them to the Tower.

Removed from view, they swiftly disappeared, and their fate has long been a cause for controversy, with the "Ricardians," or supporters of Richard III's reputation, offering ingenious accounts to seek to prove his innocence. However, given Richard's brutal and decisive character, the example of his own and his brothers' ruthlessness, particularly at Tewkesbury in 1471, and the murderous nature of politics in this period, it is likely that the princes were killed. Contemporaries believed that they were dead. Otherwise, it would have been improbable for a rank outsider like Henry Tudor, son of Margaret Beaufort, the heiress of the illegitimate Lancastrian line, to seem a viable figurehead for opposition to Richard. Belief in this murder greatly discredited Richard, a violent man.

Richard III (1483–85) had ability and determination and inspired the trust of many up to the time of his usurpation in 1483. He had invaded Scotland successfully in 1482, so his record was good. However, Richard's seizure of the throne defied political conventions and divided the Yorkists, and, as a result, Richard was left with only a slender base of support.[26] This was shown in October 1483 when the Woodvilles and Henry, Second Duke of Buckingham, rebelled. The duke, who was married to Catherine Woodville, sister of Edward IV's wife, had played a major role in Richard's seizure of the throne. In this crisis, which Shakespeare handles with economy and energy, Richard moved swiftly, dispersing the rebels, most of whom made their peace with Richard or escaped abroad. Buckingham was beheaded at Salisbury. One supporter of the rebellion, Richard Edgcumbe of Cotehele, escaped his nemesis by fooling his pursuers that the cap he had thrown into the river Tamar near Cotehele with a stone in it marked the spot of his death in the river.

These frequent changes created a sense of anarchy, seen for example in a revival of fortified architectural features, such as battlements, in the houses of the elite. The violent nature of politics was scarcely conducive to good government. The Wars of the Roses, indeed, provided the context for the working out of rivalries between the nobility in the regions—for example in Devon, East Anglia, and the North—as had also been the case in the civil war of Stephen's reign (1135–54). Moreover, the unstable politics of the period were understood by at least some in prophetic terms, as a curse visited on the country.

### SOCIOECONOMIC DEVELOPMENTS

Shakespeare does not devote much attention in his history plays to the social and economic background, but it was in fact significant. The period as a whole was one of serious difficulties in Britain because of the strains arising from economic difficulties. The Black Death was followed not by a recovery in population numbers but by a period of general stagnation, with fresh attacks of plague in 1361–62, 1369, and 1375. This stagnation reduced the market for domestic agriculture and industry, which acted as a general dampener on the economy. The fall in population resulted in many villages being deserted or shrunken, while the pattern of ridge and furrow that is still visible in many modern pastures shows the extent of ploughland that was taken out of arable agriculture and turned over to grazing by animals. The trade at most markets and fairs declined, hitting town life, which exacerbated the impact of disease. The long-term context was of a downturn in the climate. As it became colder, so the growing season of crops was limited, which reduced their yield. This would all still have been a potent memory in the sixteenth century.

At the same time, as a reminder of the variety of interests affected by economic trends, the absence of population growth fed through into the labor market and made it possible for peasants to exploit demands for labor. They were also helped by the decline of serfdom and the resulting rise in the fluidity of tenurial relations. Labor rents were commuted into money payments, and this process increased the penetration of the money economy into the rural world. The higher level of wages allowed workers more leisure time: drinking socially in alehouses became more widespread, and legislation to regulate games was prompted by the same trend. As another aspect of relative prosperity and of social change, the general rise in stock farming meant that meat eating spread further down the social scale.

Furthermore, the growth of the cloth trade provided Britain with a key economic advantage. Parts of England and Scotland, particularly East Anglia and the Southern Uplands of Scotland, had for long been centers of wool exports, providing the basic raw material for the important cloth industry in the Low Countries (Belgium and Netherlands). Describing England, John Trevisa in the fourteenth century, in his translation of Higden's *Polychronicon*, noted the presence of sheep bearing "good wool ... Flanders loving the wool of this land." This agriculturally based industry was particularly important, first because England neither produced nor, as was later to be the case, imported cotton, second because this was an age that did not have synthetic textiles, and third because the range of industrial production was far more limited than it was to be subsequently.

In the fourteenth and fifteenth centuries, there was a switch from exports of wool to exports of woolen cloth, as its manufacture now took place in England. This development brought considerable prosperity that can still be glimpsed in the magnificent churches of such towns as Lavenham and Long Melford (both in

Suffolk), although, in part, this was a matter of a change in the relative ranking of regions. For example, the wealth of East Anglia was not matched in the North, while, in eastern England, the relative importance of Lincolnshire declined in favor of Norfolk and Suffolk. By the 1540s, about 88 percent of English cloth exports went through London, enhancing the capital's wealth and political pull.

The cloth trade also provided the Crown with a key and largely reliable source of revenue, one that required a development both of government in the shape of the customs service and trade protection and of politics in the form of links with mercantile interests. The cloth trade also encouraged a close interest in the politics of the Low Countries, and this industry therefore interacted with the dynastic and political strategies that led to foreign intervention in civil war in England and, within England, to the seeking of such supporting intervention.

## THE ARRIVAL OF THE TUDORS

The Wars of the Roses climaxed with the replacement of the Yorkist Richard III by the Tudor Henry VII (r. 1485–1509) as a result of the killing of the former and victory of the latter at the Battle of Bosworth in 1485. Invading from France, Henry had been able to advance into the center of England, as Henry IV had done in 1399 and Edward IV in 1471. At Bosworth, although John, First Duke of Norfolk, the Earl Marshal and Lord High Steward, was killed by an arrow while leading his vanguard, Richard was abandoned both by the Stanleys—an important family, allied to Henry Tudor through Margaret Beaufort—who had brought their troops to the battlefield and by Henry Percy, Fourth Earl of Northumberland, who commanded his rearguard. This reflected Richard's failure to offer adequate good lordship to his supporters from the North. Henry, meanwhile, benefited from the support of skilled French mercenaries. Nevertheless, Richard's cavalry charge represented a chance for victory that reflected the chaotic and far from inevitable nature of the battle, one also shown by Richard's ability to kill many of those who were impersonating Henry Tudor in order to reduce the risk to him. In the end, Richard fell with formidable wounds.

Shakespeare depicts Richard, like Macbeth, as a scourge of God, a man devoid of integrity, who receives his just desserts at the end of a play in which there have been many murders and others shown being conveyed to judicial execution. Indeed, Henry tells his army that they are helped by the prayers of "holy saints and wronged souls" (V, iii), a reminder of the interaction of the human and the divine and of the present and the past. To Shakespeare, Richard was prone to the knowledge of his guilt, rather like Macbeth, whereas, in practice, he was a confident and inspirational figure, convinced of the rightness of his position as the head of the Yorkist clan, not least as his mother, Cecily Neville, was willing to describe Edward IV as illegitimate.[27] Shakespeare was greatly influenced by Thomas More in his representation of Richard and may have had access to oral traditions, which would still have been strong. When seeking a coat of arms, he claimed that an ancestor had been advanced by Henry VII. Richard was not alone in being a controversial figure. As King John portrayed, John could (and can) indeed also be seen as an unpleasant and murderous tyrant,[28] although it is necessary to note the black propaganda disseminated by his opponents.

The Tudors had a weak dynastic claim through their Lancastrian connections. Henry's grandfather, Owen Tudor, was the second husband of Henry V's widow, Katherine Valois, while his mother, Margaret Beaufort, was granddaughter of John of Gaunt through his third marriage, to his mistress Katherine Swynford. Henry, however, was helped by Richard's usurpation, which blew the succession wide open, and by the unpopularity of Richard, which ensured that much of the nobility did not support him. There were also the crucial defections from his side at Bosworth.[29] After the battle, more nobles rallied to Henry.

Even so, Henry had to cope with a subsequent series of Yorkist plots, including a full-scale rebellion in 1487 that was defeated at the Battle of Stoke, which was the true end of the Wars of the Roses. The Yorkist army there was ostensibly fighting for "Edward VI," Edward, Earl of Warwick, son of George, Duke of Clarence, and nephew of Edward IV, who, in fact, was impersonated by Lambert Simnel, probably the son of an Oxford tradesman. Another nephew, John, First Earl of Lincoln, son of Edward IV's sister Elizabeth, played a key role in the rising. He was killed in the battle, and the captured Simnel was given a menial role in the royal kitchens, which was an expression of Henry's contempt, one designed to convey the strength of his position. However, the battle was hard fought and larger than Bosworth, and Henry knew from Richard's fate that kings could be overthrown all too easy. If Stoke had been won by Lincoln, a Yorkist bandwagon might have begun to roll, a bandwagon that would have affected the subsequent depiction of the Wars of the Roses by Shakespeare and others.

This invasion/rebellion proved the last of a sequence that had started with Henry of Lancaster's against Richard II in 1399. Plots and royal anxiety, nevertheless, continued for decades thereafter, being centered in 1495–99 on Perkin Warbeck, another impersonator of alleged royalty and one enjoying Burgundian support. In 1499, Edward Plantagenet, Seventeenth Earl of Warwick, Clarence's son, who had been kept in the Tower since 1485, was beheaded for treason after being involved in a plot to escape. Warbeck, who claimed to be the youngest of the sons of Edward IV, was hanged for his role in the same attempt.

Plots and anxiety led, under the restlessly anxious and vindictive Henry VIII, to the execution of those with some possible claim on the throne, for example, due to the marriage of Edward IV's youngest daughter Katherine to Sir William Courtenay. Their child, Henry, Marquess of Exeter, was executed for treason in 1538, and Margaret, Countess of Salisbury, daughter of Clarence, mother of Cardinal Pole, in 1541. Pole was seen as a key figure in organizing Continental opposition to Henry VIII, who sought to have him kidnapped or assassinated.[30] In Shakespeare's *Henry VIII*, the alleged treachery of Edward, Third Duke of Buckingham, executed in 1521, is a major issue, one that looks back to the events of 1483 when his father had rebelled.

Henry VII, however, had strengthened the Tudor claim in 1486 by marrying Elizabeth of York, a daughter of Edward IV and sister of the princes killed in the Tower. Henry thus joined his branch of the House of Lancaster to that of York. This process was symbolized by the replacement of the white rose of York and the red rose of the Beauforts (and maybe of Lancaster) by the Tudor rose. At the close of *Richard III*, Henry presents a prospectus for unity under the Tudors, with him and Elizabeth

> The true succeeders of each royal house,
> By God's fair ordinance conjoin together!
> And let their heirs, God, if thy will be so,
> Enrich the time to come with smooth-fac'd peace. (V, v)

The end of civil war in England and the consolidation of royal authority in Scotland under the vigorous James IV (r. 1488–1513) each provided opportunities for stronger central government, the so-called New Monarchy. This strengthening in part took the form of new institutions, but there was also a focusing of authority and patronage on the monarch and an attempt to build up links with "new men" as part of a process in which the Crown had more direct routes to the locally powerful.[31] Although nobles, such as John, Thirteenth Earl of Oxford, a firm opponent of Edward IV, could be trusted by Henry with considerable local power,[32] a determined attempt was made to limit the private armed forces of nobles, and Henry also placed people under bonds (financial guarantees) for good behavior.[33] The battle of Nibley Green, fought in 1470 in Gloucestershire between William, Second Lord Berkeley, and Thomas, Second Viscount Lisle, turned out to be the last battle on English soil fought entirely between the private armies of feudal magnates. Berkeley deployed about a thousand and Lisle about three hundred. Lisle's death was followed by the collapse of his army.[34]

The focus on the monarch led to an increase in the effectiveness of royal justice but also in a recurrence of the pattern in earlier centuries—for example, under Henry I, Henry II, and John—to a use of this justice to advance royal interests that struck many as extortionate and unfair. This situation led to a reaction when Henry died. Two unpopular ministers, Sir Richard Empson and Edmund Dudley, were executed in 1510, a dramatic instance of the ruthless opportunism of the new king, Henry VIII (r. 1509–47), who turned to violence from the outset. A reminder of the significance of family links and the histories that they provided was John, Duke of Northumberland, Dudley's son, who sought to exclude Mary in 1553, being executed for his pains, and one of the latter's two surviving sons was Elizabeth I's favorite, Robert, Earl of Leicester: his elder brother had also been executed by Mary.

Henry VII's victory at Bosworth in 1485 is still popularly held to mark the close of the Middle Ages in England and thus the beginning of the modern age. The establishment of Henry and the Tudor dynasty was and still is an appropriate point to take stock. By ending the Wars of the Roses (albeit really at the Battle of Stoke in 1487, not at Bosworth in 1485), Henry helped to bring a measure of greater unity to the kingdom. Over the previous decades, civil strife had contributed to, as much as it had stemmed from, a serious crisis, both in law and order and, more generally, in royal governance. In turn, there was a change so that strong royal authority, as seen under Henry VII and Henry VIII, was an eventual consequence of the collapse of stability in the 1450s and 1483–85. This authority was challenged and qualified during the following century and notably repeatedly in 1536–69, but it was the basis for the political order that Shakespeare apparently respected and the effects of the earlier absence of which he so dramatically and cumulatively charted in his history plays.

## REFORMATIONS

Under the greedy and profligate Henry VIII,[35] the same process of raising revenues seen under Henry VII was renewed but on a far greater scale. In large part, the pressure to get money was to pay for Henry VIII's expensive wars with France and Scotland. Indeed, the cost of these wars led to a violent popular response in 1525 when taxes were raised in what became the far from welcome Amicable Grant. The term itself indicates that spin was scarcely an invention of the late twentieth century. Shakespeare presents the tax as the device of Thomas, Cardinal Wolsey (c. 1473–1530), archbishop of York from 1514 and Henry's principal minister as Lord Chancellor from 1515—a tax that is abandoned when Henry is informed of the true situation by Queen Katherine (of Aragon) and Thomas, Third Duke of Norfolk. In a discussion of the social consequences of misgovernment, the latter sensibly links taxation to unemployment and the threat of disorder. Shakespeare offered a more perceptive account in *Henry VIII*:

> upon these taxations,
> The clothiers all not able to maintain
> The many to them 'longing [belonging], have put off
> The spinsters, carders, fullers, weavers, who,
> Unfit for other life, compell'd by hunger
> And lack of other means, in desperate manner
> Daring th'event to th'teeth, are all in uproar,
> And danger serves among them. (*Henry VIII*, I, ii)

The opportunities for stronger government were to be greatly affected by the Protestant Reformation. This was part of a European movement, beginning in the German states in the late 1510s, with Martin Luther publicly defying papal authority at Wittenberg in 1517. The Reformation ended with England having a distinctive Church settlement, but the background was not exceptional. At the start of the sixteenth century, England and Scotland were parts of what sought to be a universal Church with standard practices. There were local variations, not least attachment to particular saints and shrines, and the local recruitment of clerics. These and other elements, however, did not detract from the wider obedience to the papacy, which, based in Rome, drew on an unprecedented institutional continuity. Furthermore, although there were clerical abuses, popular devotion to existing religious practices was undeniable.[36]

The Reformation led to change, doctrinally, liturgically, and organizationally, as both England (and, differently, Scotland) separated themselves from the self-proclaimed universal Church, in other words the Roman Catholic Church, for there were already other independent churches, including the Russian Orthodox, Greek Orthodox, Coptic, Assyrian, and Ethiopian. The Reformation also resulted, within England, Scotland, and other states, in a religious heterodoxy as many people did not accept the changes. There is the suggestion that Shakespeare or at least some members of his family were secret Catholic sympathizers and that this contributed to the "multivocality" of Shakespeare's plays.[37] Others sought different changes in the shape of a Protestantism that was not that offered by the Reformation Settlement eventually established in England. This heterodoxy was a challenge to royal authority and power, not least because religious toleration was very much treated as weakness in this period. At the same time, the idea of transferring headship of the Church from the papacy brought a major extension of the royal position.

In England, Parliament was used under Henry to assert royal control over the Church to an unprecedented degree and in a very different fashion to past action against individual popes or particular papal claims. Henry, who had initially punished Protestants as heretics and earned the title Fidei Defensor (Defender of the Faith) from Pope Leo X for writing *Assertio Septem*

*Sacramentorum* (Defense of the Seven Sacraments, 1521), a book against Luther, was angered by Pope Clement VII's refusal to give him a "divorce" from his first wife, Katherine of Aragon: in fact, an annulment declaring that no valid marriage had been contracted. By Katherine, who is presented as a strong and impressive personality in Shakespeare's play and has been successfully acted accordingly, Henry had a daughter (Mary) but not the son necessary, in his view, though not legally, to guarantee the position of the Tudor dynasty. He convinced himself that his failure to have a son was divine punishment because he had married his brother's widow. The marriage in 1509 had been permitted by Pope Julius II, despite their relationship, but Henry became increasingly mindful of the biblical injunction that a man should not have sexual relations with his brother's wife. The last should-be female ruler, Matilda, daughter of Henry I (r. 1100–35), had been prevented from getting the throne by Stephen and at the cost of a lengthy and highly destructive civil war.

The refusal of Anne Boleyn, whom he had genuinely come to love, to become Henry's mistress also played a role, as this led Henry to decide that he wanted to marry her, which pressed forward his quest for an annulment. The pope's concern with the views of the emperor Charles V (also Charles I of Spain), Katherine's nephew, who ruled important Italian principalities and whose unpaid forces had stormed Rome in 1527, ensured that, despite major and lengthy efforts by Henry, negotiations for an annulment failed.

This failure led to the fall of Henry's principal minister, Wolsey, who, in a step reflecting Henry's purposes,[38] was dismissed as chancellor in 1529. Wolsey was shown by Shakespeare trying to manipulate Henry, as in the appointment of his protégé Stephen Gardiner as Henry's secretary and a bishop. Wolsey had been charged with the offense of praemunire, namely, breaking the statutes of 1351 and 1363 restricting papal authority in England.[39] In part, Shakespeare's play *Henry VIII* is the tragedy of the cardinal, who dies at the end of act 3, having renounced ambition. Wolsey had become closely associated with the attempt to secure the annulment by papal means. Because the play closes in 1533, Wolsey plays a far more significant role than if it had closed with Henry's death in 1547.

In 1531, in reaction against the failure of the negotiations and, therefore, against papal legal jurisdiction as a whole, Henry became more assertive in limiting English independence from the Church. He was impressed by the argument that kings possessed imperial authority by divine gift so that the ruler should not submit to the power of the Church. As a result, he believed papal sanction was not required for the annulment. Henry's views were taken forward with parliamentary support in 1532, as the House of Commons was antagonistic to Church officers abusing their power, which they sought to restrict.

Henry finally publicly rejected papal jurisdiction in 1533. That year, Henry also secretly married Anne Boleyn; their meeting is depicted by Shakespeare, although, for the sake of the dramatic action, events are run together in *Henry VIII*, as so often in Shakespeare's plays. In 1533, Anne gave birth to the future Elizabeth I, and the marriage with Katherine was annulled by the new archbishop of Canterbury, Thomas Cranmer,[40] whom Shakespeare presents as defended from false accusations by Henry, which indeed happened. The annulment made valid the marriage with Anne, a Catholic who sympathized with some aspects of Protestantism. Princess Mary now became illegitimate. In 1534, by the Act of Supremacy, Henry became the "Supreme Head" of the English Church, and the Treason Act of that year made it treasonable to deny this supremacy. Conformity in belief, rather than just act, was now required. Under this statute, such prominent critics as Thomas More, the former chancellor, and John Fisher, bishop of Rochester, were executed in 1535.

The emphasis in England on policy and its defense led to the expression of what was, by the standards of the age, nationalism.

This nationalism focused not only on present politics, lay and ecclesiastical, but also on an account of the past, while the politics, in turn, encouraged a fresh interpretation of English history. In the preamble to the Act in Restraint of Appeals [to Rome] of 1533, an act that proclaimed jurisdictional self-sufficiency and rejected appeals to Rome, it was claimed that "by divers sundry old authentic histories and chronicles, it is manifestly declared and expressed that this realm of England is an empire, and so hath been accepted in the world, governed by one supreme head and king, having the dignity and royal estate of the imperial crown of the same." This assertion by Henry looked back to the House of Wessex's claims of overlordship in Britain in the tenth and eleventh centuries, an overlordship rooted in control of England but not restricted to it.

The past was a continuing presence for Henry, who was no Protestant and did not wish to see any abandonment of the Catholic faith—as was shown, after the break with Rome, by the attack on heresy, that is, Protestantism, with the Act of Six Articles in 1539. However, in accordance with a providential grasp of kingship, Henry was resolved to take charge of the Church and came to see himself as like the kings of Israel in the Old Testament.[41] In 1536, royal injunctions specified the doctrines to be taught. Henry formulated a distinctive type of Christianity while claiming to free the English Church from the evil of papal usurpation. The rejection of miracles and relics was a major change. The impact of Henry's policies was to make the ecclesiastical situation in England dependent on English politics. Moreover, such moves as the destruction of the monasteries, nunneries, and shrines also hit hard at popular devotion and practices and totally destroyed the sense of an unchanging religious practice.

The monasteries offered rich pickings to the government, as they owned vast estates across the whole of England, in towns as well as the countryside. They were dissolved (suppressed) between 1536 and 1540. The cost of wars and the pressures of patronage ensured that their land seized by the Crown did not remain with it. Had the Crown retained all or much of the land, it would have gained a permanent addition of revenue and therefore strength, enabling rulers to dispense with the financial support of Parliament. Instead, although some of the lands were used to endow six new bishoprics and cathedrals, the monastic estates were largely disposed of or sold at preferential rates to royal supporters, who, with them, acquired rights over the churches formerly held by monasteries.

Existing landowners and royal officials were able to expand their land holdings, but the process of the Dissolution of the Monasteries and the subsequent allocation of land led to much destruction and disruption. Monasteries were centers of religious practices, such as pilgrimage, and the shrines were destroyed, not only for loot but also as a rejection of what was now presented as idolatrous. The most prominent shrine, that of St. Thomas Becket in Canterbury, was a historical affirmation of a set of values that Henry wished to destroy, for Becket had opposed royal authority under Henry II and was made a saint in 1173 as a result of being murdered for doing so in 1170.

Monastic buildings were used for stone and lead, frequently for the houses of the new landowners, as with the Russells at Woburn Abbey. Thus, Walsingham Abbey provided the Puritan Nathaniel Bacon, half brother of Francis Bacon, with stone for Stiffkey Hall. Great monasteries, each representing centuries of history and religious devotion, such as Rievaulx (Yorkshire), Bury St. Edmunds (Suffolk), Glastonbury (Somerset), and Tintern (South Wales), were abruptly turned into ruins with their communities dispersed, sometimes brutally so. Indeed, the ruined monastery became one of the landscape markers for travelers, artists, and writers, notably so from the late eighteenth century onward. The Dissolution of the Monasteries was a potent demonstration of Henry's will and power. The counterpoint was the palaces he built for himself, notably what was aptly called Nonsuch, a palace that does not survive.

Shakespeare's sonnet 73 begins:

That time of year thou mayst in me behold
When yellow leaves, or none, or few, do hang
Upon those boughs which shake against the cold,
Bare ruin'd choirs, where late the sweet birds sang.

Shakespeare would have seen the chapel in Stratford-upon-Avon, the walls of which had to be whitewashed over. The sweet birds might have been monks. This sonnet at least suggests Catholic sympathies. There were also the echoes of medieval wall paintings, at least in peoples' memories. The Guild Chapel in Stratford, on the corner next to the grammar school, has a series of medieval wall paintings that were covered by limewash following the Reformation but have since been uncovered. In Westminster Abbey, two late thirteenth-century wall paintings similarly covered over were discovered on the wall of the South Transept in 1936.

However, alongside discussion of Catholic sympathies in Shakespeare's work, there is also evidence of Protestant ones. *Cymbeline* has been discussed in terms of Protestant interpretations of reconciliation, forgiveness, free grace, and the grace of Christian marriage. Despite the presence in the play of Jupiter and a soothsayer, the presence of Christian character in human relations is portrayed in the play, notably with forgiveness by both Imogen and Cymbeline and with Posthumus's remorse.[42]

Destruction was a key element of Henry VIII's policies, for much of the wealth gained was spent on military preparations and war. War with France and Scotland in the 1540s proved extraordinarily expensive in large part because of the task of fighting two simultaneously, because the conflicts were sustained, and because the burden of the war in France could no longer be covered in part from the possessions there of the king of England.

War led in England to high taxation and the debasement of the coinage. Combined with inflation, these measures ensured serious economic and social strains.

As centers of local communities, monasteries and nunneries were important providers of education and other social benefits, and these functions were greatly disrupted by their dissolution. In part, the resulting need was met by a new philanthropy, some of it centered on the foundation of grammar schools. There was also pressure for public provision that helped lead to the successive pieces of legislation of 1531, 1536, 1572, 1598, and 1601 that comprised the Tudor Poor Law (see chap. 8), although the social problems that this responded to were wider ranging in their cause.

Concern about the Dissolution of the Monasteries ensured that Henry faced a serious challenge in 1536. Opposition to his policies, particularly those toward the Church, as well as anxiety about rumors of new taxes, triggered a major rebellion in the North of England, the Pilgrimage of Grace. The reaction indicated the extent of popular concern about political and religious developments and the role of religion in helping to rally support. The army of the pilgrims was to rally round the sacred banner of St. Cuthbert, which was brought by the Durham contingent. The pilgrims contrasted "the whole body of the realm" with "evil-disposed persons" in the king's council: a contrast with a lengthy medieval pedigree but one made more complex and attractive to some by the religious dimension.

Using true faith as an element of judgment when considering claims about tyranny offered a seriously subversive means for dissent across the religious spectrum, one that greatly encouraged people to action. As with later episodes, such as the civil wars that broke out in 1638–42 in Scotland, Ireland, and then England, a general cause for opposition was combined with specific political agendas so that in 1536 there were complaints about the Treason Act of 1534, the Succession Act of 1536 (which enabled the monarch to name his successor—a measure that would deal with the argument that Henry's divorce from Katherine of Aragon was illegitimate), and other unpopular governmental practices.

As with the Peasants' Revolt in 1381 and Jack Cade's rebellion in 1450, tension in 1536 was assuaged by royal concessions, but, again as in 1381 and 1450, there was subsequent repression, as Henry, who in any case never intended to fulfil these concessions, was released from his promises by further revolts. This ensured that there was no Parliament at York to settle grievances. Furthermore, the Pilgrimage of Grace did not stop the Dissolution of the Monasteries nor the concurrent attack on saint worship. Instead, there was a brutal and bloody treatment of the former rebels, while the opportunity was taken to execute most of the survivors of the blood royal outside Henry's immediate family. This was part of a more widespread violent treatment of those whom Henry distrusted, one in which the law was manipulated by a suspicious and insecure king ready to use deceit and violence to overcome the reality of problems. None of this was touched on by Shakespeare's *Henry VIII*. Indeed, the tragic drama of the king and the consequences of his paranoid power for others and himself were not really taken up as a topic. The play, which appeared in 1613, was part of a continuing saga of popular accounts of the reign.[43]

Henry's suspicions were manipulated, as so often with figures depicted on the stage, including, in *Henry VIII*, the case of Edward, Third Duke of Buckingham, in 1521. This manipulation was seen in 1536 when the conservatives at court—joined in this case by Thomas Cromwell, Henry's key minister—(falsely) alleged that Anne Boleyn was being unfaithful in order to overthrow her. This was an episode not shown in Shakespeare's play, and unsurprisingly so. Anne was executed, and Elizabeth was declared a bastard.

In turn, Cromwell himself was to be overthrown on June 10 and executed on July 28, 1540, when the conservative faction

exploited his unwillingness to support Henry's favor for Katherine Howard, his fifth wife, whom the king married on the day of
the execution. In turn, her alleged adultery led to her execution in
1542. Katherine certainly recklessly showed favor to young courtiers. Of the other wives, Jane Seymour, the third and the mother
of his successor, Edward VI, died a natural death in 1537; Anne
of Cleves, the fourth, did not please Henry, and the unconsum-
mated marriage was rapidly annulled in 1540, while Katherine
Parr, the sixth, a widow, survived him, although only after seeing
off a major challenge to her position, one based on hostility to her
evangelical activities.[44]

More than executions were involved in Henry's politics and
suspicions. Uneasiness about the security situation far from London led the government in 1536–43 to push through union with
Wales so that it was all assimilated into the English governmental, parliamentary, and legal systems. This was not an outcome
seen with Scotland in 1603.

Religious change under Henry helped ensure that there was a
shift of psychological possibilities as far as the people were concerned: the ending of purgatory and the concomitant practice
of offering prayers for the dead destroyed the links between the
communities of the living and the dead. Chantry chapels were
dissolved in 1545 and 1547. The commissioners closing the chantries in the county of Berkshire referred to them as "purgatory
trasshe." Similarly, there was also a marked critique of the idea
and content of miracles linked to the attack on sacred places and
saints. Protestants accepted that miracles had occurred in biblical times, which confirmed the divine origin of the Bible, but
they claimed that, thereafter, they had ceased and that assertions
to the contrary by the Catholic Church were a form of false information that proved the bogus, indeed diabolical, character
of Catholicism. The denial of miracles extended to the destruction of shrines, reliquaries, and the related frescoes and carvings
that provided accounts of the miracles. Thus, the accumulated

information presented by the visual panoply of the miraculous world was desecrated and destroyed, as saints and sainthood were brutally dethroned.

Those who complained, let alone resisted, could readily become victims of coercion, even persecution, as religious life was newly scrutinized and regulated by the state in a reformulation of the confessional state. Looked at differently, it was the very weakness of the state that was an important part of the equation. This was a weakness in terms of directing opinion and regarding implementation. This weakness encouraged action by the government as it sought a semblance of control.[45]

In contrast to the destruction of images, the production of an official English Bible in 1537, followed in 1538 by the instruction to every parish church to purchase a copy, was a marked extension of the authority of print that expanded the possibilities for readers and listeners of reaching their own conclusions and also encouraged literacy. The possibilities of state direction of the Church were linked to those of the new technology of printing. Henry argued that the "word of God" supported the idea of royal supremacy, and this encouraged the translation of the Bible. The first complete translation of the Bible to be printed in English, that by Miles Coverdale, was dedicated to Henry in 1535. The authoritative nature of the Bible was taken further with the King James, or Authorized, Version of it in 1611. Shakespeare made many references to the Bible (notably, for the comedies, to the Psalms), the Book of Common Prayer, and the Books of Homilies. His own knowledge of scripture was good and resonant.[46] So would have been that of the audience.

Shakespeare did not simply write against the background of a narrative of strife that he then retold. There were also longstanding developments, important to the character of English society and politics, occurring during this period, that very much influenced his work and the perception of it. These developments, all of which had begun before the period, included the rise of the vernacular (the English language), the growth of Parliament, the role of the common law, and the increased flexibility of English society. The last has led to claims that, at least since the thirteenth century and possibly from far earlier, England was distinctly and distinctively less stratified than elsewhere in Europe and, as such, characterized by a "possessive individualism" and open to the development of capitalism and the advance of political liberty.[47] Individualism can be seen in the depiction of character and motivation in plays. It contrasts with the more formulaic nature of drama in many cultures, notably in the Orient.

In ending the continuous sequence of history plays in 1485 and *Henry VIII* in 1533, Shakespeare both provided coherent plots and invited his audience to consider the present in relation to the past. That is a consideration we need to repeat in order to understand the relation between Shakespeare's England and that within its collective memory of the period treated with by these plays, a period that was more easily recovered for contemporaries thanks to his plays. Today, these plays are more important to the collective memory of the long fifteenth century than they were in Shakespeare's day, in part because other forms of memorialization for this period have receded.

To Shakespeare and his contemporaries, the political order was grounded in morality, and the latter was very much seen in religious terms. In *Henry VIII*, Wolsey, having been dismissed, tells Thomas Cromwell:

> Cromwell, I charge thee, fling away ambition,
> By that sin fell the angels; how can man then,
> The image of his maker, hope to win by it? (III, ii)

The reference to the fall of the devil from heaven is instructive. A more pointed historical reference in the play was the depiction of Stephen Gardiner, bishop of Winchester from 1531 to 1555, as a villain, keen to have Cranmer destroyed. This depiction linked the struggle over the Henrician Reformation with the Marian

reaction and, by extension, with the Catholic Church's opposition to Elizabeth, for Gardiner was one of Mary's key advisors.
The history plays focused on the consequences of royal weakness and dynastic challenge, but there was also an historical dimension stemming from the Reformation. Brought to the fore
in *Henry VIII*, this historical dimension affected and reflected
the sense of the past in terms of broader considerations about order, morality, purpose, continuity, and the place of religion. The
historical dimension was an aspect of the representation of monarchs, one in which mystification was balanced with popularity.

The popular perception of individual monarchs depended
greatly on how their representation was perceived, and this issue
was pushed to the fore as a result of the Reformation. The latter ensured that royal authority was both significant and contested, and
each as never before.[48] Although it is not known how the audiences
experienced plays, the work of playwrights can be located in this
context of contestation, not least in terms of the degree to which
plays were open to variant readings, in part because of the way in
which language had many meanings and was perceived in that
light.[49] There was no neutrality as far as the history plays and, indeed, the more general understanding of the past were concerned.

## NOTES

1. P. Rackin, *Stages of History: Shakespeare's English Chronicles*
(London, 1990); D. G. Watson, *Shakespeare's Early History Plays: Politics at
Play on the Elizabethan Stage* (London, 1990).

2. I. W. Archer, "Discourses of History in Elizabethan and Early Stuart
London," *Huntington Library Quarterly* 68 (2005): 214.

3. P. Saccio, *Shakespeare's English Kings* (Oxford, 1977); E. Sterling,
*The Movement Towards Subversion: The English History Play from Skelton
to Shakespeare* (Lanham, MD, 1996); J. W. Velez, ed., *Shakespeare's English
Histories: A Quest for Form and Genre* (Binghamton, VT, 1996).

4. P. Rackin, *Stages of History: Shakespeare's English Chronicles* (Ithaca,
NY, 1990).

5. For a focus more on political intention, Peter Lake, *How Shakespeare Put Politics on the Stage: Power and Succession in the History Plays* (New Haven, CT, 2016).

6. For a global context, J. Duindam, *Dynasties: A Global History of Power, 1300–1800* (Cambridge, 2015).

7. N. Saul, *Richard II* (New Haven, CT, 1997).

8. D. Biggs, *Three Armies in Britain: The Irish Campaign of Richard II and the Usurpation of Henry IV, 1397–99* (Leiden, UK, 2006).

9. For comparisons between the two playwrights, R. A. Logan, *Shakespeare's Marlowe* (Aldershot, UK, 2007).

10. D. Biggs, *Royal Charter Witness Lists, 1399 to 1417* (London, 2017), xi.

11. G. Dodd and D. Biggs, eds, *The Reign of Henry IV: Rebellion and Survival 1403–13* (Woodbridge, UK, 2008).

12. C. Given-Wilson, *Henry IV* (New Haven, CT, 2016).

13. M. Vale, *Henry V: The Conscience of a King* (New Haven, CT, 2016).

14. A. Curry, *Agincourt* (Oxford, 2015); A. Curry and M. Mercer, eds., *The Battle of Agincourt* (New Haven, CT, 2015).

15. J. Bellis, *The Hundred Years War in Literature, 1337–1600* (Cambridge, 2011).

16. K. J. Lewis, *Kingship and Masculinity in Late Medieval England* (London, 2013).

17. J. Sumption, *The Hundred Years War IV: Cursed Kings* (Philadelphia, 2015).

18. C. Allmand, *Henry V* (London, 1992).

19. A. Tricomi, "Joan La Pucelle and the Inverted Saint's Play in *1 Henry VI*," *Renaissance and Reformation* 25 (2001): 5–31.

20. M. L. Kekewich, *The Good King: René of Anjou and Fifteenth Century Anjou* (Basingstoke, UK, 2008).

21. N. Murphy, "Henry VIII's First Invasion of France: The Gascon Expedition of 1512," *English Historical Review* 130 (2015): 51.

22. J. Rose, ed., *The Politics of Counsel in England and Scotland, 1286–1707* (Oxford, 2016).

23. M. Hicks, *The Wars of the Roses* (New Haven, CT, 2010).

24. M. Hattaway, "The Play: 'What Should Be the Meaning of All Those Foughten Fields?'" in Hattaway, ed., *The Third Part of King Henry VI* (Cambridge, 1993), 9–35.

25. A. Crawford, *Yorkist Lord: John Howard, Duke of Norfolk, c. 1425–1485* (London, 2010).

26. J. Gillingham, ed., *Richard III: A Medieval Kingship* (New York, 1994). For an account that criticizes Shakespeare, C. Skidmore, *Richard III: Brother, Protector, King* (London, 2017), especially 7, 369.

27. M. Jones, *Bosworth 1485: The Battle That Transformed England* (New York, 2015).

28. S. Church, *King John and the Road to Magna Carta* (London, 2015).

29. M. Bennett, *The Battle of Bosworth* (Stroud, UK, 1993).

30. S. Brigden, "'The Shadow That You Know': Sir Thomas Wyatt and Sir Francis Bryan at Court and in Embassy," *Historical Journal* 39 (1996): 9–27.

31. S. Gunn, *Henry VII's New Men and the Making of Tudor England* (Oxford, 2016).

32. J. Ross, *John de Vere, Thirteenth Earl of Oxford, 1442–1513: "The Foremost Man of the Kingdom"* (Woodbridge, UK, 2011).

33. J. Bellamy, *Bastard Feudalism and the Law* (London, 1989).

34. P. Fleming and M. Wood, *Gloucestershire's Forgotten Battle: Nibley Green 1470* (Stroud, UK, 2003).

35. S. Thurley, *Houses of Power: The Places That Shaped the Tudor World* (London, 2017).

36. E. Duffy, *The Stripping of the Altars* (New Haven, CT, 1992) and *Saints, Sacrilege, and Sedition: Religion and Conflict in the Tudor Reformations* (London, 2012).

37. Lake, *How Shakespeare Put Politics on the Stage*. For Catholicity, C. Asquith, *Shadowplay: The Hidden Beliefs and Coded Politics of William Shakespeare* (New York, 2005) and *Shakespeare and the Resistance* (New York, 2018). For a convincing criticism, P. Dean, "Crypocriticism," *The New Criterion*, November 2018, 21–24.

38. G. W. Bernard, *Power and Politics in Tudor England* (Aldershot, UK, 2000), 74.

39. P. Gwyn, *The King's Cardinal: The Rise and Fall of Thomas Wolsey* (London, 1990).

40. D. MacCulloch, *Thomas Cranmer: A Life* (New Haven, CT, 1996).

41. R. Rex, *Henry VIII and the English Reformation* (London, 1993); G. W. Bernard, *The King's Reformation* (New Haven, CT, 2005).

42. D. L. Wright, *The Anglican Shakespeare: Elizabethan Orthodoxy in the Great Histories*; P. M. Simonds, *Myth, Emblem, and Music in Shakespeare's "Cymbeline": An Iconographic Reconstruction* (Newark, DE, 1992).

43. T. Betteridge and T. S. Freeman, eds., *Henry VIII and History* (Farnham, UK, 2012).

44.  D. MacCulloch, *Thomas Cromwell: A Life* (London, 2018); D. Loades, *The Politics of Marriage: Henry VIII and His Queens* (Stroud, UK, 1994).

45.  A. Walsham, *Charitable Hatred: Tolerance and Intolerance in England, 1500–1700* (Manchester, 2006).

46.  N. Shaheen, *Biblical References in Shakespeare's Comedies* (Newark, DE, 1993).

47.  A. Macfarlane, *The Origins of English Individualism* (London, 1976) and *The Culture of Capitalism* (London, 1987).

48.  K. Sharpe, *Selling the Tudor Monarchy: Authority and Image in Sixteenth-Century England* (New Haven, CT, 2009) and *Image Wars and Rebranding Rule* (New Haven, CT, 2013).

49.  K. Sharpe, *Reading Authority and Representing Rule in Early Modern England* (London, 2013).

# THE NARRATIVE OF POLITICS

SHAKESPEARE WAS BORN SOON AFTER the accession of
Elizabeth I in 1558. At that stage, England was very much in a
midcentury crisis, as it had also been a century earlier and was
to be anew a century later. It was an unstable country, its future,
both political and religious, highly uncertain, while it had been
newly defeated by France. It could hardly have been imagined
that Elizabeth was to rule until 1603, a reign longer than any
since that of Edward III (1327–77) and only next surpassed by
that of George III (1760–1820), nor that she would overcome a
series of domestic and international crises. These achievements
would have astonished contemporaries, looking back to the
recent history of the country, and maybe would have surprised
Elizabeth.

Like Elizabeth, her father, Henry VIII (r. 1509–47), had kept
a firm grip on the domestic situation, helped by his clear right
to the throne, his unwillingness to turn too obviously to either
religious option, and by the selective employment of terror. Not
that "selective" would have been the word that came to mind to
the victims of his often arbitrary rule and brutal harshness. These
victims spanned the social ranks and the regions and included
clerics, as well as laity. Particular energy was devoted to a ruthless

tracking down and dispatching of Plantagenets like the Poles, but all opponents and might-be opponents had reason to fear.

Coercion was not the sole issue and means. Instead, Henry's use of Parliament in the 1530s and 1540s helped legitimate his objectives, while also increasing its frequency and role. Nevertheless, the idea (strongly advanced from the 1950s by Geoffrey Elton, the leading Tudor historian until the 1980s) that—alongside Thomas Cromwell's vision of the state as a sovereign nation living under a law that was controlled by Parliament—there was a revolution in government in the 1530s, notably through new bureaucratic agencies, is now seen as questionable.[1] Instead, Henry's preference for personal politics and direct control remained the dominant theme throughout his reign. Henry kept control of his aristocrats through their attendance at court, through taking the court itself traveling, through shared participation with them in military activities and the hunt, and through patronage. The seizure of Church lands gave him greater opportunities for the last than any English monarch since William the Conqueror (r. 1066–87), who had overthrown the Old English monarchy: Henry's conquest of the Church was far easier.

### EDWARD VI, 1547–53

Such processes of government, however, appeared suddenly tenuous when it became clear that the new monarch would not control the situation personally, as was the case during the minority of Henry's young son and successor, Edward VI (r. 1547–53). The last minority had been that of Edward V in 1483, and he had rapidly and murderously been supplanted by his uncle, Richard III. At the end of Henry's reign, the king turned against the powerful Howard family, executing Henry, Earl of Surrey, on a charge of treasonably quartering the royal arms, and disgracing his father, Thomas, Third Duke of Norfolk, who survived only because Henry died the day before that appointed for his execution. These moves led to the overshadowing of the more conservative faction at court, that which was closest to Catholicism. Power, instead, was grasped by Edward VI's uncle, Jane Seymour's brother, Edward, a rival of the Howards, who now became Protector and Duke of Somerset.

The legacy, however, was very troublesome. Expensive and seemingly intractable wars with France and Scotland in the 1540s had exhausted royal resources and pressed hard on the economy and on society, although without causing political crisis. Under Edward VI, both politics at the center and control of the localities were greatly complicated by religious disputes, which made it impossible to tackle the tensions within the governing elite and also within society as a whole. In many senses, the divisions and potential for disorder created by the events of Henry's reign were brought to fruition. These disputes made it harder to ensure cooperation and consensus.

During Edward's reign, England was far more open to the influence of Protestantism from the Continent, and in marked contrast with the equivocations under Henry, there was a surge of state-supported and purposeful Protestant activity. The priggish Edward is generally seen as an enthusiastic Protestant, but this has been disputed, and it has been argued that the drive to Protestantism came primarily from his ministers. Certainly, the ambitious Protector Somerset, allied with Thomas Cranmer, archbishop of Canterbury, consolidated Protestant worship in 1549, with the Act of Uniformity and the Book of Common Prayer required to be used in every parish church, producing a religious settlement very different to that under Henry. Moreover, due to Edward's minority, religious change took an institutional character that contrasted with that under Henry. The council assumed the Royal Supremacy, and the Uniformity Acts of 1549 and 1552 provided a statutory institutional character for the Supremacy.

In turn, strong Catholic hostility to religious change played a major role in the widespread uprisings in the South West of

England, especially in Cornwall and Devon, in 1549. These were known as the Prayer Book Rising.[2] However, the rising in Norfolk in eastern England that year focused not on religious change but on socioeconomic issues. Opposition to landlords, especially the enclosure of common lands and their high rents, was the key factor. So also was hostility to oppressive local governments.[3] The first issues had already led to riots in Norwich, Coventry, and Southampton over the previous seventy years.

The uprisings were crushed in battle with heavy casualties, partly by foreign mercenaries and their military experience and firearms. However, uprisings in 1549, like others before and after, indicated the extent to which developments in the 1530s through the 1560s encouraged a degree of hostile popular response that menaced or could appear to menace the political system. This menace encouraged a reliance on force and patronage on the part of government but also made necessary the development of a new language and practice of apparent consultation within the political nation.

Edward's reign saw the interaction of an embrace of Protestantism, with aristocratic factionalism and widespread popular uprisings. The last two were examples of the turmoil that was to feature in several of Shakespeare's plays. Whatever the habits of obedience that had been encouraged under Henry VIII, their impact proved limited at the first crisis. Indeed, in early 1549, Somerset's ambitious and volatile younger brother Sir Thomas Seymour was arrested and executed, for plotting to gain power by seizing Edward and marrying Elizabeth,[4] prefiguring the gamble seen with Robert, Second Earl of Essex in 1601.

In the second part of his reign, after the overthrow in October 1549 of Somerset, who had been weakened by the crises of that year and had lost the support of the council, Edward came under the influence of John Dudley. He became Duke of Northumberland in October 1551 and very much acted as the overmighty subject that featured in many plays. Northumberland had Somerset beheaded in 1552 on Tower Hill and took the development of state Protestantism further. In turn, the king's deteriorating health led Northumberland to try to act as a queen maker. The unmarried Edward was persuaded to exclude his half sisters, Mary and Elizabeth, daughters respectively of Henry's first two wives, Katherine of Aragon and Anne Boleyn. Instead, Lady Jane Grey, the Protestant granddaughter of Henry VII through his second daughter, Mary, was declared next in line. She was married to Lord Guildford Dudley, one of Northumberland's sons and, when Edward died in 1553, was proclaimed queen by Northumberland.[5]

Had Mary been captured, as Northumberland had planned, or defeated and slain, then Northumberland might well have been able to preside over a new political system, especially if Elizabeth had been imprisoned. It was not to be. In a highly dramatic fashion, the determined Mary proclaimed herself queen. Northumberland's support rapidly fell away, and Mary seized power. London joined the county elites and the council in rallying to Mary, who gained power largely due to the nobles and gentry in East Anglia being willing to fight for her. In the event, there was no need to fight a civil war. Northumberland was beheaded. This was a pace of events that matched those in Shakespeare's history plays.

MARY, 1553–58

When she rode into London, Mary (r. 1553–58) was greeted with great popularity, but Sir Thomas Wyatt's rising in early 1554, a rising directed against her forthcoming marriage to Philip II of Spain, indicated the precarious nature of the regime. London, however, proved resolute for the Crown in this crisis and Wyatt failed. Like her father, Mary was willing to use force against the innocent: Lady Jane Grey and her husband were executed in response. Jane's father, Henry, Duke of Suffolk, a zealous Protestant, was involved in the Wyatt conspiracy and was beheaded accordingly. However, against the advice of the imperial ambassador and of Bishop Gardiner, Mary's half sister, Elizabeth, was not executed despite being a Protestant.

Mary was a devout Catholic who was determined to return England to the Catholic fold. A parliamentary statute declared her power to be identical to that of a male ruler. She persuaded Parliament to repeal Edward's religious legislation and her father's Act of Supremacy. Mary restored papal authority and Catholic practice, reforming the clergy and reviving Catholic orthodoxy at the universities, although a papal dispensation from Julius III allowed the retention of the former Church lands by those who now held them, which was a prudent way to ensure the support of the social elite. Mary also married her younger first cousin Philip II, in order to ensure a Catholic succession. This led England into a war with France, which resulted in the loss of Calais in 1558, although France's ally Scotland at least did not capture Berwick.[6]

The drive for re-Catholicism was demonstrated, from February 4, 1555, by the burning of Protestants, who were treated as heretics. London, Kent, and Sussex had a disproportionately high number of Protestant martyrs, being geographically nearest to Continental Protestantism and also most exposed to royal power and attention. It was not just London but increasingly the London-centered hinterland as a whole that was influential. As a consequence, the balance of power, wealth, and influence within England shifted steadily southeastward, and the relative dominance of the subregion grew.

The public burnings of individuals who were still alive were probably highly traumatic experiences for those who were present. They certainly proved the basis for a Protestant martyrology that was effectively disseminated in *Acts and Monuments of the Church* (1563) by John Foxe, popularly known as the *Book of Martyrs*. Although Shakespeare did not write a play about Mary, Foxe's work was not the only subsequent sign of her reign in the world of print during his lifetime. In the 1600s, her opponent Wyatt emerged as a hero in the play *The Famous History of Sir Thomas Wyatt* by Dekker and Webster, both leading playwrights.

The popularity of Mary's policy of re-Catholicization and the attempt to rehabilitate her reputation are matters for scholarly controversy, as is the question of what would have happened if her reign had lasted for longer. The killing of its leaders in England certainly deprived Protestantism of both leaders and cohesion and challenged its morale and hopes for the future. At the same time, the burnings continued into 1558, which suggests, in a reminder of the multifaceted nature of evidence, not only the sustained energy of repression but also that Protestantism continued to have supporters. That repression could work as a policy, however, was to be shown in a number of states over the following century and a half, most prominently Austria, Bohemia, and France, which also experienced forcible re-Catholicization.[7]

Nevertheless, in comparison, Mary's reign was brief and her impact limited. She was sickly and had two phantom pregnancies but, more significantly, did not give birth to the hoped-for heir, whereas Philip had children by his next marriage. As a result, Mary was succeeded in 1558 by her Protestant half sister, Elizabeth. The dying queen maintained the order of succession, although she greatly disliked Elizabeth.

## ELIZABETH I 1558–1603

Had Elizabeth lived only for as long as Mary, then her reign would not have been long, and the succession would have been an even more significant issue and come to a climax earlier. Instead, Elizabeth's lengthy reign allowed for the consolidation of a relatively conservative Protestant church settlement and also contrasted both with the chaos of the preceding two reigns and with the disturbed situation in contemporary France, which suffered badly from the drawn-out Wars of Religion.

Elizabeth's personality was important but was not probed in a play by Shakespeare, who could not thereby contribute to what became a life prominent in later interpretations.[8] Like her paternal grandfather, Henry VII, she was a skillful manipulator, able to read the personality of others, and not a zealot. She had to master a court where there were many crosscurrents of personality and policy.[9] In religion, she sought to avoid extremes and would have preferred a settlement closer to that of her father, Henry VIII— namely, Henrician Catholicism without pope, monks, or friars, the last of whom appeared fairly often in Shakespeare's plays. She and then James I made mandatory changes to what was acceptable ritual, as a matter of politic policy rather than creed.

Elizabeth was, nevertheless, a supporter of the reformed Church, which, while describing itself as the true Catholic Church was in the last analysis Protestant and was understood both domestically and internationally to be so. Mary's ministers and favorites were mostly dismissed, and the domestic political situation led Elizabeth in a more Protestant direction. At Christmas 1558, Elizabeth walked out of the Mass when Owen Oglethorpe, bishop of Carlisle, the only bishop who had been prepared to crown her, elevated the host, a Catholic step, after she had told him not to do so. The following May, he and the other bishops who refused to take the Oath of Supremacy were deprived. However, there was considerable reluctance at the local level to abandon traditional customs.[10]

Religious issues were also important in international links. Negotiations in the 1560s for a marriage between Elizabeth and the Austrian Habsburg archduke Charles, brother to the Emperor Maximilian II and cousin of Philip II—negotiations that involved a diplomatic mission by Thomas, Third Earl of Sussex, in 1567—failed in part because of an unwillingness to grant Charles, a Catholic, the right to a private Mass in the royal household. These and other negotiations also provide evidence of the able and well-educated Elizabeth's skill in other languages, notably Italian and French.[11]

Attempts to persuade Elizabeth to marry and secure the succession were made by her ministers, and some were staged, for example in *Gorboduc* (1561), a play by Thomas Norton and Thomas Sackville (later First Earl of Dorset and Lord Treasurer), performed before Elizabeth in the Inner Temple in 1562, and also in the entertainment she received from Sussex when staying at his country seat in 1579. These marriage schemes all failed, and the Catholicism of the key suitors was a major issue that contributed to this failure, being an issue that divided her ministers.

Nevertheless, the Protestant settlement she introduced, with new Acts of Supremacy and Uniformity, was more conservative than that of Northumberland in 1552. Elizabeth also sought to prevent further change, and this led to repeated disputes with the more radical Protestants, the Puritans. Puritanism, a tendency within the established Church and one located along a continuum rather than a separatist movement,[12] pressed for a more severe, Calvinistic organization and theology. Angry with those who had conformed and attended Mass under Mary, including Elizabeth and William Cecil, Puritan expressions of discontent focused on the role of bishops and the nature of clerical vestments, both seen as Catholic features. Puritan activism pushing for more clearly Protestant outcomes included women and men and spanned politics, as well as religion. This offered an opportunity to develop the vitality of English Protestantism, bringing Puritan energies into line with the structures and goals of the Church of England. However, that fusion, which had appeared possible in the 1570s, proved unsuccessful, in part because of hostility on the part of the Church, notably due to the opposition of Richard Bancroft, bishop of London 1597–1604 and archbishop of Canterbury 1604–10. Believed to be part of a wide-ranging conspiracy, Puritans were prosecuted, and their plans, advanced in a secret conference movement in the 1580s, for a Presbyterian Church of England, were thwarted.[13]

What would subsequently be presented as a middle path, or *via media*, in religious matters and be applauded accordingly, not least as a characteristic of Englishness, as well as being used to praise Elizabeth, in practice proved very difficult to establish and implement. Indeed, difficulties with both helped ensure that there was an ad hoc character to this middle path, one seen in purges of JPs on religious grounds.[14] This character required decision making, elucidation, defense, and implementation, none of which was easy or free from controversy. Theologians, such as the Cambridge academic and cleric William Perkins, a Warwickshire writer (1558–1602) a bit older than Shakespeare, devoted much effort to these tasks, as did politicians, lay and clerical. Their pursuit also affected others, including literary figures,[15] and ensured a background of contention that influenced public life and private opinion.

While many issues focused on religion, the difficulties owed much to the political context—or rather, contexts—local, national, and international. These contexts created issues, opportunities, and problems, not least due to the interaction with factional politics in England. The contours of these politics are not easy to follow, especially because the surviving sources are heavily slanted toward the Cecils, William (1520–98), Lord Burghley from 1571, and his son Robert (1563–1612). William Cecil, Elizabeth's leading minister, was secretary of state from 1550 to 1553 and 1558 to 1572 and treasurer thence until his death. Robert was secretary of state from 1596 to 1608, thus bridging the reigns of Elizabeth and James I. The Cecils left copious archives, which were well looked after subsequently. This ensures that the point of view of the Cecils tends to be that which is most readily accessible, although there were other definitions of the national interest and of how best to pursue it. Burghley, a quite familiar, Polonius-style figure to the audience, presented himself as disinterested and above faction, a compound of Ciceronian virtue, Protestant commitment, and loyal service to Elizabeth.[16] However, this approach ignored his central political role, a role that opposed newer conceptions of "office" to older ones of aristocratic honor.

This was a tension seen earlier with Wolsey and one offered by Shakespeare in a comic tone with Malvolio.

Moreover, Cecil's position affected the possibility of pursuing other options. Most notably, the Puritans were supported by the Dudleys, particularly Robert Dudley, Earl of Leicester (1532–88), and his supporters, who also backed a Protestant marriage for Elizabeth, indeed a marriage with himself. There was a romantic relationship between the two for a while, one that Elizabeth clearly enjoyed, but there is no evidence of a sexual one. Leicester's first wife, Amy Robsart, died in 1560 from a mysterious fall down a flight of stairs, which left him free to remarry but did not improve his reputation. There were prominent figures who were opposed to the prospectus of a Leicester marriage, including not only Catholics and crypto-Catholics but also, for example, Thomas, Third Earl of Sussex, and Sir Christopher Hatton (1540–91), a royal favorite who became the Lord Chancellor in 1587. As chancellor of Oxford University, Leicester purged the university of Catholics. Leicester, the third son of John, First Duke of Northumberland, who had been executed in 1553, had himself been condemned to death under Mary in 1554 but had been released.

Factional and/or religious politics provided a violent theme across Elizabeth's reign. The Catholic Northern Rising of 1569 was very different in character to the failed coup by Leicester's stepson, Robert, Second Earl of Essex, in 1601, but there was a common theme in the use of violence. This was also a threat throughout the period. This threat was driven home by the frequent examples of violence abroad, notably in France from the 1560s to the 1590s and in Scotland in the 1560s. In each case, this involved murder around the Crown and civil war. Henry III of France was assassinated in 1589, while Mary, Queen of Scots, was overthrown after her husband and cousin, Henry, Lord Darnley, had been murdered in 1567. The threat of violence in England was echoed by writers' presentation of the past. A degree of political violence that might appear almost lurid in Shakespeare's plays rested on a considerable degree of reality in the reports and rumors of his lifetime.

Contemporary attitudes to Church government and to toleration ensured that decisions, once made, had to be implemented throughout the state and with the assistance of the lay authorities, which posed problems. Elizabeth's Protestant settlement aroused Catholic concern, and this at a time of growing energy in the Counter-Reformation, the Catholic effort to drive back Protestantism. Some clerics who refused to accept Elizabeth's settlement established seminaries on the Continent, most prominently at Douai, to train missionaries to reconvert England to Catholicism. This encouraged government action against Catholics, especially priests. As a result, some Catholic houses from the period still contain priest holes: hiding places in the event of raids.[17]

As significant, over time, those who had lived in an unchallenged world of Catholicism died out, and an increasing percentage of the population came to be educated in a Protestant Christianity and to be devout (or not) accordingly.[18] Furthermore, a better- and differently educated and more committed Protestant, parochial (parish) clergy developed. The universities, which played a key role in the education of the elite, were centers of Protestantization. Their academics were all clerics and saw themselves as given a role in terms of securing the new religious order.

The fragile political consensus was affected by increasing polarization in religion and foreign policy. The succession was a major issue. The situation became volatile in 1568 when Elizabeth's cousin, the Catholic Mary, Queen of Scots (1542–87), fled to England, where, as a granddaughter of Henry VII, through his elder daughter Margaret (who had married James IV and been the mother of James V, the father of Mary), she was next in line in the succession. Already while in Scotland, Mary had been the subject of designs for a Catholic succession in both countries, notably by Margaret, Countess of Lennox, the daughter of

Henry VIII's elder sister Margaret, by her second husband, who saw such a succession as possible by means of Mary's marriage to Margaret's son Lord Darnley.[19]

Mary's presence in England swiftly acted as a focus for discontent, and she was imprisoned. Once imprisoned, Mary was never to be freed. In 1569, a court conspiracy to replace Elizabeth's leading minister, William Cecil, and to marry Thomas, Fourth Duke of Norfolk, a leading religious conservative, to Mary and to acknowledge Mary as heir to the throne was thwarted; Norfolk, the sole English duke, the son of the Earl of Surrey who had been executed in 1547 and the grandson of the Third Duke of Norfolk, was imprisoned.

In November 1569, the fallout from the conspiracy triggered the last major provincial rising in Tudor England, the Northern Rising, an episode similar to those depicted in Shakespeare's history plays. The rising was led by members of two families whose family names resonated in these plays, Thomas Percy, Seventh Earl of Northumberland, and Charles Neville, Ninth Earl of Westmorland, the latter being Norfolk's brother-in-law. Their local positions were endangered by a lack of royal favor: the relationship between power in the localities and royal patronage was the crucial factor in noble power. There was a strong interaction of political and religious hostility to the government in the rising, not least resentment at the way Elizabeth was using loyal Protestants attached to the Council of the North to undermine the independent power of local aristocratic families. In addition, the bishop, dean, and chapter of Durham were all propagating Protestantism. The disclosure of the court conspiracy led Elizabeth to order the two earls to London, despite advice from Thomas, Third Earl of Sussex, the Lord President of the North, that it would lead them to rebel. The earls refused the dangerous command, which would have taken them to the Tower of London, and, with their options gone, gathered their men to resist any attempt to compel them.

The earls marked the beginning of the rising by occupying Durham Cathedral on November 14, 1569, destroying English bibles and celebrating Mass in the Latin rite. The choir sang an anthem praising the Virgin Mary, thanks to whom sin was banished. Catholic worship was subsequently restored in many other churches in the region. In County Durham, only Sir George Bowes, constable of Barnard Castle, a royal lordship, backed Elizabeth. The earls' revolt was a powerful defiance of royal power by a rising led, unlike those hitherto in the century (bar that for Elizabeth's half sister, Mary I, in 1553), from the very top of the social hierarchy. Furthermore, unlike the risings in 1536 and 1549, there was, in Mary, Queen of Scots, in 1569 a clear monarchical alternative to the sovereign. This matched the distinction in the 1450s between Cade's Rebellion and the more serious and lasting conspiratorial efforts of Richard, Duke of York.

However, the threat posed by the earls in 1569 was diminished by the absence of foreign military support, whether from Spain, France, or Scotland, and by the inability of the rebels to reach and release Mary when, with about 5,800 men, they marched south on November 15. Short of money, they could not pay their force, which was dissolving. Having turned back near Knaresborough on November 24, the earls besieged and took the surrender of Barnard Castle. Nevertheless, the advance of a strong royal army of about 12,000 men under Leicester's surviving elder brother Ambrose Dudley, Third Earl of Warwick, led the earls to disband their forces and to flee.

They and their families were hit hard. The Earl of Northumberland was handed over by the Scots in 1572 in return for £2,000 and beheaded at York for treason after having refused to renounce Catholicism. The Percy stronghold of Warkworth, at one time a major castle, was systematically pillaged of timber and fittings. Westmorland fled overseas and died in the Netherlands in 1601, but the titles and honors of the family were extinguished, and Raby Castle, the family seat, was forfeited to the Crown. The estates of the Dacre family, which also unsuccessfully rebelled, were confiscated.[20] As Shakespeare's plays made abundantly clear, this was scarcely a new policy, for previous rebellious northern earls had also been defeated and killed, notably the Percy opponents of Henry IV. Indeed, *Henry IV, Parts I and II* can in part be read in the echo of the 1569 rising, a link that would have been readily apparent to contemporaries.

Yet the fate of the two earls and their allies represented a significant change in the political geography of the country. Its failure was one of the major stages in the political unification of England, for it marked the end of any viable prospect of regional autonomy centered on a different political and/or religious agenda. This was important because the North of England was more religiously conservative than the South. Even in 1569, the rebellion had been intended to ensure a change in the policy of the central government. Thereafter, politics centered far more on nationwide attempts to influence the center rather than on local efforts to defy it. There was no longer a serious "northern problem" (resistance within northern England) for the security of governments based in southern England, as there had been for most of the previous six hundred years, going back to Northumbrian opposition to the expansion of the Old English House of Wessex in the tenth century. Moreover, some of the forfeited estates went to nobles from the South.

This change was to be consolidated in 1603 with the personal union of England and Scotland when James VI of Scotland became James I of England. The union greatly lessened the possibilities of local magnates playing the two states off against each other. Religion, instead, became more important to the political geography of both England and Scotland.

Retribution after the rising reflected the social politics of Tudor England, including the concern that elite division would provide opportunities for social instability. This retribution demonstrated that Elizabeth was alive to the need to treat the propertied rebels carefully. None of the nineteen leaders from County Durham attainted by the Act of Parliament was executed. Eleven went into exile, while eight were pardoned. The Earl of Northumberland's punishment did not destroy the Percys, for his brother, Sir Henry Percy, had served Elizabeth and became Eighth Earl (although forbidden to live in the North), and many other families were able to save their estates through such divided loyalties. Indeed, the instructions for the court-martial that tried most of the rebels were that those with freehold, copyhold, or estates of substance were to be spared execution. Instead, it was the poor who were punished: different contemporary lists give 228, 305, and 313 as the number of those hanged. Many others had to buy pardons, while the homes and villages of the rebels were plundered. The harsh treatment, however, did not last, as that in Ireland was to do.[21]

The Northern Rising was followed by a marked escalation in tension between Elizabeth's government and Catholic Europe, with the latter encouraging Catholic activism in England, an activism that was part of the Catholic Counter-Reformation.[22] Already, in 1568, Philip II had refused to permit the English envoy to have Protestant services in his home. As a result, there was no resident English envoy in Spain until the war between the two powers that was to begin in 1585 ended in 1604. This lack of an embassy removed an important means of communication, as successive Spanish envoys in London were totally compromised by their willingness to conspire against Elizabeth.

In February 1570, in a direct attack, Pope Pius V, in the bull *Regnans in Excelsis*, excommunicated and deposed Elizabeth, the anointed ruler, a step not taken with Henry VIII. Elizabeth was accused of having "removed the Royal Council, composed of the nobility of England" and having replaced them by "obscure men" who were heretics. Papal intervention in England was to be a hostile theme of Shakespeare's plays *King John* and *Henry VIII*, and this theme referred to Pius V's move.

A major step in terms of the ideology of the period, the papal move made sense of a world of Catholic alienation and exile[23] and promoted and legitimized Catholic conspiracies designed to replace Elizabeth with Mary, Queen of Scots. There were a number of unsuccessful attempts, notably the Ridolfi (1571–72), Throckmorton (1582–83), and Babington (1586) Plots. These conspiracies reflected growing Catholic desperation. Encouraged by the papal bull, the Ridolfi Plot proposed a papal-backed invasion of England by the Duke of Alba, commander of the Spanish army in the Low Countries, in order to help Mary, who was fully involved, as was the Spanish ambassador. The Throckmorton Plot was a response to the failure of marriage negotiation between Elizabeth and Francis, Duke of Anjou, a Catholic, brother to the king of France, and one of the unsuitable options (whether or not formal suitors) that helped leave her unmarried.

The government responded firmly to conspiracies in England, as well as Ireland, developing, notably under Leicester's adroit and thorough ally Francis Walsingham, an effective secret police, including a system of informers and a practice of intercepting and deciphering messages. With parliamentary support, Thomas, Fourth Duke of Norfolk, was beheaded in 1572 for conspiring with Mary, Queen of Scots, and for his role in the Ridolfi Plot. However, Elizabeth refused to back Parliament's call to debar Mary from the succession. Catholics were purged from the Lord Lieutenancy and the Commissions of the Peace, which undercut their local position, were arrested, and were fined. Torture was used. Francis Throckmorton was racked into confessing to the plot of his name and was executed in 1584. Henry, Eighth Earl of Northumberland, who had been committed to the Tower in 1571 for negotiating with Mary, was sent there again in 1582 and 1584—on both occasions because of his involvement in plotting. He died, apparently a suicide, in the Tower in 1585.

A committed Protestant, Walsingham (c. 1532–90), who had left the country during Mary's reign, became a MP in 1559 and worked with Cecil against the Ridolfi Plot. Ambassador in France from 1570 to 1573, he was in Paris during the St. Bartholomew's Day massacre in 1572. In 1573, Walsingham became joint principal secretary of the Privy Council, going on to become the sole principal secretary in 1576. Knighted in 1577, he acted as Elizabeth's spymaster.

The cautious Elizabeth was reluctant, despite pressure from her ministers, to try Mary, both a fellow ruler and a relative. At the same time, Mary's demands that she be released and associated with her son in the government of Scotland were unavailing. In 1586, the interception of Mary's letters revealed that she had agreed to Elizabeth's assassination in the Babington Plot, a conspiracy involving the French ambassador, who was linked to the pro-Spanish Catholic League in France. As a result, with Elizabeth pressed hard by her ministers, Mary was convicted of treason under the 1585 Act of Parliament. This was a questionable charge since, as a fellow monarch, she owed Elizabeth no allegiance.

Mary was beheaded at Fotheringhay Castle on February 8, 1587. Consequently, both the monarchs of Shakespeare's lifetime, Elizabeth I and James I, had mothers who had been beheaded. This throws light on some of the more violent political killings of Shakespeare's plays and underlines the fact that women were scarcely safe from the process. In *The Winter's Tale*, Hermione is unfairly accused of treasonous adultery, a crime punishable by death: here there is an obvious link with the fate of Anne Boleyn, although none with that of Mary. Elizabeth herself was angry with her ministers about the execution, to which she felt she had been driven by pressure as well as necessity. There had certainly been no enthusiasm on her part.

Alongside plots, there was propaganda, and from all sides. Polemics served to mobilize support and direct anger.[24] There were other forms of soft power that the Crown used, ranging from royal progresses around England to prayers for the Crown in church. Progresses provided a public choreography of patronage and grandeur, one that drew on more broad-ranging patterns of structured and structuring ceremonies.[25]

## IRELAND

In Ireland, the attempt to make real Henry VIII's claim to be king of Ireland and the imposition of the Elizabethan Acts of Supremacy and Uniformity led the "Old English" settlers (English who were Catholics) to ally with the native (Gaelic) Irish in defense of Catholicism. Elizabeth failed to understand the nature of Irish society and the difficulties of implementing her policies there, and she did not respond to policy problems in an adroit fashion. The assumption that the anglicization of Ireland by means of the introduction of English law, justice, and much else would work proved flawed. Obedience was no substitute.[26]

The refusal of most of the Irish to accept the Reformation was central to the divergence of Ireland from the general model of British development. Indeed, the different religion and, to a considerable extent, language of the Irish people played a major role in the failure of clientage and policies and in the depersonalizing of the Irish in the minds of the English and Scots. This situation was crucial to the process of the expropriation of much of Ireland and the related establishment of English and Scottish settlement colonies. The pace of such "plantations" increased from the late 1560s, and English rule became more military in character and intent, leading to fresh attempts to extend and enforce control but also being affected by muddled and inconsistent government policies and attitudes.[27]

These, in turn, provoked rebellions, notably in the 1570s, culminating in a major uprising in 1595 ably led by Hugh O'Neill, Earl of Tyrone. That was the probable year of *Richard II*, a play in which the king's presence in Ireland to deal with a rebellion (as indeed happened with Richard in 1399) was important to the plot. Firearms were effectively combined with infantry shock tactics by Tyrone; the wooded and boggy terrain of Ulster was well suited to guerrilla conflict, and English armies were defeated at Clontibret (1595) and Yellow Ford (1598). These defeats only encouraged the English to persist, with Elizabeth determined to suppress rebellion. Robert, Second Earl of Essex, Elizabeth's favorite, was sent with a major force in 1599, although the Irish thwarted him by avoiding battle. Elizabeth was furious with Essex for dubbing eighty-two knights, a step that compromised her control over honors and patronage and one he took in order to keep gentlemen volunteers serving. In *Henry V*, the chorus compares the return of the hero after his triumph at Agincourt in 1415 to both that of Julius Caesar after victory and to Essex, the latter very much an inappropriate comparison:

> Were now the general of our gracious empress [Elizabeth],
> As in good time he may, from Ireland coming,
> Bringing rebellion broached on his sword,
> How many would the peaceful city quit,
> To welcome him! (V, Prologue)

### WAR WITH SPAIN

Meanwhile, in 1585, English military support for Dutch Protestant rebels against Philip II of Spain in the Dutch Revolt, and English raids on Spanish trade and colonies, especially those of Francis Drake (c. 1540–96), had led to the outbreak of war between the two powers. This conflict, which lasted until 1604, saw an English military presence in the Low Countries from 1585, with the army initially commanded by Leicester, a major political commitment. The army had a mixed record; it certainly helped the Dutch but scarcely matched the achievements of Henry V in France.

The war with Spain is most famous for the Armada of 1588, a Spanish attempt to send a major fleet of 130 ships up the English Channel to cover an invasion of England from the Spanish

Netherlands (modern Belgium) by the effective Spanish Army of Flanders, under Alexander Farnese, Duke of Parma. The Armada was thwarted by a combination of poor planning, a skillful English naval response, and the weather. The latter fueled the development of belief in a providential sanction for English Protestantism. To contemporaries, the unassailable nature of divine approval was clear.

The Spanish fleet had sailed along the channel, maintaining a tight formation to protect their more vulnerable vessels, while harried by long-range English gunnery. This did scant damage, and, during nine days of engagements, the Spaniards retained their formation against attack. The English fleet, with the advantage of superior sailing qualities and compact four-wheeled gun carriages, which permitted a high rate of fire (many of the Spanish guns were on cumbersome carriages designed for use on land), suffered even slighter damage and was endangered principally by a shortage of ammunition. When the Spanish fleet anchored off Calais, it found that Parma had been able to assemble the transport vessels necessary to embark his army for England but that they would not come out from port until after the English and Dutch naval squadrons had been defeated.

Instead, the Spaniards lost the initiative. The formation of their fleet was disrupted by an English night attack using fire ships, and the English fleet then inflicted considerable damage in a running battle off Gravelines. A strong southwesterly wind drove the Armada into the North Sea. With no clear tactical objective after Parma's failed embarkation, the Spanish commanders ordered a return to Spain via the hazardous north-about route around the British Isles. However, a succession of violent and unseasonable storms lashed the fleet as it passed north of Scotland and down the rocky west coast of Ireland; ship after ship was smashed or driven ashore, and only a remnant of the fleet and a portion of its crews reached Spain. This outcome made sense of the major role that such storms played in Shakespeare's plays, notably the storm in *Othello* that wrecks the Turkish invasion fleet intended for Cyprus.

Elizabeth's reported speech to the troops assembled at Tilbury east of London in order to repel the likely invasion is well known. She stressed both her own dedication to and her identification with England, and her remarks were not idle ones: four years earlier, William of Orange, the other leading Protestant champion and opponent of Philip II, the leader of the Dutch Revolt, had been assassinated in the Netherlands, an episode that would have sat equally well in a play by John Webster:

> I am come amongst you ... not for my recreation and disport, but being resolved, in the midst and heat of battle, to live and die amongst you all, and to lay down for my God, and my kingdom and for my people, my honour and my blood, even in the dust. I know I have the body of a weak and feeble woman, but I have the heart and stomach of a king, and of a king of England too, and think foul scorn that [the Duke of] Parma or [the King of] Spain, or any Prince of Europe should dare to invade the borders of my realm.

This speech, the authenticity of which is controversial,[28] displayed some of the rhetorical practices of the period, practices best used by Shakespeare in the speech given to Mark Antony in *Julius Caesar*. However, in a contrast also seen in Shakespeare's *Henry V*, with the depiction of the brave and noble Henry very different to that of some of his army, notably Bardolph (executed for looting), Nym (also hanged for looting), and Pistol (a fraud),[29] the situation might have been less happy had the army of Flanders landed. The English defenses were inadequate: poor fortifications, insufficient and mostly poorly trained troops, and inadequate supplies. In addition, defensive coverage was patchy. The council was convinced that London was the key target, and there was particular concern about the Spaniards landing on the Essex bank of the Thames and thus not needing to fight their way through Kent and across the Thames. London Bridge could thereby be circumvented. It was scarcely surprising that Providence was seen as at work in England's survival.

England is invaded in Shakespeare's plays, in *Cymbeline, King John, Richard II, Henry VI, Part Three, Richard III*, and *King Lear,* although without any discussion of the issues involved. Nevertheless, the audience would have lived in the shadow of invasion. Indeed, the Spaniards launched two further armadas against England, in 1596 and 1597, only for them to be turned back by bad weather, which led, as in 1588, to the idea of Protestant winds protecting England. A Spanish force landed in southern Ireland in 1601 but was abandoned by its fleet, which returned to Spain. Trapped by gales and blockaded by English ships in the port of Kinsale, the force was besieged by land. The Spaniards surrendered after the decisive defeat of an Irish relief attempt.[30]

In turn, the English failed in a combined operation against Lisbon in 1589. As with so many combined operations (and, indeed, conventional land or sea ones), this was one that suffered from conflicting aims. In the event, having lost surprise by mounting an attack on the Spanish port of Corunna—the Spanish port most suitable, due to its position, for an invasion of England—the English made a successful amphibious assault (opposed landing) at Peniche on the Atlantic coast, some fifty miles from Lisbon. However, hopes that the countryside would rise in support of the pretender to the Portuguese throne (held since 1580 by Philip II), Dom Antonio, an ally of the English, proved unfounded, while the landing in part gave away the tactical and operational initiative to the Spanish defenders. This was common with combined operations. So also with the extent to which the army lost men as it advanced. Meanwhile, Drake, the English naval commander, sailed to the mouth of the Tagus estuary, only to fail to force the forts guarding the entrance to Lisbon. In contrast, an expedition that had sailed directly for Lisbon and focused its force against the forts there would possibly have succeeded.[31]

A large Anglo-Dutch combined operation, involving about 6,000 troops, achieved surprise when it attacked the Spanish port of Cadiz in 1596. In that clash, both the attacking and the defending sides relied on combined forces. The Spanish fleet was supported by the guns of the city, while the ably commanded Anglo-Dutch force fought its way into the defended anchorage and conducted a successful opposed landing followed by the storming of the city, which lacked adequate defenses. The competence of the English naval gunners was important. The expectation of reward from the city and the merchant fleet was a powerful motivating factor for the soldiers and sailors of the combined forces.[32] One of the galleons captured at Cadiz was the *Andrew* mentioned in *The Merchant of Venice*.

The attacks on Spanish ports, like those on hostile positions in France and the Low Countries, reflected a determination to defend England's maritime frontiers. Given Spanish amphibious attacks—for example, a landing, albeit small scale and unsuccessful, at Smerwick in Ireland in 1580—and attempts, notably the 1588 Armada, this was a reasonable approach. Indeed, as a result, there was an essential coherence in English war making, one in which land and naval capabilities and operations were linked. This was not only a matter of combined operations against targets abroad but also of often linked amphibious assaults specifically designed to thwart the preparations of opponents, as with attacks on Cadiz and Corunna. The latter assaults were part of a broader pattern of defense by both land and sea.

The English were less successful when they launched combined operations against Brittany and Normandy in 1590. These were designed to win success by means of allying in the French Wars of Religion with the Huguenots (French Protestants), who were opposed to Spain and to Spain's French allies. In particular, there was a need to deny Spain naval bases near England. Reality proved otherwise. The Normandy expedition rapidly failed, in part due to the impact of disease on English troop numbers. The

Breton commitment lasted longer but again with only limited results.

The English also launched assaults on Spanish possessions in the New World, notably on Hispaniola, the island that is now divided between Haiti and the Dominican Republic. Most dramatically, on New Year's Day 1586, a fleet of seven large ships and twenty-two others, under Drake, attacked Santo Domingo, the capital of Hispaniola. Having landed nearby, the English forces advanced through the plantations outside the city, before capturing it and extracting a 25,000-ducat ransom. In strategic terms, these attacks posed a threat to the transatlantic flow of silver on which Spain depended heavily. A strong element of private initiative and the hope of gain supported the English enterprises in the West Indies. Although the numerous privateering expeditions were not all a success, they were a high-risk, high-reward investment. There were some remarkable achievements, including James Lancaster's capture of the port of Pernambuco in Brazil in 1594 and George, Third Earl of Cumberland's, of San Juan in 1598. The Dutch were similarly successful in the Canary Islands in 1599. The Spanish response was multifaceted. It included the improvement of fortifications at key points, notably Panama and Portobello, the key points on the route across the Panama peninsula, as well as later replacing the *flota*, the silver fleet, with crossings by fast ships (*fragatas*) sailing alone.

## THE CRISIS-RIDDEN CLOSE OF ELIZABETH'S REIGN

Despite the defeat of the Armada, Elizabeth's reign did not end on a triumphant note. Inflation and a lack of Crown revenue created a difficult situation, one accentuated for the government and others by the fact that the war with Spain continued until 1604 while there was also a seemingly intractable struggle in Ireland in the 1590s. It was scarcely surprising that, in comparison, Henry V was much praised. This was true not only of the play of

that name, but also in *Henry VI, Part I*, in which one of his brothers, Humphrey, Duke of Gloucester, was given the role of praising
the dead leader:

> His brandished sword did blind men with his beams;
> His arms spread wider than a dragon's wings;
> His sparkling eyes, replete with wrathful fire,
> More dazzled and drove back his enemies
> Than midday sun fierce bent against their faces. (I, i)

As a woman, Elizabeth could not play that role, but neither would
the unmartial James I be able to do so.

Economic difficulties made the situation much grimmer for
government and public alike. Elizabeth preferred to address
public expenditure rather than reform the revenue system, and
demands for additional taxation and attempts to raise funds by
unpopular expedients—especially forced loans, ship money, and
the sale of monopolies to manufacture or sell certain goods—
led to bitter criticism in the Parliaments of 1597 and 1601. Using
monopolies to pass on the cost of patronage to the consumer
was a politically far more problematic course than disposing of
Church lands. Tax demands were especially unwelcome because
of harvest failures and related social tensions. In London, the city
authorities complained about the royal court's tolerance of aristocratic practices, such as rowdiness, the violent assertion of honor,
and the patronage of brothels, theaters, and gambling houses, as
well as the reprieves given for convicted felons.

As a separate issue, the Cecils had made a large fortune.
Burghley had three palaces and was able to establish each of his
two sons with substantial estates, estates linked to the dignity
of earl to which they were each raised. Similarly, Hatton made a
great fortune, in part from royal favor, and built a splendid house
at Holdenby. This situation contributed to a widespread sense of
corruption and malaise.

Meanwhile, Puritanism remained a political problem; and
Shakespeare referred to aspects of it, as in the outward compliance

of Puritan clergy in wearing "the surplice of humility over the black gown," the Anglican garb over the Calvinist Geneva gown (*All's Well That Ends Well*, I, iii).

Elizabeth had always faced a degree of unpopularity,[33] but by the 1590s, there were problems—political, social, economic, and religious—aplenty, as earlier difficulties and tensions came to the fore.[34] These problems interacted with politics, including within the regime, with contradictory demands, for example, in foreign policy or those of anti-Puritanism and antipopery, being pursued and manipulated accordingly.[35] Moreover, the government had a stopgap feel to it, in part due to the queen's longevity but apparently imminent death. Elizabeth had been born in 1533. Moreover, she was less adept and tolerant in her last years than she had been earlier in the reign. As Elizabeth survived but aged, the issue of the succession remained highly contentious, both politically and culturally. She refused to designate James as her successor, a step, she said, that would be to have her own winding sheet laid out before her eyes. However, this refusal left an uncertain James uneasily seeking to build up support, which, in turn, exacerbated tensions with Elizabeth and within the English government.[36]

These problems and issues affected the theater. In or before 1597, the "abdication" scene in *Richard II*, a sensitive presentation of the enforced overthrow of a monarch, was removed. Rumors about plays, for example, the alleged politics of *The Isle of Dogs* (1597) by Thomas Nashe, contributed to tension focused on the theater.[37] Indeed, the difficulties of the period were captured in Shakespeare's plays.[38] So also was the broader range of political opinion, one that should not be simply reduced to mixed monarchy or monarchical republicanism.[39] As a unitary state, England could not be divided to suit the views of a ruler, as King Lear did at the outset of Shakespeare's play (probably late 1605). Moreover, the division of the country depicted in *Henry IV, Part I* was readily presented as both wrong and a proof of the malign character of the conspirators against the king who quarreled over the terms of this division.

In 1601, the conspiracy of Robert, Second Earl of Essex (1566–1601), a royal favorite disgraced after his failure in Ireland in 1599, was very much set against a background of disorder and in a febrile atmosphere of rumor and uncertainty, notably over the royal succession. Policies also played a role. Continuing the emphasis shown by Leicester, Essex supported a determined prosecution of the war with Spain, as well as an emphasis on Protestantism as a basis for policy. Like Leicester, he represented military experience, although also showing the difficulties it posed to political position, since it led to a dependence on a continued success that was not at the command of the court or of individual commanders. Moreover and more specifically, Essex's loss of favor was hitting him financially. In debt, like many other aristocrats, he was threatened by the loss in 1600 of his lease of the customs revenue from imported sweet wines. Essex planned to take control of Elizabeth in order to secure his position and to destroy his rival, the chief minister, Burghley's son Sir Robert Cecil, later Earl of Salisbury. Essex sought more power for the nobility vis à vis the Crown and remarked, "To serve as a servant and a slave I know not."[40] He was supported by six other peers, including Shakespeare's onetime patron Henry, Third Earl of Southampton, who had lost his post of master of the horse as a result of losing Elizabeth's favor.

Essex failed totally. In an impetuous and mistaken act of heroic chivalry, Essex wanted to force his way into the queen's presence, overcoming the prohibition on his doing so, and then to make himself a key advisor.[41] This was a position and a means she was not prepared to accept.[42] There was no successful coup, let alone a civil war comparable to that recently in France. On February 8, 1601, Essex, ignoring the order given him the previous day to go to court and explain his conduct, detained the four members of the council who came to see him to reiterate the command and, instead, sought to raise the city, only to find that, while he had failed in that, Robert Cecil had blocked the exit from the city toward Westminster at Ludgate. Thwarted, the incompetent Essex returned to Essex House, which was besieged until he surrendered. Aside from Essex, five others were executed but none of the peers who had backed him. The pattern offered by Essex was dangerous, which was why an example had to be made of him.

Essex had supported the revival of Tacitus, a Roman writer critical of imperial tyranny, a theme offered to the public in Ben Jonson's play *Sejanus* (1603 or 1604), about the Roman emperor Tiberius's dominant minister. John Hayward made much use of Tacitus. Henry Savile, translator of Tacitus, was a protégé of Essex, who may well have been guided by Tacitean concepts (derived from republican sympathies in the period of imperial Rome) of the need to resist tyrants and to drive out evil ministers. These ideas had also been pushed to the fore by Huguenot writers during the French Wars of Religion and were more generally associated with Calvinism. Others might have shared these thoughts, but Essex was ready to act, and without the motivation of a Catholicism linked to the excommunication of Elizabeth. Yet his attitude cut across the ethos of political order, the respect for monarchy, and political prudence.[43]

Essex's rising did not prove a major crisis, but it was staged in London and it touched Shakespeare's own position: the Lord Chamberlain's Men, the company of actors with whom he was linked, was paid by the conspirators to revive *Richard II*, including the deposition scene that had been prohibited in the published version, on the eve of the rebellion. Indeed, Elizabeth told William Lambarde soon after: "I am Richard II, know ye not that."[44] In 1600, John Hayward had been arrested and imprisoned for his *The First Part of the Life and Reign of Henry IV,* a history, including an account of the deposition of Richard, that was published in 1599 and fulsomely dedicated to Essex. Hayward was released after Essex's execution and found it prudent to display conspicuous loyalty. The continued resonance of Shakespeare's play was seen when Nahum Tate's adaptation of *Richard II* (1680) was banned because of its potential relevance during the Exclusion Crisis (1679–81). This was an attempt to exclude James II (a grandson of James I) from the succession to his brother Charles II because James was a Catholic. In the words of one modern historian, Shakespeare more generally had "bought rather heavily into the Essex project" and "got things spectacularly wrong."[45]

Later in 1601, the government faced criticism in Parliament, including about taxation and monopolies. As a result, concessions were made, with the most unpopular monopolies abolished. Elizabeth felt it appropriate to give an audience to the members of the House of Commons in which she spoke of her love for them.

The increasing widespread politicization that was a feature of sixteenth-century England did not, in the event, present insuperable problems. Essex's failure can even contribute to the argument that the crisis of the 1590s has been exaggerated, both in a relative sense and regarding contemporary perceptions about English politics and, in particular, political ideology and practice. This tension in the evaluation of crisis and success, the fact that both were present, is of considerable relevance in considering the background to Shakespeare's work. At any rate, the Stuart succession was inaugurated in 1603 without a civil war, even though England was still at war with Spain.

Instead, very differently, the long war with Spain influenced and focused antipopery[46] and contributed to a stronger national consciousness, one seen with Shakespeare's plays and also with the focus on the vernacular and not on Latinity. This cultural change had a political background, one in which, from the Reformation, there was a clear anglicization in political purpose and reference, while, more specifically, parliamentary management became increasingly important during the long reign of Elizabeth. This was an aspect of a shift in the politics of the country away from a focus on relations between Crown and aristocracy and, instead, toward relations between Crown and gentry, a pattern that offered a new version of the policies followed by Henry VII.

At the center, although the royal court remained the major focus of politics, notably at the elite level, this process led to a greater role for Parliament and a stress on ideas of representation and, in the localities, to the growing importance of the gentry as justices of the peace. The rise of a numerous and independent gentry with a sense of obligation to public duty, a process mocked in *Henry IV, Part II*, in the person of Justice Robert Shallow, was linked to the failure of the peerage (aristocracy) to be the prime beneficiary of the sociopolitical changes of the period. The creation of stronger links between Crown and gentry was fundamental to the achievement of the Elizabethan period and helped ensure that the problems of the last fifteen years of the reign did not lead to instability on the level of the mid-sixteenth or the mid-seventeenth centuries.

The emphasis on the gentry rather than the aristocracy had possible echoes in Shakespeare's plays. This was not least in the apparent qualification of heroism, seen for example in *Antony and Cleopatra*, which was probably first performed in late 1606 and which very much differed from that in *Henry V*, probably first staged in 1599. More particularly, England had moved from war to peace in 1604, and this may have affected the choice of values for praise. There was also the particular need to confront Mark Antony's career and reputation. Unlike Henry V, he could be presented as a self-indulgent opponent of order and prudence.

With the gentry playing the key role in the House of Commons, Parliament was a national body, whereas the nearest equivalent in France, the Estates-General, had less impact (and was not summoned between 1614 and 1789) than the regional estates, which kept strong a sense of regional difference, for example in Brittany and Languedoc. In his *De Republica Anglorum* (1565), Sir Thomas Smith argued that the consent of the Parliament was taken to be every man's consent and that the source of sovereign authority was the Crown in Parliament. In the 1580s, William Lambarde noted the "stacks of statutes" that the justices of the peace were told to implement. Indeed, they came to have a greater contact with the expectations and demands of central government.

James was the only child of Mary, Queen of Scots, which raises interesting questions as to what the consequences would have been had she had a daughter. Having followed the enforced abdication of his mother by ruling Scotland as James VI from 1567 (initially as a baby), James came to the throne of England as James I in 1603, in a coronation in which English was used in place of Latin. Already a monarch who, in Scotland, had had to cope with the shifts and expedients of a weak position, notably bitter aristocratic factionalism, James was the beneficiary of Tudor-Stuart dynastic links. He inherited the English throne as a result of the marriage of Henry VII's elder daughter Margaret with James IV, combined with the failure of all three of Henry VIII's legitimate children, only one of whom had married, to have children of their own and the execution of his mother.

When James went south to claim his new crown in 1603, the transition was managed with far less difficulty than had been anticipated, and he stayed in England for the rest of his reign, except for one visit back to Scotland. He was therefore less exposed than his Scottish predecessors to the impact of quarrels between Scottish lords or to their defiance of royal authority. Scotland, however, remained an independent state, governed by the Scottish Privy Council and with a separate parliament. Despite contemporary interest in the example of the union of Poland and Lithuania[47] and James's hopes for a "union of love," or, at least, a measure of administrative and economic union between England and Scotland, the union remained essentially personal. There was fear in England about the legal and constitutional implications, and the Westminster Parliament rejected a parliamentary or legal bond. The union of Portugal and Spain (1580–1640) was similarly personal.

James was Shakespeare's second monarch. He proved a figure whom it was difficult to incorporate into heroic accounts. As ruler both in Scotland and in England, a success that had eluded his predecessors and that represented a major triumph for the Stuart dynasty, James, nevertheless, lacked charisma and found it difficult to win respect or affection. As *Henry V* chronologically succeeded *Henry IV, Parts I and II*, the dissolute Prince Hal was shown by Shakespeare as rising to the occasion and to the need for majesty, when he came to the throne as Henry V. However, there was to be no such clear transition for James in 1603.

James was certainly well educated, well read, perceptive, thoughtful, and conciliatory, as well as complex and self-indulgent. His conciliatory, albeit stubborn, character and his appreciation of the constraints of his position helped limit religious tensions. More generally, presenting himself as moderate, James castigated opponents as extremists. His different self-images included an authoritarian Constantinian image that had little time for opposition, linked to his commonplace stress on royal authority as having a religious role. With his emphasis on authority, James therefore offered a model of sacral kingship, which paralleled that on the Continent, including in Catholic states.[48] At the same time, he was interested in other writers and could be receptive to their arguments.[49]

However, with James, the contrast between image and reality was more abrupt and harsher than with Elizabeth. The bisexual and spendthrift king presided over a corrupt and sleazy court that did little to foster the prestige of either James or the monarchy or to win support for his policies. As he was no warrior king and preferred to pursue controversy in print, for example, in favor of the divine right of kings, James did not gain glory through victory. None of the biblical models of kingship was truly present in James. The range of associations offered by James's kingship both provided multiple and conflicting contexts for Shakespeare's plays and ensured that these plays could be seen as supportive or critical or disengaged with aspects of this kingship.

The Gunpowder Plot of 1605 was the headline event in James's reign, although the King James Version of the Bible was a more important lasting legacy. The plot was the culmination of a series of conspiracies relating to power and religion before, with, and after James's accession, as hopes were advanced and thwarted.[50] In general, religious tension diminished, helped by the end of war with Spain in 1604, a measure in line with Elizabethan policy, and by James's attempts to lessen differences between Protestants, although that was not how Puritans saw it. At the Hampton Court Conference of 1604, James allowed theologians of various Protestant views to participate. He himself had strong views on religious observance and on appropriate behavior on Sundays and backed moderate church reform, as well as being interested in the reunion of Christendom or, at least, of Protestantism and Catholicism.

In the Gunpowder Plot, however, a small group of Catholics had put gunpowder in the cellars under Parliament, planning to blow it up when James opened the session on November 5, 1605 and hoping that the destruction of the royal family and the Protestant elite would ignite rebellion. The attempt to warn a Catholic peer, William, Fourth Baron Monteagle, to be absent, led to the exposure of the plot. Seized with the gunpowder, Guy Fawkes was tortured (a vicious process) to reveal the names of his coconspirators and then brutally executed. A number of conspirators, including Robert Catesby, died resisting arrest. Henry Percy, Ninth Earl of Northumberland, was sent to the Tower and held there until 1621, although his crime was Catholicism rather than conspiracy.

The exposure of the Gunpowder Plot was not followed by any attempt to extirpate Catholicism, but it launched the rhetoric of anti-Catholicism into an apocalyptic overdrive that, in turn, underlined the providential account of England's role in God's particular purpose.[51] This was a conflict different from that recently ended with Spain but more threatening. Shakespeare was influenced by this context. In *Macbeth*, there is mention of "an equivocator, that could swear in both the scales against either scale; who committed treason enough for God's sake, yet could not equivocate to heaven" (II, iii). This is a reference to the trial of the Jesuit father Henry Garnet for complicity in the Gunpowder Plot, a trial that led to his conviction and execution for treason in 1606. The eclipses in *King Lear* and the mention accordingly of "mutinies," "discord," and "treason" (I, ii) have also been linked with the plot.

James, however, sought a Christian reunion, a goal linked to his desire for peace. His wish for an ecumenical church council got nowhere,[52] and he failed to mediate successfully in the European crisis of the Thirty Years' War (1618–48). The embassy of James, Earl of Doncaster, that he sent to Germany in 1619 was mocked for its large size and failed to prevent the spread of the conflict.[53]

Catholic zealots were a target of writers, but so also was Puritanism. Puritans could be satirized, as with the hypocritical zealot, Zeal-of-the-Land Busy, in Ben Jonson's *Bartholomew Fair* (1614), an exuberant account of a lively London, and with "we of the separation" in his *The Alchemist* (1610); and Shakespeare glanced at them in *Twelfth Night* with Malvolio, albeit briefly. At the same time, the Puritans highlighted a set of values, including self-restraint and family cohesion, against which the royal court appeared morally and emotionally corrupt. Little Moreton Hall, with its biblical texts decorating the chapel and the parlor frieze depicting the story of Susannah and the Elders, was a world away from James's tastes.

In spite of a maintaining a love match with Anne of Denmark (1574–1619), herself a convert to Catholicism,[54] and fathering three children, the bisexual James was also keen on a series of pretty and greedy young men. This had serious political implications because of his willingness to promote them into the aristocracy and at court. In what became a major scandal, one favorite, Robert Carr, Earl of Somerset, and his wife were found guilty of poisoning Sir Thomas Overbury in the Tower of London in 1613 but were reprieved by James. Overbury knew too much about the seamy side of court intrigues. Another unpopular and greedy favorite, George Villiers, the handsome son of a minor gentleman, became royal cupbearer in 1614, a gentleman of the bedchamber in 1615, master of the horse and a viscount in 1616, and Duke of Buckingham in 1623, only to be assassinated in 1628 in the next reign. Such activity greatly helped affect the depiction of court life in the plays of the period.

A challenge to this style of the court was that of James's eldest son, Prince Henry, who became Prince of Wales in 1610, notably with an impressive parliamentary installation that was popularly seen as a quasi coronation.[55] Henry offered the muscular kingship that James conspicuously lacked, was a keen supporter of Protestantism and also a patron of the arts, and was linked to the world of theater himself, taking the lead role in Ben Jonson's masque *Oberon, the Fairy Prince* (1611). From 1603 to 1612, the Admiral's Men, the principal rivals of Shakespeare's company of players, was known as Prince Henry's Men. However, Henry, who would have been Henry IX, predeceased his father in 1612, dying of typhoid.[56]

This left the way clear for his less flexible and intelligent brother Charles, who became Charles I in 1625, with many claiming that Buckingham had murdered James in order to make way for his friend. There was no evidence for this charge, but it reflected the uneasiness about court life that was to the fore, as well as concern about Spanish influence,[57] concern that looked back to the reign of Mary in the 1550s. Buckingham had unsuccessfully backed a Spanish marriage for Charles, the two men going to Madrid to that end in 1623. In the event, Charles did make a Catholic marriage, soon after his accession, but with Henrietta Maria, a French princess, the sister of Louis XIII.

James himself had some significant interest in drama, although more in masques than in plays. He established the King's Men, and *Measure for Measure* may reflect his taste. Queen Anne was also a patron of court masques. Plays offered very different views of life, although criticism of royal courts was an important theme in many. There could be even more dramatic attacks. In 1621, a play written by Jasper Garnett, a local schoolmaster, and put on in Kendal Castle led to Garnett being accused in Star Chamber of making subversive comments. He responded: "What was then acted was a representation of ravens feeding off poor sheep in Hell, which ravens were compared to greedy landlords and the sheep to their poor tenants . . . but the same was not intended against any of the County of Westmorland than against other counties and all in general."

More commonly, there was a sense of decline from a better past, a sense that is a frequent theme in drama but one that is important for all that. Thus, in *All's Well That Ends Well*, which probably appeared in 1604, the elderly Countess of Rossillion, the king of France, and his adviser, Lord Lafeu, all look to the past, remembering an age of past honor and meaning. They are concerned with reality as opposed to appearance, with the king stating:

> Good alone
> Is good, without a name; vileness is so:
> The property by what it is should go,
> Not by the title. (II, iii)

Language is thereby used to decry the lack of meaning in words.

James's policies were mistrusted, and he could not avoid mounting debts. He did not understand the character of Parliament, while MPs did not greatly appreciate his views. However, although the Addled Parliament of 1614 proved acrimonious and short, James acquired a degree of competence in the difficult management of English parliamentary and religious politics, as he had earlier done with the hard world of Scottish factionalism.[58] In England and Scotland, there was no breakdown of control or stability akin to those in France and the Holy Roman Empire

(Germany) in the 1610s and early 1620s. Nevertheless, James's accession helped bring the issue of Britishness forward, both politically and culturally,[59] and very differently from the situation under Mary, Queen of Scots. Britishness, consciousness that drew in part on Welsh nationalism,[60] posed difficulties, notably with Ireland in the 1590s and early 1600s. Thanks to crises for British-level policies of anglicization and for local policies of a new order, first in Scotland in the late 1630s and then in Ireland in 1641, Britishness was to help provoke political breakdown across the British Isles as a whole.[61]

Nevertheless, in the shorter term of Shakespeare's life, with James I's accession peaceful and the Irish rebellion defeated, the king appeared to present success and stability, and notably so after the suppression of the Gunpowder Plot in 1605. Opportunities for prosperity and success seemed improved. In addition, the punishment of opinion continued to fall from the peaks under Henry VIII and Mary.[62] Given the prominence of violence in the plays of Shakespeare and his contemporaries, both in high-political terms and as an aspect of the life of the public and of political expression at that level,[63] a prominence that reflected reality,[64] this was a reassuring close to the playwright's life.

## NOTES

1. G. Elton, *The Tudor Revolution in Government: Administrative Changes in the Reign of Henry VIII* (Cambridge, 1953), *Reform and Renewal: Thomas Cromwell and the Common Weal* (Cambridge, 1973), and *Policy and Police: the Enforcement of the Reformation in the Age of Thomas Cromwell* (Cambridge, 1973); D. Loades, *Thomas Cromwell: Servant to Henry VIII* (Stroud, UK, 2014). For recent skepticism, M. Everett, *The Rise of Thomas Cromwell: Power and Politics in the Reign of Henry VIII* (New Haven, CT, 2015).

2. M. Stoyle, "'Fullye Bente to Fighte Oute the Matter': Reconsidering Cornwall's Role in the Western Rebellion of 1549," *English Historical Review* 129 (2014): 549–77.

3. D. MacCulloch, "Kett's Rebellion in Context," *Past and Present*, no. 84 (1979).

4. G. W. Bernard, *Power and Politics in Tudor England* (Aldershot, UK, 2000), 134–60.

5. J. Loach, *Edward VI* (New Haven, CT, 2002); S. Alford, *Kingship and Politics in the Reign of Edward VI* (Cambridge, 2002).

6. A. Blakeway, "The Anglo-Scottish War of 1558 and the Scottish Reformation," *History* 102 (2017): 201–24.

7. R. J. W. Evans, *The Making of the Habsburg Monarchy, 1550–1700: An Interpretation* (Oxford, 1979).

8. M. Dobson and T. S. Freeman, eds., *England's Elizabeth: An Afterlife in Fame and Fantasy* (Oxford, 2002).

9. S. Doran, *Elizabeth I and Her Circle* (Oxford, 2015).

10. E. Baskerville, "A Religious Disturbance in Canterbury, June 1561: John Bale's Unpublished Account," *Historical Research* 65 (1992): 340–41.

11. C. Bajetta, G. Coatelen, and J. Gibson, *Elizabeth I's Foreign Correspondence: Letters, Rhetoric, and Politics* (Basingstoke, UK, 2014).

12. A. Ryrie, *Being Protestant in Reformation Britain* (Oxford, 2013).

13. P. Collinson, *Elizabethan Puritan Movement* (London, 1967) and *Richard Bancroft and Elizabethan Anti-Puritanism* (Cambridge, 2013); J. Crawford, *Mediatrix: Women, Politics, and Literary Production in Early Modern England* (Oxford, 2014).

14. A. Wall, "Religion and the Composition of the Commissions of the Peace, 1547–1640," *History* 103 (2018): 223–42.

15. W. B. Patterson, *William Perkins and the Making of a Protestant England* (Oxford, 2014).

16. N. Jones, *Governing by Virtue: Lord Burghley and the Management of Elizabethan England* (Oxford, 2015).

17. G. Kilroy, *Edmund Campion: A Scholarly Life* (Farnham, UK, 2015).

18. J. Martin and A. Ryrie, eds., *Private and Domestic Devotion in Early Modern Britain* (Farnham, UK, 2012); N. Mears and A. Ryrie, eds., *Worship and the Parish Church in Early Modern Britain* (Farnham, UK, 2012).

19. M. King, *So High a Blood: The Life of Margaret, Countess of Lennox* (London, 2017).

20. K. J. Kesselring, *The Northern Rebellion of 1569: Faith, Politics and Protest in Elizabethan England* (Basingstoke, UK, 2007).

21. Kesserlring, *The Northern Rebellion*.

22. A. Walsham, *Catholic Reformation in Protestant Britain* (Farnham, UK, 2014).

23. B. Lockey, *Early Modern Catholics, Royalists, and Cosmopolitans: English Transnationalism and the Christian Commonwealth* (Farnham, UK, 2015).

24. P. Lake, *Bad Queen Bess? Libels, Secret Histories, and the Politics of Publicity in the Reign of Queen Elizabeth I* (Oxford, 2016).

25. D. Rutledge, ed., *Ceremony and Text in the Renaissance* (Newark, DE, 1996).

26. B. Kane and V. McGowan-Doyle, eds., *Elizabeth I and Ireland* (Cambridge, 2014).

27. M. A. Hutchinson, *Calvinsim, Reform and the Absolutist State in Elizabethan Ireland* (London, 2015).

28. B. T. Whitehead, *Braggs and Boasts: Propaganda in the Year of the Armada* (Stroud, UK, 1994).

29. For the bleak reality, P. Thomas, "Vagabond Soldiers and Deserters at Elizabethan Northampton," *Northamptonshire Past and Present* 9 (1995–96): 101–10.

30. D. Elkin, *The Last Armada: Queen Elizabeth, Juan del Águila, and Hugh O'Neill; The Story of the 100-day Spanish Invasion* (London, 2016).

31. R. B. Wernham, ed., *The Expedition of Sir John Norris and Sir Francis Drake to Spain and Portugal, 1589* (London, 1986).

32. Wernham, "Amphibious Operations and the Elizabethan Assault on the Spanish Atlantic Economy 1585–1598," in *Amphibious Warfare 1000–1700*, ed. D. Trim and M. Fissell (Leiden, UK, 2005), 203–7.

33. J. Walker, ed., *Dissing Elizabeth: Negative Representations of Gloriana* (Durham, NC, 1998).

34. J. Guy, ed., *The Reign of Elizabeth I: Court and Culture in the Last Decade* (Cambridge, 1995).

35. P. Lake, "A Tale of Two Episcopal Surveys: The Strange Fates of Edmund Grindal and Cuthbert Mayne Revisited," *Transactions of the Royal Historical Society* 18 (2008): 162.

36. J.-C. Mayer, ed., *The Struggle for the Succession in Late Elizabethan England: Politics, Polemics and Cultural Representations* (Montpellier, Fr., 2004).

37. M. Teramura, "Richard Topcliffe's Informant: New Light on *The Isle of Dogs*," *Review of English Studies* 68 (2017): 44–59.

38. J. Shapiro, *1599: A Year in the Life of William Shakespeare* (London, 2005).

39. J. F. McDiarmaid, ed., *The Monarchical Republic of Early Modern England* (Farnham, UK, 2007); R. Rapple, "Elizabethan Absolutism and

Tamburlaine's Tents: Sir Humphrey Gilbert Reads *De Republica Anglorum*," *English Historical Review* 132 (2017): 38–40.

40. W. Camden, *Annales London* (1635), 494.

41. P. Hanmer, "Shakespeare's *Richard II*, the play of 7 February 1601 and the Essex Rising," *Shakespeare Quarterly* 59 (2008): 1–35.

42. J. Dickinson, *Court Politics and the Earl of Essex, 1589–1601* (London, 2012).

43. A. Gajda, *The Earl of Essex and Late Elizabethan Political Culture* (Oxford, 2012).

44. Jason Scott-Warren, "Was Elizabeth I Richard II? The Authenticity of Lambarde's 'Conversation,'" *Review of English Studies* 64 (2012): 208–30.

45. P. Lake, *How Shakespeare Put Politics on the Stage: Power and Succession in the History Plays* (New Haven, CT, 2016), 602.

46. J. Lock, "'How Many Tercios Has the Pope?' The Spanish War and the Sublimation of Elizabethan Anti-Popery," *History* 81 (1996): 197–214.

47. S. Sobecki, "John Peyton's *A Relation of the State of Polonia* and the Accession of King James I, 1598–1603," *English Historical Review* 109 (2014): 1079–97.

48. R. Asch, *Sacral Kingship between Disenchantment and Re-enchantment: The French and English Monarchies, 1587–1688* (Oxford, 2014).

49. J. Rickard, *Writing the Monarch in Jacobean England: Jonson, Donne, Shakespeare and the Works of King James* (Cambridge, 2015).

50. M. Nicholls, *Investigating the Gunpowder Plot* (Manchester, 1991) and "Treason's Reward: The Punishment of Conspirators in the Bye Plot of 1603," *Historical Journal* 38 (1995): 821–42.

51. H. Hirschfeld, "'Wildfire at Midnight': The *Revenger's* Tragedy and the Gunpowder Plot," *Review of English Studies* 68 (2017): 60–78.

52. W. B. Patterson, *King James VI and I and the Reunion of Christendom* (Cambridge, 1997).

53. E. McCabe, "England's Foreign Policy in 1619: Lord Doncaster's Embassy to the Princes of Germany," *Mitteilungen des Instituts für Osterreichische Geschichtsforschung* 58 (1950): 457–77.

54. M. Meikle and H. Payne, "From Lutheranism to Catholicism: The Faith of Anna of Denmark (1574–1619)," *Journal of Ecclesiastical History* 64 (2013).

55. P. Croft, "The Parliamentary Installation of Henry, Prince of Wales," *Historical Research* 65 (1992): 177–93.

56. R. Strong, *Henry, Prince of Wales and England's Lost Renaissance* (London, 1986).

57. A. Bellany and T. Cogswell, *The Murder of James I* (New Haven, CT, 2015).

58. D. Newton, *The Making of the Jacobean Regime: James VI and I and the Government of England, 1603–1605* (Woodbridge, UK, 2005); T. Harris, *Rebellion: Britain's First Stuart Kings* (Oxford, 2014).

59. G. Burgess, R. Wymer, and J. Lawrence, eds., *The Accession of James I: Historical and Cultural Consequences* (Basingstoke, UK, 2006).

60. P. Schwyzer, *Literature, Nationalism and Memory in Early Modern England and Wales* (Cambridge, 2004).

61. A. Hadfield, *Shakespeare, Spenser and the Matter of Britain* (Basingstoke, UK, 2003).

62. D. Cressy, *Dangerous Talk: Scandalous, Seditious, and Treasonable Speech in Pre-Modern England* (Oxford, 2010).

63. R. A. Foakes, *Shakespeare and Violence* (Cambridge, 2003).

64. R. Rapple, *Martial Power and Elizabethan Political Culture: Military Men in England, 1558–1594* (Cambridge, 2009).

# THE POLITICAL IMAGINATION

O piteous spectacle! O bloody times!
Whilst lions war and battle for their dens,
Poor harmless lambs abide [endure] their enmity.

—Henry VI in *Henry VI, Part III* (II, v)

THE AUDIENCE OF *HENRY VI, Part III*, seeing a son who has unwittingly killed his father during the Wars of the Roses in its most bloody battle, Towton in 1461, would have been very familiar with the idea that civil war meant breakdown and horror. Strife within the family went back to the Bible, while civil war as a key historical factor went back to the classical world, notably the collapse of the Roman republic, and could readily be presented in Shakespeare's Roman plays. The predictions of disorder surrounding the assassination of Julius Caesar were given added force when anointed and rightful monarchs were killed, as with the murder of Duncan in *Macbeth* and of Richard II and Henry VI, although not of Richard III. Fears about anarchy and disorder were represented in the plays as an aspect of the depiction of the "great chain of being" that linked everything in a divinely ordained order.

The fear of disorder drove control and repression; and much of the drama of the Reformation and of Tudor politics was played out in London, Shakespeare's backdrop as a dramatist. Those who opposed the royal will met with summary punishment and very much as a public spectacle. The heads of those who had been executed were often displayed on top of the south gate of London Bridge, as a warning visible to all those entering the city, and the display is shown in Visscher's view of the city published in 1616. As in everything else, there was a social hierarchy. Tyburn was where criminals and traitors of mean or common status met their fate by hanging. In contrast, Tower Hill, literally in the shadow of the royal might of the Tower of London, was generally reserved for the demise of more noble offenders, and their end came by beheading. Noble status led to the relative dignity and mercy of beheading, as with the Earl of Essex in 1601, rather than the slow strangulation of hanging. The beheading of women was usually reserved for the intimacy of Tower Green.

The linkage of domestic rebellion and foreign threat was made very clear in the depiction in *Henry V* of the unsuccessful 1415 French-backed conspiracy of Richard, Earl of Cambridge. This is described twice in act 2, first by the chorus in a preface and then in real time. Both descriptions link hell to treason, Henry V stating that revolt is "like another fall of man," a comparison pregnant with existential religious meaning and carefully drawing the contrast between concern with self and with the kingdom. This is a contrast that weak and/or immoral rulers, such as Richard II in the opening acts of the play of that name, are repeatedly shown as unable to make. Henry declares:

> You have conspired against our royal person,
> Joined with an enemy proclaimed, and from his coffers
> Received the golden earnest [advance payment] of our death;
> Wherein you would have sold your king to slaughter.
> His princes and his peers to servitude,
> His subjects to oppression and contempt

And his whole kingdom into desolation.
Touching our person seek we no revenge;
But we our kingdom's safety must so tender [cherish],
Whose ruin you have sought, that to her laws
We do deliver you. (II, ii)

*Henry V* is frequently presented today as an antiwar play, and the savage aspects of the war with France are clearly depicted. This theme was much reprised in performances during 2014–18, the centenary of World War I. However, Shakespeare's references to hell or "Perdition" are very much those of treason, not war. Indeed, this is an instance when the presentation by modern directors searching for relevance is highly misleading and can be a lazy, as well as convenient, echoing of popular contemporary views rather than an engagement with the text or the likely views of contemporaries.

Elizabeth I's preference for stability was a matter of more than personality and prudence. There was also need for it. The fifteenth-century legacy of the Wars of the Roses, as discussed in chapter 5, was of a bitterly contested succession. More recently, the period between 1530 and 1569, as considered in chapter 6, had seen instability and rebellions, and government was repeatedly hit by a lack of continuity in personnel, institutions, and policy. This lack of continuity could be found in religion, politics, and much else, including the buildings that formed the background to Shakespeare's London. For example, Westminster Abbey, a Benedictine foundation, was seized by Henry VIII in 1540 as part of the general Dissolution of the Monasteries. It was then reestablished by Henry as a cathedral for the new bishopric of Westminster. Ten years later, when the diocese was abolished, the abbey became a second cathedral for London, only for its monastic status to be restored by Mary in 1556 during the Catholic reaction. In 1560, Elizabeth refounded the abbey as a collegiate church enjoying exemption from episcopal control, an arrangement that has been maintained ever since.

With time, Elizabeth became the most experienced politician in her kingdom: certainly far more experienced than was Mary, Queen of Scots, in Scotland or in England. Anxious to preserve the royal prerogative and presiding through the impact of majesty and power on and via personal relationships,[1] Elizabeth knew when to yield without appearing weak. She had favorites, especially her master of the horse, Robert Dudley, Earl of Leicester (a son of John, Duke of Northumberland, who had been executed in 1553), whom she visited at his castle seat at Kenilworth, and, later, Robert, Second Earl of Essex. However, Elizabeth never gave them power, she never married as Leicester wanted her to, and she had Essex executed. Shakespeare possibly witnessed Elizabeth's visit to Leicester's seat in 1576, as Kenilworth was near Stratford; he would certainly have heard much about it. Oberon's account of the "fair vestal" has been accounted for accordingly (*A Midsummer Night's Dream*, II, i).

Although longevity was very important, the contrast with Mary of England's reign rested on much more. Claiming that she was an exceptional woman, because chosen by God as his instrument, Elizabeth was pragmatic and generally more successful in coping with and often exploiting aristocratic factionalism and ministerial divisions than her predecessors had been. She had Henry VII's watchfulness and caution and did not need to rely on frequent recourse to the executioner's axe that Henry VIII had felt that he had to do. Despite being the target of many conspiracies and rebellions, Elizabeth executed fewer people per year than either Henry VIII or Mary had done.

It was not surprising that the long-lived Elizabeth played a major role in the political imagination of her subjects. Her reputation later helped to overshadow the less impressive character and impact of James I's kingship, which also suffered from Elizabeth becoming a figure recalled in a golden hue. The response to individuals was part of a more general engagement with the role of the monarch, an engagement given religious force by the significance of the kings of Israel in the book of Kings in the Old Testament of the Bible. This text was a frequent source for church sermons and readings. Political culture stressed the ideal of a Christian community, with monarchs presiding actively in defense of the faith and their subjects. The obligation of monarchs included an oath at their coronation to defend religious orthodoxy. They were the key figures in the health, both physical and spiritual, of their kingdom. In *Hamlet*, Guildenstern refers to

> those many many bodies . . .
> That live and feed upon your Majesty.

Rosencrantz adds:

> the cease of Majesty
> Dies not alone, but like a gulf doth draw
> What's near it, with it. It is a massy wheel
> Fix'd on the summit of the highest mount,
> To whose huge spokes, ten thousand lesser things
> Are mortis'd and adjoin'd: which when it fall,
> Each small annexment, petty consequence
> Attends the boisterous ruin. Never alone
> Did the King sigh, but with a general groan. (III, iii)

Ironically, each man is defending a murderous usurper, Claudius, whom the spectators know to be a murderous usurper, which may affect how the lines are supposed to be taken. That is a problematic point throughout the interpretation of the plays and one in which consistency in approach is far from easy.

Royal authority rested on divine right, the divine right to the Crown and its authority, with providential support significant and in part to be gauged by interpretations, notably by astrological signs. Validation by the Church at the coronation and its subsequent backing were also important. That makes the views of individual clerics of interest, notably (offstage) Pope Innocent III in *King John* and (onstage) Cardinal Wolsey and Archbishop Cranmer in *Henry VIII*. At the same time, the partisan character of some senior clerics is fully revealed, as with Richard Scrope, Archbishop of York, in *Henry IV*; Henry Beaufort, Bishop of Winchester and Cardinal in *Henry VI, Parts I and II*; and Stephen Gardiner, Bishop of Winchester, in *Henry VIII*, each of whom is presented as a malicious and dangerous politician. However, except where necessary for the historical record, Shakespeare tended to downplay the potential role for clerics. This was the case, for example, in *Hamlet, Macbeth, Othello, Measure for Measure, Two Gentlemen of Verona*, and *As You Like It*, to draw attention to a range of his plays.

Royal authority was also limited by a rule of law that maintained both royal prerogative powers and the liberties of the subject, with this rule of law at the same time being strengthened for the monarchs by divine right. Rights, duties, responsibilities, and obligations were therefore based on religious belief, the belief shared by both sovereign and subjects that was set within a divinely decreed and monitored order, one in which natural law was still important. The latter offers a fresh way to approach Shakespeare's work.[2] The common law had moral weight, and its presentation drew heavily on moral assumptions. In the latter, there was a shared ownership that reflected not only this background but also a sense of common interest.[3] Order is also represented by the gardener in *Richard II* who, in a moment at once light and powerfully evocative, compares the kingdom to the garden, referring to "fruits of duty" and to the need to remove "the noisome weeds," while the First Servant asks why the garden should be kept in "law and form and due proportion" when the

> whole land
> Is full of weeds. (III, iv)

The dystopian reverse of order is frequently depicted and discussed by Shakespeare, ranging most bluntly from the presentation of Scotland under a Macbeth ready to order the slaughter of children to the fevered imaginings of a Timon made misanthropic by adversity. In *Timon of Athens*, he offers a terrible vision for an ungrateful Athens, in which political and social disorder are linked to a fear of sexual freedom and excess:

> Matrons, turn incontinent!
> Obedience fail in children! slaves and fools,
> Pluck the grave wrinkled senate from the bench,
> And minister in their steads! To general filths
> Convert, o' the instant, green virginity!
> Do 't in your parents' eyes! Bankrupts, hold fast;
> Rather than render back, out with your knives,
> And cut your trusters' throats! Bound servants, steal!
> Large-handed robbers your grave masters are,
> And pill [pillage] by law. Maid, to thy master's bed;
> Thy mistress is o' the brothel! Son of sixteen,
> Pluck the lin'd [padded] crutch from thy old limping sire,
> With it beat out his brains! Piety, and fear,
> Religion to the gods, peace, justice, truth,
> Domestic awe, night-rest and neighbourhood,
> Instruction, manners, mysteries and trades,
> Degrees, observances, customs and laws,
> Decline to your confounding contraries,
> And let confusion live. (IV, i)

And so on.

Individualism is potentially destructive and, indeed, an aspect of the fragility of society in the face of self-will.[4] In *The Tempest*, Antonio, the usurper of Milan, seeking to encourage Sebastian to murder the latter's brother Alonso, king of Naples, responds to reference to his conscience by asking:

> where lies that?
> . . . . . . . . . . . . . .
> I feel not
> This deity in my bosom: twenty consciences
> That stand 'twixt me and Milan, candied [crystallized] be they,
> And melt ere they molest! (II, i)

What may appear rational to such individuals as Aaron, Angelo, Iago, Macbeth, Lady Macbeth, Richard III, and Don John—and that is a selective list of highly dangerous but very different characters—is shown in practice to be deeply irrational. This individualism causes social damage, and, in the case of tragic figures to whom we are given interior and reflective insight, the damage is also strongly felt by them personally.[5] The individual drives of Macbeth and his wife, both focused on concepts of manhood, lead Macbeth to fail to discern correctly the spirits that are competing in and through and thereby against both him and society.[6] His humanity is lost, followed by his sensitivity. In *Othello*, the villainous Iago very much puts the self to the fore in rejecting Roderigo's mention of virtue:

> Virtue? A fig! 'Tis in ourselves that we are thus, or thus. Our bodies are our gardens, to the which our wills are gardeners, so that if we will plant nettles or sow lettuce, set [plant] hyssop and weed up thyme, supply it with one gender [species] of herbs or distract [spoil] it with many—either to have it sterile with idleness, or manured with industry—why, the power and corrigible authority of this lies in our wills. If the balance of our lives had not one scale of reason to poise [balance] another of sensuality, the blood and baseness of our natures would conduct us to most preposterous conclusions. But we have reason to cool our raging motions, our carnal stings, our unbitted [unbridled] lusts. Whereof I take this that you call love to be a sect or scion [cutting or shoot]. (I, iii)

Strains within the self are described in political terms by Brutus in *Julius Caesar*:

> Between the acting of a dreadful thing
> And the first motion, all the interim is
> Like a phantasma or a hideous dream:
> The genius and the mortal instruments
> Are then in council; and the state of man,
> Like to a little kingdom, suffers then
> The nature of an insurrection. (II, i)

These strains are traced to nature, not nurture, both as an aspect of the dominance of "humours" and because of related astrological influences. Hamlet takes this view:

> So, oft it chances in particular men,
> That for some vicious mole of nature in them,
> As, in their birth—wherein they are not guilty,
> Since nature cannot choose his origin—
> By the o'ergrowth of some complexion,
> Oft breaking down the pales and forts of reason,
> Or by some habit that too much o'er-leavens
> The form of plausive manners; that these men,
> Carrying, I say, the stamp of one defect,
> Being nature's livery, or fortune's star,
> Their virtues else, be they as pure as grace,
> As infinite as man may undergo,
> Shall in the general censure take corruption
> From that particular fault . . . (I, iv)

The model of good kingship was of rulers guided by God and provided with willing obedience by their loyal subjects. Patronage lubricated the system. It could have a benign quality, in that it was a social and political relationship that placed obligations on both parties, even though they were greatly differentiated by status, obligations seen in patterns of gift giving and in practices of service.[7] Indeed, as a result, there was no simple distinction of government and subjects. This model of good kingship was matched but also complicated by the reality of the monarch not always being willing to listen to good counsel. In part, this failure was due to the politics of patronage in the shape of the monarch not confiding in appropriate supporters and advisers.[8]

The social privileges of the aristocracy made the lack of a simple distinction between monarchs and subjects particularly apparent, for rulers and greater aristocrats shared glorious lineages and a similar lifestyle, which encouraged aristocrats to expect that they would not be classified and dealt with like other subjects. This was a factor in the outbreak and development of the Wars of the Roses. Political tension could focus on royal favor for ministers who appeared to reject this scenario, notably by lacking aristocratic support and breaching the conventions of aristocratic society. At the more minor level of an aristocratic household, Malvolio, the steward in *Twelfth Night*, is an illustration of this in his treatment of Sir Toby Belch, his mistress's kinsman, and Belch's friend and dupe, Sir Andrew Aguecheek, and in the critical and condescending stance toward both men he plans to take if he marries Olivia.

Political tension could also focus on relations within families, notably the problems caused by younger sons and illegitimate sons. These, indeed, are matters both for kingdoms, as with *Richard III* and *King Lear*, and for nonroyal households, as in *As You Like It*. In the latter case, the two issues arise with Orlando, the impoverished younger son who is mistreated, and the old Duke, who has been disinherited by his discontented younger brother, Frederick. In *The Tempest*, there is a similar usurpation. Primogeniture (inheritance by the eldest son), its impact on status, and the responses of others link royalty and other ranks and can be seen both in the plays and in the lives of much of their audience.[9]

In contrast to modernizing forms of bureaucratic, information-led governance, the continued importance, in practice, of informal channels of authority in political and government systems, in which bureaucracy played only a limited role, focused attention on the ruler's ministers and also ensured that the role and skill of individual monarchs were critical. Having "the ear of the king" was crucial, and reports about other states frequently focused on royal health, intentions, and advisors and those of the likely successor. That is an important aspect of *Hamlet* and of the history plays. Repeatedly, Shakespeare showed that having the king's ear and using it to manipulate patronage and policy for personal gain were causes of instability. This was certainly the message of *Richard II*, of all the parts of *Henry VI*, and of *Henry VIII*. *Measure for Measure* offered the same for a ducal court. Moreover, having the ear of a patron could be important in more modest courts, such as those of the Duke and of Olivia in *Twelfth Night*.

Although monarchy and the monarchs dominated the political imagination, and notably that of Shakespeare's plays, they were not the sole images of power. Shakespeare engaged with republics, with two plays set in the Venetian world (*The Merchant of Venice, Othello*) and a concern also with the republics of antiquity: Athens, the setting of *Timon of Athens*, and Rome. Indeed, the fall of the Roman republic, the subject of two of his plays and potentially of a third (*Coriolanus*), enabled Shakespeare to discuss the strengths and weaknesses of republics. The fickleness of popular support is a theme right from the outset in *Julius Caesar*, with Marcellus, one of the tribunes, criticizing the willingness of those who had shouted earlier for Caesar's opponent Pompey now being intent on applauding his overthrow by Caesar. Marcellus declaims:

> O you hard hearts, you cruel men of Rome,
> Knew you not Pompey? Many a time and oft
> Have you climbed up to walls and battlements,
> To towers and windows, yea, to chimney-tops,
> Your infants in your arms, and there have sat
> The livelong day, with patient expectation,
> To see great Pompey pass the streets of Rome
> . . . . . . . . . . . . . . . . . . . . . . . . . . . . . .
> And do you now put on your best attire?
> And do you now cull out a holiday?
> And do you now strew flowers in his way,
> That comes in triumph over Pompey's blood? (I, i)

More brutally and threateningly, the death of history through popular action is offered by Jack Cade in *Henry VI, Part II*: "Away, burn all the records of the realm: my mouth shall be the Parliament of England." The social ordering envisaged by Cade is clear: "and henceforth all things shall be in common" (IV, vii).

There is also a coverage of political organizations in a demotic context, notably in a comic setting but (unlike Bottom's players in *A Midsummer Night's Dream*) one crucial to the plot and the eventual success of virtue, with the Watch in *Much Ado About Nothing*. Its members represent an aspect of citizenship, at once comic and impressive: "good men and true... honest neighbours" (III, iii). Their actions unravel the conspiracy.

Caliban in *The Tempest* provides an opportunity to consider order and authority in another aspect, that of control over those who were not human or fully human. Having earlier tried but failed "to violate the honour" of Miranda, Caliban is ready to "swear upon that bottle" to be a "true subject" and is even ready to let Stephano be his "god" (II, ii). Caliban is held up as an instance of malign nature defeating the influence of benign nurture, a process encouraged by his turning to the distorting nurture of alcohol. Miranda describes him as an

> Abhorred slave,
> Which any print [imprint] of goodness wilt not take. (I, ii)

And Prospero refers to Caliban as

> A devil, a born devil, on whose nature
> Nurture can never stick: on whom my pains,
> Humanely taken, all, all lost, quite lost. (IV, i)

Although Shakespeare left scant guidance over how best to understand remarks beyond the explicit level, these remarks are given to people who, in treating Caliban as a slave, have an interest in disparaging him. On the other hand, Caliban's behavior and intentions, as shown and presented, do not challenge these remarks.

The relations of Prospero with Ariel in the same play and the position of Puck in *A Midsummer Night's Dream* offer different accounts of control. Indeed, in *The Tempest*, exposure to an island that lacks a weight of history comparable to that of Europe leads to reflections on purpose. Gonzalo considers what he would do if the island was his territory. He proposes to create and rule a new, model society of equality and thus to end division:

> no kind of traffic [commerce]
> Would I admit; no name of magistrate;
> Letters should not be known; riches, poverty,
> And use of service, none; contract, succession [inheritance],
> Bourn [land boundary], bound of land, tilth [agriculture], vineyard,
> none;
> No use of metal, corn, or wine, or oil;
> No occupation; all men idle, all
> And women too, but innocent and pure; . . .
> All things in common nature should produce
> Without sweat or endeavour; treason, felony,
> Sword, pike, knife, gun, or need of any engine,
> Would I not have; but nature should bring forth,
> Of its own kind, all foison [plenty], all abundance,
> To feed my innocent people.
> . . . I would with such perfection govern, sir,
> T' excel the Golden Age. (II, i)

Although offered by a meritorious individual, this utopian prospectus of a return to the idyllic, mythical earliest of ages is, in practice, so illusory as to be almost magical. That, indeed, provides another way to look at the island: as a setting not just of reconciliation but also of illusion. However, in *The Tempest*, magic is real and illusion is reality, as well as having meaning. Gonzalo's prospectus is given a different meaning when a drunken Caliban outlines to Trinculo and Stephano what he will do as their "subject":

> I show thee the best springs: I'll pluck thee berries:
> I'll fish for thee and get thee wood enough . . .
> will dig thee pignuts [edible roots]:
> show thee
> a jay's nest and instruct thee how
> to snare
> the nimble marmoset: I'll bring thee
> to clust'ring filberts [hazelnuts] (II, ii)

In offering differing perspectives in and on his plays, Shake-speare could question them or allow his audience to do so. How-ever, the process was not always pushed home. Thus, the selfishness of those who brought down Julius Caesar is not discussed.[10] Ques-tioning could arise from those who suffer misfortune, such as Cali-ban, or experience prejudice, such as Shylock in *The Merchant of Venice* (a less unsympathetic character than Marlowe's *The Jew of Malta*), as well as from figures within the system. In *All's Well That Ends Well*, the king of France, rejecting Bertram's snobbish disdain for his allocated wife as "a poor physician's daughter," a view that would have hit Shakespeare's descendants, replies:

> 'Tis only title thou disdain'st in her, the which
> I can build up. Strange is it that our bloods,
> Of colour, weight, and heat, pour'd all together,
> Would quite confound distinction, yet stand off
> In differences so mighty. . . . Good alone
> Is good. . . . honours thrive
> When rather from our acts we them derive. (II, iii)

Social ambition in marriage was frequently shown, as in *Much Ado About Nothing* when Leonato holds it "as a dream" that his daughter, Hero, should marry Don Pedro, Prince of Aragon. This is a commoner marrying into royalty. In *The Taming of the Shrew* and *The Merchant of Venice*, however, the heroines reject social ambition and wealth as their marital goals.

Shakespeare devoted much attention to the reality of power and to its consequences. His was a world of courts but also of lo-calities. In the former, as he showed, royal advisers were crucial. In the latter, members of the social elite owned and controlled much of the land and were the local notables, enjoying social prestige and effective governmental control. This control was bluntly displayed in the history plays. In *Henry VI, Part III*, the Duke of Warwick, again a would-be "king-maker," responds to Edward IV's invasion, in 1471, by calling on aristocratic strength:

In Warwickshire I have true-hearted friends,
Not mutinous in peace, yet bold in war;
Those will I muster up; and thou, son [son-in-law] Clarence,
Shalt stir up in Suffolk, Norfolk, and in Kent,
The knights and gentlemen to come with thee:
Thou, brother Montague, in Buckingham,
Northampton, and in Leicestershire, shalt find
Men well inclin'd to hear what thou command'st:
And thou, brave Oxford, wondrous well-belov'd
In Oxfordshire, shalt muster up thy friends. (IV, viii)

More generally, central government lacked the mechanisms to intervene effectively and consistently in the localities, unless with the cooperation of the local elite. Power in the localities was delegated, as with the rise in county administration of the Lord Lieutenancy, from 1585. The Lord Lieutenants provided a royal representative in each county. This was a rise in which Protestants benefited by being chosen.[11]

Indeed, in what was in large part a prestatistical age, the central government of England found it difficult to produce coherent plans for domestic policies based on the premise of change and development, with the significant exception of the ability to push through religious matters for which there was a force for implementation in the ecclesiastical structure. In contrast, in most matters, without reliable information concerning population, revenues, economic activity, or landownership and lacking land surveys and accurate and detailed maps, government, both in England and elsewhere, operated in what was, by modern standards, an information void, although, at the time, it would have seemed normal. This situation increased the central regime's reliance on the landed elite.

There were changes, however, in the nature of government. In particular, the political imagination had to engage with new challenges, notably the Reformation, which affected relations within families, communities, and the nation and state as a whole. Nevertheless, much remained traditional, notably the impact of social norms and structures and the nature of governance. The marvelous representation of a Commission of Array at work raising troops in Shakespeare's *Henry IV, Part II* (III, ii), involving Bullcalf, Mouldy, and so forth, although fictional, was not a depiction of a well-oiled administration. In practice, although the situation was not that grim, there was a lack of funds to provide the necessary muskets.[12] Indeed, lacking a developed war machine comparable to that of Spain, let alone that of the Ottoman Turks, Elizabeth I had to contract with adventurers and mercenaries in order to raise and sustain forces. Aside from serious administrative problems, including corruption, this situation ensured that the government had only limited control over military operations, a position that was matched in many other fields. Moreover, instead of embarking upon a risky attempt to reform governmental structures in order to make financing and fighting the war easier, Elizabeth resorted to expedients that squandered goodwill and kept the war effort hand-to-mouth.

It was difficult, anyway, due to problems with communications, to provide instructions that would comprehend all eventualities or, alternatively, to respond adequately at a distance to fast-changing developments. The slow and uncertain nature of communications ensured that considerable discretion had to be left to those in the field and the localities. The nature of communications encouraged the spread of rumor, which overlapped with news because of the difficulties of checking reports. On land, speed was determined by animal (and human) endurance and muscle, while the weather played a key role there, as at sea. As a result, government was at the mercy of rumor and speculation, which hindered confident decision making. The emphasis on secrecy as the best means to thwart enemies exacerbated this situation. Communications were not only slow and uncertain but also frequently such that information could only be confirmed by waiting for subsequent messages, a situation that was ably captured by Shakespeare. Moreover, disaster faced those characters who would not or could not wait for more news to test their impressions. This was most conspicuously so with Romeo, who had not heard that Juliet was drugged and dead only in appearance. The audience, but not Romeo, knows this, which provides both suspense and a way to assess the response of individuals.

Without the reach of modern governments, those of Shakespeare's lifetime relied on other bodies and individuals to fulfil many functions that are now discharged by central government, and these bodies and individuals very much reflected the interests, ideology, and personnel of the social elite. Religion, education, poor relief, health, and public order were all focused on the parish, a link that underlined the significance of the Church. The essential element for stable government was to ensure that the local notables governed in accordance with the wishes of the center; but means and outcome were achieved largely by giving them the instructions that they wanted. For the notables, it was necessary both that they received such instructions and that they got a fair share of governmental patronage. This system worked—and its cohesion, if not harmony, was maintained—not so much by formal bureaucratic mechanisms as by the patronage and clientage networks that linked local notables to those wielding national influence and enjoying access to the monarch.

However, patronage and clientage could be the means for disorder and violence, a point that was presented both historically and with reference to the present. That was very much the theme of the three parts of *Henry VI*, but also of other plays. Thus, at the end of *Romeo and Juliet*, the Prince contemplates the murderous consequences of his earlier failure to quiet the "discords" in Verona between Capulets and Montagues, a feud that affected more than just these two rival families:

> And I, for winking at your discords too,
> Have lost a brace of kinsmen. (V, iii)

Mercutio was the most important of these kinsmen. That he is not a Capulet or a Montagu provides some of the interest in his fate and pushes friendship to the fore.

Central government lacked the facilities, techniques, and understanding to oversee officials in an effective fashion. Disobedience, disaffection, and corruption characterized much government business. Office was widely seen as a source of personal and family profit, and financial irregularities flourished as officeholders sought to profit from those they dealt with and from the funds under their control, as with corruption, tax farming, and the awarding of monopolies of production, importation, or sale. Thus, the potential for power created by notions of sovereign authority and arising from the resource base could not be realized by government. Instead, it was necessary to turn to the compromises and exigencies of partnerships between sovereigns and others, principally the social elite but also within government as a whole. As a result, there was no "big bang" of new forms of government or a Tudor "Revolution in Government," other than in the very important sphere of the Church (where the Crown, in the 1530s, essentially took over much of the papal position, established total control, and ended monasticism). Meanwhile, the administration of justice remained a key element of government, albeit one that, as earlier, had to respond to social and other changes. This process interested such writers as Shakespeare,[13] as well as providing the means and vocabulary for a range of social and political ideas and practices.[14]

Given the social and cultural context, it is unsurprising that there was little in the way of a distinct bureaucratic ethos. Concepts of fidelity and clientage and attitudes of status, all characteristics of the aristocratic social system, illuminated policy and provided much of the texture of administration. This was in a situation in which social rank, patronage, and inheritance, in combination, defined merit, led to appointment and promotion, and greatly affected marital choices.

Custom was a key guide to rights and practice, one that was important at all levels of the community.[15] For example, the relationship between host and guest is repeatedly seen in Shakespeare's plays, and the duties of being a host often take a major part in the action and the remarks made. Macbeth's personality is shattered by his murderous failure as the host, first, of Duncan, his monarch and patron, and, later, of Banquo, his friend and companion in arms. *Pericles* begins with a total failure of royal hospitality on the part of Antiochus. Guests, however, could themselves be problematic. This was notably and dangerously so with Don John in *Much Ado About Nothing* but sometimes to comic effect, as with Sir Toby Belch in *Twelfth Night*.

The failings of government and of human conduct as a whole, a duality captured in *Measure for Measure*, contrasted with assumptions about the value of order and the possibilities for improvement, notably by public action.[16] Looking back to classical and biblical roots, these assumptions were strengthened by the vitalization of each in the Renaissance and Reformation. Moreover, a quest for order reflected the attempt to understand the world. Renaissance thought represented both an attempt to understand new (and revived) information and an attempt to systematize it in order to provide a natural philosophy that could be used to comprehend and expound knowledge. The aim of rationalizing the world, using the study of the natural world and Christian devotion to understand each other, was intended to ensure a harmony that would bring peace and fulfill divine goals. This purpose linked intellectual speculation with religion and also with alchemy and magic. Harmony, the counterpoint of order, was believed to be inherently a good, as well as being a means of good.

This harmony was challenged by a lack of self-control, both individual and collective, and that is repeatedly a theme of the plays. Pride is an obvious instance, as conspicuously with Julius Caesar but so also with Lear's wish to hear praise from his daughters. Self-indulgence is seen in *Romeo and Juliet* with the willingness of the protagonists to turn to suicide, an action that Hamlet notes is banned by God. The temptation of Gloucester, apparently by a fiend, to suicide is very important to his redemption in *King Lear*.

More broadly, there is repeatedly the case of what Horatio, at the close of *Hamlet*, terms

purposes mistook,
Fall'n on the inventors' heads. (V, ii)

This is both a dramatic device, found in tragedies, comedies, and history plays, and a moral point, the latter a context for the use of this device but also the end judgment on the individuals involved. Hamlet's reflections on the skulls in the graveyard are another instance of the judgments he so frequently and powerfully offers, as with that of the skull of Yorick, the king's jester. Morality in *Hamlet* is a matter not only of the serious and nervy protagonist but is also linked with any hope of order in the world he and the audience inhabit. This approach was made more serious by the use of the play within the play to offer insight and of the main play thereby to provide criticism.

Political ideas were inseparable from wider considerations of social and cultural norms. Each can be glimpsed in the use of language, not only in the words and images employed, even invented, but also in the timbre of their use. The political imagination was not a question of the particular politics on offer but rather one of the application of morality in the story of the characters depicted. As a result, the hubris of individuals was at once both political and moral, both narrative device and basis of judgment, or story and understanding. Politics was not *politique* in the sense of being a convenient mechanism to avoid strife but rather a quasi-spiritual activity. Plays provided the public with imaginative access to what it was like to be a king, a courtier, a counsellor, a magnate, a justice of the peace, and so on and thus to enter into the challenges, dilemmas, and temptations of power. Politics, perhaps even more than now, was theatrical. The plotting, intrigues, dissimulation, and impression management by rulers of the state, which one glimpsed by means of rulers on the stage, reflected and informed the politics of the age.[17] The stage offered a political education, notably of the interplay between an ideology of governmental command and a need, in practice, to respond to and exploit contingent situations. This need was seen both in the narrative presented and in the plays themselves. The depiction of characters, including rulers, seeking support and popularity, and the audience response, contributed to the role of the theater as a participatory public space.[18] The audience role has been presented as constitutive to the understanding that is offered of the constitution.[19]

## NOTES

1. S. Doran, *Elizabeth I and Her Circle* (Oxford, 2015).

2. R. S. White, *Natural Law in English Renaissance Literature* (Cambridge, 1996); G. Burgess, *Absolute Monarchy and the Stuart Constitution* (New Haven, CT, 1996).

3. M. L. Kaplan, *The Culture of Slander in Early Modern England* (Cambridge, 1997).

4. D. Margolies, *Monsters of the Deep: Social Dissolution in Shakespeare's Tragedies* (Manchester, 1992).

5. R. Hillman, *Shakespearean Subversions: The Trickster and the Play-Text* (London, 1992).

6. R. V. Caro, "Rules for Discernment: Another Context for *Macbeth*," *Notes and Queries* 245 (2000): 455–58.

7. F. Heal, *The Power of Gifts: Gift-Exchange in Early Modern England* (Oxford, 2014).

8. M. O'Callaghan, "'Talking Politics': Tyranny, Parliament, and Christopher Brooke's *The Ghost of Richard the Third* (1614)," *Historical Journal* 41 (1998): 120.

9. Louis Montrose, "'The Place of a Brother' in *As You Like It*: Social Process and Comic Form," *Shakespeare Quarterly* 32 (1981): 28–54.

10. T. P. Wiseman, *Julius Caesar* (Stroud, UK, 2011), 100–113.

11. N. Younger, *War and Politics in the Elizabethan Counties* (Manchester, 2012).

12. A. J. King, ed., *Muster Books for North and East Hertfordshire, 1580–1605* (Hertford, UK, 1996).

13. B. Cormack, *A Power to Do Justice: Jurisdiction, English Literature, and the Rise of Common Law, 1509–1625* (Chicago, 2008).

14. C. W. Brooks, *Law, Politics and Society in Early Modern England* (Cambridge, 2008).

15. A. Wood, *The Memory of the People: Custom and Popular Senses of the Past in Early Modern England* (Cambridge, 2013).

16. P. Slack, *The Invention of Improvement: Information and Material Progress in Seventeenth-Century England* (Oxford, 2014).

17. G. Wills, *Making Make-Believe Real: Politics as Theatre in Shakespeare's Time* (New Haven, CT, 2014); N. Millstone, "Seeing Like a Statesman in Early Stuart England," *Past and Present* 22 (2014): 77–127.

18. J. Doty, *Shakespeare, Popularity and the Public Sphere* (Cambridge, 2017).

19. I. Ward, "A Kingdom for a Stage, Princes to Act: Shakespeare and the Art of Government," *Law and Critique* 8, no. 2 (1997): 189–212, esp. 212.

# EIGHT

—ɯ—

# SOCIAL CONDITIONS, STRUCTURES, AND ASSUMPTIONS

IT IS ALL TOO EASY when watching modern productions of Shakespeare's plays to assume that his society was similar to ours. This is a process much encouraged by the use of modern dress, music, and settings and one that is explicitly sought by many directors. It is also stimulated by references to Shakespeare's plays and characters by other writers. Many such references cascade through time, creating or adapting assumptions. For example, Nikolai Leskov's *Lady Macbeth of Mtensk District* (1865), a story about a discontented and ultimately violent young bride whom Leskov compared with Lady Macbeth, inspired both an opera by Dmitri Shostakovich (1932) and *Lady Macbeth*, a film of 2016. Leskov's story drew on Shakespeare, but it is an adaptation, not a reproduction, of Shakespeare's plot.

Despite such similarities, it must be emphasized that modern society rests upon a very different set of basic assumptions and experiences, most notably about life and death, meaning and purpose. The sixteenth-century Protestant Reformation, with its strong emphasis on a vernacular Bible, ensured that good and evil became more literary and less oral and visual than hitherto. Nevertheless, that did not diminish the need for people to understand their world in terms of the existential struggle between the two, as noted in chapter 1. Evil, malevolence, and the inscrutable workings of the divine will all continued to seem the only way of explaining the sudden pitfalls of the human condition.

Harvests were hit by bad weather, while the cold and damp exacerbated disease. Buildings and trees provided some shelter from the rain, but, as part of the key rhythm of the seasons, there was little escape from the cold. This helped ensure that reference to the latter was particularly common in the plays when Shakespeare is trying to set the scene. Such scene setting extended to mood, as very much in *The Winter's Tale*. A particularly memorable evocation of winter occurs in the song at the close of *Love's Labour's Lost*, one that links winter to the poor and names them:

> When icicles hang by the wall,
> And Dick the shepherd blows his nail,
> And Tom bears logs into the hall,
> And milk comes frozen home in pail,
> When blood is nipp'd, and ways be foul,
> Then nightly sings the staring owl,
> To-whoo;
> To-whit, to-whoo—a merry note,
> While greasy Joan doth keel the pot.[1] (V, ii)

As a contrast, although lessened in Shakespeare's plays by the use of settings in the Mediterranean and by his generally making little mention of creature comforts, fire was a protection against the cold, as well as a source of light. In both respects, fire provided comfort. Characters were not generally presented as huddled round the fire, but there was frequent reference to fire. This was accentuated by the usage of fire as a metaphor for love and desire and by remarks reflecting knowledge of how fires burn, as with Lucetta's comment "Fire that's closest kept burns most of all" (*Two Gentlemen of Verona*, I, ii). Yet the tempting nature of fire also led people astray, for the devil was referred to as ever keeping a "good fire." In *Macbeth*, in an arresting speech, the drunken

Porter pretends he is guarding the entrance to "the everlasting fire," again hell (II, iii).

The major role of agriculture ensured that much of the population lived in the most fertile areas. Nevertheless, this role also meant that a greater percentage than today lived in areas that were less attractive for farming, so long as a living could still be wrenched from the soil. The detailed pattern of land use was far more complex than might be suggested by the pattern of upland pasture and lowland arable discussed in chapter 3. In upland areas, grain was grown, with whatever difficulty, in small quantities as a subsistence crop, while livestock were kept in lowland areas to provide meat, milk, manure (animal waste for fertilizer), wool, and motive power. At the level of the individual farmstead and again of the village, there was a degree of self-reliance that is totally unknown to modern farmers. This self-reliance reflected the relative difficulties of preservation and transport in an age before refrigeration and motor vehicles and also the degree and intensity of local systems of exchange, as well as the degree to which self- and local-reliance made more economic sense than in the modern age of specialization as a result of the knowledge today of comparative profit margins. Where there was a combination of poor soils, steep slopes, a limited growing season, and high relief, then dependence on animal rearing was pronounced. In steep areas, this meant sheep; on flatter (and lower) land, cattle. Neither, especially sheep rearing, offered a form of agriculture that could support the population levels of arable regions or that encouraged their nucleated (village) settlements. Instead, dispersed settlement was the norm, frequently in the form of isolated farmsteads.

"To grunt and sweat under a weary life"—Hamlet's observation (III, i)—was pertinent for most of the population, even though relatively few of them were seen in the plays as characters, let alone probably being in the audiences. Agricultural labor was arduous and repetitive and took much of the waking day. Agricultural work was generally daylight to dusk in winter, and six a.m.

to six p.m. in summer. Industrial employment was also hard, for example, up to sixteen hours being worked daily in the Yorkshire alum houses where the dye fixative for woolens was produced.

Work was also often dangerous. Each occupation had its own hazards, hazards that challenged the self-sufficiency that was important to reputation, identity, and survival and that affected life expectancy. Millers worked in dusty and noisy circumstances, frequently suffered from lice, and often developed asthma, hernias, and chronic back problems. Disorders could result from the strain of repeated motions and unusual physical demands or postures, such as those required of tailors and weavers; and Shakespeare made frequent reference to the particular character of individual trades, as in the Porter's speech in *Macbeth*. The opening scene of *Julius Caesar* refers to the distinctive signs of particular professions, notably the leather apron and ruler of the carpenter. In *A Midsummer Night's Dream*, Bottom takes this further, in having the Wall acted: "some man or other must present Wall; and let him have some plaster, or some loam, or some roughcast about him" (III, i).

Many places of work were damp, cold, badly ventilated, poorly lit, and unsafe. Work frequently involved exposure to dangerous substances, such as arsenic, lead, and mercury, or was dangerous and even deadly in itself, particularly construction, fishing, and mining. The first could be backbreaking, while the last involved much work with pickaxes. Most industrial processes, moreover, were dangerous or at least unpleasant, and to others besides the workers: dressing and tanning leather polluted the water supplies, while the kilns of brick and tile works produced smoke and fumes. There were restrictions on individual noxious practices, for example, the pollution of water supplies by some industrial processes, but there was no systematic scrutiny of them or drive for improvements. Urine was widely used in cloth making.

At a more mundane level, uncertainty was a matter not only of demographics and injuries but also an aspect of the contemporary world of space, not least of transport conditions. This uncertainty, striking in comparison with modern life, was captured most vividly by the abrupt shift from light to darkness, which is discussed in chapters 1 and 2.

There were still virulent outbreaks of the bubonic plague, as in 1499–1500, 1518, 1538, 1563, 1603, 1605, 1625, 1636, and 1665. The last was the Great Plague, in which between 70,000 and 100,000 people died, and possibly more, as the parish registers could not be kept up. About one-quarter of the population of London died in 1563 and about one-fifth of the population of Manchester in 1605. There were also local outbreaks, as in Newcastle in 1589, in which 1,727 people were reported dying, out of a population of about 9,000 in 1548. These sudden deaths underlined the precariousness of life, at both the individual and the collective level. About 3,750 immigrants annually were needed in London in the late sixteenth century simply to maintain its population and prevent it from falling. A significant channel of such immigration for young men was apprenticeship, although most immigrants were probably not taken on as apprentices.

As mentioned earlier, there was also a major rise in population across England as a whole, from under 2.5 million in 1500 to about 5 million in 1650. The analysis of past population trends is far from easy, but it has been the subject of much research for several decades, including the development of family reconstitution studies and the methodical analysis of parish registers. It seems clear that the increase in population was due largely to a fall in mortality, not least the retreat of the plague. A rise in fecundity, stemming from a small decrease in the average age of women at marriage, was probably also important.

The increase in population affected the structure of society by leading to overpopulation. This was definitely so as far as the distribution of resources was concerned and certainly in comparison with the fifteenth century. An increasing population led to greater demand, which encouraged a persistent rise in prices in the sixteenth century, a process further encouraged by a serious debasement of the coinage. The increase in food prices did not automatically result in a rise in rents, because rents were commonly unalterable, with many small tenant farmers on long leases that the gentry could not easily break. Nevertheless, the demand for food caused the rents of agricultural land to rise proportionately more rapidly than wages. This gap affected both tenants and those with little or no land, while the fact that the increase in food prices was higher than that in wages hit the poor, both rural and urban.

In a volatile and strained situation, agrarian capitalism became more intense and was widely perceived as harsh and immoral. In *Julius Caesar*, Brutus reproaches Cassius with corruption, adding:

> I can raise no money by vile means:
> By heaven, I had rather coin my heart,
> And drop my blood for drachmas, than to wring
> From the hard hands of peasants their vile trash
> By any indirection. (IV, iii)

Benefiting from price inflation and the cheaper relative cost of labor, landlords tried to increase the yield of their estates, both from their tenants and from the land that they worked directly, and they sought to destroy the system of customary tenure. As a result, more land came to be rented or leased out at market rates—not that this was a new tension or process. Much of the peasantry lost status and became little different from poorly paid wage laborers. Shakespeare himself sought to pursue the opportunities provided by economic change by buying up local property and, possibly, supporting enclosures and speculating in grain.[2]

The poor in general were unable to share in the greater affluence of the period, unless through crime, charity, or as servants. They ate less, and less well, and their food was prepared in a different way to that of the wealthy and eaten in a different context. For example, the poor tended to eat rye or barley bread and not bread made from wheat.[3] Moreover, the poor were affected by the disruption, if not dismantling, of traditional forms of social welfare, as so many Church assets were reorganized or seized during the Reformation. While some hospitals (a term including buildings that provided care for the destitute as well as for the sick), such as that attached to St. Mary Spital in London, were dissolved, others were reestablished on more secular lines.

The increasing mobility of labor, with young people moving from home with expectations of employment, helped to translate more difficult economic conditions into vagrancy. The growing number of paupers and vagrants greatly concerned successive governments, although more for reasons of law and order, in both town and country, than because of humane concern about the poor. There was scant understanding of the many and serious problems posed by unemployment and underemployment. Indeed, such hardships were frequently treated as self-inflicted and thus deserving only of neglect or punishment.

The standard precept of care was that it should discriminate between the deserving and the undeserving. This religio-moral principle was applied on grounds of age, health, and gender and not with reference to employment or income. Thus, the infirm, the elderly, the young, and women with children were the prime beneficiaries of poor relief, albeit often in a harsh fashion, such as putting young children to work.[4] In contrast, the able-bodied were denied poor relief, whether they were in low-paid employment/underemployment or unemployment.

The condition of the poor was often extremely difficult and notably so if they were mentally ill. In *King Lear*, a play that develops in and through its protagonist to provide a social conscience, Edgar comments on itinerant, insane beggars:

The country gives me proof and precedent
Of Bedlam beggars, who, with roaring voices,

Strike in their numb'd and mortified bare arms
Pins, wooden pricks, nails, sprigs of rosemary;
And with this horrible object, from low farms,
Poor pelting villages, sheep-cotes, and mills,
Sometimes with lunatic bans, sometimes with prayers,
Enforce their charity. (II, iii)

At the same time, government action in many aspects sought to benefit all. For example, as a major aspect of the "moral economy" of the period, there was intervention in the grain market, which was regularized with the issue of Books of Orders from 1586. In response to the threat of grain shortages—a serious challenge to public order as well as raising issues of health and even survival—justices of the peace were required to determine the availability of surplus grain and to ensure that it was brought to market. Focusing on distribution and allocation, as cause and solution, ensured a need for information about grain supplies. There was, however, no possibility of alleviating the situation by imports. The days of grain imports from the New World were long in the future and came only after the development of large steamships in the late nineteenth century, as well as of railways to move the grain on land.

A series of Poor Law statutes was passed in England, in 1531, 1536, 1547, 1572, 1576, 1598, and 1601, in an attempt to respond to popular mobility and social dynamism[5] by regulating and providing for concern about the poor—or, rather, those of the poor who were to be helped. In place of occasional aid, there were to be regular payments, with all the structures and guidance that this required. National direction and pressure were key elements. Compulsory poor rates were introduced in 1572, and in 1598 the relief of poverty was made the responsibility of individual parishes. This was a reflection of the "parish state," the local nature of education, health and welfare provision, and the maintenance of basic law and order and also of the lack of any comprehensive or even extensive system of direct agents of the central government.[6]

Social strains, exacerbated by a sequence of disastrous harvests in 1596–98, led to a national Poor Law and not a major rebellion. However, despite the efforts of government, bad harvests were difficult to counter. They may have been responsible for the increased reference to debt in wills of the period drawn up in the county of Essex. Rumors of probable rebellion were widespread, there were preparations for one in Oxfordshire in 1597, and the 1598 Poor Law did not prevent the Midlands' rising of 1607, which affected Leicestershire, Northamptonshire, and Warwickshire. The rising achieved nothing.

In London, the former royal palace of Bridewell was acquired by the city's corporation in 1553 as a house of correction, an important component of an attempt to restructure the system of social welfare. Bridewell indeed served as a model for institutions elsewhere. The able-bodied were made to work, with some also sent in chain gangs to clean streets and ditches and others, later, as indentured servants, to Virginia in order to provide controlled labor.

More generally across England, there was policing by parish constables, watchmen, and churchwardens as part of the attempt to clear the streets and to contain what was seen as disorder or immorality. In *Much Ado About Nothing*, Dogberry tells the Constable of the Watch to "comprehend all vagrom men," in other words, seize any vagrants (III, iii). This was a version of the "rounding up all the usual suspects" seen in the film *Casablanca* (1942). This was an approach that, in England, as in Vichy-run Morocco, pressed particularly hard on poor strangers.

Rural parishes that attracted immigration tended to be those that offered opportunities for cottage industry. The availability of common land (land to which all had access) could also be a very important factor as it eased the problem of feeding the increased population by giving them access to this land.

Yet, at the local level, there were major variations in employment, prosperity, and charity. These variations reflected the extent to which a national demographic regime was both super-imposed on and mediated through very varied local patterns of activity. However, poverty pressed on the neighborliness within the parish community that was important to social cohesion and to the maintenance of order.

At the same time that poverty was one major issue, economic growth and diversification led to an increasingly complex social pattern, with hierarchical assumptions complicated and even challenged. This affected not only relations within and between social groups but also in families. Wives could find themselves do-ing an increased variety of tasks and, in part, defining themselves accordingly. Witness statements in Church courts indicated that women deployed occupational descriptors about themselves less often than men ("spinsters" being one of the commoner terms), but, nevertheless, they gave verb-oriented accounts of what they did, and many women claimed to be able to maintain themselves and others.[7]

Urban expansion was a product of the role of towns as cen-ters of manufacturing, trade, government, and leisure. Yet all four were also pursued in the countryside, just as there was much market gardening within town walls, as well as orchards and pastures—the latter particularly for milk, which could not be refrigerated, treated, or preserved. With the exception of London, cities were small, and the countryside, even for London, was always nearby. For example, in 1523, Worcester ranked sixteenth among England's towns by population, but this was then only about 4,000 people and had risen to only about 6,000 in 1646. Evesham, the next biggest town in Worcestershire, a prosperous county next to Shakespeare's native Warwickshire, had only about 1,400 people—the size of a modest village of today—in the mid-sixteenth century.

Rural fairs remained important for trade, but their episodic character was a reminder of the rhythm of seasonal activity that framed life, and not least the economy. Their impact was spread by peddlers. In *The Winter's Tale*, the Clown is sent "to buy for our sheep-shearing feast 'Three pound of sugar; five pound of currants; rice ... saffron ... mace ... nutmegs ... a race [root] or two of ginger ... four pound of prunes ... raisins'" (IV, iii). This is a reminder of the social role of feasts and how they gave access to food that was out of the ordinary. The Clown meets Autolycus, a courtier-turned-peddler who, having picked his pocket, then goes to the feast, with a servant praising his wares:

> He hath songs for man or woman, of all sizes—no milliner can so fit his customers with gloves. He has the prettiest love-songs for maids.... He hath ribands of all the colours i'the rainbow; points [laces] ... inkles [coarse linen tape], caddisses [ribbons], cambrics, lawns [fine linen]. (IV, iv)

The life and government of towns with their relatively small population put an emphasis on the views, alignments, and commitments of a limited group of individuals and of the families they represented, the pattern also seen in the countryside. In this context, feuds could be longstanding, a characteristic Shakespeare brilliantly captured for Verona in his *Romeo and Juliet*, where they shape life, convey and affirm status, and are repeatedly revealed as not only murderous but also inherently meaningless. In England, these feuds looked back to national, as well as local, political differences and divisions. This process was greatly exacerbated, first, by the Wars of the Roses and then by the Reformation. Nevertheless, in England, family feuds rarely led to significant violence, and this situation became more the case as royal authority was imposed under the Tudors. Instead, feuds were increasingly pursued by means of appealing to royal authority and power and via the law courts.[8] As a consequence, Shakespeare's plays that were based on Italian stories often reflected social arrangements, especially family structures, that, although meaningful to English audiences, would still have appeared somewhat exotic.

Feuds were an aspect of a more general, widespread, and insistent pursuit of status. This pursuit was seen in positive as well as negative senses (for example, marriages as well as violence) but with competition as a common theme. Status was pursued in dynasticism, notably marital strategies, for both individuals and their heirs and connections (as in *Romeo and Juliet*), and also in the physicalities of land acquisition and building for display, as well as in aspects of prestige that were differently real and intangible. The latter was seen in particular in heraldry and the related organization of the grants and regrants of arms, the production of pedigree rolls, and the expression and policing of pretension. Heraldry proved a way for the newly arrived to demonstrate status and, in part in response, for those longer established to maintain and strengthen theirs. As a result, quarterings on coats of arms increased, and heraldry was stamped into decorative schemes and displayed and demonstrated at funerals. Greed and snobbery played significant roles in this process, and Ben Jonson was to criticize the College of Heralds accordingly. However, heraldic visitations ensured that only those qualified to do so used armorial bearings.[9]

Alongside any emphasis on elements of economic (and other) continuity in Shakespeare's England, it is necessary to draw attention to the many signs of economic change. There was an important social dimension to this change. The poverty of the majority was counterpointed by the growing comfort that characterized the wealthier, including the increase in the range of household effects bequeathed in wills, which was apparent, for instance, in the wills drawn up by Bristol citizens in the 1590s. Probate inventories for the Warwickshire village of Stoneleigh indicate more furniture, including beds.[10] More generally, alongside periodic food shortages for the many, there were imported luxury goods and products for the few. The tax assessments of the better-off were low, both on capital and on income, which helped to sustain their consumption patterns.

This contrast was also seen in political and religious change, with the bulk of the population neither consulted nor considered, other than in terms of control. The absence of consultation was more disruptive than it had been ever since the Norman Conquest of 1066. Change was not simply a matter of monarchs and aristocratic factions competing for the spoils of power and privilege but, with the Reformation, also a deep-seated and divisive transformation in the nation's ideology, culture, and, in the case of the monasteries, the built landscape. As later with the impact on the constitution and broader culture of the Glorious Revolution of 1688–89, the extent of this transformation has been largely overlooked because, from the reign of Elizabeth, the Reformation was seen as the national destiny and as central to national identity. English became the language of God's work, and the monarch was now head of the Church, even if, from Elizabeth I onward, referred to as Supreme Governor rather than Supreme Head. The change with Elizabeth was deeply symbolic, as well as being important both ecclesiastically and politically.

The symbolic and practical, cultural, and ideological disruption of the Reformation was intense however. For example, the assertion by the English Church that purgatory did not exist and the consequent abolition of prayers for the dead destroyed the potent links between the communities of the living and the dead. These links had had a range of consequences including the widespread belief in ghosts. The attack on purgatory, however, did not end this belief.

The loss of the monasteries in the 1530s also brought much disruption, including, in many localities, the breakdown of poor and medical relief. Nevertheless, although in the short term monastic charity was ended, Protestant-influenced patterns of charitable giving developed quite soon. Instead of bequests for masses for the dead and chantry priests, they were now more frequently left for parish charities, educational provision, and almshouses, all of which were significant.[11] Hospitals were refounded, for example that in Norwich in 1549, now placed under the control of the city.[12]

Another charitable impulse was the establishment of many grammar schools, such as that at Stratford, refounded in 1553, where Shakespeare was very likely educated and with an impact on his creative practice.[13] Although education had played a major role already in late medieval towns, and without there being any connection to printing, the new importance attached to schooling, as a means to approach and use the world of print, encouraged a greater emphasis both on education and on the role of learning in education. Yet, this was also socially divisive, since access to learning (for example, in the grammar schools) developed in terms of existing social structures and practices. Because so many children went out to work, their access to formal education was limited. Education was not supported by taxation, central or local, but had to be paid for by the pupil's family (which was generally the case in grammar schools) or by a benefactor, dead or alive. There were many small, local charity schools. Attendance at school was lower in summer, which was the high point, with harvesting, of agricultural work.

Education was also linked to social mobility. On the one hand, a higher (although still small) proportion of boys went to university at this time than at any other period before the 1960s. But for every child who acquired some formal education, there were others who received little or none. Girls, the rural population, and the poor—each had fewer educational opportunities. Most people could neither read nor afford books; most men and, even more, women lacked formal education, and the difficulty, even inability, of the poor to express themselves was accentuated, not least in terms of the vocabulary available. This difficulty was captured by Shakespeare, although often in comic fashion rather than by making the poor the emotional or psychological centers of attention in his plays. Even for those who received some schooling, the classical teaching offered by the grammar schools—including very probably to Shakespeare in Stratford—was not available in most schools.

The connections between education in the broadest sense and the theater were very close. The plays necessarily emphasized appearing to be the right person by fine talking, smooth manners, the right clothes, and so on.

Shakespeare devoted an enormous amount of attention in his plays, whether comedies, tragedies, or histories, and in his sonnets to relations between the sexes. For both genders, relations within families, and between the generations were a crucial dynamic. The situation, nevertheless, was very different from that in modern England, including in sexuality, courtship, marriage, divorce, and relations between the generations. Marriage was central to household structure, sex, procreation, and the upbringing of children. Most childbearing was within marriage, although, as the dialogue of many of Shakespeare's plays points out, adultery was a major anxiety, and by both men and women. Barring occasional bigamies and illegal wife sales, marriage, as a religious act, was irreversible and not to be ended by divorce. As a consequence, marriage ended only with the death of one of the partners or with a desertion that involved flight from the community: either real flight or the flight of a pretend death. The latter was a theme brilliantly explored by Shakespeare, although very differently, as in *The Winter's Tale* and *Romeo and Juliet*.

In *Othello*, in the person of Emilia, Iago's wife, a frequently underrated character, Shakespeare makes a powerful call for women to be treated equally, one in which emotion, affection, and sexual fidelity are intertwined:

I do think it is their husbands' faults
If wives do fall. Say that they [the husbands] slack their duties [sexual
    responsibilities]
And pour our treasures into foreign laps,
Or else break out in peevish jealousies,
Throwing restraint upon us; or say they strike us,

Or scant our former having in despite
Why, we have galls [spirit to resent injury], and though we have
    some grace,
Yet have we some revenge. Let husbands know
Their wives have sense like them. They see and smell
And have their palates both for sweet and sour,
As husbands have. What is it that they do
When they change us for others? Is it sport?
I think it is. And doth affection [passion] breed it?
I think it doth. Is 't frailty that thus errs?
It is so too. And have not we affections?
Desires for sport? and frailty? as men have?
Then let them use us well; else let them know,
The ills we do, their ills instruct us so. (IV, iii)

She is far from being the only forthright and perceptive wife in
Shakespeare's plays. Julius Caesar is given good advice by his wife,
Calphurnia. She urges him not to leave their house in Rome on
the Ides of March. In his pride of purpose and reputation and also
in accordance with his fate, Caesar ignores her and is murdered.
At a different level, in *The Merry Wives of Windsor*, Mistress Page
and Mistress Ford humorously outmaneuver male characters.

As Shakespeare makes clear, gender and generational relations
could also be greatly affected by social status. This issue could be
addressed, both dramatically and humorously, by confusion as to
identity and intention, as with gender relations in *Twelfth Night*,
a theme also explored in the films *Shakespeare in Love* (1998) and
*All Is True* (2018). Nevertheless, there were serious questions
about the relationships between gender, rank, and virtue—and
for both men and women. Sexuality was a key element, but the
pursuit or defense of status involved far more. In *Twelfth Night*,
Malvolio is mocked, both by other characters and by the playwright, for seeking to pursue enhanced status by marrying his
employer; but this is an honest attempt.

The absence of effective and available contraceptives and of safe, let
alone legal, abortion could lead to infanticide as a form of postbirth

contraception: action in 1624 against the concealment of the deaths of newborn children was specifically aimed at unmarried mothers. There may have been awareness of the capacity of ergotism—poisoning through eating cereals affected by the ergot fungus—to act as an abortifacient. Although there could be doubts over female chastity, and therefore over the identity of fathers, doubts frequently referred to in plays, recorded illegitimacy rates were low. This was despite marriage on average not being until both parties were in their twenties, whatever the impression of young marriage created by *Romeo and Juliet* and sustained by film versions of the play. Premarital sexual activity rates were low by modern standards, especially for women.[14] In addition, many men and women never married.

At the same time, as noted by Shakespeare, for example, in *Measure for Measure*, celibacy did not satisfy all. Indeed, aside from seduction, there was prostitution, which was the prime form of casual sex. Prostitutes were frequently depicted in Shakespeare's plays, as with the courtesan in *The Comedy of Errors*, whom Antipholus of Ephesus favors, while his twin brother, Antipholus of Syracuse, rejects her as "the devil's dam" (IV, iii). Shakespeare provides observations on the conduct of prostitutes, as when, in *Othello*, he has Iago describe Bianca:

A huswife that by selling her desires
Buys herself bread and cloth. It is a creature
That dotes on Cassio (as 'tis the strumpet's plague
To beguile many and be beguiled by one). (IV, i)

Bianca subsequently denies being a "strumpet." There were many puns relating to prostitutes, as with the use of the term "laced mutton" in *The Two Gentlemen of Verona* (I, i).

Prostitution was commonplace in Tudor England, notably in the towns. In London, it was particularly prevalent in Southwark, the prime theater area. Shakespeare's treatment of prostitution in his plays throws a very critical light on male conduct, most obviously in *Pericles*, where Marina, a Cordelia-like character, is sold by pirates to a brothel in Mitylene. The bawd, the woman who keeps a brothel, has a harsh attitude:

> BAWD: We were never so much out of creatures. We have but poor three, and they can do no more than they can do; and they with continual action are even as good as rotten. . . . The stuff we have, a strong wind will blow it to pieces, they are so pitifully sodden.
> PANDAR: Thou sayest true; they're too unwholesome, o'conscience. The poor Transylvanian is dead, that lay with the little baggage.
> BOULT [servant to Pandar]: Ay, she quickly pooped him; she made him roast-meat for worms. (IV, ii)

The Bawd then tells Boult to shout around town that she has a new girl whose virginity will go to the highest bidder, adding, "Such a maidenhead were no cheap thing, if men were as they have been." The Bawd tells Marina: "If it please the gods to defend you by men, then men must comfort you, men must feed you, men must stir you up." The interest of a Frenchman in Marina is referred to and also the fact that he has venereal disease (IV, ii). Lysimachus seeks a woman "that a man may deal withal, and defy the surgeon," in other words, not catch venereal disease from. He asks Marina if she has been a prostitute since being five or seven. After he has been repelled by her virtue, the Bawd tells Boult to "take her away; use her at thy pleasure; crack the glass of her virginity, and make the rest malleable" (IV, vi).

Venereal disease, the "pox," is often referred to in the plays, as in *Timon of Athens*, where the spread of syphilis from prostitutes and the harshness of the cures are mentioned by Timon as aspects of his unbalanced horror with the world:

> This fell whore of thine
> Hath in her more destruction than thy sword
> For all her cherubin look.
> Be a whore still; they love thee not that use thee;
> Give them diseases, leaving with thee their lust.
> Make use of thy salt hours; season the slaves
> For tubs and baths; bring down rose-checked youth
> To the tub-fast and diet. (IV, iii)

Of course, the prostitutes had got their diseases from men. The death of Nell, a character from *Henry IV*, from the "malady of France," is mentioned in *Henry V* (V, i). Venereal disease is discussed in many other plays, including *Troilus and Cressida*. In *Measure for Measure*, all the brothels in Vienna's suburbs are pulled down at the behest of Angelo, but lust is scarcely affected, notably as he is shown to be a would-be seducer. Again, the theme in that play is that of a maiden under threat from a predatory and dangerous male.

Law and social convention gave authority to fathers and husbands, as the unmarried Luciana discusses with her married sister, Adriana, in *The Comedy of Errors*. Adriana complains that men have more liberty, but Luciana replies:

> There's nothing situate under heaven's eye
> But hath his bound, in earth, in sea, in sky
> The beasts, the fishes, and the winged fowls,
> Are their males' subjects and at their controls.
> Men, more divine, the masters of all these,
> Lords of the wide world, and wild wat'ry seas,
> Imbu'd with intellectual sense and souls,
> Of more pre-eminence than fish and fowls,
> Are masters to their females and their lords:
> . . . . . . . . . . . . . . . . . . . . . . . . . . . . . . . . . . . . . .
> Ere I learn love, I'll practise to obey. (II, i)

Patriarchalism was strongly entrenched in laws and, if women could turn to law, then that process involving appealing to men to police patriarchal practices.[15] In practice, however, male authority was often tempered by the dynamics of family life, the moral authority of wives and mothers, the play of personality, the need for cooperation between men and women—however grudging, if families were to cope with challenges—and the extent to which patriarchal authority was subverted and compromised by the individual and collective character of female culture.[16]

The play of personality was a key element in enhancing the position of individual women. This was notably so in Shakespeare's plays, as in *Antony and Cleopatra, Macbeth,* and *The Taming of the Shrew,* and also more generally. In *Othello,* Iago complains to Emilia, his wife:

> You are pictures [silent] out of door,
> Bells in your parlours, wildcats in your kitchens,
> Saints in your injuries [look innocent when about to attack], devils
>     being offended. (II, i)

Their relationship is poor, with Iago suspicious of a past affair between Othello and Emilia, which gives fire to his anger and jealousy and energy to his sexual references. Emilia offers Desdemona a jaundiced account of marriage:

> Tis not a year or two shows us a man.
> They are all but stomachs, and we all but food;
> They eat us hungerly, and when they are full,
> They belch us. (III, iv)

The stages in a relationship are also significant, as Rosalind notes in *As You Like It*:

> Say "a day" without the "ever." No, no, Orlando,
> Men are April when they woo, December when they wed;
> Maids are May when they are maids, but the sky
> Changes when they are wives. (IV, i)

Courtship and marriage were linked to social politics, which were hierarchical and often harshly so. This politics could be the subject of humorous overturning on the stage. In Francis Beaumont's lively comedy *The Knight of the Burning Pestle* (1607), an apprentice, Jasper, marries Luce, the daughter of his master, a merchant, against the latter's will, as he favors another suitor. Luce is seized by her parents and locked up. Feigning death, Jasper is taken into the house in a coffin, where he frightens the merchant by appearing as a ghost and thus gains his consent. Thomas Dekker's comedy *The Shoemaker's Holiday* (1599) has a nobleman disguise himself as a shoemaker to pursue his love for another shoemaker's daughter.

Hierarchies could clash with personal favor. This was shown to comic effect in *Twelfth Night*. The clash could also be savagely disruptive, as in *Othello*, which begins with Iago complaining:

> Why, there's no remedy. 'Tis the curse of service:
> Preferment goes by letter and affection,
> And not by old gradation, where each second
> Stood heir to th'first. (I, i)

Age was an important aspect of hierarchy but scarcely one without tension. The Shepherd remarks in *The Winter's Tale*: "I would there were no age between sixteen and three-and-twenty, or that youth would sleep out the rest; for there is nothing in the between but getting wenches with child, wronging the ancientry, stealing, fighting" (III, iii).

Quite apart from its role in his sonnets, courtship is a major theme in Shakespeare's plays: the leading one in several plays and one that ranges within and across social, national, and religious divides. Courtship offers a range of contexts, dynamics, and moods, from wit to tragedy, with both present in *Much Ado About Nothing*. The courtship that Shakespeare depicts reflected social norms but would also have given ideas of how to behave.

Shakespeare depicted many strong women, including Cleopatra, Margaret of Anjou, Katherine of Aragon, Lady Macbeth, Volumnia, and Joan of Arc. Their fates vary greatly, but several are allowed to show character, bravery, purpose, and poise.[17] A number of traditions and prototypes are brought into play in the treatment of these and other women, notably stories from the classical world (most prominently, of Antony and Cleopatra), together with the ideas and language of medieval chivalry. Far from becoming outdated, let alone disappearing, each tradition had enjoyed a revival as a consequence of Renaissance court culture, as well as the revival and dissemination of established ideas by means of printing. A female ruler, such as Elizabeth, made the situation more significant and yet complex,[18] as did other royal women, especially Mary, Queen of Scots. The court context of so many of the plays underlined these themes and facilitated their presentation, not least in wordplay between the protagonists, as well as in stories of love that was eventually successful (or not).

Other themes also played a role. Straightforward power was one. There was a degree of menace, not just as well as but also alongside some of the talk of courtship. This menace could reflect the pernicious, if not evil, nature of particular characters, such as Richard III. His successful wooing of Anne Neville (1456–85)—daughter of Warwick the "King-Maker" and young widow of Edward, Prince of Wales (1453–71), who was slaughtered at Tewkesbury in 1471—is that of a woman whose own first husband he had murdered. In a very sinister fashion, Richard also approaches Edward IV's widow, Queen Elizabeth, to woo her daughter Elizabeth, his niece, on his behalf. She points out that he has been responsible for the death of her sons, the Princes in the Tower: Edward V and his younger brother, Richard, Duke of York:

> ELIZABETH: thou didst kill my children.
> RICHARD: But in your daughter's womb I bury them:
>   Where, in that nest of spicery, they shall breed
>   Selves of themselves. (IV, iv)

This menace could also be a correct assessment of the abuse of authority, which is, indeed, the major theme in *Measure for Measure*, with Angelo focusing this abuse on obtaining sexual control over the sister of a man condemned to death. Aside from menace, violence itself is often seen as likely to lead to rape, both in the case of war and with reference to brigands.

In England, the statute against rape was restored in 1562, and those convicted of rape were exempted from a general pardon in 1609. Rape was a felony but was often prosecuted as assault, abduction, and as a property crime, especially if by men of high status. The penalties for conviction of rape were severe, including life imprisonment and heavy fines, and under the law of Elizabeth I, the death penalty was added. Rape was also prosecuted as a moral offense in Church courts, as a form of fornication or adultery.[19] Another aspect of power is represented by the use of women as prostitutes. The latter did not have to be presented as victims and could be depicted in an attractive or, at least, exciting light, but, as Shakespeare makes clear and is discussed above, they can also be or become victims of authority, power, and abuse and commonly indeed were or became so.

The sphere of straightforward propositioning was different, but can be presented as resting on a degree of violence or almost intimidatory wooing. This was not least because, on the longstanding pattern of the hunt of animals, the loss of virginity and chastity[20] is often seen as an element—a forceful element indeed—of propositioning and courtship. This focus can leave modern audiences very uncomfortable. For example, in *The Tempest*, Ferdinand remarks on meeting Miranda, who, due to being stranded on an island with her father and with no other, has never herself seen a young man:

> O, if a virgin,
> And your affection not gone forth, I'll make you
> The Queen of Naples. (I, ii)

The eventual submission of Katherine to her husband in *The Taming of the Shrew* has the same effect on modern audiences. It appears as a submission that is both a culmination of the play and almost a betrayal of the play's theme of female independence, such that the submission is sometimes played ironically:

> Thy husband is thy lord, thy life, thy keeper,
> Thy head, thy sovereign; one that cares for thee . . .
> [He] craves no other tribute at thy hands
> But love, fair looks, and true obedience. (V, ii)

Reality was generally far bleaker than that of willfulness or foolish obstacles overcome. Queen Elizabeth herself was furious that, in 1560, her cousin Lady Catharine Grey, daughter of Henry, Duke of Suffolk, and sister of Lady Jane Grey, had secretly married Edward, Earl of Hertford, the eldest surviving son of Protector Somerset. She had them both sent to the Tower of London and the marriage annulled and did not recognize Catharine's children. The eldest son, Edward, Lord Beauchamp, born in the Tower, inherited the Suffolk claim to the royal succession.

The plight of young love, at the mercy of the power of parents or guardians, was a frequent theme in drama, as in Thomas Middleton and Thomas Dekker's *The Roaring Girl* (1610). Repeatedly, status and authority were both involved. In Philip Massinger's *A New Way to Pay Old Debts* (c. 1622), the greed of the villain, Sir Giles Overreach, is focused on the calculation of social advantage through family marriages, and failure leads to his becoming mad. In *The Witch of Edmonton* (c. 1621) by William Rowley, John Ford, and Dekker, Susan Carter is murdered by Frank Thorney. He had bigamously married her to secure his inheritance, as she is his father's choice. However, he has a secret wife, the servant Winifred. In *Pericles*, the prologue reveals that King Antiochus is having a secret incestuous affair with his daughter, and that is the setting for the deceit and menace at the outset. Indeed, the play as a whole offers a varied but insistent palette of menace. In *Othello*, Brabantino sees his daughter Desdemona's pursuit of her love with Othello as

> treason of the blood!
> Fathers, from hence trust not your daughters' minds
> By what you see them act. (I, i)

Brabantino is convinced that his daughter has been beguiled "by spells and medicines bought of mountebanks" but finds her ready to "confess that she was half the wooer" (I, iii).

Attitudes to women also affected the response of contemporaries to Queen Elizabeth, although, in that, there was the very recent example of her half sister, Mary Tudor.[21] Elizabeth's court preachers emphasized traditional stereotypes of feminine weakness and depicted the queen as a woman rescued by God rather than as a warrior queen, although she created a iconographical and political space for herself and was presented by supporters as an exceptional woman who had qualities above the ordinary and therefore deserved the obedience that was her just deserts as ruler.[22] Presented in the Bible as masculine, God's masculine attributes were unsurprisingly underlined since clergy were men, and social pressures were certainly hostile to female independence. Much in Elizabethan society was traditional, for example, in the different standards applied to male and female premarital and extramarital sex and in the strictures against homosexuality, which was viewed as immoral and considered illegal. More particularly, homosexual sex was regarded as a sin and was treated harshly in the legal systems of the age. Ironically, in light of the practice of giving all the female roles onstage to male actors, there was no social acceptance of changing gender identities.

Double standards in sexual behavior were clear, with men content to ignore their illegitimate children and/or have a reputation for having illegitimate children, as with Gloucester at the start of *King Lear*; whereas, in a culture of sexual honor that women played a key role in maintaining (including by gossip), women who lacked chastity were usually castigated. In *King Lear*, Gloucester's harsh fate, as a result of betrayal by his bastard, Edmund, however, is a return on his feckless conduct, which is a sin. If he is more sinned against than sinning, the latter is the cause of the former. Nevertheless, justice ensures that Gloucester is allowed to redeem himself: a process that brings him nobility of spirit.

Aside from Edmund in *King Lear*, Faulconbridge in *King John*, a far more positive figure, is another bastard who has a dynamic impact and who challenges conventional hierarchies. The illegitimate son of John's brother and predecessor, Richard I (the Lionheart), he is shown to have more character than John.

Faulconbridge is a fictional creation based on Richard's illegitimate son, Philip of Cognac, although, unlike in the play, where he is presented as the son of Lady Faulconbridge, his mother is unknown.[23]

Independence in women was not encouraged and, indeed, was disapproved of. Elizabeth had frequently to cope with slanderous and politically compromising rumors about her preferences for men. Aside from women not acting in plays, women letter writers were constrained by the conventions of the genre.[24] At the same time, Shakespeare's depiction of women is scarcely one of weakness or inconsequence. Nor is their position that of men's shadows dependent for their significance on the position of the latter. In the historical plays, there are patriarchal stances, character, and lines but also, as discussed above, significant women, such as Cleopatra, Joan of Arc, Queen Margaret in *Henry VI*, and Queen Katharine in *Henry VIII*. All fall victim to men, the first two losing their life, but none can be described as a cypher. Indeed, Cleopatra commits suicide.[25]

Nuns, a group discussed by Shakespeare, for example, with the Abbess in *The Comedy of Errors* and also in pre-Christian reference in the shape of Diana's vestals in *Pericles*, were probably the group that lost most from the Reformation. At the same time, the Reformation offered new opportunities to female spirituality, and women were able both to claim and to exercise a right to conscience and self-determination in religious matters. Martyrdom was a key instance, with Foxe, in his *Book of Martyrs*, recording forty-eight female martyrs, who were presented as strident and not as domesticated. More generally, Foxe employed female imagery.[26] These opportunities, however, did not fully transcend gender limitations. The attitudes of Protestant sects largely represented traditional social ideals and practices, and few women rose to positions of authority within them.

The Reformation did lead, however, to a more sympathetic attitude toward marriage and sexual love within marriage, one that was reflected and considerably strengthened by the fact that clergy now could be married, as most soon were. Nevertheless, concern about the disruptive nature of sexual desire continued to focus on single and adulterous women rather than on men. At the same time, there was an important shift from regarding moral misdemeanors as matters for the Church courts to bringing them under secular authority so that prostitutes and women of ill repute were increasingly dealt with by the justices of the peace. This process preceded but was greatly furthered by the Reformation and matched the concern with social control expressed by moves against vagrancy.

The sexual standards of the day nevertheless reflected female as well as male views, suggesting that women, at least to some degree, supported the maintenance of patriarchy. This is a theme that is difficult to investigate but one that is not therefore less significant. Women punished as witches by a male-dominated legal system suffered terribly. However, women were not simply the victims of witchcraft accusations; they were also actively involved in bringing prosecutions and acting as witnesses and searchers for marks supposedly revealing witches. Furthermore, there were also male witches. More generally, women could be harshly punished for crimes, but most convictions were of men, and most penalties were inflicted on men. For example, with the exception of the killing of infants, women were less often guilty of homicide than men.[27] In general, women were more active in legal processes as a whole and thus had more control or, at least, influence over their lives than patriarchal nostrums might suggest.[28]

This was also the case with the informal legal processes, those of denunciation and proof, that played such a major part in many of Shakespeare's plays, and notably those near their close. In effect, within a world in which responses to contracts, oaths, pledges, and vows helped to define relationships and provide the occasions, energies, and turnabouts of plot,[29] there is a denouement or revelation. This is on the pattern of much detective fiction, a later genre that provides stories in which morality, justice, and redemption are often to the fore. In *Othello*, Emilia, denouncing Iago, responds to her husband's order that she go home, in his attempt to make her be silent and take her away from the apparent protection of a semipublic setting. She declares:

> Good gentlemen, let me have leave to speak.
> 'Tis proper I obey him, but not now.
> Perchance, Iago, I will ne'er go home.
> ... I will speak as liberal as the north [wind].
> Let heaven and men and devils, let them all,
> All, all, cry shame against me, yet I'll speak. (V, ii)

Emilia is not intimidated, even when threatened by Iago with his sword. In response to this threat, Gratiano has to intervene on her behalf, but that does not prevent the vicious Iago from killing her in a close to a play that, like *Hamlet*, has too many deaths.

Similarly, women played a greater role in inheritance than was legally essential. Many husbands showed confidence in their wives in the phrasing of a will; and the interest in the well-being of widows indicates the degree of matrimonial love.[30] Wives were not normally allowed to make wills, because in law they could not own property separately from their husbands. Spinsters and widows, however, had independence,[31] and wealthy ones could be of considerable importance, as was indicated by educational and religious bequests, for example, to a number of the colleges at Oxford and Cambridge. An act of Parliament in 1540 permitted the widows of peers to appoint two chaplains. Moreover, women had a number of ways to advance their views, not least because they were quite often an executor of their husband's will.[32] The particular status of widows played an important role in the dynamics of family structure and inheritance patterns, but so also did the high rate of maternal mortality. This situation led men to remarry and thus ensured numbers of stepmothers. Widowhood was a condition to which Shakespeare was sensitive, as in *All's Well That Ends Well*. Social practice and legal assumptions ensured that the household was seen as a particular space for women and, within that, that the domestic sphere was carefully delimited. At the same time, there was a variety of practice and presentation.[33]

Shakespeare depicts closeness in many marriages, although that in turn could create issues, most obviously with Lady Macbeth's destructive and seductive sway over her husband. Indeed, there is destructiveness in her seduction, as well as seduction in her destructiveness. Claudius and Gertrude in *Hamlet* are less close but also have a destructive mutual appeal. So, very differently, do Antony and Cleopatra, Othello and Desdemona, and, to a degree, Hamlet and Ophelia.

Whatever their personal circumstances and legal position, hard work was the fate of most women. This was commonly alongside their husbands. At the same time, domestic service was a common form of work for single people, both men and women. As household tasks were arduous and manual and the technological contribution minimal, such service was the life of many. Jobs such as the disposal of human excrement were unpleasant. Moreover, water carrying from the well and from other sources could cause physical deformity, while cleaning and drying clothes involved considerable physical effort. In *The Tempest*, Prospero sets Ferdinand to the heavy work of carrying wood, a regular task necessary for heating and cooking. Caliban is referred to by Prospero as a slave, one who will be punished if he does not work. Prospero tells him:

> Fetch us in fuel, and be quick . . .
> If thou neglect'st or dost unwillingly
> What I command, I'll rack thee with old cramps. (I, ii)

Wages for servants were poor and paid largely in kind. This made life very hard for those who wished to marry and leave service, for married servants were relatively uncommon. In addition, female servants were often sexually vulnerable to their masters and to others.[34]

The difficulties and complexities of the relationship between masters and servants were captured frequently by Shakespeare. Many servants enjoyed considerable independence, at least in what they said and in being trusted to undertake tasks, as with the two Dromios in *The Comedy of Errors* and the nurse in *Romeo and Juliet*. Servants were often presented as the confidants of their masters and their mistresses. At the same time, the latter could chastise them; and this chastisement could be depicted as violent, at least in threat. Not only male employers were harsh. In *The Two Gentlemen of Verona*, a servant, Lucetta, is struck by her mistress, Julia, for being "too saucy" (I, ii). Later in the play, Launce refers to the harsh treatment he has received because of his dog: "I have sat in the stocks, for puddings he hath stolen, otherwise he had been executed; I have stood on the pillory for geese he hath killed, otherwise he had suffered for't" (IV, iv). In *All's Well That Ends Well*, the Clown has recently been whipped. In *The Comedy of Errors*, the two Dromios are beaten, the Dromio of Ephesus saying:

> I would I were senseless, sir, that I might not feel your blows. . . . I have served him from the hour of my nativity to this instant, and have nothing at his hands for my service but blows. When I am cold, he heats me with beating; when I am warm, he cools me with beating; I am waked with it when I sleep; raised with it when I sit; driven out of doors with it when I go from home; welcomed home with it when I return; nay, I bear it on my shoulders. (IV, iv)

Part of the role of being a master was the ability to threaten and to carry out threats, and notably so within a household and over economic dependents, such as apprentices. Although the contrast between threat and action was frequent, a contrast shown in the plays, there was no suggestion of equality between masters and servants. At the same time, as with relations within families, the situation was made more complex by the favor shown

to confidants of real or apparent noble bearing, as with Viola—
"parentage above my fortunes" (I, v)—in *Twelfth Night*. In that
play, the problems of status were taken further in the presentation of Malvolio, the steward, who is encouraged to see himself
as the equal of his mistress, Olivia, a countess, due to her alleged
willingness to marry him. In turn, once the delusion is exposed,
he is treated with great cruelty, and his position as an underling
is driven home.

Alongside (and as an aspect of) concern about the socializa-
tion of children,[35] physical chastisement was a frequent fate of
children. Julia points out in *The Two Gentlemen of Verona*

> how wayward is this foolish love,
> That (like a testy babe) will scratch the nurse,
> And presently all humbled kiss the rod! (I, ii)

In the same scene, Julia strikes her servant Lucetta. Most
servants could be treated as if children and thus as vulnerable.
Children could be loved, but love often included a focus on the
driving out of sin and the instilling of discipline that could be
chilling and/or violent.[36]

This situation extended more widely with rulers and their subjects. Whether the monarch possessed a true and fit mastery was
crucial, as with the doubts of and harsh fate of the Fool in *King
Lear*. Relations between masters and servants were thus aspects
of the broader tensions of those within society as a whole. This
was notably so in the microcosm offered by the family, including
ruling families, as in *Hamlet*. Many of Shakespeare's plays focused on relations between fathers and either sons or daughters.
*King Lear*, with the king and Gloucester each as key figures, offers relations with both daughters (Lear) and sons (Gloucester).
Separately, although not in *King Lear*, the dynastic and thus political theme generally helped push relations between fathers and
sons to the fore, as in *Henry IV*, although not in the other English
history plays.

In part, the role of the father was an aspect not only of hierarchy and deference but also of a more general weight of the past. This weight was given theatrical force with the setting of actions in or alongside tombs and funerary monuments, as in *Romeo and Juliet*, *The Winter's Tale*, and, to comic effect, by "old Ninny's tomb," in the play within a play in *A Midsummer Night's Dream*. These settings reflected the major role of memorialization in English culture of the period, one seen in funeral services and preaching, as well as in charities, tombs, coats of arms, plate, and portraits.[37] Shakespeare captures this role not only in his history plays but also in the dialogue and settings of his other dramas.

Memorialization can be related to tension between the generations and notably between duty and inclination. Thus, at one level, *Romeo and Juliet* is a clash between young love and old-established family alignments; although, with the richness repeatedly seen in Shakespeare's plots and characterization, more than that is involved on both sides. In *Hamlet*, the generational clash is far more complex, but, again, there is a sense of the weight of the past, of the selfishness and malice of at least some of the previous generation, and of the victimhood of the young. The history plays, therefore, were not the only ones that offered a history. Indeed, the relationship between the different types of history plays is instructive. It throws light on the imaginative pressure exerted by the past, both real and fictional.

## NOTES

1. The call is that of the tawny owl. Joan is pouring in cold water to cool off the pot to avoid a boil over.

2. S. Schoenbaum, *Shakespeare: A Documentary Life* (Oxford, 1975); R. Bearman, *Shakespeare in the Stratford Records* (Stroud, UK, 1994).

3. P. Lloyd, *Food and Identity in England, 1540–1640: Eating to Impress* (London, 2015).

4. P. Crawford, *Parents of Poor Children in England, 1580–1800* (Oxford, 2010).

5. S. Hindle, A. Shepard, and J. Walter, eds., *Remaking English Society: Social Relations and Social Change in Early Modern England* (Woodbridge, UK, 2013).

6. M. K. McIntosh, *Poor Relief in England, 1350–1600* (Cambridge, 2012); A. L. Beier, *The Problem of the Poor in Tudor and Stuart England* (Lancaster, UK, 1983), *Masterless Men: The Vagrancy Problem in England, 1560–1640* (London, 1985), and *Social Thought in England, 1480–1730, from Body Social to Worldly Wealth* (Chicago, 2016).

7. A. Shepard, *Accounting for Oneself: Worth, Status and the Social Order in Early Modern England* (Oxford, 2015).

8. Hugh Vaux, "Violence and the Law in Tudor Cumberland: 'The Malice of the Lowthers,'" *Transactions of the Cumberland and Westmorland Antiquarian and Archaeological Society* 17 (2017): 121–35.

9. N. Ramsay, ed., *Heralds and Heraldry in Shakespeare's England* (Donington, UK, 2014).

10. S. Lang and M. McGregor, *Tudor Wills Proved in Bristol, 1546–1603* (Bristol, 1993); N. Alcock, *People at Home: Living in a Warwickshire Village, 1500–1800* (Chichester, UK, 1993).

11. A. Nicholls, *Almshouses in Early Modern England: Charitable Housing in the Mixed Company of Welfare, 1550–1725* (Woodbridge, UK, 2017).

12. E. Phillips, ed., *Health and Hygiene in Early-Modern Norwich: Account Rolls of the Great Hospital, Norwich, 1549–50 and 1570–71* (Norwich, UK, 2013).

13. L. Fox, *The Early History of King Edward VI School, Stratford-upon-Avon* (Stratford-upon-Avon, 1984); N. Rhodes, *Shakespeare and the Origins of English* (Oxford, 2004).

14. P. Laslett, *The World We Have Lost* (London, 1965) and *The World We Have Lost: Further Explored* (London, 1983).

15. R. Fritze, "'His Evel Life, His Troublesome Behavior': George Puttenham and His Marital Problems," *Archives* 29 (2004): 38–49.

16. A. Wilson, *Ritual and Conflict: The Social Relations of Childbirth in Early Modern England* (Farnham, UK, 2013).

17. T. Jankowski, *Women in Power in the Early Modern Drama* (Urbana, IL, 1992); I. Bell, *Elizabethan Women and the Poetry of Courtship* (Cambridge, 1998); G. Greer, *Shakespeare's Wife* (London, 2007); R. Houlbrooke, *Love and Dishonour in Elizabethan England: Two Families and a Failed Marriage* (Woodbridge, UK, 2017).

18. C. Bates, *The Rhetoric of Courtship in Elizabethan Language and Literature* (Cambridge, 1992).

19.  C. Dunn, *Stolen Women in Medieval England: Rape, Abduction, and Adultery, 1100–1500* (Cambridge, 2013).

20.  B. Johnson, *Chastity in Early Stuart Literature and Culture* (Cambridge, 2015).

21.  J. M. Richards, "Mary Tudor as 'Sole Quene'?: Gendering Tudor Monarchy," *Historical Journal* 40 (1997): 895–924.

22.  R. B. Waddington, "Elizabeth I and the Order of the Garter," *Sixteenth-Century Journal* 24 (1993): 97–113.

23.  H. V. Bonavita, *Illegitimacy and the National Family in Early Modern England* (Abingdon, UK, 2017); K. Pritchard, "Legitimacy, Illegitimacy and Sovereignty in Shakespeare's British Plays" (PhD, Manchester, 2011).

24.  J. Daybell, *Women Letter-Writers in Tudor England* (Oxford, 2006); G. Schneider, *The Culture of Epistolarity: Vernacular Letters and Letter Writing in Early Modern England, 1500–1700* (Newark, DE, 2005); J. M. Gray, *Oaths and the English Reformation* (Cambridge, 2013).

25.  N. Levine, *Women's Matters: Politics, Gender, and Nation in Shakespeare's Early Plays* (Newark, DE, 1998).

26.  M. Hickerson, *Making Women Martyrs in Tudor England* (Basingstoke, UK, 2005).

27.  J. Sharpe and J. R. Dickinson, "Revisiting the 'Violence We Have Lost': Homicide in Seventeenth-Century Cheshire," *English Historical Review* 131 (2016): 302–3.

28.  J. Kermode and G. Walker, eds., *Women, Crime and the Courts in Early Modern England* (London, 1994).

29.  J. Kerrigan, *Shakespeare's Binding Language* (Oxford, 2016).

30.  E. Spring, *Law, Land, and Family: Aristocratic Inheritance in England, 1300 to 1800* (Chapel Hill, NC, 1994).

31.  J. Spicksley, ed., *The Business and Household Accounts of Joyce Jeffreys, Spinster of Hereford, 1638–1648* (Oxford, 2012).

32.  S. James, *Women's Voices in Tudor Wills, 1485–1603: Authority, Influence and Material Culture* (Farnham, UK, 2015); B. Moring and R. Wall, *Widows in European Economy and Society, 1600–1920* (Woodbridge, UK, 2017).

33.  M. Wiesner-Hanks, ed., *Mapping Gendered Routes and Spaces in the Early Modern World* (Farnham, UK, 2015).

34.  J. Whittle, ed., *Servants in Rural Europe, 1400–1900* (Woodbridge, UK, 2017).

35.  M. Bailey, *Socialising the Child in Late Medieval England, c. 1400–1600* (Woodbridge, UK, 2012).

36. A. Fletcher, *Growing Up in England: The Experience of Childhood, 1600–1914* (New Haven, CT, 2008).

37. I. Archer, "The Arts and Memorialization in Early Modern London," in *Imagining Early Modern London: Perceptions and Portrayals of the City from Stow to Strype, 1598–1720*, ed. J. F. Merritt (New York, 2001), 89–113, esp. 96–113.

# HEALTH AND MEDICINE

BECAUSE OF LOW LIFE EXPECTANCY, the average experience of life and of life events for the people of the period necessarily came at a younger age than for the average person today.
This experience was shaped within a context of an ever-present
threat of death, disease, injury, and pain. There was still the joy
and pleasure, exultation and exhilaration of life, and Shakespeare
provides much on these; but the demographics were chilling.
Alongside a lucky few individuals who lived to old age and acquired a venerable status accordingly, there were many lives
quickly cut short, in the case of women especially in childbirth.
Child mortality figures continued to be high, indeed very high by
modern standards. For example, 38 percent of the children born
in Penrith in the Northwest of England between 1650 and 1700
died before reaching the age of six.

The heavy human toll was seen in Stratford with Shakespeare's
family, notably with the death of his two older siblings, Joan and
Margaret, both as babies, of his sister Anne in girlhood, and
of his son Hamnet, who died aged eleven. So also in London,
where his younger brother, Edmund, an actor, died. After giving
birth to a stillborn child, Ann, the wife of the poet John Donne
(1572–1631), died in 1617, and her husband, who became dean of

St. Paul's Cathedral in 1621, long remained depressed. Suffering was a frequent theme in his poetry, not least as he moved from the mythological staging of his early works, and his last sermon was on the theme of "Death's Duel." Donne coined the famous line "send not to know for whom the bell tolls; it tolls for thee." The bell is a reference to the church's funeral bell. There is no evidence that Donne and Shakespeare knew each other.

Despite the awareness of the arbitrary nature of fate and possibly an understanding and acceptance of it, it is probable that suffering, misery, and loss were an experience of many people. Defenses against disease remained flimsy, not least because of the limited nature of medical knowledge, a topic that playwrights noted. Such treatments as blistering, bloodletting, and mercury (the last for syphilis) were often painful, dangerous, enervating, or all three. Surgery was primitive and painful, was performed without anesthesia, and frequently led to death through blood poisoning. Bizarre ideas circulated, as in the claim in *All's Well That Ends Well* that sex with a virgin was a cure.

More generally, health and medicine were troubling issues for contemporaries, playwrights and other writers. There was nothing akin to the modern expectation that there should be a medical cure for everything; and people were forced to resort to quack medicines, folk remedies, and prayer. However, modern attitudes toward holistic approaches to medicine, as well as current knowledge of placebo effects, suggest that these remedies may have been far from worthless. Indeed, they might have been more potent than today, given contemporary beliefs in their appropriateness, if not efficacy.

The deadly plague, the "pestilence" of *Much Ado About Nothing* (I, i), closed the theaters in 1593—and not only then. The plague, however, was not the sole dangerous illness. As smallpox, one of the most serious diseases, was, unlike the plague, airborne, growing urbanization and a rise in population increased vulnerability to the disease. In major urban areas, the disease became endemic as well as epidemic, and this proved especially deadly to infants and children. Survivors bore scars. Like much else, smallpox was also socially selective, with the poor far more vulnerable, although Elizabeth I herself came close to dying from it in 1562. The poor lived at a higher population density than the wealthy. In addition, smallpox viruses remained active for up to a year and could be contracted via clothing or bedding. The poor were less able to afford to destroy clothing and bedding after a death and so were more vulnerable. Inoculation had not yet been developed.

Typhus, typhoid, influenza, dysentery, chicken pox, measles, scarlet fever, and syphilis were all serious threats. Other conditions that can now be cured or held at bay were debilitating. In *All's Well That Ends Well*, the king languishes from "a fistula" (I, i), an abnormal channel or passageway in the body. The hazards of venereal disease were to the fore, with many references in Shakespeare's plays, both humorous (albeit cruelly so) and not humorous at all. This situation conditioned the treatment of prostitution and of illicit sex, making it harsh, with morality sharpened by the element of fighting disease and by its very public signs.

Living conditions contributed to the problem, although, since Shakespeare was not writing "Condition of England" plays, they were not to the fore in his work. The sharing of beds for sleeping (not sexual purposes), which was normal given the relative rarity of beds, helped spread disease, particularly respiratory infections. Most dwellings were neither warm nor dry, and sanitary practices were a major problem. There were few baths, washing in clean water was limited, and louse infestation was serious:

> The multiplying villainies of nature
> Do swarm upon him

The description of a rebel, "the merciless Macdonwald ... from the western isles," in *Macbeth* (I, ii), referred to vermin. A similar point could have been made for many other characters in Shakespeare's plays. Although outer clothes were worn for long periods and were not washable, those who could afford it wore linen or cotton shifts next to their skin, and these shifts could be regularly laundered. However, most people wore the same clothes for as long as they could, which meant that they were still worn when rags.

Bedbugs and rats were real horrors, and, by modern standards, breath and skin must have been repellent. It is difficult to recreate an impression of the smell and dirt of the period, and the former in particular eludes the modern imagination, not least as it cannot be shown in films or on television. However, ventilation was limited. Humans lived close to animals and dunghills, and this closeness damaged health. Manure stored near buildings was hazardous and could contaminate the water supply, while effluent from undrained privies and animal pens came into houses through generally porous walls. Privies with open soil pits lay directly alongside dwellings and under bedrooms. In *Much Ado About Nothing*, Don John's follower Borachio is employed "for a perfumer" (I, iii), who deals with unpleasant domestic smells by burning sweet-smelling woods.

Despite efforts to enhance the urban environment,[1] rich and poor alike were exposed to the polluted environment. John Stow, in his *Survey of London* (1598), noted the filthy state of the Fleet River in London, clogged with human waste. In 1633, Charles I complained about the effect of brewing on the air at St. James's Palace: the coal smoke that was produced was noxious. In his *Fumifugium: or the Inconvenience of the Air and Smoke of London Dissipated* (1661), John Evelyn wrote of "the hellish and dismal cloud of sea-coal" (coal with a high sulphur content) that perpetually enveloped London. He proposed to banish such trades as brewing, dyeing, soap and salt boiling, and lime burning to a distance of several miles. Evelyn referred to the city as wrapped "in clouds of smoke and sulphur, so full of stink and darkness," which is not how it is presented on canvas or in engravings. In practice, little happened to deal with the problem.

The poor suffered a much harsher life, as King Lear came to appreciate:

> Poor naked wretches, whereso'er you are,
> That bide the pelting of this pitiless storm,
> How shall your houseless heads and unfed sides,
> Your looped and windowed raggedness, defend you
> From seasons such as these? O, I have ta'en
> Too little care of this. Take physic, pomp;
> Expose thyself to feel what wretches feel,
> That thou mayst shake the superflux to them,
> And show the heavens more just. (III, iv)

In *The Winter's Tale*, Hermione has "the childbed privilege denied" (III, ii), as if she was poor. In *Pericles*, the protagonist says of Thaisa, his supposedly dead wife: "A terrible child bed hast thou had . . . no light, no fire" (III, i). Poor nutrition, moreover, lowered resistance to disease, stunted growth, and hit energy levels.[2] Fruit and vegetables were expensive, their supply determined by seasonal availability, and they played only a minor role in the diet of the urban poor. In both town and country, the poor ate less meat than the rest of the population. Poor diet encouraged parasitic infection of the colon, hepatitis, salmonella, and many other medical problems. The limited availability of food helped ensure that feasts played a major role in stories, which shows the grip of hopes of plenty on the imagination.

Moreover, the situation could get much worse. Plant stocks had not yet been scientifically improved to resist disease and adverse weather conditions in order to increase yields, and poor harvests drove up death rates. The terrible harvests of 1555 and 1556 were followed by a disastrous epidemic, probably of influenza. This pattern was repeated in the 1590s, as bad harvests from 1594 onward led to high death rates, especially so in the winter and in the late spring when food was particularly scarce and costly. In addition, the poor were generally ill clad and often had holes in their shoes (*The Two Gentlemen of Verona*, II, iii).

Shakespeare's medical knowledge was extensive. He offered the medical doctrines of the age, notably that of the humors (that bodies were composed of the four elements of fire, air, earth, and water); presented long lists of diseases, as in *Troilus and Cressida* (V, i); and was aware of many of the forms of treatment. Clyster pipes are referred to in *Othello*. Shakespeare's son-in-law, John Hall, was a physician who practiced in Stratford and was only seven years younger than the playwright.

Doctors played only a relatively minor role in the plays and not always a favorable one. In *Much Ado About Nothing*, Beatrice, using a medical analogy for the costs of a disastrous friendship, remarks, "It will cost him a thousand pounds ere 'a be cured" (I, i). Health, however, was important in the plays. The doctor in *King Lear* recommends rest for the disturbed king: "Our foster nurse of nature is repose" (IV, iv). In *Macbeth*, a Scottish doctor accurately observes Lady Macbeth's sleepwalking, describing what most in the audience would never have seen:

> A DOCTOR OF PHYSIC: A great perturbation in nature, to receive at once the benefit of sleep, and do the effects of watching! In this slumbery agitation, besides her walking and other actual performances, what, at any time, have you heard her say? . . . Her eyes are open.
> GENTLEMEN: Ay, but their sense is shut. (V, i)

The doctor goes on in his observations to say that the case is beyond him and needs handling by a higher body, God and, when pressed by Macbeth, refers to help by means of the patient's ability to confront their own situation, a confrontation that will be assisted by divine favor:

> This disease is beyond my practice: yet I have
> known those which have walked in their sleep who
> have died holily in their bed.
> . . . Unnatural deeds
> Do breed unnatural troubles; infected minds

To their deaf pillows will discharge their secrets.
More needs she the divine than the physician.
God, God forgive us all! Look after her;
Remove from her the means of all annoyance. (V, i)

Macbeth urges the doctor to cure her, significantly choosing a doctor and not a cleric in a play in which Scotland does not appear to offer that option:

Cure her of that:
Canst thou not minister to a mind diseased,
Pluck from the memory a rooted sorrow,
Raze out the written troubles of the brain,
And with some sweet oblivious antidote
Cleanse the stuffed bosom of that perilous stuff
Which weighs upon the heart?

He receives the reply:

Therein the patient
Must minister to himself.

To this, Macbeth peremptorily responds:

Throw physic to the dogs; I'll none of it. (V, iii)

Lady Macbeth's eventual suicide reveals that that patient was unable to minister to herself, which was a result of an unparalleled sin, a version indeed of the deicide represented by the Crucifixion.

Sleeplessness itself appears to have been a problem for Shakespeare:

I haste me to my bed,
But then begins a journey in my head . . .
And keep my drooping eyelids open wide. (Sonnet 27)[3]

Medicine overlapped with a form of white magic in assessing problems, understanding the essence of properties, and addressing cures by an active means. Thus, Cornelius, the doctor in *Cymbeline*, is able to trick the Queen from her plan of suicide by picking drugs that, instead, will bring about a deep sleep:

Will stupify and dull the sense awhile;
Which first, perchance, she'll prove on cats and dogs,
Then afterward up higher; but there is
No danger in what show of death it makes,
More than the locking-up the spirits a time,
To be more fresh, reviving. She is fool'd
With a most false effect; and I the truer,
So to be false with her. (I, v)

Romeo and Juliet lacked this benign control, in part due to their impulsiveness, but also so as to provide a drama centering, in the end, on a hostile, "star-crossed" fate.

Medicine as true knowledge is linked to an account of social worth and individual purpose in the portrayal, in *Pericles*, of Cerimon, a doctor but also a nobleman:

CERIMON: I hold it ever,
Virtue and cunning were endowments greater
Than nobleness and riches: careless heirs
May the two latter darken and expend,
But immortality attends the former.
Making a man a god. 'Tis known, I ever
Have studied physic, through which secret art,
By turning o'er authorities, I have,
Together with my practice, made familiar
To me and to my aid the blest infusions
That dwell in vegetives, in metals, stones;
And can speak of the disturbances
That nature works, and of her cures; which doth give me
A more content in course of true delight
Than to be thirsty after tottering honour,
Or tie my treasure up in silken bags,
To please the fool and death.

SECOND GENTLEMAN: Your honour has through Ephesus pour'd
  forth
  Your charity, and hundreds call themselves
  Your creatures, who by you have been restored:
  And not your knowledge, your personal pain, but even
  Your purse, still open, hath built Lord Cerimon
  Such strong renown as time shall ne'er raze. (III, ii)

At the same time, religious remedies were regarded as part of
the equation and notably so with mental issues. This usage was
employed in different contexts. Comic effect could play a role, as
in *The Comedy of Errors*, when the schoolmaster, Pinch, tries to
exorcise the devil from Antipholus of Ephesus:

I charge thee, Satan, housed within this man,
To yield possession to my holy prayers,
And to thy state of darkness hie thee straight,
I conjure thee by all the saints in Heaven. (IV, iv)

Pinch argues that the "pale and deadly looks" (IV, iv) of Antipholus and Dromio of Ephesus show that they are possessed. So also
with the harsh treatment of Malvolio, treated as a lunatic from
whom Satan should be driven, in *Twelfth Night* (IV, ii). In a contrasting context, Henry VI adopts a similar course:

O thou eternal Mover of the heavens!
Look with a gentle eye upon this wretch;
O! beat away the busy meddling fiend
That lays strong siege unto this wretch's soul,
And from his bosom purge this black despair. (*Henry VI, Part II*,
  III, iii)

Ill health could be understood in spiritual terms and be seen
as a challenge to faith as well as a test of personality.[4] Disease,
moreover, served a variety of political purposes, as in *Troilus and
Cressida*, where "the rotten diseases of the south" are itemized by
Thersites (V, i). This approach matched and exemplified English
contempt for the Mediterranean. As both means and metaphor,

health and disease were important to the plots and atmosphere of Shakespeare's plays.

NOTES

1. C. Rawcliffe, *Urban Bodies: Communal Health in Late Medieval English Towns and Cities* (Woodbridge, UK, 2013).

2. D. Gentilcore, *Food and Health in Early Modern Europe: Diet, Medicine and Society, 1450–1800* (London, 2016).

3. See more generally S. Handley, *Sleep in Early Modern England* (New Haven, CT, 2016).

4. O. Weisser, *Ill Composed: Sickness, Gender, and Belief in Early Modern England* (New Haven, CT, 2015).

# TEN

# CULTURAL TRENDS

They say miracles are past.

—Lafeu in *All's Well That Ends Well* (II, iii)

THAT THE CULTURE OF THE Tudor age still echoes today is in large part thanks to Shakespeare. This was drama written and performed in English. Indeed, the use of English in its standard form was a fourteenth- and fifteenth-century development that was pushed further under the Tudors, when it became both the language of authority and of culture. The rise of the vernacular, always significant for popular culture,[1] lessened the role of both Latin and Anglo-Norman, the French spoken in England. The English language was increasingly identified with an English people and nation in the thirteenth century and became more important in literature in the fourteenth, not least with William Langland's *Piers Plowman* (different versions, 1362–92) and Geoffrey Chaucer's *Canterbury Tales* (c. 1387–1400).

In many respects, the Hundred Years' War with France (1337–1453) offered a cultural precursor to the Reformation of the sixteenth century. At the start of the Hundred Years' War, the aristocracy of England was international in outlook, and French was the language at court and of anyone with upwardly mobile aspirations. However, as politics drove the two realms into a long war, so it became awkward that high society in England aped French style, manners, and customs. The government also built up patriotic characteristics and, in so doing, deliberately harnessed linguistic awareness. The earliest parliamentary petition in English was in 1386. Henry V himself switched to writing in English in 1417, a significant year given the intensity then of the war with France. From 1420, Chancery clerks were pushing English as the official language of government.

National distinctiveness was also seen in the perpendicular style, a native architectural form of the fourteenth and fifteenth centuries that left an impressive legacy to Shakespeare and his contemporaries, and in an equally distinctive style of English music. Pre-Reformation England was part of an international cultural world and notably so with the Church and Latinity but one that had become far less dependent on Continental, especially French, influences than hitherto. Moreover, there were elements of Church life that were national in tone, as in the veneration of Henry VI as a saint and martyr; miracles were attributed to him.

England played a role, albeit not a central one, in the European Renaissance. Henry VII's court was visited by such leading luminaries as Castiglione (1503) and Erasmus (1499), and the latter spent several years at Cambridge. Henry VIII's court also had an international flavor with, for example, the painters Hans Holbein and Vincenzo Volpe working there. In 1519, Henry appointed the Bavarian astronomer Nikolaus Kratzer, already an academic at Oxford, as court astronomer and horologist.

The Reformation ensured a religious and intellectual and thus cultural shift in England's connections from southern to northern Europe, although links with Italy remained significant, not least for the purchase of paintings. Cultural and intellectual change had elements of transformation in and after the

Reformation. This situation, however, also encompassed the continuation of existing circumstances and practices, such as the cult of St. George, although not that of Henry VI, which provides a context for Shakespeare's plays about the reign.[2] There was also the development of new practices. In particular, alongside a new interest in Anglo-Saxon England, including its language,[3] an interest that reflected a rejection of Latinity—the English language was developed by Tudor playwrights and was staged accordingly. Written English became homogenized in the age of print, which saw much translation into English and the wholesale borrowing of foreign words. This process provided a context for Shakespeare's plays, which expressed the aspirations and tensions of the emerging nation-state, while their vocabulary and phrases came, in turn, to occupy a major position in the language.

So also with the Bible. Its translation into English under Henry VIII and its mandatory use in churches had a great impact, as can be seen in Shakespeare's employment of so many biblical phrases. In 1604, James I established the panel that in 1611 produced the King James, or Authorized, Version, intended as a definitive translation of the Bible. Like Shakespeare's plays, the Authorized Version was to prove very important in the overall development of the English language, as well as giving currency to many phrases.

The process of presenting established works in English was also seen with the classics, for example, the publication in translation of Ovid's *Metamorphoses*.[4] Another major source for Shakespeare was Erasmus's *Adages*, a collection of passages translated from the classics. The English translation by Sir Thomas North of Plutarch's *Lives of the Noble Grecians and Romans* (in fact a translation of a French translation) was published in 1579, and the first part of George Chapman's translation of the *Iliad* in 1598, the complete work appearing in 1611. Chapman also wrote plays, as well as a poem, *De Guiana*, on English transoceanic enterprise. Translation was seen as a patriotic task.[5] Shakespeare was able to draw on a great range of sources that were available in translation, including French and Italian stories. He used North's edition of Plutarch, notably in *Coriolanus* and *Antony and Cleopatra*. Classical motifs were very important in other aspects of the English culture of the period, including rhetoric, illustrations, and motifs. For some critics, indeed, Shakespeare's works could appear insufficiently located in classical forms.[6]

In his plays, Shakespeare very much engaged with the past, notably of England but also of Rome and of Scotland. There was, in his lifetime, a greater sense of the past as distinctive and separate from the present. This sense was linked to the emergence of a particular awareness of history, derived above all from the Renaissance typology and progression of historical eras (classical-medieval-modern) and the related Protestant proposal of early Church–medieval Church–reformed Church, with the medieval Church (i.e., Roman Catholicism) as a location of iniquity. In part, this emergence of a particular awareness of history was an aspect of the general impact of humanism and, specifically, of the emphasis that was placed on literal rather than allegorical interpretations of scripture and the classics, as well as on the accuracy and clarity of the text.

The significance of time, the separation between past and present, came to be more strongly asserted and more readily understood. Historical maps, maps drawn to depict past events, were conscious historical statements dependent on a sense of the past as a separate sphere. John Speed's *A Prospect of the Most Famous Parts of the World* (1627) included "A Briefe Description of the Civil Wares and Battails fought in England, Wales, and Ireland," illustrated by a double-page black-and-white map titled "The Invasions of England and Ireland with all their civil wars since the [Norman] Conquest," a map first published in about 1601. This map had faults, particularly in its depiction as simultaneous of events greatly separate in time, indeed from over half a millennium, which was a traditional device and one that should lessen criticism of Shakespeare's treatment of historical time. Speed's county maps also included historical information, for example, sites of battles.

The first historical atlas appeared in Shakespeare's lifetime. It was the work of one of the leading cartographers, Abraham Ortelius (1527–98). Published in Antwerp in 1570, Ortelius's *Theatrum Orbis Terrarum* (*Theatre of the World*), an atlas of the contemporary world, had about forty editions by 1612. John Dee and Richard Hakluyt owned copies, and in 1609 James I bought a library that contained copies. Ortelius, who visited London in 1577 and was familiar with and corresponded with the antiquaries William Camden, John Dee, and Humphry Llwyd, was also interested in the geography of the ancient world and specifically the period of Shakespeare's Roman world. From 1579, Ortelius provided the most significant spatial depiction of this world in the "Parergon," a historical section of the *Theatrum* that grew from twelve plates in the 1584 Latin edition to thirty-eight in 1603. The accompanying text was also by Ortelius. The "Parergon" was translated into French, Italian, German, and English, the English edition of the *Theatrum*, containing forty-three plates in the "Parergon" section, appearing in 1606. The classical world was presented in great detail, although the "Parergon" maps centered on Rome rather than Greece.

There was no sense of chronological progress in the organization of the maps. Thus, the map of the campaigns of Alexander was followed by that of the travels of Ulysses: history succeeded by myth, in a mixture commonplace in this period. Ortelius was affected by current concerns and present-day images, just as was Shakespeare. Alexander's fleet was depicted as comprising sixteenth-century boats, while the Low Countries, in Ortelius's map of them in the Roman period, consisted of the seventeen provinces belonging to the Hapsburgs. This created a sense of territorial coherence that was misplaced for the earlier period.

The "Parergon" reflected the degree to which knowledge of the worlds of the Bible and the classics was seen by pedagogues and princes alike as a vital aspect of genteel education. This point was clear from the focus of Sir Walter Raleigh's *History of the World*, which ended its coverage in 168 BCE.[7]

Moreover, alongside continuing interest in medieval themes, genres, and literature,[8] there was also an element of the new textualism of the Renaissance in the character of antiquarian studies. The Anglo-Saxon scholar and cartographer Laurence Nowell (d. c. 1576), in his thirteen-section manuscript mid-sixteenth-century map of England and Wales, gave place-names in Old English and used Old English letter forms. The Kentish antiquary and mapmaker William Lambarde (1536–1601), a pupil of Nowell, not only produced the first English county history, the *Perambulation of Kent* (1576), but also drew a map of the Anglo-Saxon kingdoms. This process looked toward Lear's division of his kingdom. In 1601, Elizabeth made Lambarde keeper of the records in the Tower of London, and she discussed history with him.[9]

In addition, a wish to relate time to place was becoming more common. There had been many remarks to the effect that geography was an important ancillary to history—a kind of second eye—but these were essentially rhetorical before about 1580, and possibly later. However, there are signs of important shifts in interest and perception, notably with an understanding of close relations between history and geography, as with Peter Heylyn's *Microcosmus, or a Little Description of the Great World. A Treatise Historical, Geographical, Political, Theological* (1621), a book based on his university lectures.

Shakespeare's plays assume some knowledge of classical geography or, at least, a willingness not to be put off by it. Thus, *Pericles* is entitled more fully *Pericles, Prince of Tyre*, and introduces, as the initial major characters, Pericles and King Antiochus the Great, whose palace is in Antioch, which the prologue correctly identifies as in Syria. Ephesus, Tharsus, and Mytilene also feature as locations. The play, which ultimately derives from the Greek romance of Apollonius of Tyre, is located in the pre-Christian world, with Diana's temple playing a role. The Mediterranean (including the Aegean) is very important in *Pericles*, not simply in the shape of the plot device of storms but also because it serves as the way to link places, as also with *Antony and Cleopatra* and *The Comedy of Errors*. Thus, Pericles alters his course to Tarsus because he is off its coast. His daughter, Marina, is kidnapped by pirates on the seashore and taken to Mytilene, where she is sold for prostitution. After she is reunited with Pericles, they follow a vision sent by Diana and sail to Ephesus where Pericles finds his long-lost wife. Such references are made easier because the Mediterranean was not only the setting of the ancient world known to the English and depicted in maps but also a setting of their contemporary world.

The geography of the ancient world also plays a role in the other plays set there. Thus, *Antony and Cleopatra* is organized conceptually and politically in terms of the contrast between Rome and Egypt. However, far more is involved in the play's geopolitics. In the second scene, Antony, who has been seduced by his relationship with Cleopatra, Queen of Egypt, is warned about the threat to the Roman Empire:

> Labienus—
> This is stiff news—hath, with his Parthian force,
> Extended Asia from Euphrates;
> His conquering banner shook, from Syria
> To Lydia and to Ionia. (I, ii)

This account in fact is a major exaggeration of the challenge that was posed by the Persian-based Parthians, but to contemporaries it captured a sense of Oriental power, as well as locating the geography in terms of the known landscape of the classical world. The Parthians are presented as advancing from Iraq (where the river Euphrates flows) to Ionia, which is the part of modern Turkey on the Aegean Sea. In turn, Ventidius, the Roman victor over the Parthians in Syria, in fact Publius Ventidius Bassus, a protégé of Julius Caesar and ally of Mark Antony, is described as having the option of chasing them through Media and Mesopotamia, meaning present-day Iran and Iraq. So also when Alexandria in Egypt is mentioned: its location is well known.

## MAPS

The printing of maps began in Europe in the 1470s and became central to most map production in the sixteenth century. Thanks to the use of woodblocks, maps could be more speedily produced and more widely distributed and could therefore be profitable as a format designed for a mass market. From midcentury, woodblocks gave way to engraved copper plates, as the latter were easier to correct and revise, both important factors in a mapmaking world that emphasized novelty and precision. Meanwhile, different map projections were devised in response to the extension of Western knowledge about the physical shape of the world, most crucially the work of the Flemish mathematician and mapmaker Gerhardus Kramer (1512–94), whose name was Latinized as Mercator. In 1569, Mercator produced a projection that treated the world as a cylinder so that the meridians were parallel rather than converging on the poles, as they actually do. In this projection, the poles were expanded to the same circumference as the equator.

Maps became a key form of applied knowledge, one in which, like geography books, knowledge could be accumulated, organized, and deployed. As Shakespeare shows, this issue could become contentious. In *Troilus and Cressida*, Ulysses responds to the criticisms of Greek war making made by Ajax and Achilles, criticisms that extend to "mappers":

> They tax our policy, and call it cowardice;
> Count wisdom as no member of the war;
> Forestall prescience, and esteem no act

But that of hand: the still and mental parts,
That do contrive how many hands shall strike,
When fitness calls them on, and know by measure
Of their observant toil the enemies' weight—
Why, this hath not a finger's dignity:
They call this bed-work, mappery, closet-war;
So that the ram that batters down the wall,
For the great swing and rudeness of his poise,
They place before his hand that made the engine
Or those that with the fineness of their souls
By reason guide his execution. (I, iii)

Maps were an increasingly significant form of national political and cultural expression. Under the Tudors, maps grew in potency, both as a symbol and as reality. Their authority increased when one illustrating the Exodus route of the Bible was printed in 1535. The Bible story could thus be fixed. The visual splendor of maps encouraged their display, but maps were also produced and used for practical purposes, including governmental, military, and economic ones.

The development of mapmaking can be seen in the attractive maps produced by Christopher Saxton. Little is known about his early life. Born in about 1542–44 in Yorkshire, Saxton learned surveying and was commissioned by Thomas Seckford, surveyor of the Court of Wards and Liveries, to produce his maps of individual counties. Seckford was close to Burghley, who had a substantial collection of maps, some annotated in his own hand, and who had been a patron of Laurence Nowell in his mapping and other scholarly work in the 1560s. In 1576, the Privy Council instructed the justices of the peace and mayors in Wales to give Saxton all assistance in traveling and viewing the country there.

Saxton's maps were copied with few, if any, changes for two centuries, largely because the cost and effort of new surveys appeared redundant not only for commercial reasons but also due to the authority of the Saxton maps. As a result, map publishers took over from mapmakers. Saxton's surveys were the basis for maps by others, such as John Norden (1548–1629). Their maps further helped to establish and consolidate the visual images and awareness of counties. This was an important aspect of the extent to which particular images were propagated in introducing maps to a wider public and in encouraging map use. So also with plays, which shared with maps and geometry the need to make conventions of representation work.[10]

Shakespeare's characters are shown making some use of maps. In the first scene in *King Lear*, the protagonist calls for the map in order to display his division of his kingdom between his daughters. Lear tells one of them, Goneril:

> Of all these bounds, even from this line to this,
> With shadowy forests and with champains [pastures] rich'd,
> With plenteous rivers and wide-skirted meads,
> We make thee lady. (I, i)

Located in pre-Christian history, this story depicted the use of a map that could not have occurred then. However, for Shakespeare's audience, such a use of a map would have appeared possible, not least because maps of England, however imprecise, were adequate for such purposes.

Partition on a map clearly interested Shakespeare. In *Henry IV, Part I*, the conspirators against Henry IV meet in Bangor, with "Hotspur," Harry Hotspur, at first angry that he has "forgot the map." Already bitter with each other, Hotspur and the Welsh leader, Owen Glendower (Owain Glyndŵr), then row over the distribution of their projected gains:

> GLENDOWER: Come, here's the map: shall we divide our right
>     According to our threefold order ta'en?
> EDMUND MORTIMER: The archdeacon hath divided it
>     Into three limits very equally.
>     England, from Trent and Severn hitherto,
>     By south and east, is to my part assign'd:
>     And westward, Wales beyond the Severn shore,
>     And all the fertile land within that bound,

> To Owen Glendower; and dear coz [Hotspur], to you
> The remnant northward, lying off from Trent.
> HOTSPUR: Methinks my moiety, north from Burton [upon Trent] here,
> In quantity equals not one of yours:
> See how this river comes me cranking in,
> And cuts me from the best of all my land
> A huge half-moon, a monstrous cantle out.
> I'll have the current in this place damm'd up,
> And here the smug and silver Trent shall run
> In a new channel, fair and evenly:
> It shall not wind with such a deep indent,
> To rob me of so rich a bottom here.
> GLENDOWER: Not wind! it shall, it must; you see it doth.
> MORTIMER: Yea, but
> Mark how he bears his course, and runs me up
> With like advantage on the other side;
> Gelding the opposed continent as much,
> As on the other side it takes from you.
> THOMAS PERCY [HOTSPUR'S UNCLE]: Yea, but a little charge will
> trench him here,
> And on this north side win this cape of land;
> And then he runs straight and even.
> HOTSPUR: I'll have it so; a little charge will do it.
> GLENDOWER: I will not have it alter'd. (III, i)

Their quarrel makes the division appear ridiculous, as does the idea of changing the course of the river Trent. However, the use of a map is instructive.

In practice, the conspirators would not have done this in 1403, when the conspiracy took place: maps were not then widely used and were, anyway, generally of insufficient quality to enable the detailed comments attributed to the conspirators. By contrast, to the audience of 1597, benefiting from the fixing of visual images through printing and also reflecting the greater use of maps in the Elizabethan period, it was perfectly credible that the three conspirators should refer to a map and entirely possible to understand the anger of Harry Hotspur, the Percy from the North of England, about the impact of the river Trent's course on his share.

More generally, audiences were expected to know or at least accept geographical references as part of a broader encounter with Britain,[11] for example, in *Cymbeline* that Milford Haven was in Wales; in *Richard III* that Haverfordwest, Milford Haven, and Brecon were in Wales; and in *Henry V* that Harlech was in Wales. In *Richard II*, the audience was given an account of the campaign that led to the overthrow of the king, with Bolingbroke, the future Henry IV, landing at "Ravenspurgh" in Yorkshire. Subsequently, "in the Gloucestershire Wolds," in other words the Cotswolds, Bolingbroke asks Henry Percy, the First Earl of Northumberland (father of the "Hotspur" killed at Shrewsbury): "How far is it, my lord, to Berkeley now?" receiving the reply:

> Believe me, noble lord,
> I am a stranger here in Gloucestershire:
> These high wild hills and rough uneven ways
> Draw out our miles and make them wearisome. (II, iii)

Ironically, to a Percy, the Cotswolds would not in fact have seemed "wild hills": they scarcely compared with the Cheviots or the northern Pennines. This was very much a case of Shakespeare taking his own limited experience as his benchmark. To an inhabitant of Stratford who had traveled to London, the Cotswolds might have appeared "high" and "wild" but not to someone more familiar with English geography, notably with the Pennines, let alone the Lake District. In *Richard II*, Bolingbroke, outside Berkeley Castle, resolves to attack Richard's supporters in Bristol Castle. The campaigning then switches to Wales, and the audience is assumed to know where Flint Castle is.

## STAGING RELIGION AND THE RISE
### OF A DIFFERENT THEATER

Religious change was a more abrupt and transformative changing element in the development of a national culture. For example, the Reformation had a direct impact on existing forms of drama, notably with the end of mystery plays. Like wall paintings, these depicted the world of good and evil in a traditional light. The Coopers' pageant in the 1415 York Corpus Christi play showed "Adam and Eve and a tree between them, a serpent deceiving them with apples, God speaking to them and cursing the serpent, and an angel with a sword casting them out of Paradise." Religious vitality had been clearly exemplified in pre-Reformation local culture and in many forms. Linked to the activity and re-ligious and corporate ethos of guilds and enabling guildsmen to take a role in the social and political agenda of their towns,[12] mystery plays developed in the period, although not in London. The York ones were written down in the 1460s or 1470s and those of Towneley/Wakefield in the 1520s, while the Chester and Coventry plays were reworked in the 1530s.

Under Elizabeth, these mystery plays largely came to an end. The last recorded performances at York, Coventry, and Chester were in 1569, 1571, and 1575 respectively, and attempts to revive performances at York in 1579 and Chester in 1591 were abortive. There was, however, opposition to this change. In Tewkesbury, not far from Stratford, plays were still being performed inside the church in 1600, and as late as 1576 the chalice had not been re-placed with a communion cup. Mystery plays lasted in Lancaster and Preston (both in Lancashire) into the reign of James I.[13]

There were other forms of public theater, as with annual shows, such as the Lord Mayor's Pageant in London, probably from the 1520s. Royal entries also saw grand pageantry. In 1599, Henry Hardware, the mayor of Chester

> caused the giants in the Midsummer-show not to go, the devil in his feathers not to ride for the butchers, but a boy as the others, and the cuppes, and cannes, and dragon, and naked boy to be put away; but caused a man in compleat armour to go before the showe in their stead.

This mayor altered many ancient customs, for example, the shooting for the sheriff's breakfast and the display of the giants at Midsummer, and would not permit plays, bearbaiting and bullbaiting; only for the next mayor to restore all the ancient pageants, which included one on St. George's Day.[14]

There were important links between the mystery plays, traditional pageants, the plays performed for the London guilds, and aspects of the theater of Elizabethan England, including the works of Shakespeare. The links included the mental universe, for example, the role of the devil, story lines, the character of staging, the objects available for drama, notably theatrical properties, and the music.[15] Similarly, there was continuity in the case of other arts, including church music, with polyphonic singing continuing in many parishes until the 1580s.[16]

By weakening or at least challenging patterns of control over expression, the Reformation provided new opportunities for the theater, notably in what could be covered, although that was not the intention of the reformers. Theater was an indigenous development, with London the prime setting for the changes in drama. The professional theater was very much connected with London. The Theatre, the first purpose-built public playhouse in England, was opened in 1576 in Shoreditch by James Burbage, an actor and master carpenter, and it was followed by his Curtain in 1577, the Rose in 1587, and the Globe in 1599. Burbage's lease ran out in 1597, and he dismantled the Theatre, using some of its timbers for the Globe.

Unlike the new public buildings in the city, notably Gresham's Exchange and the Bourse, these theaters were all located outside the city walls, the Theatre and the Curtain being in Shoreditch and the Rose and the Globe in Southwark. This was due to measures against plays by the city authorities, measures that had been encouraged by preaching. A ban on public playing in the city was pressed for from the 1570s and was realized in the 1590s. Nevertheless, in 1595 about 15,000 people visited the London theaters weekly, a figure that included many who were not at the height of society. The Globe, with its capacity of 2,800, could take a larger audience than earlier theaters. Modern safety requirements mean that the reconstruction, opened in 1997, holds only 1,400 spectators.

All of these theaters were open-air amphitheater-type places based on the model of galleried innyards. The more expensive places in the theaters were in the galleries, which were covered, while the yards, for which admissions was commonly one penny, lacked cover, exposing those there to rain. The theaters represented an institutionalization of drama similar to that of the economic market in the Exchange and the Bourse.[17]

As an alternative, there were smaller, entirely covered hall playhouses, which had a smaller capacity and cost more to enter, usually sixpence. The first, the Paul's Theater, for the pupils of St. Paul's boys' school, opened in 1575, while Burbage's company used another, in Blackfriars, from around 1606, providing new staging opportunities for Shakespeare. Due to its monastic background, Blackfriars was a site that represented the crisis of the Reformation.[18] Despite contrasts in cost, there was considerably overlap in the audience of the two types of theater.[19] Purpose-built premises encouraged specialization, and that meant a need for more plays in order to bring in audiences. Shakespeare was one playwright who rose to the challenge.

The private patronage of the wealthy, as seen with the sponsored musicians and actors in the Earl of Leicester's Men and other theatrical companies, and of wealthy institutions was important. Alongside them, public patronage and the exigencies and opportunities of the commercial marketplace were crucial to the development of culture and notably of the theater. The numerous plays that were produced ranged widely in their subject matter, but the vitality of contemporary London was a frequent theme, as were the wealth and social pretension of groups in urban society. Londoners could see themselves and those they recognized depicted on the stage. This depiction was a matter not only of the presentation of London but also of that of other cities. Thus, the social dynamics of such cities as Athens, Ephesus, Messina, Milan, Mitylene, Rome, Venice, Verona, and Vienna, each of which was a setting for action in Shakespeare's plays, were, at least in the subplots, the social dynamics of London. At the same time, setting the plays abroad provided a sense of difference that, alongside Shakespeare's sources, helped make the plays more interesting. The listing of the cities makes clear the dependence of the plots on the Mediterranean, both ancient and modern, and thus the significance of the assumption that it was in many respects similar to England, at least to the extent of being part of the same culture.

The identification with London was also true of other playwrights. Probably born in Westminster and educated at Westminster School, Ben Jonson (1572–1637) was made city chronologer in 1628, succeeding Thomas Middleton.[20] Set in London, his vigorous play *Bartholomew Fair* (1614) depicted the outwitting of a country squire, as well as the attraction of the stall selling roast pork.

Although the plight of the poor could be shown, the theater and its morality were primarily located within a world of affluence, which was an aspect of its escapism. This location was so even if the audience was invited to mock the corrupt and lecherous wealthy, such as Sir Walter Whorehound in Middleton's comedy *A Chaste Maid in Cheapside* (1611), again set in London. Social distinction was a theme of plays, but there was also a pride and self-identification of communities and nation, both in plays and with other cultural forms. Books played a major role in this, as with John Stow's *Survey of London* (1598).

Books were significant because the Reformation, with its emphasis on a vernacular and therefore more accessible and easier to read Bible, ensured that, alongside the significance of preaching, representations of good and evil became more literary and less oral and visual than hitherto. This change in the contours of information about religion was socially slanted toward the literate and thus was disorientating to many. Moreover, that change did not diminish the need for people to understand their world in terms of the struggle between good and evil. Indeed, the shock of change may even have encouraged it.

Shakespeare's work reflected not only spiritual themes, such as atonement, resurrection, and temptation, but also more specific biblical stories, episodes, and language; and the audience response drew on the collective religious experience. For example, the idea of resurrection is seen with the reawakening of Juliet in the last scene of *Romeo and Juliet*.[21] As a consequence of this setting in a world of Christian belief, believers, references, and controversies, the plays can frequently be read in terms of religious controversies as well as beliefs, as with the roles of contingency and ghosts in *Hamlet*. These roles were linked to differences between Catholicism and Calvinism, notably over free will and transubstantiation but also over much else.[22] At the risk of overanalyzing a play that derives its energy from being a drama, Hamlet's agonized dilemmas in large part rest on the need to develop and keep the story going, building up dramatic anxiety while focusing on the issues involved in rejecting one's mother, in committing murder within the family, and in killing a usurper. The complexities of moral dilemmas in a divided Christendom were also very important. Separately, the complexities of moral dilemmas were taken further by the need to reconcile Christian with classical teachings, assumptions, images, and examples.[23] This was readily apparent in the plays that were set in the ancient world.

At the same time, care is required, as also in the search for political references. The limited evidence for audience views and for their understanding of analogies is such that "might" and "maybe" should be key terms in analysis. Political and religious references were really or potentially troubling and legally problematic in a world that was divided and fearful over both; but what specific references meant to contemporaries is far less clear. These points also reflect on modern presentations of the plays. For example, the dynamic 2017 production of *Othello* by the Tobacco Factory, a most impressive Bristol company, was described in the publicity leaflet as follows:

> One of Shakespeare's most startling contemporary plays, *Othello* is a masterful depiction of a life torn apart by racism and the destructive nature of prejudice. Venice, a western colonial power, employs the newly-married Othello, a Muslim general, to lead their army against Turkish invasion. The difficulties of assimilating into a society riven by discrimination, fear and mistrust soon began to take their toll on Othello: manipulated by Iago, his life quickly unravels, and he turns on all he holds dear. A truly timeless play, *Othello* speaks afresh to each society that comes to it: a warning weaved within the fabric of the tragedy, more urgent than ever, compelling us to look beyond divisions of race, religion or culture and acknowledging our universal humanity.[24]

This may be so for today, but does this tell us much about the audience when *Othello* appeared in 1604? And that question leaves aside the somewhat misleading description in the leaflet of Venice as a Western colonial power, especially in its resisting Ottoman plans for Christian Cyprus, let alone the extent to which individual betrayal and personal dynamics are to the fore in the play. Regarding Othello, it is surely the fact that he is Moorish, not Muslim, that is the issue.

Shakespeare's religious beliefs have been a matter for claims and controversies, not least as he has been moved from being the national hero of a Protestant state to becoming, in some accounts, a Catholic and even a Counter-Reformation activist, although others contest this interpretation. In practice, the evidence for his views and position is fragmentary, indirect, and ambiguous: there is no conclusive evidence of Shakespeare's religious beliefs. Shakespeare's writing can be read in terms of the defense of integrity in the face of state-imposed religious change, a Catholic approach,[25] although that interpretation can also be questioned. So too with the argument that the representational eucharistic doctrine presented by the Book of Common Prayer provided Shakespeare (and others) with a political template that encouraged the separation of political symbols from realities.[26] The background, experience, and legacy of the period included both Protestant and Catholic elements, and this situation helped underline the ambiguity of pieces of evidence. Dramatic effect rather than theological sophistication and coherence comes to the fore in the plays, as with the treatment of the occult—for example, ghosts.[27]

A traditional and religious theme that remained powerful, as well as providing dramatic strength, was that of free will versus determinism. Helena observed in *All's Well That Ends Well*:

Our remedies oft in ourselves do lie
Which we ascribe to heaven; the fated sky
Gives us free scope; only doth backward pull
Our slow designs when we ourselves are dull. (I, i)

The tension between free will and determinism extended to the theater and its audience, notably the extent to which the playwright, the actors, and the setting sought to lead the response but at the same time had to confront the agency of the audience. Words and settings could appear like drugs, with the theater a setting for the sleeping potions offered by the plays.[28]

More centrally and often providing modesty and wit as well as clarity and meaning, the prologues and afterwords made the free response of the audience a key element. Prospero's epilogue in *The Tempest* presses for such applause as a major plot enabler:

I must be here confined by you [the audience],
Or sent to Naples. Let me not,
Since I have my dukedom got
And pardoned the deceiver, dwell
In this bare island by your spell,
But release me from my bands [bonds]

With the help of your good hands [applause]:
Gentle breath of yours my sails
Must fill, or else my project fails. (V, i)

We can see Londoners, in addition to their depiction on stage, as individuals, as we frequently cannot see their fifteenth-century predecessors, thanks to more lifelike and more numerous portraits. Portraits painted by Hans Holbein (1497–1543) earlier in the sixteenth century are more famous, but it is the production of more numerous portraits later in the century that is more significant. These include not only major figures of state and court, most dramatically Elizabeth I, but also representations of those of humbler position. One of Shakespeare was produced during his life, a portrait that shows him wearing an earring. Indeed, male decoration and display were particularly significant in this period, not least colorful clothes that displayed both status and ambition for status, the latter very much the case with Malvolio in *Twelfth Night*.[29]

## THE WORLD OF PRINT

The printing of vernacular Bibles gave ordinary individuals an opportunity to consider God for themselves and to question traditional teachings from the perspective of their own understanding of scriptural authority. Thus, knowledge was not so much freedom as a cause of the demand for freedoms. The populace was not a passive recipient of policies and initiatives from the more powerful. Yet, while the Reformation was heavily dependent on the ability of publications to overcome traditional constraints on discussion and the spread of ideas, it also reflected the power of the state. Protestant worship was introduced by means of the Book of Common Prayer (1549), which contained the forms of prayer and Church services requisite for every religious event. Parliament passed a Uniformity Act decreeing that the Book of

Common Prayer alone was to be used for Church services, which were all to be in English. After an order of Convocation (the clerical parliament of the established Church) of 1571, cathedral churches also acquired copies of Foxe's *Book of Martyrs*, a highly potent account of the Protestants killed during Mary's reign;[30] and many parish churches chose to do likewise.

As yet, the impact of popular literacy and the print revolution upon oral culture was, while important, still limited. Visual experiences remained highly significant, including with books. Foxe's *Book of Martyrs* was illustrated, and these images were arguably more potent than the text, a point also true of images of witches. While these images fueled the anxieties of the age, other images could be celebratory and consoling. Important aspects of visual culture included pageantry and costume.

About 80 percent of London craftsmen were literate by the 1600s, but literacy rates were lower, much lower, for the poor, for women, and for the rural population. Most people could neither read nor afford books. Thus, printing exacerbated social divisions and gave an extra dimension to the flow of orders, ideas, and models down the social hierarchy. The inability of the poor to express themselves was accentuated. Yet there were also possibilities of expression even if they could be mocked. In *A Midsummer Night's Dream*, Bottom awakes from his encounter with the fairy world, proclaims its uniqueness, and seeks to fix it for posterity in a work of poetry that will be recited:

> The eye of man hath not heard, the ear of man hath not seen, man's hand is not able to taste, his tongue to conceive, nor his heart to report what my dream was! I will get Peter Quince to write a ballad of this dream; it shall be called "Bottom's Dream," because it hath no bottom. (IV, i)

The literate Quince, the carpenter, allocates the parts in "Pyramus and Thisbe," and writes and speaks the prologue. Bottom's muddling of the senses has biblical provenance, and even he dimly realizes it is a mystery.

Education, the world of print, the impact of government, and the role of London all encouraged the gentry increasingly to view politics and society in national terms. London dominated printing, and language was standardized through London-based printing, which reduced the impact of regional linguistic differences. Standardization was related to the interlinked authority of print and the capital.

The impact of print was often indirect and subtle but was nevertheless significant in establishing assumptions. For example, printing changed the law by easing and encouraging the processes by which injunctions, information, and outcomes were recorded and stored. In place of the variations of the oral transmission of information and custom, there came a demand for certainty and precision linked to the written record. With customary law, a largely oral system was transformed into a written one. Such changes enhanced the prestige of text and its capacity to act as a system of validation and thus of arbitration and settlement. Shakespeare referred to a new world in *All's Well That Ends Well*:

> They say miracles are past; and we have our philosophical persons to make modern [everyday] and familiar, things supernatural and causeless [inexplicable]. Hence is it that we make trifles of terrors, ensconcing ourselves into seeming knowledge when we should submit ourselves to an unknown fear. (II, iii)

There were textual variations with printing, notably as a result of errors, changes introduced in new editions, and also censorship. Printing, nevertheless, represented a way to fix texts in a fashion different from the instability arising from the continual alterations that resulted from hand-copied texts and, even more, by the oral transmission of information and opinion. Thus, the character of textual memory and of memory as a whole was changed. The more fixed character of print was linked to the more public response to what was published, a response also seen with the development of printed commentary.

REPORT AND RUMOR

It is important to note both the still-thriving manuscript culture of the period[31] and the contemporary understanding of printed texts as unreliable.[32] Nevertheless, at the same time, the culture of print brought new authorities and new processes of authorization. The prestige of print, it has been suggested, was linked to a new stage in the relationship between reality and the fictional in the shape of the perception and strength of particular fictional ideas.[33] Authorization was in part a matter of censorship, which served a range of goals from religious and political control to attempts to regulate the book trade as a business activity. Censorship and licensing, however, were not simply means of restriction but also of legitimation, marking the boundary of what was respectable. Licensing included the granting of commercially valuable privileges to publish, which was a variant on monopoly rights.

This was to be important in the development of novel forms of news reporting. As Shakespeare's plays made clear, much news was not in a form that would be regarded as central today. Instead, it could be repetitive and cyclical, as with the cycle of days on which parish bells were rung and the telling and retelling of familiar tales and superstitions. These activities afforded some security in an insecure world. A sense of news as frequent, even daily, did not represent a secular rejection of a religious world view but, instead, with some similarities to a play, was a common theme in society, offering interest and explanation in the form of narrative continuity. At the same time, print, drama, and greater interest in recording and "telling" time were all aspects of a cultural shift. The development of time-based forms of publishing, such as astrological publications, news pamphlets, and newspapers, was part of this shift.

As a result, gossip was given new forms and authority. In more conventional forms, gossip was a key element in many of

Shakespeare's plots, notably the comedies, and was shown as le-thal in *Othello*. Present at all social levels, gossip, as in *Othello*, frequently played on the anxieties of the powerful and forceful.

In England, government concern with rumors was seen in 1580, when a proclamation was issued against the spreading of rumors that invasion by Philip II and the pope was imminent, rumors that were indeed inaccurate. The world of report was shaped by government regulation, entrepreneurial activity, and the pur-chasing, reading, and viewing decisions of many, for whom such choices were acts of political and/or religious affirmation, as well as signs of interest. In a pattern reminiscent of Casca's speech in the second scene of *Julius Caesar*, branches of knowledge fed by (new) information, such as astrology and the journalistic genre of "strange newes," could be used as vehicles for articulating topi-cal grievances. So also with the use of the occult in *Henry VI, Part II* (I, iv).

However expressed, including on the stage, the information and opinion that circulated were not confined to a system of government-directed control or to hierarchic patterns of defer-ence, and Ben Jonson was to sound a warning in his play *The Staple of News* (1626). Attempts to control the flow and dissemination of unwelcome material stemmed from concern about the political, religious, and, to a lesser extent, social possibilities of print and drama, including its influence on those who could not read or, indeed, afford to go to the theater but who might be swayed by those who could. The nature of the intelligence gathering required by governments was affected by print and the theater.

The development of pamphlets, newspapers, and theater was located within a wider cultural shift that focused attention on what could be presented as news: news from elsewhere. This in-formation became more prominent in the sixteenth century, not only with the increase of public or semipublic forms, such as man-uscript newsletters, but also as a result of a greater internalization of news, apparent with the growing number of diarists, many of whom recorded public news. The extent to which this process of engagement with clearly defined news, especially from distant places, was related to institutional developments—such as the increase in public postal links and of mercantile correspondence systems—as opposed to cultural changes, is unclear.

Entrepreneurial activity helped foster a process in which different media joined, overlapped, or separated. In England, the genre of "strange newes" was used to provide accounts of providential tales, and this possibility attracted entrepreneurial publishers. Plot devices in plays that to us may appear far-fetched would scarcely have done so to the readers of such tales. However, although providential tales remained an important topic for report, news and fact were increasingly differentiated from exemplary prose in which morality was seen as defining accuracy, for example, sermons. So also with plays, although they responded to the possibilities of a range of genres. Political information became a valuable commodity that was turned to profit by the writers of newsletters, as well as providing material for satirical works that, in part, dwelt on the contents and implications of morality.[34]

The interest in new developments both at home and abroad, the latter notably due to religious conflict and even warfare from the 1520s, ensured that information circulated more widely. This was a process encouraged by governmental and ecclesiastical activity and by translations of items. Publications, like plays, contributed to and drew on a heightening, focusing, and, to a degree, polarization of public opinion. They brought a new intensity to the political contention already seen there, notably in the 1580s, 1590s, and 1620s, and both reflected and sustained the particular issues of specific political moments. Thus, Thomas Dekker argued the case in 1606 for a militant Protestantism, one in which anti-Catholicism was taken to the fore, in both domestic and international affairs, in the aftermath of James I's accession in 1603 and the Gunpowder Plot in 1605.[35] Rumor, which Shakespeare brings onstage at the start of *Henry IV, Part II*, was an aspect of public (and private) opinion. It was seen under Elizabeth, but James's court and his personal style of rule through favorites encouraged rumor still more.[36]

## CONCLUSION

A key element in the world of print was provided by the publication of plays. This was very much a way in which Shakespeare's works could be fixed, and he could be identified and also criticized. In 1598, there was the first appearance of Shakespeare's name on the title pages of his printed plays, in the shape of a quarto printing of *Love's Labour's Lost*. The original authored "Complete Works" appeared only after Shakespeare's death, in the "First Folio" text of 1623, that is, a large "Folio" format. This was assembled by Shakespeare's colleagues John Heminges and Henry Condell, both actors in the King's Men, for whom Shakespeare wrote.

The dimension of publication was important, but the plays were staged; they were not appreciated primarily as written texts. This staging involved adaptation to the constraints of contemporary productions and theaters, but these constraints both offered opportunities and could be pushed against. Moreover, the theatricality included the display that could provide an important component in the visual appeal of the plays. This display was notable in terms of the solemn processions or dances that could end plays: tragedies and comedies respectively. Neither solemn processions nor dances were new features of the culture of the period, but their setting in theaters, in which people were paying to see plays written for commercial ends, was new. The context and the content of national culture were changing.

## NOTES

1. D. Gray, *Simple Forms: Essays on Medieval Popular Literature* (Oxford, 2015).

2. J. Good, *The Cult of St George in Medieval England* (Woodbridge, UK, 2009).

3. R. Brackmann, *The Elizabethan Invention of Anglo-Saxon England: Laurence Nowell, William Lambarde and the Study of Old English* (Cambridge, 2012).

4. J. Bate, *Shakespeare and Ovid* (Oxford, 1993); A. Taylor, ed., *Shakespeare's Ovid: The "Metamorphoses" in the Plays and Poems* (Cambridge, 2000).

5. L. Oakley-Brown, *Ovid and the Cultural Politics of Translation in Early Modern England* (Aldershot, UK, 2006); R. S. Miola, *Shakespeare and Classical Tragedy: The Influence of Seneca* (Oxford, 1992). For the broader context, K. Newman and J. Tylus, eds., *Early Modern Cultures of Translation* (Philadelphia, 2015).

6. J. Armitage, *Arbella Stuart: The Uncrowned Queen* (Stroud, UK, 2017), 170.

7. N. Popper, *Walter Raleigh's "History of the World" and the Historical Culture of the Late Renaissance* (Chicago, 2012).

8. G. McMullan and D. Matthews, *Reading the Medieval in Early Modern England* (Cambridge, 2007).

9. R. Warnicke, *William Lambarde: Elizabethan Antiquary* (Chichester, UK, 1973).

10. H. S. Turner, *The English Renaissance Stage: Geometry, Poetics and the Practical Spatial Arts 1580–1630* (Oxford, 2006).

11. J. Cramsie, *British Travellers and the Encounter with Britain, 1450–1700* (Woodbridge, UK, 2015).

12. G. Rosser, *The Art of Solidarity in the Middle Ages: Guilds in England, 1250–1550* (Oxford, 2015); N. R. Rice and M. A. Pappano, *The Civic Cycles: Artisan Drama and Identity in Premodern England* (Notre Dame, IN, 2015).

13. D. George, ed., *Records of Early English Drama: Lancashire* (Toronto, 1991).

14. Anne Lancashire, *London Civic Theatre: City Drama and Pageantry from Roman Times to 1558* (Cambridge, 2002) and, ed., *Records of Early English Drama: Civic London to 1558*, 3 vols. (Cambridge, 2015); Anon., *History of the City of Chester* (Chester, UK, 1815), 282, 284–85.

15. H. Cooper, *Shakespeare and the Medieval World* (London, 2010); K. A. Schreyer, *Shakespeare's Medieval Craft: Remnants of the Mysteries on the London Stage* (Ithaca, NY, 2014).

16. J. Willis, *Church Music and Protestantism in Post-Reformation England: Discourses, Sites and Identities* (Farnham, UK, 2010).

17. D. Bruster, *Drama and the Market in the Age of Shakespeare* (Cambridge, 1992).

18. J. Shapiro, *1606: The Year of Lear* (London, 2015); S. Dustagheer, *Shakespeare's Two Playhouses: Repertory and Theatre Space at the Globe and the Blackfriars* (Cambridge, 2017).

19. A. Gurr, *Playgoing in Shakespeare's London* (Cambridge, 1987).

20. S. Gossett, ed., *Thomas Middleton in Context* (Cambridge, 2011).

21. B. Groves, *Texts and Traditions: Religion in Shakespeare, 1592–1604* (Oxford, 2007).

22. J. E. Curran, *Hamlet, Protestantism, and the Mourning of Contingency: Not to Be* (Aldershot, UK, 2006).

23. A. F. Kinney, ed., *Hamlet: New Critical Essays* (London, 2002).

24. Flyer for production at Exeter Northcott Theatre, May 9–13, 2017.

25. C. Asquith, *The Hidden Beliefs and Coded Politics of William Shakespeare* (New York, 2005).

26. T. Rosendale, *Liturgy and Literature in the Making of Protestant England* (Cambridge, 2007).

27. D. S. Kastan, *A Will to Believe: Shakespeare and Religion* (Oxford, 2014).

28. T. Pollard, *Drugs and Theater in Early Modern England* (Oxford, 2005).

29. E. Goldring, *Nicholas Hilliard: Life of an Artist* (New Haven, CT, 2019).

30. T. Freeman, "Fate, Faction and Fiction in Foxe's *Book of Martyrs*," *Historical Journal* 43 (2000): 601–23.

31. H. R. Woudhuysen, *Sir Philip Sidney and the Circulation of Manuscripts, 1558–1640* (Oxford, 1996).

32. F. E. Dolan, *True Relations: Reading, Literature and Evidence in Seventeenth-Century England* (Philadelphia, 2013).

33. H. Turner, *The Corporate Commonwealth: Pluralism and Political Fictions in England, 1516–1651* (Chicago, 2016).

34. A. McRae, *Literature, Satire and the Early Stuart State* (Cambridge, 2004).

35. J. C. White, "Militant Protestants: British Identity in the Jacobean Period, 1603–1625," *History* 94 (2009): 154–75.

36. D. Coast, *News and Rumour in Jacobean England: Information, Court Politics and Diplomacy, 1618–25* (Manchester, 2014).

# ENGLAND AND EUROPE

You write as if you were a foreign prince, seeking to meet
the king or his commissioners on foreign soil. It is so long
since we forshook the usurped power of the bishop of Rome
that these things seem very strange. . . . Experience shows
nothing lost to us by the open enmity or doubtful friendship
of France and Scotland; we are accustomed to fight both
and win. . . . We hope all princes will realise their authority
and detest Rome's usurped power. . . . Friendship between
nations should not be hindered by difference in [religious]
ceremonies, since we all believe in one God and Christ.

—Protector Somerset to Cardinal Pole, in
C. S. Knighton, ed., *Calendar of State Papers
Preserved in the Public Record Office*, 108–9

WRITING TO REGINALD, CARDINAL POLE, a papal legate
(an English exile, indeed a scion of the Yorkists), who was appointed archbishop of Canterbury under Mary,[1] Edward, Duke
of Somerset, Protector of England for his nephew Edward VI,[2]
captured the significance of the aftermath of the Reformation for
England's subsequent history. England simultaneously became
both more engaged and more disengaged with the Continent.

Alongside an increasing sense of national identity, there was ambiguity, an ambivalence that was also to be seen in the later treatment of Elizabeth's reign.

The idea and practice of national independence sat as part
of the degree to which Elizabethan England was very Europe
conscious. Politically and militarily, there was the threat from
Rome and Spain and the need to develop positions (including
military intervention) in relation to the French Wars of Religion
and the Dutch Revolt. The combination of the Catholic Counter-
Reformation, the power of Philip II's Spain (particularly thanks
to the civil wars in France), the issue of the English succession,
and the fate of Scotland and Ireland ensured together that it was
impossible to cut England off from her neighbors. Indeed, in part,
the very assertion of Englishness under Elizabeth, as under Henry
VIII, was an anxious response to the serious challenges posed by
a hostile international context. Economically, there were explora-
tions of opportunities in a broader Europe, including Russia as
well as the Mediterranean.[3] In religious terms, many of the English
were looking to Protestant or Catholic Europe, specifically Geneva
or Rome. Culturally, there was a great fascination with French and
Italian culture, as well as the beginnings of the Grand Tour.

A hostile international context was not new. As Shakespeare
showed, foreign rulers had interfered in past episodes of domestic division, notably during John's reign and in the Wars of the
Roses. Such interventions are presented by Shakespeare as dishonorable. In *King John*, Count Melun of the invading French
army reveals to the rebels against John that the French leader, the
Dauphin, is out to betray them:

> Fly, noble English; you are bought and sold;
> Unthread the rude eye of rebellion,
> And welcome home again discarded faith.
> Seek out King John and fall before his feet;
> For if the French be lords of this loud day,

He means to recompense the pains you take
By cutting off your heads. (V, iv)

Would-be foreign intervention was accentuated as a result of the Reformation, which both represented an assertion of national independence and met with a hostile response. In the first, the case was put strongly on behalf of Henry VIII. In the Act in Restraint of Appeals (1533), England was declared "an empire" sufficient to itself and therefore not subject to the pope or to Emperor Charles V. Shakespeare captured this approach in his presentation of the reign in his *Henry VIII* (1613), a play cowritten with John Fletcher that in the twentieth century was for long unduly neglected but that brought the history plays up dangerously close to what was then the present.

During the first production of the play, the Globe was burned down as a result of the thatch catching light after cannon were fired to mark an entry of the actor playing Henry. This deprived that audience of Archbishop Thomas Cranmer's (fictional) eulogy on the infant, born in 1533, who was to become Elizabeth I, a eulogy he was bid speak by heaven, in which it was foretold that her virtues would be reborn, phoenix-like, in James I (then on the throne), and that

He shall flourish,
And like a mountain cedar, reach his branches
To all the plains about him. (V, iv)

This was a very different context to Macbeth being shown by the witches the dynastic future in the shape of Banquo's descendants. History, as staged in *Henry VIII*, provided not only Katherine of Aragon's drama but also a glorious anticipation and justification of the present, indeed a potent form of legitimation in the shape of a very different female ruler.[4]

Necessarily so, as England itself was in a hostile world, one made much more so by the Reformation, which linked royal legitimacy to the struggles of the present and gave them an historical resonance. Most obviously, the historicity and therefore legitimacy of the Protestant Church that had been established in England became a matter of debate between Protestant and Catholic controversialists. Seeking to minimize the role of the papacy, Matthew Parker, archbishop of Canterbury from 1559 to 1575, emphasized the antiquity of the British Church in his *De Antiquitate Britannicae Ecclesiae* (1572). The Church insisted on the apostolic succession of its bishops, so emphasizing its continuity with the past. Papal authority was presented as an intrusion. Catholics, in contrast, stressed the conversion by St. Augustine, who had been sent from Rome by Pope Gregory the Great. Such debates were far from abstract. They were linked to the legitimacy of the papal excommunication and deposition of Elizabeth and to anti-Catholic legislation, notably that of 1585 and the 1591 proclamation against seminary priests and Jesuits.

A new national history differentiating England from the Continent was being developed. This was expounded in a number of books, most notably in Ralph Holinshed's *Chronicles* (1577), in reality a collaborative book, a successful publication that was reissued in a larger edition in 1587. This traditional format for history writing provided a mass of material for playwrights and others, one made more complex and varied by the number of writers involved.[5] To a degree, Shakespeare's work fitted into this context.

The war with Spain (1585–1604) fostered national consciousness, providing a new focus for the commemoration of national history, as with annual celebrations for the defeat of the Armada. In the last speech in *King John*, probably written in 1596, Philip the Bastard, the illegitimate son of the heroic Richard I, declares:

> This England never did, nor never shall,
> Lie at the proud foot of a conqueror,
> But when it first did help to wound itself.
> Now these her princes are come home again,
> Come the three corners of the world in arms,
> And we shall shock them. Nought shall make us rue,
> If England to itself do rest but true. (V, vii)

Celebrations for the defeat of the Armada in 1588 were an aspect of the advancing of new national days of celebration recalling recent Protestant history and replacing the earlier dominance of the year by the commemoration of saints' days, which remained dominant in affirming identity in Catholic countries.[6] Church bells were rung every November 17 to celebrate the accession of Elizabeth in 1588 and thus the end of Catholic rule. The failure of the Catholic Gunpowder Plot in 1605 provided a new annual celebration on November 5, one with a message of threat and providential rescue.

Links between England and the Continent were varied and developing. Translations and other publications brought information on other countries, as with George North's *The Description of Sweden, Gotland and Finland* (1561). An active world of newspapers drew closer in Elizabeth's reign with the publication in London of news pamphlets, especially by the publisher John Wolfe. These and other pamphlets fostered a lower-cost marketplace of print and encouraged entrepreneurs to seek profit in ephemeral publications. In 1620, the first English-language newspapers were imported from Amsterdam into London. These encouraged the publication of "corantos" (newsbooks or newspapers) in London from 1621. They were soon widely distributed across England, using weekly postal services from London, and thus enhanced London's importance as a center of news, both its disseminator and indeed its image.

At the same time, the long territorial links with the Continent had been sundered. After the loss of the French territories in 1453, which had a last aftershock in 1558 with the fall of Calais (a possession of the kings of England since 1347), England was insular to a degree that had not been true for centuries. This had consequences for England's diplomatic situation and significance. Under the Treaty of Nonsuch of 1585, England had garrisons in Brill and Flushing, which were "cautionary towns" held, as a result of help to the Dutch in their War of Independence with Spain, until 1616. England was also to occupy Dunkirk from its capture from Spain in 1658 until it was sold by Charles II to Louis XIV of France in 1662. With these exceptions, England did not have any Continental possessions from 1558 until the conquest of Gibraltar from Spain in 1704, and Gibraltar was very much a maritime base.

More significantly, the concern with Continental possessions and pretensions that had motivated her medieval monarchs and that still played a major role for Henry VIII were of little consequence for Elizabeth and for her Stuart successors. Elizabeth sought the return of Calais in 1562 but abandoned the attempt in failure two years later. She again sought its return during her marriage negotiations with the Duke of Anjou, the brother of Francis II, Charles IX, and Henry III of France, and on other occasions, but the issue was not pressed. Though still claiming to be kings of France (as they did until the reign of George III), the rulers of England were now insular in their possessions and concerns in a fashion that had not been seen since the Norman Conquest of 1066.

And yet the rulers and political elite of England remained bound closely to Continental affairs and in some respects more so than over the late fifteenth century. Two important aspects of this were the consequences of the Reformation and the growing strategic significance for England of the Low Countries as a result of the rise of French power and the struggle between the Hapsburgs and the rulers of France.

The effect of the Reformation on religious ties with the Continent was ambiguous. A distinct and distinctive independent English Church was created, but, in addition, new religious links with Protestant northern Europe rather than with Rome led to the establishment of important new ties with that region. Furthermore, English foreign policy now acquired a religious dimension. From the 1550s, as it became apparent that the Reformation would not be universally successful and that the Catholic church and its allies were striking back determinedly, so a sense of community of interests with Protestants abroad developed rapidly, notably with the principalities of northern Germany and with Denmark.[7] The early 1560s, moreover, saw the outbreak of confessional violence in France, and this was followed by the Dutch Revolt in which England formally intervened from 1585.

The plight of French Protestants (Huguenots) excited much attention, and English troops were sent to France in 1562 and from 1589 to 1597. Elizabeth gave the Huguenot leader, Henry of Navarre, eventually crowned as Henry IV in 1594, considerable support, although her continued support after his reconversion to Catholicism in 1593 suggests that religion was not her top priority: she supported Henry in large part because he was opposed to Spain, with which he remained at war until 1598. In *Love's Labour's Lost*, the French Wars of Religion are registered in the names of most of the play's male characters, including Navarre. It has been observed that the name Navarre is employed in a context that reflects concerns about unreliability at the level of linguistical use, including postponed ends.

The interaction of principle and prudence, as in English foreign policy, was part of the complex nature of politics that provided the context for Shakespeare's audiences. However, they did not always have to employ this context when watching his plays. This interaction was not usually brought to the fore, because Shakespeare frequently offered wise authority figures, as in the rulers brought on stage in *The Comedy of Errors* and *Romeo and Juliet*, rather than exploring the ambiguities of power. Furthermore, when he tackled the latter, it was frequently in moral terms, as in *Measure for Measure* and *Hamlet*. The interaction of principle and prudence on the part of rulers and their advisers was not generally the crucial issue. Instead, moral characterization was at issue, notably in the drive to power, as by Antonio and Sebastian in *The Tempest*. Once Macbeth and Richard III have grasped power, its retention, not its use, becomes their purpose. Guilt is an element of this moral characterization, but that again is part of the morality of politics, one that is dramatized by ghosts.

In responding in these and other issues to the present, Shakespeare drew on the assumptions of his audience, as well as his own knowledge. Thus, for example, probably using John Florio's guides to Italian, he profited from Italian tragicomic models, while also domesticating them.[8] So also with Shakespeare's historical sources.

War and politics were not the sole ways in which national identity was established or expressed. In *Othello*, the mood is temporarily lightened when Iago sings a drinking song he learned in England. Presumably in order to get a cheer from the audience, Iago adds that the English are

> most potent in potting [good at drinking]. Your Dane, your
> German, and your swag-bellied Hollander—
> Drink, ho!—are nothing to your English.
> CASSIO: Is your Englishman so exquisite in his drinking?
> IAGO: Why he drinks you with facility your Dane dead
>   drunk; he sweats not to overthrow your
>   Almain [German]; he gives your Hollander a vomit ere the
>   next pottle can be filled. (II, iii)

The state boundaries, indeed the national ones, in so far as that term can be employed, were not those of the present, which ensures the need for care in responding to names for countries or states or peoples. To take 1564, the year of Shakespeare's birth, and compare it to the present underlines the need for caution in readily applying modern names for countries or states as if there has been scant change. There are examples of continuity since then. As far as European frontiers are concerned, Portugal has remained largely unchanged, although an area east of the Guadiana River was gained by Spain in 1801. However, "Spain" is used as a short term for the territories of the king of Spain, which were very different from the situation today. The division of the wide-ranging inheritance of the Emperor Charles V / Charles I of Spain, ensured that, at Shakespeare's birth, the dominions ruled by Philip II of Spain included half of Italy (Sicily, Sardinia, Naples, the Milanese—Lombardy and the Tuscan coastal presidios—fortified towns), as well as the Burgundian inheritance as enlarged by Charles: Franche-Comté (the region around Besançon, now in France) and the Low Countries (essentially modern Belgium, Netherlands, and Luxembourg but including parts of modern France, especially Artois, while excluding the prince-bishopric of Liège).

The last was one of the many ecclesiastical states that showed that the idea of rule by a cleric continued to seem a viable option to Catholics. This was not an issue that Shakespeare considered. He brought historically powerful English clerics onto the stage, such as Henry Beaufort (bishop of Winchester) in *Henry VI, Parts I and II* and Thomas Wolsey in *Henry VIII*, but not villainous Catholic prince-bishops in modern Europe, as Webster did with the Cardinal in *The Duchess of Malfi* (1612–13).

The strong Hapsburg presence in the Low Countries had been of strategic importance to Henry VIII when he was seeking allies against France but under Philip II helped ensure that English concern in the Low Countries was the tinder to what became a major conflict between Spain and England. Spain's great rival in Shakespeare's lifetime might to the English seem to be England but was really France. This was readily apparent in the 1600s when its power revived under Henry IV. Indeed, in 1595, when Spain had 100,000 men under arms, England had only 20,000. England, however, was the key enemy when France weakened in the 1580s and the early 1590s. In 1585–1604, the English fought Spain at sea, as well as in the Low Countries, France, and Ireland. In total, 106,000 troops were sent overseas during the war years with Spain. Earlier, thy ofte severithe threat posed by the alliance of France and Spain against England in 1539–40 had been readily apparent. Given that Shakespeare wrote many of his plays during a long, difficult, and apparently intractable war, that of 1585–1604, it is striking that he did not make more use of the theme, present or historical, of the nation under threat, although war is important to many of the plays and can be part of the background of those not generally considered in that light, such as *Much Ado About Nothing*.

Shortly before Shakespeare's birth, France had expanded under Henry II, gaining the prince-bishoprics of Metz, Toul, and Verdun in 1552 and Calais (from England) in 1558; Boulogne, lost to English siege in 1544, was regained by the French in 1550. Nevertheless, France had not yet made the major advances that were considerably to change its eastern frontier: the independent duchy of Savoy (a composite state with Piedmont and Nice) still reached to the Saône until 1601; Lorraine was an independent duchy until 1766 and ruled by hostile dukes until 1737; and France only gained Alsace in 1648, Artois and Roussillon in 1659, and Franche-Comté in 1678. Much of this expansion was into what had been part of the middle kingdom created in the ninth century from the Frankish inheritance.

In the fifteenth century, the period of Shakespeare's history plays, much of this onetime middle kingdom had been given international vitality as an expanding state by the Dukes of Burgundy, who played a significant role in the events described in those plays. A large part of the Burgundian inheritance had been acquired by Charles V and, subsequently by his son Philip II. As a result, the struggle between Hapsburg and Valois, Spain and France, was, in part, a conflict between Burgundy and France that continued a long-established struggle. However, due to his militant Catholicism, Philip could not take the favorable role that Burgundy had generally done, notably for Henry V and the Yorkists.

In northern Europe, the collapse in 1523, as a result of a Swedish war of liberation, of the Union of Kalmar, which had joined Denmark, Sweden, Norway, Finland, and their ancillary territories, had left not the situation depicted in *Hamlet* but two competing states. Finland was part of the kingdom of Sweden, while the king of Denmark also ruled Norway, Schleswig and Holstein, and parts of modern Sweden, especially the island of Gotland and the Scania region of southern Sweden. Poland was a large composite state that included modern Lithuania and much of modern Ukraine, Belarus, and Latvia, as well as suzerainty over the duchy of Prussia (East Prussia), which was ruled by a branch of the house of Hohenzollern.

Germany, Italy and southeastern Europe in 1564 were very different from today's position. The Balkans were ruled by the Ottoman (Turkish) Empire, an Islamic monarchy based since 1453 at Constantinople (modern Istanbul) that also ruled Syria (from 1516), Egypt (from 1517), much of southwest Asia, including Iraq, and the northern shores of the Black Sea, where the khanate of the Crimea was, from the 1470s, a dependent state. The Ottoman conquest of much of Hungary, after Süleyman the Magnificent's victory at Mohacs in 1526, had brought them into direct contact with Hapsburg power and dramatically so when the Ottomans unsuccessfully besieged Vienna in 1529.

Their historical setting ensured that Othello, but not many other of Shakespeare's warriors, could fight the Turks. In *Richard II*, however, the fate of Thomas Mowbray, First Duke of Norfolk, in 1398–99 is discussed. In reality, he certainly died in Venice having merely gone on a pilgrimage to Jerusalem, but for the bishop of Carlisle in Shakespeare's play

> Many a time hath banish'd Norfolk fought
> For Jesu Christ in glorious Christian field,
> Streaming the ensign of the Christian cross
> Against black pagans, Turks, and Saracens;
> And toil'd with works of war, retired himself
> To Italy; and there at Venice gave
> His body to that pleasant country's earth,
> And his pure soul unto his captain Christ,
> Under whose colours he had fought so long. (IV, i)

In a comparison with the Turks, Carlisle also predicts chaos in England if Richard is overthrown:

The blood of English shall manure the ground
And future ages groan for this foul act;
Peace shall go sleep with Turks and infidels. (IV, i)

This was also a warning for the present, one encouraging support for Elizabeth.

The Hapsburgs also benefited from Mohacs as the kingdoms of Bohemia and Hungary had been united under the same crown from 1490, and, with the death of king Louis II at Mohacs, the Hapsburgs were able to acquire what the Ottomans did not conquer. As a result, the Hapsburg position in most of what is now Austria and Slovenia was enhanced by the acquisition not only of what became Hapsburg Hungary (much of modern Slovakia and parts of modern Croatia and Hungary) but also of Bohemia and Moravia (the modern Czech Republic), as well as Silesia (southwest modern Poland) and Lusatia (to the southeast of Berlin).

Since 1438, each successive Austrian Hapsburg ruler had been elected Holy Roman Emperor, which provided him (it was only ever a man) with a measure of authority, although less power, in the empire. Sometimes called the Holy Roman Empire, this was an area roughly coterminous with modern Germany, Austria, the Netherlands, Belgium, Switzerland, the Czech Republic, and much of northern Italy. In these areas, sovereignty was divided, and a large number of territorial princes, mostly lay but some ecclesiastical, and imperial free cities, such as Frankfurt and Hamburg, exercised effective power within the loose bounds of an imperial constitution.

Most of Europe was ruled by hereditary monarchs, and its politics was therefore affected by what has been termed proprietary dynasticism. The most important Christian dynasty, in both their own eyes and those of most other commentators, was the Hapsburgs. During Shakespeare's lifetime, the Valois and then, with the accession of Henry IV in 1589, the Bourbons ruled France; the Tudors and then Stuarts, England; the Vasas, Sweden; the Stuarts, Scotland; the Hohenzollerns, Brandenburg; the Wettins, Saxony;

the Wittelsbachs, Bavaria; the Medici, Tuscany; and so on, down to small principalities in Germany and Italy. These principalities might not confer much power, but the families that ruled them, for example, the Gonzaga of Mantua and the Farnese of Parma, followed dynastic goals of their own with just as much ambition as their more prominent counterparts. Indeed, their very lack of power helped lead to an emphasis on the careful manipulation of alliance systems, a manipulation seen by dramatists as an aspect of Machiavellian deceit and revenge tragedies.

The Holy Roman Empire and the papacy were the most prominent of the elective monarchies, a group that included Bohemia, Hungary, and, from the 1570s, Poland but never England. Nor was elective monarchy ever going to be a solution to disputes over the succession to the English Crown. The Swiss Confederation, Venice, and Genoa were the leading republics. Venice ruled a still-extensive empire that, in 1564, included Cyprus, Crete, the Ionian Islands, Dalmatia, and much of northeastern Italy, notably the cities of Brescia, Cremona, Padua, Verona, and Vicenza. Genoa ruled Corsica and Liguria.

Shakespeare's birth in 1564 coincided with a new wave of wars of religion that came to affect much of Europe. This was most notably the case in the 1560s in France, the Low Countries, and the British Isles. In each, rebellion was linked to religious disaffection, although other factors also played a role, especially tensions within the elite. In addition, as an instance of an apparent Islamic threat, a rising in Granada in 1568 was eventually brutally suppressed, with a large number of the Moriscos (apparent Moorish converts from Islam) involved slaughtered.

In the Low Countries (modern Belgium and the Netherlands), the unpopular religious and fiscal policies of the ruler, Philip II of Spain (brother-in-law to Elizabeth as husband of her predecessor, Mary I), and his neglect of the views and interests of the Dutch nobility, led to riots in 1566–67 and then to the reimposition of order by a powerful Spanish army under the Duke of Alba. To the English, this reimposition became a potent image and reality of tyrannical military power and of misrule at its most brutal. Over 1,000 people were executed in the Low Countries and about 60,000 went into exile. The English exiles of Shakespeare's history plays appeared mirrored by the Protestant exiles from continental Europe in Shakespeare's lifetime.

England's response to the Dutch Revolt was a key question for government during most of Shakespeare's life. It also became a political issue due to contrasting views among ministers and wider public concern. In particular, Burghley urged caution, while Leicester and Walsingham supported intervention.

The sense of Catholic cruelty seen in the attempt to suppress the Dutch Revolt was taken further by the killing of the Huguenot (Protestant) leaders in France and several thousand of their followers in the St. Bartholomew's Day Massacre on the night of August 23–24, 1572, as king Charles IX, the brother-in-law to Mary, Queen of Scots, turned against them. This gave Marlowe the subject for his disturbing play *The Massacre at Paris*, printed in about 1594. Moreover, this event provided an instance of a plot point frequently made by Shakespeare, notably in his history plays—namely, the relationship of developments in different countries: freed from the risk of French intervention, Alba focused on the fresh wave of Dutch rebel activity in 1572.

War involved not just fighting on the battlefield but a broader range of activities, some of which captured the darker side of human interaction. Religious activity, education, publications, censorship, marriage, the household, and poor relief were all battlefields and were regarded and linked as such. The conflict was as much about "soft" power as "hard" power, an element Shakespeare captured in his discussion of power, and it is no accident that the Society of Jesus, or Jesuits, was established by Ignatius Loyola in 1534 as a quasi-military Catholic order. The first Jesuit missionaries, Edmund Campion and Robert Parsons, reached England in 1580, much to the alarm of the government. Captured

the following year, Campion held out against persuasion and torture and was executed for treason. In 1594, Parsons published *A
Conference about the Next Succession to the Crown of England*, in
which he pressed the case for a Spanish infanta as the successor
to Elizabeth.

"Hard" and "soft" power overlapped, for example, when clerics
were slaughtered by both sides in the Low Countries and France
and when worshippers were intimidated, if not killed. Similarly,
image breaking was important to the process by which Protestants seized control of churches. Crucial to all religious conflict
was a degree of popular engagement, including in the form of
riots and massacres. Concern about popular action led governments to erect fortifications. Shakespeare's consideration of such
rioting related, however, to political and not religious violence.

The Dutch Revolt led in the long term to the overthrow of
Philip II's rule in the northern provinces, the basis of the modern
Netherlands, but in the then more populous and economically
advanced south, the basis of modern Belgium, it proved possible
for him to regain control. This owed much to the achievements
from 1579 of the Army of Flanders, the Spanish regional force, under its brilliant commander, Alexander Farnese, Duke of Parma,
including the capture of Antwerp in 1585. However, it was also
necessary for Philip's representatives to make concessions, producing a settlement acceptable to the influential and Catholic
Walloon nobility. In contrast, the Dutch state was dominated
economically by the towns of the province of Holland, especially
Amsterdam, and this dominance led to a different social politics
from that in the southern provinces.

Parma's successes overshadowed earlier ideas that the oppo-
nents of Spain might seek safety by offering the sovereignty of the
Low Countries to Francis, Duke of Anjou, the surviving brother
of Henry III of France, who was himself a suitor for the hand of
Elizabeth. In 1580, he was given this sovereignty, and in 1581 the
French sought to negotiate the marriage. Elizabeth responded in

a distinctly ambiguous fashion, making it clear that she wanted an alliance with France rather than the marriage. Henry III replied that the two had to be linked, but Elizabeth was only willing to give Anjou, who came to England in 1581–82, money and a kiss. The politically incompetent Anjou proved a failure in the Netherlands, leaving for France in 1583 and dying in 1584. The following year, Elizabeth agreed to provide the Dutch with 7,400 troops as well as £126,000 annually until the end of the war, although this contribution was mishandled in 1585–87 by the commander, Robert, Earl of Leicester.

Meanwhile, the root causes of dissension in France persisted, notably religious division, aristocratic factionalism, and royal weakness. Foreign intervention complicated the situation, with the Catholic League formally allying with Philip II in December 1584. Royal power and authority collapsed in France in the 1580s, reaching their nadir in 1589 when the childless Henry III (another brother-in-law to Mary, Queen of Scots), the Catholic king, was assassinated by a Catholic zealot while unsuccessfully besieging Paris, from which he had been driven by the more radical urban elements of the Catholic League.

Spain and England then intervened on opposite sides in the war in France, the English to significant local effect in Brittany and Normandy but without fulfilling the high hopes that were held. However, having converted to Catholicism, Henry of Navarre, the first of the Bourbon dynasty, consolidated power and was crowned, as Henry IV, in 1594. Although it is disputed by modern scholars whether he actually used the phrase "Paris is worth a Mass," the sentiment it expressed was a reflection of his political pragmatism. Buying off the major Catholic aristocrats with a recognition of their provincial power bases and thus neutering the Catholic League and satisfying the Huguenots by concessions to Protestant worship in the Edict of Nantes (1598), Henry achieved domestic peace, but the condition of peace with Spain that year was an acceptance of Spanish hegemony. The latter ensured that pressure could be brought to bear on the Dutch and English in the continuing war. However, James I settled with Spain in 1604, while Spain's financial burdens helped lead to the negotiation of the Twelve Years' Truce with the Dutch in 1609.

To a degree, there was a change in the second half of Shakespeare's life, with the end of both the French Wars of Religion and the war between France and Spain in 1598, the wars between England and Spain in 1604, between Austria and the Turks in 1606, and between the Dutch and Spain in 1609. England was not engaged in war after 1604 during the rest of Shakespeare's lifetime, while the beating of drums was subdued on the Continent.

Yet "alarums" continued. In 1610, the Jülich-Cleves succession crisis in the Rhineland appeared to presage large-scale conflict between France and Spain, and that was only averted when Henry IV of France was stabbed to death by François Ravaillac, a Catholic fanatic, in the Rue de la Ferronnerie in Paris, in a scene that would have done credit to a Shakespeare play, as would the punishment for this regicide: Ravaillac was pulled apart by four horses. Although large-scale war over Jülich-Cleves was avoided, there was campaigning involving Dutch, French, and imperial forces, as well as those of the Protestant Union of German princes. Moreover, prior to the outbreak of the Thirty Years' War in 1618, there was instability in the Holy Roman Empire (Germany and the Hapsburg lands), northern Italy, and France. In 1611, the Estates (Parliament) of Bohemia clashed with an army raised by Archduke Leopold, a Hapsburg prince. Venice fought Austria in 1613–16, Charles Emanuel I of Savoy-Piedmont invaded the Monferrato in 1613, and in 1614 Dutch and Spanish forces confronted each other in the Rhineland. Also in 1614, Henry's son, Louis XIII of France, marched south with his army to impose his authority on Béarn, an independent territory in southern France that was a royal fief but where Catholic worship was not permitted. Opposition was overawed, and Béarn was formally annexed. Béarn had a common border with one territory mentioned by

Shakespeare, Navarre, and was close to another to which he referred, Roussillon.

So, given all these conflicts, it is easy to understand why Shakespeare's contemporaries would have seen the wider world as troubled, with violence an ever-present prospect, and this situation a context for the pursuit of other aspects of life, such as romance and trade. However, it was not until the outbreak of the Thirty Years' War in 1618 and its major broadening out in 1620–21 that anxiety and the theme of religious confrontation revived strongly in England.[9]

Further afield, Russia was expansionist under Ivan IV, "the Terrible" (r. 1533–84), with whom England developed trade links in the 1550s. He conquered Kazan in 1552 and Astrakhan in 1556, but he failed to win a dominant position on the Baltic. Ivan's attempt to annex Livonia (much of modern Latvia) was thwarted by Stephen Báthory, the dynamic king of Poland (r. 1576–86), who campaigned successfully from 1578, forcing Ivan to peace in 1582. Russia also failed to defeat the Swedes. In *The Winter's Tale*, the accused Hermione notes: "The Emperor of Russia was my father" (III, ii).

Christian IV of Denmark was the brother-in-law of James I, and, in 1606, he paid a three-week state visit to England. Given the confusion of Baltic power politics, it is scarcely surprising that, in *Hamlet*, Shakespeare displays a troubled situation, with Fortinbras, nephew of the king of Norway (then in fact part of Denmark), being obliged by his uncle not to attack Denmark but, instead, encouraged to turn against the Poles. Hamlet questions a captain in Fortinbras's army as to the goal, to be told:

> We go to gain a little patch of ground
> That hath in it no profit but the name:
> To pay five ducats, five I would not farm it. (IV, iv)

The political geography of Europe scarcely exhausted the range of spatial awareness and expression in Shakespeare's

England. Indeed, the basic forms of awareness were reiterated weekly, both in Church and at market day. The former ensured that the geography of a world view that spanned heaven and hell was fully expressed. So also with a wider confessional geography that included the Islamic world, not least Algiers and Jerusalem, as well as the geopolitics of a Protestantism that spanned from an allegedly papist Antichrist to Protestant co-religionists. Venice brings in interaction with Jews in *The Merchant of Venice*, and *Othello* is set in Cyprus while it was a Venetian colony before the Turkish conquest of 1570–71. Indeed, the plot comes from the *Hecatommithi* (1565), a collection of tales by the Italian writer Giambattista Giraldi Cinzio. The plot of *Othello* incorporates another aspect of difference, in the shape of the protagonist, a Moor who has converted to Christianity.

Market days offered a very different geography. They focused the local understanding of spatial links, notably between towns, like Stratford and Warwick, and their hinterlands. These could then be supplemented by links between the towns themselves. These spatial links both complemented county divisions and clashed with them. At a higher level, there was the question of regional identity within England. The end of the Council of the North meant that there was no specific institutional formulation, comparable, for example, to an area covered by an individual French *parlement* or an imperial (German) circle. The great magnates did not control affinities that were sufficiently powerful to provide regional political action, a point demonstrated by the total failure of the rising of the Northern Earls in 1569. Nevertheless, there could still be an idea of a region, for example in East Anglia, the West Country, or "the North," the last an area made troublesome in the history plays, notably *Henry IV, Parts I and II*, at the same time that there were many divisions within these areas, whether economic, political, governmental, social, and/or religious. The links within and between regions were not affected by developments in transportation, because there was nothing that matched the situation in the century after Shakespeare's death. Road links remained poor, few canals were built, and distance affected experience and set a ready bound to certainty and confidence.

Another idea of space, one that was very different from that of physical movement, was provided by that of kinship groups or extended families, for example, that of the Cecils. Cousinhood was important. This was an aspect of the dynasticism that was repeatedly discussed in Shakespeare's plays with reference to lineage, parentage, and marriage, as with *Romeo and Juliet*. These links could have a spatial dimension as well, with figures from different areas being brought into a relationship. Space and time were thus related, with kinship a matter of lineage. Because families generally stayed in the same area for a long time, this process was linked to neighborliness.

Overall, there was the assumption on Shakespeare's part that his audience was familiar with the geography of Europe. Shylock says of Antonio: "He hath an argosy bound to Tripolis [Tripoli in Libya], another to the Indies; I understand, moreover, upon the Rialto [in Venice], he hath a third at Mexico, a fourth for England" (I, iii). The assumption is that these references are understood, as is the reference, with the Prince of Morocco, to his complexion (I, vii) and to his fighting on behalf of Sultan Süleyman the Magnificent (r. 1520–66) against the Safavids of Persia (Iran).

Possibly the details were less significant for audiences, indeed far less significant, than the sense of distance and difference. So also for other references, as at the beginning of *The Winter's Tale*, where there is mention of "great difference betwixt our Bohemia and your Sicilia," which, today, would be the Czech Republic and Sicily. In reality, in Shakespeare's lifetime, these were ruled by different branches of the Hapsburg family, the Austrian and Spanish branches respectively, and their relationship was not hostile. Shakespeare was also wrong to describe Bohemia as "a desert country" (III, iii), on the coast of which Antigonus's ship had touched: Bohemia is both fertile and far inland. He draws on his source, but all available maps would have shown it to be wrong.

In *Measure for Measure*, the lengthy case involving Elbow, Froth, and Pompey leads Angelo to remark:

> This will last out a night in Russia,
> When nights are longest there. (II, i)

The sense of distance is sometimes given poetic effect, as, in *Richard II*, when the king banishes his cousin Bolingbroke and also the latter's opponent, Thomas Mowbray, First Duke of Norfolk. Bolingbroke discusses this banishment with his father, John of Gaunt, Duke of Lancaster. The latter urges Bolingbroke to take it as a travel for pleasure, adding:

> All places that the eye of Heaven visits
> Are to a wise man ports and happy havens.

He encourages him to experience places in part by reimagining them. Bolingbroke replies, questioning:

> who can hold a fire in his hand
> By thinking on the frosty Caucasus? (I, iii)

The Caucasus was then an area of imperial contention, which the Ottomans (Turks), Safavids (Persians), and Russians sought to dominate. The tone could also be lighter even if still harsh, as in *The Comedy of Errors* when Dromio of Syracuse describes Nell the "kitchen-wench," who is a version of "Greasy Joan" from *Love's Labour's Lost* (V, ii). Nell is so greasy "I warrant her rags and the tallow in them will burn a Poland winter"—in other words, one that is very long and very cold. As with the Bolingbroke quotation, cold helps fix place. Comparing the spherical Nell to a globe, Dromio claims:

> I could find out countries in her.
> ANTIPHOLUS: In what part of her body stands Ireland?
> DROMIO: Marry, Sir, in her buttocks: I found it out by the bogs.

ANTIPHOLUS: Where Scotland?

DROMIO: I found it by the barrenness; hard in the palm of the hand.

ANTIPHOLUS: Where France?

DROMIO: In her forehead; armed and reverted, making war against her heir.

ANTIPHOLUS: Where England?

DROMIO: I looked for the chalky cliffs, but I could find no whiteness in them: but I guess it stood in her chin, by the salt rheum that ran between France and it.

ANTIPHOLUS: Where Spain?

DROMIO: Faith, I saw not; but I felt it hot in her breath.

ANTIPHOLUS: Where America, the Indies?

DROMIO: O, sir! Upon her nose, all o'er embellished with rubies, carbuncles, sapphires, declining their rich aspect to the hot breath of Spain, who sent whole armadoes of caracks [ships sent to the Indies to acquire precious stones] to be ballast at her nose.

ANTIPHOLUS: Where stood Belgia, the Netherlands?

DROMIO: O, sir! I did not look, so low. (III, ii)

Ephesus, Messina, Verona, and Vienna are scarcely crucial locations for particular plays and, instead, are sketched in with economy. For Ephesus in *The Comedy of Errors*, this is notably so as a city where the occult allegedly plays a role (in practice it does not) rather than as a detailed townscape. At the same time, there is, for Ephesus, as for the locations for other plays, a setting described that is necessary both for the action and for the particular dynamics of characterization, description, and drama. At times, the departure from geography is readily apparent, even if that does not disrupt the plot. In *The Two Gentlemen of Verona*, there is marked lack of specificity as to place and, indeed, as to the identity of the ruler, whether duke or emperor.

Repeatedly, the places in question in the setting are courts, quays, and marketplaces rather than cities as a whole. The first, in particular, permits a disengagement from context, one also seen when rulers are exiled, as with *As You Like It* and *The Tempest*. That *The Tempest* is set on a deserted island, its location lost in a magical storm, while *Much Ado About Nothing* is set in Messina in

Sicily, is far less consequential than that they both address types of court. So also with *Hamlet*, a revenge tragedy that could have been set in Italy or anywhere else rather than having to be in Denmark. Its major source was a Norse folk tale that had been written down by a Danish historian and then translated into French. In *Henry VI, Part I*, the list of losses in France that is announced to Henry V's funeral party is designed to impress rather than to be accurate and to establish a context of failure:

> Guienne, Champaigne, Rheims, Orleans
> Paris, Guysors, Poictiers, are all quite lost. (I, i)

This was an exaggeration at that stage and also a foreshortening. Henry died in 1422, but the second messenger brings news of the crowning of Charles VII at Rheims, which, in fact, occurred in 1429, as did Talbot's defeat at Patay reported by the third messenger. Paris was not lost to the French until 1436.

This does not mean that there is a placelessness to Shakespeare's plays, notably the nonhistory plays, but rather that the spectators did not have to bring too much to the occasion. Yet that point directs attention to what they did bring: an awareness (and degree of knowledge) of a world that was changing rapidly, as exploration revealed more while the politics of Europe were greatly in flux. Geography, history, and politics came together to provide the setting for human dramas that were fictional and factual.

### NOTES

1. J. Edwards, *Archbishop Pole* (Farnham, UK, 2014).
2. C. S. Knighton, ed., *Calendar of State Papers Preserved in the Public Record Office: Domestic Series, Edward VI, 1547–1553* (London, 1992), 108–9.
3. M. Fusaro, *Political Economies of Empire in the Early Modern Mediterranean: The Decline of Venice and the Rise of England, 1450–1700* (Cambridge, 2015).
4. T. Merriam, *The Identity of Shakespeare in "Henry VIII"* (Tokyo, 2005).

5. P. Kewes, I. Archer, and F. Heal, eds, *The Oxford Handbook of Holinshed's Chronicles* (Oxford, 2012). For an antiquary who did not seek publicity, J. D. Alsop, "William Fleetwood and Elizabethan Historical Scholarship," *Sixteenth Century Journal* 25 (1994): 155–76.

6. J. A. Marino, *Becoming Neapolitan: Citizen Culture in Baroque Naples* (Baltimore, 2011).

7. D. S. Gehring, *Anglo-German Relations and the Protestant Cause: Elizabethan Foreign Policy and Pan-Protestantism* (London, 2013).

8. J. Lawrence, *"Who the Devil Taught Thee So Much Italian?": Italian Language Learning and Literary Imitation in Early Modern England* (Manchester, 2005); M. Marrapodi, ed., *Shakespeare, Italy and Intertextuality* (Manchester, 2004).

9. S. Brietz Monta, *Martyrdom and Literature in Early Modern England* (Cambridge, 2005).

# THE WIDER WORLD

*Locating Prospero*

THE WIDER WORLD WAS GRASPED for Shakespeare's audiences by the development of London as a transoceanic port. While anchored in the river Thames, ships engaged in trade, and from there they sailed forth to obtain and sell goods. There were as yet no proper wet docks where ships could unload safely at any state of the tide or river. Small vessels could still make their way upstream through London Bridge to berth at the many smaller wharves near Queenhithe and the Vintry, but as ship size increased, the quays below the bridge became more and more important. Indeed, London's first dry dock was built at Rotherhithe in 1599, followed by another, for the expanding East India Company, at Blackwell in 1614–17. The movement of anchorages downriver, from Queenhithe and Billingsgate to Deptford, Wapping, and Ratcliffe, provided more space for shipping and thus more capacity for trade.

The founding of trading companies made it easier to raise capital from and share risk among a wide range of participants. The first English expedition to the Indian Ocean, sent in 1591, had been a total failure, but Dutch voyages dispatched in 1598 and

1599 had yielded a profit, and this led to fresh English effort. Established in London in 1600, the East India Company was one of the most important long-term developments in Shakespeare's lifetime. It proved the basis for the extension of English, later British, power and influence in the Indian Ocean and in nearby lands and seas. The company sent its first voyage in 1601, following with another in 1604. The time taken by the return voyages delayed profits, which entailed cash-flow issues that were helped by the joint-stock structure. This spread risk, in a way that would have greatly benefited Antonio in *The Merchant of Venice* by saving him from Shylock. The Lord Chamberlain's Men was also a joint-stock company, with the profits being distributed among its investors, who included Shakespeare. This remarkably cohesive theatrical company was a relatively stable form of organization.

The company, a chartered monopoly trading body, was, like the privateering war with Spain, an example of the "partnership" approach to government that was more generally seen in domestic terms with the growth in the role of the gentry. Other such companies included the Muscovy Company to Russia (1555) and the Levant Company to the Ottoman Empire (1581), as well as several that were not so successful, such as the Guinea Company to West Africa (1618). In 1609, James I came to watch the launch of the East India Company's ship *Trade's Increase*, part of a major expansion in English shipping that was seen in the period and notably from the 1580s. This increase was helped by England's plentiful wood supplies, but it also put pressure on them. Trade brought in goods from near and far, some exotic, such as "the perfumes of Arabia" referred to by Lady Macbeth (V, i). Dutch competition was also a serious issue in the quest for the goods of "the rich East" (*Macbeth*, IV, iii). Tobacco arrived in the Elizabethan period from the New World, being introduced by John Hawkins and/or his crew in the 1560s. Tobacco smoking in England followed, being mentioned in 1573.

In Shakespeare's lifetime, the world was changing greatly as a result of Western exploration. This contributed much, at least for some people, to an awareness of change through time as a transformative—rather than, as had been generally believed, cyclical—process and thus of a sense of modernization and modernity. The latter, a coming to the present, offered an account of time and thus of space in which there was marked difference between the two criteria.

The medieval background set the context of inherited values in Tudor England. Traditionally, Jerusalem came at the center of the world, just as it was the inspiration of Christian pilgrimage. Jerusalem represented the key event in history, that of Christ's redemptive mission, and was also central to human space. In 1421 Henry V talked of going on an expedition to Jerusalem, although, as with his father, who had promised to do the same, events prevented him. However, by Shakespeare's lifetime, Jerusalem was of far less consequence in cultural references and political discussion. He never tackled the English monarchs who went on Crusade: Richard I and (as heir) Edward I.

Alongside the religious symbolism, there were wondrous creatures depicted in medieval *mappae mundi* (world maps), as well as in other accounts of lands outside Europe, notably in sub-Saharan Africa. These creatures echo in *Othello*, when the protagonist describes his earlier travels, including his having

> being taken by the insolent foe
> And sold to slavery.

He had seen

> hills whose heads touch heaven
> ... the Cannibals that each other eat,
> The Anthropophagi, and men whose heads
> Do grow beneath their shoulders. (I, iii)

Such accounts went back to the classics and suggested a known world that was shadowed by a mysterious present.

The Renaissance encouraged interest in the classical world, which ensured a greater degree of knowledge of its geography, knowledge that Shakespeare had absorbed through his education. In *Antony and Cleopatra*, Augustus is shown in Rome telling his principal advisors that Antony in Cleopatra's capital, Alexandria in Egypt, had divided up the Middle East:

> Unto her [Cleopatra]
> he gave the 'stablishment of Egypt; made her
> Of Lower Syria, Cyprus, Lydia,
> Absolute queen . . .
> His sons [by Cleopatra] he there proclaim'd the kings of kings;
> Great Media, Parthia, and Armenia
> He gave to Alexander; to Ptolemy he assign'd
> Syria, Cilicia, and Phoenicia.
> . . . who [Antony and Cleopatra] now are levying
> The kings o'the earth for war.
> He hath assembled
> Bocchus, the King of Libya; Archelaus,
> Of Cappadocia; Philadelphos, King
> of Paphlagonia; the Thracian king, Adallas;
> King Malchus of Arabia; King of Pont;
> Herod of Jewry; Mithridates, King
> of Comagene; Polemon and Amintas,
> The Kings of Mede and Lycaonia,
> With a more larger list of sceptres. (III, vi)

This is a version of limitless Oriental power that linked Renaissance interest in the ancient world to the Oriental-style drama conjured up by Marlowe in his play *Tamburlaine the Great*, which was performed to great success in London in 1587. Herod brings in the Christian story.

Meanwhile, exploration and travel provided and confirmed new geographical information. This was impressively offered, supposedly in Messina in Sicily, by Benedick in *Much Ado About Nothing*, when affirming his wish to travel far rather than to talk with Beatrice:

> I will go on the slightest errand now to the Antipodes [opposite side of the Earth] that you can devise to send me on. I will fetch you a

tooth-picker [toothpicks were made of precious materials] now from the furthest inch of Asia; bring you the length of Prester John's foot; fetch you a hair off the great Cham's [Emperor of China] beard; do you any embassage to the Pigmies. (II, i)

The last was a reference to sub-Saharan Africa, as was that to Prester John. In *Twelfth Night*, Fabian says: "you are now sailed into the north of my lady's opinion, where you will hang like an icicle on a Dutchman's beard" (III, ii). This is a reference to the voyage of William Barents around the north of the Arctic island of Nova Zembla in 1596–97.

Interest in gold had encouraged Portuguese explorers to sail south along the coast of West Africa in the fifteenth century. Religion was also a dynamic, with the Portuguese, notably under Prince Henry the Navigator, seeking allies against Islam in the drive to reconquer Jerusalem. This was a reconquest seen as a crucial preliminary to the Second Coming of Christ, which was the promise of the Church and the goal of millenarian thinkers. Similarly, Christopher Columbus, in his *Book of Prophecies* compiled before his fourth voyage to the Caribbean, in 1502, argued that the end of the world would occur in 155 years and that his own discoveries had been foretold in the Bible. By sailing west to discover a route to Asia, he hoped to raise money to retake the Holy Land and thus to redeem the Christian world. The recovery of Jerusalem was a key theme, one that indicated the continuing significance of crusading ideology into the sixteenth century.

Columbus had set sail westward in 1492, bound, he thought, for Japan, but instead reached the West Indies. Information was rapidly disseminated, with the second voyage, that of 1493, being significant as it helped establish a viable and repeatable route. The first circumnavigation of the world, in 1519–22, commenced by Ferdinand Magellan (although he was killed on the island of Cebu in the Philippines en route), greatly affected an understanding of its shape. This was the first voyage (in late 1520) to round the southern point of South America and subsequently achieved the first recorded crossing of the Pacific, although Polynesian travelers had already made long voyages across that ocean. Reports of a Chinese circumnavigation are erroneous.

The circumnavigation started by Magellan also exemplified how new information required new ways to display and consider it. It made the globe a more obvious tool, indeed the basic map, for understanding the world and thus emphasized the need to give greater attention to the projections used in depicting that world. The idea of a globe was repeatedly used in Shakespeare's plays. Appearing at the start of *Henry IV, Part II*, Rumour—who would have worn a cloak sporting the image of tongues—announces:

> I, from the orient to the drooping west,
> Making the wind my post-horse, still unfold
> The acts commenced on this ball of earth.

Oberon remarks in *A Midsummer Night's Dream*:

> We the globe can compass soon,
> Swifter than the wandering moon. (IV, i)

As a nighttime sphere, the moon was also a symbol of mystery. In the same play, Hermia offers an arresting image but one that she sees as inherently implausible, of the moon passing through a hole in the earth:

> I'll believe as soon
> this whole earth may be bored, and that the moon
> May through the centre creep, and so displease
> Her brother's noontide with th'Antipodes. (III, ii)

In *Troilus and Cressida*, Ulysses refers to the danger that disorder will "make a sop of all this solid globe" (I, iii). In *The Comedy of Errors*, at a more popular level, Dromio of Syracuse describes Nell the "kitchen-wench": "No longer from head to foot than from hip to hip: she is spherical, like a globe" (III, ii).

New information clarified how much more had to be discovered, for the globe had to be filled. By drawing attention to the size of the Pacific, the circumnavigation clarified not only the size of the earth but also how much remained to be mapped. The possibility that landmasses existed to the north or south of Magellan's route across the Pacific encouraged attention, the southern landmass being seen as necessary in order to balance the greater known landmass in the northern hemisphere. Despite not having actually been found, a southern continent was depicted on maps and sometimes even shown with a full set of place-names. As observers on ships could only see the distance allowed by the human eye, and then the eye supplemented by the telescope, most of the Pacific remained a matter of speculation.

For Shakespeare's audiences, it was English exploration that was most to the point. Aside from news of exploration by others, a great extension of direct English interaction with the world occurred during Shakespeare's lifetime, one in which the key names were Drake, Cavendish, Frobisher, Davis, Hudson, and Raleigh. This exploration left echoes in the plays, as when Sir John Falstaff in *The Merry Wives of Windsor* contemplates the appeal and wealth of the two women he mistakenly thinks desire him: "she is a region in Guiana, all gold and bounty. I will be 'cheator to them both, and they shall be exchequers to me: they shall be my East and West Indies, and I will trade to them both" (I, iii). Thus, South America is referred to in Windsor, a very different geography to that offered by Falstaff in *Henry IV*.

In this, Shakespeare draws on Raleigh's exploration of modern Venezuela in 1595, exploration that had led to his *The Discovery of the Large, Rich and Beautiful Empire of Guiana* (1596). Raleigh knew the playwright Marlowe and the mathematician Harriot and advised Hakluyt, who compiled information on overseas travel. Searching for El Dorado, Raleigh claimed to have found gold in the Orinoco Valley. He continued committed to his quest, for example, sending out ships in 1596 and 1597, and that helped to maintain English interest in the region. In the 1610s, Raleigh focused on the issue even though in 1604 peace had been negotiated with Spain, which claimed the whole area. The expedition he organized in 1617 attacked the Spaniards, ignoring James I's insistence that he was not to do so; and it did not find any gold mines. Raleigh was beheaded on his return, an abrupt breach with the ethos of the Elizabethan world.

## MARITIME DESTINY

In *The Two Gentlemen of Verona*, Panthiro referred to young men who sought to better themselves:

> Some to the wars, to try their fortune there;
> Some to discover islands far away. (I, iii)

Initially, the English had done less well than other nations in Western Europe. To sail west from the British Isles was to be exposed in those latitudes to prevailing westerlies (i.e., winds from the west), which hindered navigation toward America. In contrast, the Portuguese and Spaniards, farther south, benefited greatly from supporting winds when they sailed to the Caribbean. Moreover, the peoples of the British Isles lacked the "stepping stones" into the Atlantic provided the Portuguese and Spaniards by the islands of the Azores, Madeira, and the Canaries, as, to the north of the British Isles, the Vikings had earlier benefited from the islands of the Faroes, Iceland, and Greenland. In addition, there was nothing comparable to the tradition of expansion at the expense of the heathen that the Portuguese and Spaniards had acquired from their long wars against the Muslims and that both then took forward when expanding into Africa from 1415 onward.

Nevertheless, Britain's island character and the prominence of fishing and foreign trade ensured that maritime traditions were well developed. Fishing, both at sea and inland, was far more widespread than in the twentieth century, let alone the twenty-first, which helps explain the resonance of images relating to it. Shakespeare devotes less attention to fishing than to trade.

However, in *Pericles*, the shipwrecked prince is rescued by three fishermen, who are helpful and hospitable. Pericles reflects:

> How from the finny subject of the sea
> These fishers tell the infirmities of men. (II, i)

London received fish from the Thames estuary and the North Sea.[1]

Inshore maritime experience was far more readily translated to deep-sea activities than is the case today. By the late fifteenth century, over a hundred English boats every year were braving the North Atlantic, as well as making round trips lasting six months, sailing to Iceland to fish or to buy cod. These voyages encouraged the development of English shipbuilding and also led to greater knowledge of currents and winds in the North Atlantic, in particular of the brief season of easterlies from March to May, which permitted ships to sail to Iceland. This trade was dominated by Hull, East Anglia, especially King's Lynn, and Bristol but with a role some years also for a range of other ports on both the east and west coasts of the country, including Boston, Dartmouth, Grimsby, Newcastle, and Scarborough.

In the sixteenth century, fishing off more distant Newfoundland developed. Building on the methods of the Icelandic fishery, which continued strong into the seventeenth century, the Newfoundland fisheries eventually led large numbers of ships and men to cross the Atlantic and return each year, and this resulted in two important foundations for future activity: first, knowledge about Atlantic navigation, specifically the currents, winds, and coastlines of the North Atlantic, and, second, a sense that sailing across the Atlantic was normal. The Portuguese, French, and Basques were initially most active in the Newfoundland fisheries, but the English came to play a more prominent role from the 1570s, and by the end of the century, several hundred English ships were sailing there each year. The conflict between England and Philip II of Spain (from 1580 also Philip I of Portugal) was in part played out in these distant waters, with the English and French generally winning at the expense of the Portuguese and the Basques.

Cod was the principal target and was brought back in sufficient quantities to hit the North Sea cod fishery. The Newfoundland fisheries involved not only fishing but also activity on land, especially the salting and drying necessary to preserve fish, activities that led to the development of a coastal infrastructure, with wharves, washing cages, drying platforms, and oil vats for the cod liver oil. Salting and drying also increased the labor demand of the fishery, and this could not rely on the Beothuk natives, who were few in number and in competition with the Europeans for the fish. The natives were seen as creatures like Caliban in *The Tempest*, who is described by Trinculo as like "a strange fish," indeed like a dried hake (II, ii). Similarly, visiting Paris in 1865, the Dutch painter Frederik Kaemmerer referred to "the street-mender, whose coat of cowhide makes him look like a wild beast."[2]

As a result of the hostile stance of the natives, there was a reliance on labor from Southwest England. This reliance helped spread the impact of maritime activity, because, aside from experienced or "specialized" fishermen, there was also a tapping of the general labor market that took advantage of the widespread need for money and of the extent to which fishing was also part of a less specialized labor world. Thus, farmers and tradesmen turned to the sea in order to supplement their income, and the Newfoundland fisheries helped to introduce to the transoceanic world the seasonal migration of labor that was so important for English employment, although the lengths of the voyages ensured that the ships and seamen were less available for other activities than was generally the case with fishing. The labor needs of the fisheries and the length of the voyages also increased the requirement for capital.

With time, the fisheries became more complex, as sources for fish and technical and market possibilities were probed, and investment was directed to what was proving an important source of profit. Initially, boats sailed from England, moored in harbors, and then sent out shallops (twenty-five- to thirty-foot boats that had been transported in sections) to fish, while, once caught, the cod was salted lightly, washed, and dried. Some ships, however, came to sail to the offshore banks, where they preserved the cod in the hold by heavily salting it: this was the "wet" or "green" fishery, which led to a more perishable product but required less labor. The need for salt, which was obtained from Iberia or the Mediterranean, notably Sardinia, increased the diverse sailing patterns that the fisheries gave rise to, as well as underlining the capital needs of the industry. These capital needs extended the impact of the fisheries within England, and although boats and men came often from small ports, merchants in larger ones, especially and increasingly London, were important in financing and marketing the trade. This was to look toward a degree of specialization by the late seventeenth century, with the use then of larger ships based in a smaller number of larger ports.

The fish trade was not simply bilateral between England and Newfoundland. Instead, benefiting greatly from the injunctions on Catholics not to eat meat on Fridays and in particular seasons, fish was also exported to Spain, Portugal, and Italy. This played an important role in English trade. Furthermore, the Newfoundland fisheries were seen as important to the strategic strength of the country as a "nursery" (or training place) of sailors, for war and peace, while the fish that were caught provided food not only for the fishermen but also for the navy. Although largely separate from subsequent patterns of Atlantic trade, the Newfoundland fisheries helped establish methods of organization, particularly capital support for transoceanic expansion, that were to be important to other trades.

Monarchs played a role in transoceanic expansion. Edward IV (r. 1461–83) was interested in trade and shipping, encouraging the development of both. Henry VII backed the Italian John Cabot,

who sailed west from Bristol in the *Mathew* in 1497. Like Columbus, he hoped to reach the wealth of East Asia but arrived instead probably in Newfoundland, his "new found land." In 1498,
Cabot set out on another voyage but did not return, probably
falling victim to a savage storm. In 1508, Cabot's son Sebastian
set out to find a passage to Asia around the new continent and
may have reached Hudson Strait before wintering further south,
possibly in Chesapeake Bay. He returned to find the supportive
Henry VII replaced by Henry VIII, who was focused, instead,
on Continental power politics. There was then a lack of support
for several decades.

The situation changed in midcentury as merchants unsuccessfully attempted to break into Portugal's trade with West Africa.
Privateering voyages led the English into waters that were new
to them, including, in 1555, the earliest recorded English voyage
into the southern hemisphere. In turn, mercantile horizons expanded. In the 1560s, the attempt to take a share in the profitable
slave trade between Africa and the Spanish New World was an
important aspect of a search for overseas opportunities. The English, however, failed to establish a settlement with the expedition
mounted to Florida in 1565. The Spaniards keenly defended their
interests there. John Hawkins sold slaves to the Spanish Caribbean on two voyages until, at San Juan de Ulúa near Vera Cruz
in 1568, on the third voyage, the presence of the viceroy of New
Spain led to a Spanish attack on what was, in the official view, an
unwelcome interloper, helping ensure that the venture made a
large loss.

As tension rose between England and Spain in the 1570s, privateering attacks on Spanish trade and settlements in the New
World became more frequent, while greater lawlessness at sea
affected those who tried to maintain a peaceful trade. William
Winter raided the Spanish base at St. Augustine in Florida in
1571, while Francis Drake attacked the Spanish silver route across
the Panama isthmus in 1571–73. This was not a pushover. Drake

encountered serious difficulties, including yellow fever and a stronger resistance than had been anticipated. In 1576, Drake's former companion John Oxenham was defeated when he sought to capture Panama.

At this stage, however, as England and Spain were not at war, Elizabeth I was hesitant about overly offending Spain, especially as relations between the two states improved in the mid-1570s. For example, Sir Richard Grenville's attempt to mount an expedition in 1574–75, probably in order to establish a colony in the southern reaches of South America, was unwelcome to the government. Moreover, although Elizabeth invested in Drake's 1577 voyage to the Pacific, he was not given a formal commission. Nevertheless, Drake was supported by many key political figures, including the Earl of Leicester, Sir Francis Walsingham, Sir Christopher Hatton, and the Lord Admiral, Edward, First Earl of Lincoln, of the Clinton family. However, the more cautious Burghley was kept in the dark. In 1577–80, Drake became the first Englishman to circumnavigate the world, a formidable feat of seamanship and only the second circumnavigation in history, following that of some of Magellan's crew in 1519–22. Spanish shipping and positions in the Pacific were not expecting attack, and this vulnerability yielded an excellent return to the investors, especially Elizabeth. In April 1581, she knighted Drake on board his ship, the *Golden Hind*, at Deptford on the river Thames. This occasion was an important display of heroism, one that linked personal courage, enterprise, and bellicosity with monarchy and Protestantism. The occasion was also to be often cited subsequently in accounts of the reign.

English exploration had become more active from midcentury. The search for a northeast passage to the riches of the East Indies delayed the quest for a northwest passage north of North America. Sir Hugh Willoughby died in 1552 on the coast of Lapland, but Richard Chancellor reached the White Sea, before traveling on to Moscow, opening up a tenuous trade route. This was explored further by Anthony Jenkinson in 1558–62, when he traveled thence to Central Asia and to Persia on behalf of the Muscovy

Company. Established in 1555, this company developed economic links with Russia but not a territorial position. The Siberian coast and the nearby Arctic islands were not a promising destination for the establishment of bases or for colonization: furs were to be obtained instead by trading with the Russians.

From 1576, explorers again probed icy seas to the northwest of Newfoundland in pursuit of what it was hoped would be the tremendous commercial opportunity of a northwest passage, from the Atlantic to the Pacific. Martin Frobisher, John Davis, and Henry Hudson entered major bodies of water: Baffin Bay and Hudson Bay. In 1576 Frobisher found what he called Frobisher Strait, which he saw as the opening to the route to "the West Sea" (Pacific) and "Cathay" (China). In fact, he had found a bay on the coast of Baffin Island, now named Frobisher Bay. Frobisher also thought he had discovered a gold-bearing ore, and this was the focus of expeditions in 1577 and 1578, in the second of which he entered what was later to be called Hudson Strait. The ore was mined, and a large quantity was brought back to England, but it was discovered to be iron pyrites (fool's gold), and this collapse led to the failure of the Company of Cathay, which had provided the finance for the expeditions.

John Davis found Cumberland Sound in 1585 and Davis Strait in 1587, while Henry Hudson wintered in Hudson Bay in 1611–12, before being cast adrift by his mutinous crew the following June, which led to his death. In the 1610s, Thomas Button and William Baffin, and, in the 1630s, Luke Foxe and Thomas James established that the passages that had been discovered led to further shores, not open ocean. Nevertheless, these voyages accumulated valuable information that was to be used by those who sought trading opportunities, especially in furs and whales.

War with Spain from 1585 to 1604 encouraged a different placing of England from the traditional one of trade with Europe, particularly the Low Countries. In the new ordering, a global, notably transatlantic, role appeared necessary and inevitable. Maritime destiny and strength were fused with the anti-Catholic nationalism of confrontation with Spain. Providence, power, and profit all had a role to play. The sense of a maritime destiny, at once political and religious, was encouraged by the writings of the geographer and armchair traveler Richard Hakluyt (c. 1552–1616). His *Principal Navigations, Voyages, and Discoveries of the English Nation made by Sea or over Land to the most remote and farthest distant quarters of the Earth* appeared in 1589 and, as a longer work, in 1598–1600.[3] John Dee's *General and Rare Memorials Pertaining to the Perfect Act of Navigation* (1577) argued for England's position as an Atlantic power.

Geography offered a new ideal of science as a tool for understanding and controlling nature, and this potential made the subject popular. Service of the state encouraged an interest in mathematical geography, while descriptive geography helped readers to regard the world as a source of wondrous tales and new goods, thus creating attitudes that encouraged the exploitation of foreign peoples. There was a close relationship between the study of geography and the development of ideas of English power and imperial growth, and such a relationship was especially pronounced at the court of James I's eldest son, Prince Henry, before his early death in 1612. At least thirty-seven men who were connected with his circle had an interest in some aspect of geography.

The link between navigation and mathematics epitomized that between practice and theory. The need for mathematical knowledge in navigation and cartography linked the voyages with the pursuit of truth in mathematics. Edward Wright (d. 1615), who was engaged in both mathematical research and voyages of exploration, provided a mathematical rendering of Mercator's projection, calculating the position of parallels, and helped to disseminate the necessary information by publishing a table of meridian parts for each degree. As a result, mapmakers could produce accurate projections. Wright produced a map of the world that was published in the second edition of Hakluyt's *Principal Navigations* (1599): this was the map referred to in 1602 in the description of the smiling face of Malvolio in *Twelfth Night* (III, ii).

Thomas Harriot (1560–1621) and other mathematicians used a rhetoric of geographical discovery in order to present mathematicians as explorers of the structure of geometrical figures. The potent rhetoric and topic of geographical voyages of discovery was applied to the search for truth in the natural world, as well as to personal relationships and the development of the printing press. The theme of new discoveries in the accounts of voyages of exploration encouraged a call for new discoveries on the part of experimental philosophers and with these discoveries grasped through experience. In short, knowledge was not to be referential to the past but to be focused on the new. Francis Bacon explicitly compared both forms of discovery, those from exploration and those from scientific experiments.

Whereas Dee offered a deductive mathematics based on Euclid's *Elements*, the key classical model, Harriot took a bolder line toward the geometrical continuum, adopting an atomistic approach that lent itself to an engagement with knowledge as a developing field for intellectual application. In place of the classic Euclidean proof, which relies on rigorous deductions from first principles, came an attempt to look into the inner structure of geometrical figures. Thus, in contrast to the scholasticism of traditional mathematics, in which conclusions are implicit in the assumptions and geometry is focused on relations between apparent features, there came an emphasis on scrutiny and the exploration of hidden secrets, an approach appropriate for Prospero. The mathematical indivisibles, the objects of discovery, led directly, later in the seventeenth century, to the calculus of Isaac Newton and Gottfried Leibniz.

### THE AMERICAS

One major development in Shakespeare's lifetime was the foundation of English colonies in the New World, notably Virginia. Both Virginia and Bermuda have been presented as the inspiration for *The Tempest* (first produced at the royal court in 1611), and this attribution reflects the role of exploration in the imagination of the period. Shakespeare captured the sense of spreading knowledge when, in *Twelfth Night* (1602), he has Maria say of the duped Malvolio "he does smile his face into more lines than is in the new map with the augmentation [addition] of the Indies" (III, ii). That map therefore contained more information than its predecessors, and whether or not they had seen the new map, Shakespeare's London audience was expected to appreciate the fact. In *Henry VIII*, he also commented on the fascination in London with the arrival of Native Americans: "have we some strange Indian with the great tool [penis] come to court, the women so besiege us?" (V, iv). Popular curiosity was presented by Shakespeare as focused on novelty. In *The Tempest*, Trinculo sees the displaying of Caliban to the public as likely to earn money in England:

> not a holiday fool there but would give a piece of silver: there would this monster make a man; any strange beast there makes a man. When they will not give a doit [lift a finger] to relieve a lame beggar, they will lay out ten to see a dead Indian. (II, ii)

In Philip Massinger's play *The City Madam* (c. 1632), the villain is ready to sell his sister-in-law and nieces to the heroes who are disguised as "Indians" seeking women for sacrifice. Alongside comments by Shakespeare on imperial expansion in the present, the empires of antiquity also provided him with appropriate material.[4]

Initial steps had not been encouraging, despite many attempts to establish English claims. On his circumnavigation of the world in 1577–80, Drake missed the entrance to San Francisco harbor but claimed "Nova Albion," the Californian coast, for Elizabeth. Humphrey Gilbert claimed Newfoundland for the queen in 1583, but it proved difficult to transform a scattering of fishing stations into an English settlement colony. In 1610, the Newfoundland Company established a settlement at Cupid's Cove in Conception

Bay, and the company granted plots of land to settlers on the Avalon peninsula, but it was difficult to make a success of them as the climate was too harsh for farming. Nevertheless, the Newfoundland settlements showed that it was possible to overwinter there, and this provided the basis for a strengthening of the fisheries as the fishing season was extended.

On the eastern seaboard of the mainland of North America, an attempt was made to establish a colony called Virginia in honor of the unmarried sovereign. Her status was a key element of the iconography of the period. Moreover, the emphasis on the queen's virginity presumably underlined the threats to virginity depicted in Shakespeare's plays, notably in *Measure for Measure*, *Pericles*, and *The Tempest*. In 1585, 108 colonists were landed on Roanoke Island off the coast of what is now North Carolina, but they found it difficult to feed themselves and were taken off in the following year. A second attempt was made in 1588, but when a relief ship arrived in 1590, it found the village deserted: disease, starvation, or natives may have wiped out the colonists. Indeed, a forceful native response was offered by Caliban in *The Tempest*:

> This island's mine, by Sycorax my mother,
> Which thou tak'st from me . . .
> For I am all the subjects that you have,
> Which first was mine own king: and here you sty me
> In this hard rock, whiles you do keep from me
> The rest o' th'island. (I, ii)

However, the positive impression created by Harriot's *A Brief and True Report of the New Found Land of Virginia* (1588) and other reports encouraged fresh efforts to establish a colony, although it was not until a base was established by the Virginia Company at Jamestown on the Chesapeake in 1607 that a permanent colony was founded. Spain regarded this colony as an invasion of its rights and protested its foundation, but, although the defenses at Jamestown were prepared to resist Spanish attack, it

did not come: Virginia was too distant from the centers of Spanish naval power, Cadiz and Havana, and, indeed, from the outli-
ers of the Spanish Empire, notably St. Augustine. Despite heavy
initial losses, largely due to the impact of disease in an unfamiliar
environment, the colony expanded, and Native American resistance was overcome. The continued arrival of new settlers was
important to this success, and this continued arrival depended on
knowledge of the colony back in England and the dissemination
of a positive impression of it. The arrival, from 1619, of African
slaves, a practice that drew on Spanish and Portuguese roots,
assumptions, and practices, was also significant for the development of the colony.[5]

Farther north, the term "New England" was coined in 1614 by
Captain John Smith when he described the coastline north of
the Hudson. His *Description of New England* (1616) popularized
the idea that the land was comparable to that in England.[6] Already, and possibly as early as 1597, the discovery of fish stocks off
the coast of New England had led to a pattern of activity similar
to that in Newfoundland, with offshore fishing and an onshore
settlement at Sagadhoc in Maine in 1608, although this was soon
abandoned. In 1602, a settlement was created by Bartholomew
Gosnold, on an island near what he had named Cape Cod. However, his failure to develop initial trading contacts with the Native
Americans helped ensure the hostility of the latter, and the settlement had to be abandoned. In 1620, the Pilgrim Fathers, a group
of Protestant nonconformist separatists, sailing from Plymouth
in Devon on the *Mayflower* made a landfall at Cape Cod. They
established a settlement at New Plymouth. Seeking to create a
godly agrarian world, they believed that their righteousness made
them more entitled to the land than the Native Americans.

Meanwhile, in the West Indies, opposition from native Caribs
helped lead to the failure of settlements founded on the island
of St. Lucia in 1605 and on Grenada in 1609. In contrast, when a
fleet sent by the Virginia Company to resupply the colony was

scattered by storms, the flagship, *Sea Venture*, was wrecked on hitherto unknown Bermuda in 1609. Although Thomas Gates, the incoming governor of Virginia, pressed for the building of a boat and for continuing to the mainland—which was achieved in 1610—some wanted to stay on Bermuda. In the event, the island was settled in 1612. The dramatic account of this episode by William Strachey (1572–1621), a survivor, *A True Reportory of the Wracke*, was probably known to Shakespeare and to some of his audience. Not printed until 1625, a manuscript version circulated in England from 1610. It surely provided a background for *The Tempest* in that there were parallels between Strachey's account and the play, for example, in the description of St. Elmo's fire.[7]

The English presence in no way matched that of Spain, which was well established, notably in Cuba, Hispaniola, and Puerto Rico. Nevertheless, English settlements in and near the Americas reflected the sense of the world as changing and of offering new opportunities accordingly. This was not a process that was exclusive to London life but was certainly one much of which was enacted on its riverbanks and talked about in its streets. Despite the significance of struggles with Spain in the Caribbean, notably in the 1580s and 1590s, exploration was not to the fore in national concern while England was involved in a life-and-death struggle with Spain in Europe. However, the situation changed in the 1600s, and the extra-European world increasingly came to the fore in discussion. Although the classical world and English history were more pressing as topics, Shakespeare to a degree reflected this change not in details but with respect to new horizons and worlds becoming knowable.

The audiences were certainly given a range of references. Othello's last proper speech, delivered supposedly in Cyprus, referred to himself as "like the base Indian" who "threw a pearl away richer than all his tribe," compared tears to dropping "as fast as the Arabian trees. Their med'cinable gum [sap]," and to killing a hostile Turk who beat a Venetian at Aleppo (V, ii).

## AFRICA

Exploration was opening up to European eyes a world beyond Europe, but most of this world was still obscure and the stuff of vague report.[8] To take Ethiopia, otherwise known as Abyssinia, there had been direct contact in 1541 when the Portuguese sent four hundred musketeers to help against the Turks and their local allies. The Ethiopians rewarded these musketeers with land in order to retain their services, and these musketeers (and their descendants) continued to play an important military role into the following century.

Subsequent developments, however, were scarcely well known in Europe, let alone in England. Under pressure from the local Islamic sultanate of Adal and from its Turkish supporter, Ethiopia was also put under pressure by the expansion northward of the Oromo peoples, nomadic pastoralists who made effective use of horses, which increased their mobility. This helped them live off the land, outmaneuvering the more cumbersome Ethiopian forces.

However, in confronting these problems, Ethiopia benefited from vigorous leadership by Serse-Dingil, the Ethiopian emperor from 1562 to 1597. Utterly different in his leadership style compared with Elizabeth I, he serves as a reminder of the variety of effective forms of rulership. Commanding his forces in person, Serse-Dingil defeated Adal in 1576, following this up three years later with victory over an alliance of Turkish forces with Bahr Nagash Ishaq of Tigre and the ruler of Harar. This ended Turkish attempts to overrun Ethiopia from the Red Sea. Serse-Dingil then also expanded Ethiopia to the west, while he defeated the Oromo in 1572 and 1586. He also changed Ethiopia's military system, complementing the traditional reliance on the private forces of provincial governors and other regional potentates by an extension of the troops who were directly under royal control.

In *Pericles*, the first of the six knights who compete is a knight of Sparta, a clear classical reference:

And the device he bears upon his shield
Is a black Ethiop reaching at the sun. (II, i)

Susenyros of Ethiopia (r. 1607–32) continued the expansion to the west. He also incorporated many of the Oromo into his army and settled many in his dominions. However, Susenyros's conversion to Catholicism led to serious rebellions, and he abdicated, a pattern similar to the earlier Scottish reaction to Mary, Queen of Scots, and the Swedish one to Sigismund Vasa.

Ethiopia was not the only part of Africa that was vaguely known to Shakespeare's audiences or at least mentioned in his plays, as in *Romeo and Juliet*, *The Merry Wives of Windsor*, and, alongside "tawny Tartar," as an insult in *Midsummer Night's Dream* (III, ii). So also with Morocco.[9] In 1578, one of the most significant battles in Shakespeare's lifetime occurred at al-Qasr-al-Kabir/ Alcazarquivir, when the Moroccans crushed a Portuguese invasion. King Sebastian led a poorly prepared army of 18,000–20,000 men, crucially short of cavalry, into the interior in order to challenge the sharif, Abd al-Malik, who had a force of about 70,000 men. As so often with Shakespearean plays, rifts within a ruling family were a key issue. Sebastian sought to benefit from division within Morocco by helping Muhammad al-Mutawakhil, the former sharif, who had appealed for Sebastian's assistance (having been deposed by his Turkish-backed uncle, Abd al-Malik). For his part, Sebastian hoped to establish a client ruler.

Sebastian sought battle, believing that his infantry would successfully resist the Moroccan cavalry. In the event, the skillful, well-disciplined Moroccan force won a crushing victory thanks to superior leadership and discipline, more flexible units and tactics, and the contingent events of the battle. The entire Portuguese army was either killed or captured, and Sebastian killed, although

there long circulated legends about his survival in secret, possibly within a mountain.[10] Again this battle was Shakespearean
in scale, redolent of Actium, the key engagement in *Antony and
Cleopatra*, or of the Wars of the Roses as described in the history plays, although Marlowe was more suited to describe such
a battle.

As a result of al-Qasr-al-Kabir, Philip II of Spain, the uncle of
the childless Sebastian, seized Portugal in a rapidly successful
campaign in 1580. In turn, the English came to back Don Antonio, a pretender to Portugal, and to seek the support of Morocco
against Spain. English traders sold cast-iron artillery to Morocco,
buying saltpeter, a crucial constituent of gunpowder.

Morocco itself staged a near-legendary campaign. Only about
half of the 4,000 troops sent south in 1590 across the vast, dry ex-
panse of the Sahara Desert by Sultan Mūlāy Ahmad al Mansūr of
Morocco survived the crossing. In *Troilus and Cressida*, Ulysses
referred to being "parch in Afric sun" (I, iii). The sultan wanted
to secure gold, as well as recognition for his claim to be caliph,
the Muslim chief civil and spiritual ruler. The Moroccans benefited from the Portuguese arms seized in 1578, while many of the
troops sent were renegades: Christians who had become Muslims, notably 2,000 musketeers. The English defeat of the Spanish
Armada in 1588 lessened the chance of Spanish intervention in
Morocco, which, in turn, encouraged the Moroccan expedition
across the Sahara.

The resulting Moroccan victory, under Judar Pasha, at Tond-
ibi on the river Niger in 1591, led to the collapse of the Songhai
Empire there. In this battle, Moroccan musketry defeated the
12,500-strong Songhai cavalry and about 30,000 infantry, an army
equipped with spears and bows and lacking firearms. The Moroccans also benefited from the poor leadership of their opponents.
The flight of the Songhai emperor, Ishāq II, helped lead to a collapse of his army, and the Moroccans soon afterward captured
the cities of Gao and Timbuktu without resistance. It was no

wonder that Morocco appeared potent and fabulous. Octavius's conquest of Egypt after Actium stands parallel.

Most of Africa did not have this resonance. The slave trade was developing from West Africa, but, as yet, English participation was far smaller than it was to become by the late seventeenth century. The English made an attempt, from the 1550s, to break into Portugal's trade with West Africa and into the profitable slave trade from there to the Spanish New World. Plymouth-born John Hawkins obtained his slaves in West Africa on the coast of modern Sierra Leone by raiding rather than through purchase, losing men in the process to poisoned arrows and other hazards, as well as by piracy against Portuguese ships. He then shipped the slaves across the Atlantic and sold them to the Spaniards at considerable profit, which was a means of gaining access to the Spanish-controlled bullion of the New World. Thus, the slaves were not sold to England, where, indeed, there were increasing numbers of free black people. Henry VII was one of many prominent Europeans who kept some black domestic servants, but the lack of evidence of many others would suggest that black slaves were not at all common in England. The few exceptions were probably gifts and not sold on.

Hawkins's slaving voyages were stopped by the Spaniards in 1568, and in the late sixteenth century, the English commitment to the slave trade was far less than it was to become a century later. Most English voyages to West Africa were for pepper, hides, wax, and ivory and in search of gold rather than of slaves, on whom English trade with West Africa did not focus until the mid-seventeenth century. As far as West Africa was concerned, relatively little was known in England, although many people came to stereotype black Africans, and many African cultural practices were misunderstood and recast in a negative light. Denigration of them as inferior and uncivilized was related to associating Africans with occupations linked to physical prowess and thus appropriateness to enslavement.[11] So more mildly with the disparaging associations of being weather-beaten and tanned.

Rule in West Africa was segmented among a number of local states, and most polities were not far-flung. This segmentation helped encourage widespread conflict, conflict that was to feed the slave trade, both within the continent and also to the Atlantic and Islamic worlds. There was a major flow of slaves northwards across the Sahara, with such cities as Tripoli and Alexandria acting as important slave markets. There was also a significant slave flow from East Africa to the Middle East. The Islamic world had a large demand for slaves.

As *Othello* indicated, slavery did not prevent a range of attitudes toward Africans. Moors were particularly problematic as they were associated with North Africa, a Muslim area. In *Titus Andronicus*, Aaron, a Moor, the black servant and lover of Tamora, the queen of the Goths and new empress of Rome, suggests the rape of Lavinia and the murder of Bassiamus and blames Titus's sons for the murder. The play closes with the new emperor resolving that justice be done on Aaron, "that dam'd Moor" and the cause of all the mishap (V, iii).

Aaron is a far more dangerous, vicious, and crude character than Othello and lacks the tragic status and dramatic complexity of the latter. Both characters should be taken into account. Earlier in the play, however, cruelty of a different type is revealed when Tamora seeks the death of the baby she has had by Aaron. The nurse declares the baby is

> Our empress' shame, and stately Rome's disgrace!
> ... A joyless, dismal, black, and sorrowful issue:
> Here is the babe, as loathsome as a toad
> Amongst the fairest breeders of our clime:
> The empress sends it thee, thy stamp, thy seal,
> And bids thee christen it with thy dagger's point.

Aaron refuses and declares:

> Coal-black is better than another hue,
> In that it scorns to bear another hue;

For all the water in the ocean
Can never turn the swan's black legs to white,
Although she leave them hourly in the flood. (IV, ii)

He kills the nurse, the killing being almost casual, which matches
Tamora's vile request. Sycorax, the "damned witch" in *The Tem-*
*pest*, has been banished from Algiers "for mischiefs manifold and
sorceries terrible" (I, ii).

Less problematically, King Alonso of Naples is shipwrecked by
Prospero in *The Tempest* on his return from marrying his daughter Claribel to the king of Tunis, "an African." The evil Antonio
rejects her as a plausible successor to Naples on the grounds that
she "dwells ten leagues beyond man's life" (II, i). Tunis had been
the scene of major clashes in 1535 and the early 1570s, finally becoming part of the Ottoman (Turkish) system in 1574. Apart from
religion and geopolitics, it was in fact a relatively easy journey by
sea from Naples to Tunis and an even easier one from Sicily or
Malta.

## ASIA

The drama of Christopher Marlowe's play *Tamburlaine the Great*
(1587) offered London audiences an account of Asian power politics in which the rise and fall of empires was brought vividly to the
stage, while mapmaking is referred to by Tamburlaine:

> Here at Damascus will I make the point
> That shall begin the perpendicular. (Part I, IV, iv)

A contemporary of Richard II and Henry IV, although far more
powerful and ambitious than either, Tamburlaine had died in
1405 when planning to invade China. His achievements appeared to link the conquests of Alexander the Great with more
recent dramas, such as the rise of the Ottoman (Turkish), Safavid
(Persian), and Mughal (Indian) Empires. Marlowe has the dying Tamburlaine call for a map. This was not so much so that he

could contemplate his former successes, which had taken him from northern India to the Aegean, the conquest of Delhi to the victory over the Turks in 1402, which led to the capture of the sultan. Instead, the intention was to consider what more there might be to seize:

> Give me a map; then let me see how much
> Is left for me to conquer all the world,
> That these, my boys [sons], may finish all my wants. (Part 2, V, iii)

In reality, there was no map available for Tamburlaine to use, but the audiences of Shakespeare's days could have found maps that enabled readers to follow his successes. The dying Tamburlaine reflects on his inability to compass all of the world: "And shall I die, and this unconquered?"[12]

While willing for Puck in *Midsummer Night's Dream* to say he goes "swifter than arrow from the Tartar's bow" (III, ii), Shakespeare did not focus on a comparable figure. He preferred to anchor his conquerors in the classical inheritance, notably with Julius Caesar and (very differently) Octavius/Augustus, the victor over Mark Antony. The battles Shakespeare depicted or described—Philippi and Actium, where Pompey and Mark Antony, respectively, were defeated in *Julius Caesar* and *Antony and Cleopatra*—were located in a known history. There was a limit to the other figures he could have readily considered. Tamburlaine had been done and all too well by Marlowe, and little was known of Genghis Khan. Others were less reluctant.[13]

## CONCLUSION

Shakespeare played for the safety of clear sources by seeking classical and English backgrounds rather than the current-day drama of developments elsewhere. The exciting stories of the sixteenth century—the overthrow of the Aztecs and Incas, the Turkish advance in Europe, the establishment of the Mughal Empire in India, the unification of Japan, and Hideyoshi's invasion of Korea in the 1590s—were put to one side. The doings of Caesar, Mark Antony, and Cleopatra, by contrast, were known, and their plots were easier to construct and explain. The geographical context was also better understood. Thus, Shakespeare's foreign world was less novel and strange than it might have been. The imagination was engaged in a different fashion to that of narratives of exploration.

## NOTES

1. J. Galloway, "Fishing in Medieval England," in *The Sea in History: The Medieval World*, ed. M. Balard (Woodbridge, UK, 2017), 638–40.

2. Displayed information, special exhibition on Dutch painters in Paris, Van Gogh Museum, Amsterdam, 2017.

3. D. Carey and C. Jowitt, eds, *Richard Hakluyt and Travel Writing in Early Modern Europe* (Farnham, UK, 2012).

4. H. James, *Shakespeare's Troy: Drama, Politics, and the Translation of Empire* (Cambridge, 1997).

5. M. Gausco, *Slaves and Englishmen: Human Bondage in the Early Modern Atlantic World* (Philadelphia, 2014).

6. R. M. Lawson, *The Sea Mark: Captain John Smith's Voyage to New England* (Lebanon, NH, 2015).

7. V. Bernhard, *A Tale of Two Colonies: What Really Happened in Virginia and Bermuda?* (Columbia, MO, 2011).

8. S. Davies, *Renaissance Ethnography and the Invention of the Human: New Worlds, Maps and Monsters* (Cambridge, 2016).

9. G. MacLean and N. Matar, *Britain and the Islamic World, 1558–1713* (Oxford, 2011); J. Brotton, *This Orient Isle: Elizabethan England and the Islamic World* (London, 2017).

10. W. F. Cook, *The Hundred Years War for Morocco: Gunpowder and the Military Revolution in the Early Modern Muslim World* (Boulder, CO, 1994).

11. M. Catherine, S. Alexander, and S. Wells, eds., *Shakespeare and Race* (Cambridge, 2000).

12. C. Bartolovich, "Putting *Tamburlaine* on a (Cognitive) Map," *Renaissance Drama* 28 (1997): 29–72.

13. L. Niayesh, *Three Romances of Eastern Conquest* (Manchester, 2018).

# AS WE LIKE HIM

"THIS HAPPY BREED OF MEN... this England"—Shakespeare's lines from *Richard II* found a place in *1588 to 1914: Album-Atlas of British Victories on the Sea. "Wooden Walls to Super-Dreadnoughts"* (1914). Rapidly published after the outbreak of the First World War and approved by the Official Press Bureau, the atlas included details on how to join the navy, as well as an autographed portrait of the first lord of the admiralty, Winston Churchill, a note on Nelson, and, on the inside page, "Signatures of the Brave. A Place for the autographs of officers and men who served Britain by land and sea in the Great War of 1914," set above Shakespeare's lines. For this atlas, the first map of which was of the Armada of 1588, Shakespeare was very clearly a national icon alongside Nelson.

That Shakespeare was also the playwright of Elizabeth I's reign, a period of resolve and glory was significant. The *Times* of May 22, 1917, carried a report of a speech by Douglas Freshfield, president of the Royal Geographical Society, in which he referred to "the recent sea-fight against odds off Dover—a fight that recalls the glorious traditions of the days of Queen Elizabeth." The war with Spain had been transposed onto that against Germany.

In this case, the setting was of the Spanish Armada, just as, for Shakespeare, Dover was the site of past French invasions as in *King John* and *King Lear*.

Having lost favor across the seventeenth century, in part due to the different style that was to the fore in the English baroque, and then been extensively adapted accordingly with major changes to his plots, Shakespeare became the national poet and a central figure as an English literary canon was defined in the eighteenth century. Nevertheless, even if he had lost favor, Shakespeare's words, phrases, scenes, and plots echoed in seventeenth-century literature,[1] with references being frequent.

Seventeenth-century adaptations of his plays can appear flawed, as in Dryden's *All For Love; or, The World Well Lost* (1678), his version of the story of *Antony and Cleopatra*, but they happened. Dryden also adapted Shakespeare in *Troilus and Cressida; or, Truth Found Too Late* (1679), in which Cressida remains faithful, although both the protagonists die, and with Sir William Davenant, *The Tempest; or, The Enchanted Isle* (1667), which gives Ariel a sweetheart and Caliban a sister. Davenant's *The Law against Lovers* (1662) joined the Beatrice and Benedick story from *Much Ado About Nothing* to *Measure for Measure*, while, in his *Macbeth* (1664), he brought in "Three Witches Flying." Davenant adapted *Two Noble Kinsmen* as *The Rivals* (1664), providing a happy ending.[2] *The History of King Lear* appeared in Nahum Tate's version of 1681 with a happy ending in which Cordelia survives and is betrothed to Edgar. Although attacked by Joseph Addison in the *Spectator*, this version remained popular for over a century. This was unlike Tate's *The Ingratitude of a Commonwealth* (1681), which was a bloody version of *Coriolanus* in which the Roman plebeians were compared with the Whigs, to the discredit of both. *The Jew of Venice* (1701) by George, Lord Lansdowne, did not present Shylock as a tragic or dignified figure.[3]

Ridicule of these adaptations should be held at bay, given the tendency today to present Shakespeare in ways that, while arresting and thought provoking, would have greatly surprised his contemporaries, for example, with a female Hamlet and a black Iago—the latter an approach that, alongside the continued depiction of *Othello* as black, underplays the issue of racialism in the play. The changes to the plays in the seventeenth century, however, extended to complete rewrites of the text and major alterations to the plots, a practice that continued in the eighteenth century.

In part, treating Shakespeare as the national poet in the eighteenth century was a question of the definition of a national style that was not dependent on the set of classical norms that had been so dominant in the late seventeenth century and that remained important into the early eighteenth. For failing to abide by such norms, Shakespeare was criticized by Charles Gildon in *The Laws of Poetry* (1721). The situation gradually changed, with Shakespeare becoming more prominent and more praised. No fewer than six major editions of his complete works appeared in the eighteenth century: by Nicholas Rowe (1709), Alexander Pope (1725), Lewis Theobald (1733), William Warburton (1747), Samuel Johnson (1765), and Edmond Malone (1790). The printing of Shakespeare's plays suggests that his work played a role in the growth of literacy. Other Shakespearean editors and commentators included Edward Capell (1768) and Isaac Reed and John Monk, both of whom published works in 1785.

A Shakespeare revival gathered pace from the late 1730s and early 1740s, beginning with William Kent's memorial to him in Westminster Abbey of 1740. This was an aspect of a cultural nationalism that was strengthened with the pressure from war with Spain that led to the War of Jenkins's Ear of 1739–48. Shakespeare was a key aspect of a newfound support for the age of Elizabeth I, which was repeatedly adopted by self-styled patriots as a way to criticize the government of Sir Robert Walpole (1721–42) for a lack of robustness toward Spain, notably in 1729 and, even more, 1738.

The period after Britain's crushing victory over France in the Seven Years' War (1756–63) saw a particular vogue for Shakespeare. In *The Vicar of Wakefield* (1766), Oliver Goldsmith referred to "other fashionable topics, such as pictures, taste, Shakespeare and the musical glasses." David Garrick was responsible for Shakespeare's plays being staged more frequently, and he actively promoted the Shakespeare Jubilee at Stratford in 1769, the year of the publication of Elizabeth Montagu's *An Essay on the Writings and Genius of Shakespeare*. The jubilee was wrecked by poor weather, but Garrick then staged a play about the jubilee at London's major theater in Drury Lane. Interest in Stratford as a cultural shrine developed.[4] A more naturalistic approach to acting led the Irish-born Charles Macklin (1699–1797) to make his name playing Shylock as a tragic character from 1741 and to play Macbeth in Scots' clothing in 1773. A Shakespeare forgery industry started up, with William Ireland producing what he stated were original manuscripts of hitherto unknown Shakespeare plays: *William the Conqueror*, *Henry II*, and *Vortigern and Rowena*, the last of which was unsuccessfully staged at Drury Lane in 1796.

Acting and editing were not always separate activities: James Dance (1722–74), who assumed the surname Love, was a comic actor of note, who was particularly successful as Falstaff, but he also sought to improve Shakespeare, publishing an altered *Timon of Athens* in 1768. Editions and commentary led to much debate, as with Thomas Edwards's attack, in *The Canons of Criticism* (7th edition, 1765), on Warburton's edition. Shakespeare interested other writers too, for example, John Wesley, who in his history was critical of Shakespeare's treatment of Richard III: "It is evident from the conduct of Shakespeare, that the house of Tudor retained all their Lancastrian prejudices, even in the reign of Queen Elizabeth." He pressed on to compare *The Winter's Tale* with the events of Henry VIII's reign, seeing Hermione as Anne Boleyn and "the unreasonable jealousy of Leontes, and his violent conduct in consequence" as "a true portrait of Henry the

Eighth, who generally made the law the engine of his boisterous passions." Wesley also argued that Shakespeare's account would have far greater influence than those of historians[5] and was critical of Elizabeth's treatment of Mary, Queen of Scots.

Shakespeare was also important for neo-gothic writers, notably Ann Radcliffe, who quoted him in her highly popular novels, as did Horace Walpole and Matthew Lewis. In 1798, Radcliffe was referred to by the critic Nathan Drake as "the Shakespeare of Romance Writers."[6] George Colman the Younger used Shakespeare as a model for his plays *The Battle of Hexham* (1789) and *The Surrender of Calais* (1791) and also borrowed ideas for particular scenes.

Shakespeare's works could also be presented as part of a wider cultural engagement on a pattern that remained highly significant to the present. Thus, on August 11, 1791, *Swinney's Birmingham and Stafford Chronicle* carried an advertisement for the New Street Theatre in Birmingham the following night that offered *Henry IV, Part I* followed by

> A pantomimical interlude, consisting of singing and dancing, called Harlequin at All; or The Whim of a Moment. The whole to conclude with The Humours of Bromsgrove Races to which will be added A Farce (performed here but once) written by Mrs [Elizabeth] Inchbald called Animal Magnetism.

Moreover, Shakespeare and his plays attracted attention across the arts, especially from painters. William Hogarth's *Falstaff Examining His Recruits* (1730), the first known painting of a Shakespeare scene, may also have been the depiction of a performance. Subsequently, many painters responded to Shakespeare, Angelica Kauffman producing the allegorical *The Birth of Shakespeare* (c. 1770), as well as a Miranda and Ferdinand in *The Tempest* (1782). Francis Hayman, George Romney, and Thomas Jones all painted Prospero and Miranda spying the shipwrecked Ferdinand from *The Tempest*. Romney was especially interested in Shakespeare,

*King Lear in the Tempest Tearing Off His Robes* being one of his first major paintings. Joshua Reynolds, William Blake, and, particularly, Henry Fuseli were active interpreters, as with Fuseli's unsettling *Titania's Awakening and Bottom* (1790), a topic that also attracted other painters. So also with his *Macbeth, Banquo and the Witches* (1793–94). In the 1790s, John Boydell used his Shakespeare Gallery in London to display paintings of Shakespeare's plays.[7]

Actors were frequently depicted in Shakespearean roles, for example, John Henderson as Macbeth by Romney, whose portrait captured the intensity that tragic actors increasingly sought. *Swinney's Birmingham and Stafford Chronicle* of May 2, 1776, carried an advertisement offering illustrations of thirty-six leading actors in Shakespearean roles. Similarly, individuals were depicted "in character," as with Emma Hamilton, who was shown as Miranda by Romney.

Samuel Johnson was an active protagonist, although also gullible when it came to forgeries. Shakespeare was the most frequently cited authority in his *Dictionary*, and, in the preface to his edition of Shakespeare's plays, he provided a criticism of Joseph Addison's play *Cato* (1711) that made clear how tastes had changed: "Cato affords a splendid exhibition of artificial and fictitious manners, and delivers just and noble sentiments, in diction easy, elevated and harmonious, but its hopes and fears communicate no vibration to the heart."[8] Shakespeare was important to Johnson's shaping of a national cultural identity as his work and popularity supported the development of Johnson's idea of a public.[9] Shakespeare's role from the eighteenth century has been compared to that of Homer in the history of Greek, with each seen as summing up the tradition of a part of national culture.[10] In her novel *Mansfield Park*, Jane Austen described Shakespeare as "part of an Englishman's constitution. His thoughts and beauties are so spread abroad that one touches them everywhere; one is intimate with him by instinct."

Interpretations of Shakespeare, in turn, were debated. The noted travel writer Thomas Pennant concluded his account of a journey from London to Dover in 1787 by taking aim at Johnson:

> I shall conclude this journey with mention of the cliff immortalised by Shakespeare in his tragedy of King Lear. It is a vast precipice of chalk, impending over the sea; a lapse has robbed it of part of its height; but still there is enough left to terrify those who have curiosity to peep over the brink. Doctor Johnson, amidst a waste of notes on this celebrated author, observes, that the overwhelming idea is dissipated and enfeebled by the minutiae of the description; the choughs, the crows, the samphire-men, and the fishers. With all respect to so exalted a name, had Shakespeare divested it of these images, it would not have been any description whatsoever; but the reader would have been as divested of ideas as poor Gloucester, had Edgar permitted the good old man to have taken his desperate leap. But I can still sympathise with the terror which must affect every reader at the extraordinary imagery, the fine creation of our match-less Poet:
>
>> How fearful
>> And dizzy 'tis, to cast one's eyes so low!
>> The crows and choughs that wing the midway air
>> Show scarce so gross as beetles: half way down
>> Hangs one that gathers samphire, dreadful trade!
>> Methinks he seems no bigger than his head.
>> The fishermen, that walk upon the beach,
>> Appear like mice; and yond tall anchoring bark,
>> Diminish'd to her cock; her cock a buoy
>> Almost too small for sight. The murmuring surge,
>> That on the unnumber'd idle pebbles chafes,
>> Cannot be heard so high. I'll look no more;
>> Lest my brain turn, and the deficient sight
>> Topple down headlong.[11]

This is the powerful end to the volume, one that is preceded by an engraving of "Shakespeare's Cliff."

The bluestocking Elizabeth Montagu observed to a friend in 1762: "Few people know anything of the English history but what they learn from Shakespeare; for our story is rather a tissue of personal adventures and catastrophes than a series of political events."[12] This became even more true as the plays not only became canonical (with their stage business becoming traditional) but also were the prime form of literature taught in school when universal free education was introduced and then expanded in the nineteenth century. Shakespeare was, as it were, necessary but also convenient. Written in English, his plays covered a broad range of types, and all or part of them could be read across the ages of school life. It was possible to drop unpopular ones, such as *Henry VIII*, from the theatrical repertory and still have many others from which to choose. They could also be adapted. Thomas Bowdler's *The Family Shakespeare* (1818) launched a determined assault on apparent improprieties, culling them from his edition. Shakespeare, meanwhile, remained important in the visual arts, as with Daniel Maclise's *The Play Scene in "Hamlet"* (1842).

His plays were also a worthwhile text for study and commemoration across the British Empire. They contributed to its shared character and to its Englishness.[13] This Englishness encompassed native peoples as in India where Shakespeare's plays were publicly staged from midcentury and also adapted in Urdu. Praise for Shakespeare was to be described in 1901 by George Bernard Shaw as "bardolatry."

At the same time, the plays were of interest abroad outside the empire and, indeed, the Anglophone world, being praised as an intensely emotional experience, notably by the French composer Hector Berlioz.[14] That was also the approach adopted by Giuseppe Verdi in his opera *Macbeth* (1847). He said of his opera *Don Carlo* (1867): "Nothing in the drama is historical, but it contains a Shakespearean truth and profundity of characterisations." In Giacomo Puccini's opera *Tosca* (1900), Baron Scarpia, the villainous chief of police, compares his actions to those of Iago. Romantic painters frequently depicted Shakespearean scenes as in *Daydreaming (Ophelia)*, a painting of about 1850 by the Dutch painter Josef Israëls (1824–1911).

The twentieth century brought not only more editions of the works[15] but also a wealth of critical approaches as the plays were considered in light of a range of concerns and theories. There was also the further adaptation of Shakespeare for cinema, radio, television, and, indeed, advertising, Hamlet famously becoming the name of a popular light cigar, introduced in 1964, that was advertised on British television from 1966 to 1991 and at the cinema from 1996 until 1999. However, simply putting Shakespeare on or in was no guarantee of success. It was still necessary to provide good acting and directing: each era has needed its own revitalized approach.[16] Again, the range of what was written provided opportunities for very different treatments, while the prominence of the plays encouraged this process.

The world wars saw Shakespeare pushed to the fore as his lines were deployed to strengthen resolve, most prominently with Laurence Olivier's title performance in the film *Henry V* (1944) during the Second World War. The St. Crispin's Day speech about Agincourt was particularly dramatic. The links were very varied. In November 1917, General Maude, the British commander in Mesopotamia, invited the newly arrived US war correspondent Eleanor Franklin Egan, a onetime actress, to accompany him to a performance of *Hamlet* to be performed in Arabic by a Jewish school in Baghdad.[17] Joseph Conrad's novel *The Shadow-Line* (1917) had echoes of *Hamlet*.

More generally, Shakespeare was totemic of Englishness, prevalent, for example, in school curricula but also potentially different. As far as the first was concerned, the use of Shakespeare in commonplace literature, notably with quotations, was characteristic of Englishness and certainly so prior to the cultural discontinuity of the 1960s. In Agatha Christie's *The Body in the Library* (1942), Miss Marple reflects: "It *is* so important, isn't it, to be quite *sure*—'to make assurance doubly sure,' as Shakespeare has it."[18] By 1962, Christie, who made frequent references to the playwright, had surpassed Shakespeare in book sales and, by 1959, in the number of languages that her books had been translated into. He was the only comparator.

Other detective novelists also made extensive references to Shakespeare, as with *Hamlet* being used to characterize a key figure in John Masterman's *An Oxford Tragedy* (1933).[19] *Hamlet, Revenge!* (1937) was one of Michael Innes's more successful detective novels, with the Lord Chancellor being murdered while playing Polonius, in an amateur production. Innes was the pseudonym for the literary scholar J. I. M. Stewart. A more inventive Shakespeare-centered detective novel is Edmund Crispin's *Love Lies Bleeding* (1948). The murders focus on the discovery of Shakespeare's long-lost *Love's Labour's Won*. This play appears in truth to have existed, but no copies of the text survive.

Playwrights made frequent reference to Shakespeare, both to establish character and to provide plot references. Thus, in Terence Rattigan's *Live in Idleness* (1944), it was assumed that the audience would understand the strong characterization of the young man in terms of Hamlet. In contrast, Tom Stoppard, in his successful *Rosencrantz and Guildenstern Are Dead* (1966), provided a play within and without *Hamlet* in which the "attendant lords" feel trapped by the enveloping plot of Shakespeare's play. As poet, critic, and playwright, T. S. Eliot referred to Shakespeare notably in his 1919 critical reading "Hamlet and His Problems," published in *The Sacred Wood* (1921), and in the echoes of *The Tempest* in *The Waste Land* (1922). Eliot remarked, "Dante and Shakespeare divide the world between them. There is no third."[20]

A very differently humorous account of Shakespeare was provided in *Theatre of Blood* (1973), a horror-comedy in which Edward Lionheart, a ham actor played by Vincent Price, furious that the critics do not appreciate his renditions of Shakespeare, sets out to murder them in scenes based on deaths in Shakespearean

plays. Price delivers famous lines from Shakespeare, and the criti-
cally acclaimed film is one of Price's best.

Images of Shakespeare were also disseminated by means of
stamps. The British Shakespeare Festival series had stamps devoted to Puck and Bottom, Feste, the Eve of Agincourt, the Bal-
cony Scene, and Hamlet contemplating Yorick's skull. The 1995
Reconstruction of Shakespeare's Globe Theatre series depicted
the Swan, the Rose, the Hope, and the Globe, both in 1599 and in
1614. In contrast, the role of Shakespeare in the spread of British
influence was shown in the 1998 stamp from the Bicentenary of
Australian Settlement series depicting Shakespeare, John Len-
non, and the Sydney Opera House. A different form of "diaspora"
recollection was provided by the five hundred New Zealand
women embroiders who produced the curtains for the rebuilt
Globe Theatre, which were unveiled there in 1994. Two years
earlier, the first regional Shakespeare Festival in New Zealand
schools was held.[21]

The widespread support for the new Shakespeare Memorial
Theatre, opened in Stratford in 1932 in the presence of the future
Edward VIII and of the prime minister, Ramsay MacDonald,
was presented as an action at once British, imperial, and global.
Two-thirds of the cost was met by American donors.

Translations were an aspect of Shakespeare not being coterminous with Englishness. So also with dramatic foreign adaptations, such as Kurosawa's Noh version of *Macbeth* (1957) in
Japanese and the Zulu version *Umabatha* (1972). Furthermore,
the plays provided directors plentiful opportunities to make
their own political or social points. Examples are legion but see,
for example, the Royal Shakespeare Company (RSC) 1984 presentation of *Henry VIII* as the depiction of a Stalinist Britain or
Ian McKellen's *Richard III* with tanks, a production that linked
Richard to Hitler. In the production of *The Tempest* that toured
Britain in 1985–86 and went on to the Hong Kong Festival, the
directors, Nigel Jamieson and Anthony Quayle, had the actors

dressed in the late Victorian period as part of a critique of impe-rialism. In 2001, the RSC production of Hamlet was an attack on Tony Blair's spin-doctored government of Britain, with Claudius as a television manipulator. In 2012, the same company presented *Julius Caesar* in terms of the Arab Spring, with Caesar's murder drawing on echoes of the murder of Libya's dictator Colonel Gad-dhafi. That play itself has proved particularly pointed as a political symbol. In 2012, there was a production at the Guthrie Theater in Minneapolis in which Caesar was a Barack Obama figure. In 2011, the RSC's modern-day version of *Coriolanus* was seen in terms of the Arab Spring.

The range of adaptation continues to the present. Thus, in 2017, the Globe Theatre in London staged Matthew Dunster's produc-tion of *Much Ado About Nothing*, which was set in Mexico in 1910 with Hero returning from the first wave of the revolution. The play was advertised as "a fusion of Latin music, desert flowers and revolutionary politics."[22] Somewhat differently Philomena Cunk, in her satirical "Cunk on Shakespeare," addressed the question of whether there was anything of relevance in Shakespeare "to the world of Tinder" or whether it was just gibberish. Her rather lame jokes included the claim that "school was easier then," as pupils did not have to study Shakespeare. The program was nominated for a BAFTA award in 2017.[23] Also in 2017, Delta Air Lines and Bank of America withdrew their support from Oskar Eustis's Central Park (New York) production of *Julius Caesar* on the grounds that he was presented to suggest Donald Trump.[24] A similar treatment of the play was offered in London and has affected recent scholar-ship.[25] The 2018 RSC production of *Timon of Athens* staged it with overtones of the recent crisis of the Greek economy.

There is scant reason to imagine that Shakespeare will fall from favor, even though his writing is not immediately accessible to the young. The language is a challenge for many, but the vigor of the plotting and the appeal of the characterization both remain strong and attractive.

## NOTES

1. A. Walkden, *Private Lives Made Public: The Invention of Biography in Early Modern England* (Pittsburgh, 2016), 16.

2. M. Raddadi, *Davenant's Adaptations of Shakespeare* (Uppsala, Sweden, 1979).

3. J. H. Wilson, "Granville's Stock-Jobbing Jew," *Philological Quarterly* 13 (1934); S. Clark, ed., *Shakespeare Made Fit: Restoration Adaptations of Shakespeare* (London, 1997).

4. F. De Bruyn, "Shakespeare, Voltaire and the Seven Years' War: Literary Criticism as Cultural Battlefield," in *The Culture of the Seven Years' War: Empire, Identity and the Arts in Eighteenth Century Atlantic World*, ed. De Bruyn and S. Regan (Toronto, 2014), 147–68; J. Bate, *Shakespearean Constitutions: Politics, Theatre, Criticism, 1730–1830* (Oxford, 1989); M. Dobson, *The Making of the National Poet: Shakespeare, Adaptation and Authorship, 1660–1769* (Oxford, 1992); J. Brewer, *The Pleasures of the Imagination: English Culture in the Eighteenth Century* (London, 1997), 406–23.

5. J. Wesley, *A Concise History of England, from the Earliest Times, to the Death of George II*, 4 vols. (London, 1776), 2:139–40.

6. C. Desmet and A. Williams, eds., *Shakespearean Gothic* (Cardiff, UK, 2009).

7. J. Martineau, ed., *Shakespeare in Art* (London, 2003); S. Sillars, *Painting Shakespeare: The Artist as Critic, 1720–1820* (Cambridge, 2006).

8. S. Johnson, *Mr. Johnson's Preface to His Edition of Shakespeare's Plays*, vol. 1 (London, 1765), xxxv.

9. N. Hudson, *Samuel Johnson and the Making of Modern England* (Cambridge, 2003).

10. N. Ostler, *Empires of the World: A Language History of the World* (London, 2005), 473–74, footnote.

11. T. Pennant, *A Journey from London to the Isle of Wight* (2 vols. in one, London, 1801), 1:205, act 4, scene 6.

12. Montagu to Elizabeth Carter, July 16, 1762, Huntington Library, San Marino, California, Montagu papers, no. 3079.

13. L. Colley, *Shakespeare and the Limits of National Culture* (Hayes Robinson Lecture Series, 2, London, 1999), 17; J. Bate and D. Thornton, eds., *Shakespeare: Staging the World* (London, 2012).

14. J. Bate, ed., *The Romantics on Shakespeare* (London, 1992).

15. A. Murphy, *Shakespeare in Print: A History and Chronology of Shakespeare Publishing* (Cambridge, 2003).

16. K. S. Rothwell, *A History of Shakespeare on Screen: A Century of Film and Television* (Cambridge, 1999).

17. P. Knight, *The British Army in Mesopotamia, 1914–18* (Jefferson, NC, 2013), 140; E. Egan, *The War in the Cradle of the World* (New York, 1918).

18. A. Christie, *The Body in the Library* (London, 1942, 1962 ed.), 179.

19. J. Masterman, *An Oxford Tragedy* (London, 1933, 1939 ed.), 178.

20. J. Harding, "T. S. Eliot's Shakespeare," *Essays in Criticism* 62 (2012): 160–77.

21. D. Sanders, *Very Public Hangings: The Story Behind New Zealand's Gift to the Globe Theatre, London* (Wellington, NZ, 1992); M. Stocker, "'Look Here upon This Picture': Shakespeare in Art at the Papa," *Tuhinga* 28 (2017): 41–45. I would like to thank Mark Stocker for discussing this with me.

22. *Summer of Love*, brochure for summer season 2017, p. 9.

23. https://www.youtube.com/watch?v=9YeCpHoy9EQ, accessed on May 26, 2017 (183,502 views).

24. See also, regarding the RSC, D. Aaronovitch, "Trump Is Mark Antony with a Twitter Feed," *Times*, March 14, 2017, section 2, 8.

25. S. Greenblatt, *Tyrant: Shakespeare on Power* (London, 2018) and "Shakespeare Explains the 2016 Election," *The New York Times*, October 8, 2016; A. Marr, "Shakespeare Warned Us about the Dangers of a Political Vacuum," *Evening Standard*, February 2, 2018, 16.

# SELECTED FURTHER READING

The Open Source Shakespeare website is of great value. Key words can be readily searched.

Ackroyd, P. *Shakespeare: The Biography.* London, 2005.

Archer, John. *Sovereignty and Intelligence: Spying and Court Culture in the English Renaissance.* Stanford, CA, 1993.

Barton, Anne. *The Shakespearean Forest.* Cambridge, 2018.

Bate, Jonathan. *Soul of the Age: The Life, Mind and World of William Shakespeare.* London, 2008.

Bergeron, David, ed. *Reading and Writing in Shakespeare.* Newark, DE, 1996.

———. *Shakespeare's London, 1613.* Manchester, 2018.

Black, Jeremy. *Mapping Shakespeare: An Exploration of Shakespeare's World through Maps.* London, 2018.

Bullough, Geoffrey, ed. *Narrative and Dramatic Sources of Shakespeare.* London, 1957–75.

Cressy, David. *Bonfires and Bells: National Memory and the Protestant Calendar in Elizabethan and Stuart England.* Berkeley, CA, 1989.

Deats, Sara, and Robert Logan, eds. *Christopher Marlowe at 450.* Farnham, UK, 2015.

Doran, Susan. *Elizabeth I and Her Circle.* Oxford, 2015.

Doty, Jeffrey. *Shakespeare, Popularity and the Public Sphere.* Cambridge, 2017.

Dubrow, Heather. *Shakespeare and Domestic Loss: Forms of Deprivation, Mourning, and Recuperation.* Cambridge, 1999.

Franssen, Paul. *Shakespeare's Literary Lives: The Author as Character in Fiction and Film.* Cambridge, 2018.

Gilbert, Anthony. *Shakespeare's Dramatic Speech*. Lewiston, NY, 1997.

Goldring, Elizabeth. *Nicholas Hilliard: Life of an Artist*. New Haven, CT, 2019.

———. *Robert Dudley, Earl of Leicester, and the World of Elizabethan Art: Painting and Patronage at the Court of Elizabeth I*. New Haven, CT, 2014.

Greenblatt, Stephen. *Tyrant: Shakespeare on Power*. London, 2018.

Harkness, Deborah. *The Jewel House: Elizabethan London and the Scientific Revolution*. New Haven, CT, 2007.

Hirschfeld, Heather. *The End of Satisfaction: Drama and Repentance in the Age of Shakespeare*. Ithaca, NY, 2014.

Howard, Jean, and Phyllis Rackin. *Engendering a Nation: A Feminist Account of Shakespeare's English Histories*. London, 1997.

Hyland, Peter. *An Introduction to Shakespeare: The Dramatist in His Context*. Basingstoke, UK, 1996.

Jones, John. *Shakespeare at Work*. Oxford, 1995.

Kerrigan, John. *Shakespeare's Originality*. Oxford, 2018.

Kisery, Andras. *Hamlet's Moment: Drama and Political Knowledge in Early Modern England*. New York, 2016.

Lake, Peter. *Bad Queen Bess? Libels, Secret Histories and the Politics of Publicity in the Reign of Queen Elizabeth I*. Oxford, 2016.

———. *How Shakespeare Put Politics on the Stage: Power and Succession in the History Plays*. New Haven, CT, 2016.

Lake, Peter, and Michael Questier. *The Antichrist's Lewd Hat: Protestants, Papists and Players in Post Reformation England*. New Haven, CT, 2002.

Lemon, Rebecca. *Treason by Words: Literature, Law and Rebellion in Shakespeare's England*. Ithaca, NY, 2006.

Marsh, Christopher. *Popular Religion in Sixteenth-Century England*. New York, 1999.

Mullaney, Steven. *The Place of the Stage: License, Play and Power in Renaissance England*. Ann Arbor, MI, 2004.

Parry, Glyn. *The Arch-Conjuror of England: John Dee*. New Haven, CT, 2012.

Reid, Robert. *Renaissance Psychologies: Spenser and Shakespeare*. Manchester, 2018.

Rhodes, Neil. *Shakespeare and the Origins of English*. Oxford, 2004.

Schoenbaum, S. *Shakespeare's Lives*. Oxford, 1991.

Smith, Molly. *Breaking Boundaries: Politics and Play in the Drama of Shakespeare and his Contemporaries*. Aldershot, UK, 1998.

Spevack, Marvin. *Complete and Systematic Concordance to the Works of Shakespeare*. Hildesheim, Ger., 1974.

Thick, Malcolm. *Sir Hugh Plat: The Search for Useful Knowledge in Early Modern London*. Totnes, UK, 2010.

Whitfield, P. *Illustrating Shakespeare*. London, 2013.

Wills, Garry. *Witches and Jesuits: Shakespeare's "Macbeth."* Oxford, 1995.

Woolf, Daniel. *The Idea of History in Early Stuart England: Erudition, Ideology, and "The Light of Truth" from the Accession of James I to the Civil War*. Toronto, 1990.

# INDEX

JEREMY BLACK is Professor of History at the University of Exeter. He is author of many books, including *Charting the Past: The Historical Worlds of Eighteenth-Century England*, *London: A History*, and *Mapping Shakespeare: An Exploration of Shakespeare's World through Maps*.